I0886576

From Homer to Hatzi-Yavrouda

DEDICATION

In memory of Dan Ben-Amos, leading folklorist of our times, devoted academic teacher, dear friend.

From Homer to Hatzi-Yavrouda – Aspects of oral narration in the Greek tradition

Acts of a conference held at The Danish Institute at Athens in September 2018

Edited by

Marianthi Kaplanoglou, George Katsadoros,

Birgit Olsen, and Christos Zafiropoulos

Monographs of the Danish Institute at Athens, 26

From Homer to Hatzi-Yavrouda – Aspects of oral narration in the Greek tradition
© Aarhus University Press and The Danish Institute at Athens 2024

Monographs of the Danish Institute at Athens, Volume 26

Series editor: Sanne Hoffmann
Type setting: Ryevad Grafisk
This book is typeset in Minion Pro and printed on Arctic Matt 115g.
Cover: Jørgen Sparre
Cover image: Illustration from *Griechische und albanische Märchen* by Johann Georg von Hahn, 1864
Printed at Narayana Press
ISBN 978 87 7597 293 7 (printed book)
ISBN 978 87 7597 612 6 (e-book)
ISBN 978 87 7597 613 3 (e-pub)

The publication of this book was financed by:
The Carlsberg Foundation and The Danish Institute at Athens

AARHUS UNIVERSITY PRESS
Helsingforsgade 25
8200 Aarhus N
www.unipress.au.dk

Oxbow Books Ltd.
The Old Music Hall 106–108
Cowley Road Oxford, OX4 1JE
United Kingdom
www.oxbowbooks.com

ISD
70 Enterprise Drive
Bristol, CT 06010
USA
www.isdistribution.com

MIX
Paper | Supporting responsible forestry
FSC® C010651

PEER REVIEWED

/ In accordance with requirements of the Danish Ministry of Higher Education and Science, the certification means that a PhD level peer has made a written assessment justifying this book's scientific quality.

Contents

Preface

Orality is a prominent concept in contemporary folkloristics, philology, and other related fields in the humanities and the social sciences, and it is among the basic concepts for the study of culture from a historical and critical perspective. The definition of orality has long been debated in different disciplines, as has its communicative value and use. The present volume provides an opportunity for a multidisciplinary discussion of the concept, in the framework of Greek narrative tradition. The papers of the volume were initially presented at an international conference co-organized by the Danish Institute at Athens and the Faculty of Philology at the National and Kapodistrian University of Athens (29-30 September 2018). The focus was on various aspects of orality in the Greek tradition, from Antiquity to the 21st century. It provoked many discussions, which kept the participant scholars connected during the years of the pandemic. Following this preliminary work, the present volume includes the contributions of researchers from around the world, representing different perspectives and academic fields (classics, Byzantine studies, folklore studies, comparative literature), who study the nature of orality, its interrelationship with written literature, cross-cultural and transhistorical influences, and the articulation of orality in different genres, as well as specific narrators and their role in their communities. Representing different perspectives, orality is viewed variously as a tool for research, a body of texts, an entity of vernacular practices, or a series of communication strategies. The Greek tradition was taken as a point of departure for a diachronic analysis of orality, from Homer to the enigmatic figure of a female folk narrator, Hatzi-Yavrouda of Kos, both considered as emblematic manifestations of the *homo narrans* in different times and contexts. We hope that the analysis of the Greek case will contribute to discussions about the concept on a larger scale. This volume also shows that orality, in its old and new forms, is continuously present in modern and post-modern discourse and still dominates everyday communication, despite our growing dependence on digital and iconic universes.

We owe gratitude to many individuals and institutions who contributed to the organization of the conference and the realization of this volume.

The Danish Institute at Athens hosted the conference. Its staff and then Director, Kristina Winther-Jacobsen, were essential to the success of the conference, and we wish to thank all of them warmly. We are also grateful for the support of the Faculty of Philology at the National and Kapodistrian University of Athens and especially Professor Eleni Karamalengou, Dean of the School of Philosophy, Professor Amphilochios Papathomas, Chair of the Faculty of Philology at the time, and Professor Dionisios Kalamakis, Director of the Department of Byzantine Philology and Folkloristics. Thanks also go to The British School at Athens – especially its Director at the time, John Bennet – for finding the means for a live storytelling performance and for hosting the event.

We are deeply grateful to the Carlsberg Foundation for the generous financial support of not only the conference but also the publication of this volume. Without this support, neither would have materialized.

We thank all the participants at the conference, especially the keynote speakers, Professors Minna Skafte Jensen, Carl Lindahl, and Michalis Meraklis, and the colleagues who kindly chaired the sessions.

We also owe thanks to the many volunteer students for their help with the organization of the conference.

Last but not least, we would like to extend our gratitude to the artists who added another dimension to an academic meeting with their live performances: the British storytellers Hugh Lupton and Daniel Mordon who performed a re-telling of *The Odyssey*, and the Greek Shadow Theatre player Tasos Konstas who rounded off the conference with a performance of a traditional *Karagiozis* play.

Finally, we would like to thank the contributors to this volume for their inspiring contributions – oral and written – and the anonymous peer-reviewers for their valuable remarks and comments on each paper.

Introduction

Marianthi Kaplanoglou, George Katsadoros, and Christos Zafiropoulos

As the title of the volume suggests, any *θεράπων* and any student of classical studies is familiar with the core and charter standing thesis/point that orality holds in any attempts to give voice to our sources. A quick search in bibliographic databases, such as *L'Année philologique* or the *Gnomon*, confirms the pervasiveness and vividness of the theme across almost the entire range of research in Classics, from the Archaic times to Late Antiquity. It also discloses shows the wide scope for stimulating future research and discussion. Orality in Greece and Rome emerges all through our readings of ancient literature and culture: first and foremost in epic and lyric poetry, in their composition, articulation, and diffusion; in historiographical accounts from Herodotus to Roman Historians; in rhetoric and its confluence with the political; in institutional and legislative procedures in general; in ancient drama, from its performance to its diffusion; in the conducting of philosophy, in the streets or in philosophical schools, in a continuous heritage from the Pre-socratics and Socrates and from the Academy; in its dialectics with literacy; at the cradle of the alphabet and at the heart of educative practices; but also in folktale and myth, gnomic and wisdom literature, the novel, biographical accounts, as well as in religious texts and practices, and even in medical accounts.

Possibly unfair to many – yet unintentionally and under the Damocles' sword of word limits – one cannot fail to mention the pioneering and still inspiring work of Milman Parry and Albert Bates Lord, as well as the work of Walter Ong, of Egbert Bakker, Irene de Jong, Marcel Detienne, William Harris, Eric Havelock, Richard Janko, Minna Skafte Jensen, Geoffrey Kirk, Oswyn Murray, Gregory Nagy, Barry Powell, Ruth Scodel, Deborah Steiner, Jesper Svenbro, Rosalind Thomas, Martin West, Timothy Wiseman, Harvey Yunis, to name just a few. The "Orality and Literacy in the Ancient World" volumes in the *Mnemosyne, Supplements* from Brill, and the related volumes in the *Hellenic Studies* series from the Center for Hellenic Studies published by Harvard University Press, are invaluable readings on the aforementioned themes and sub-themes. All these research *topoi* and many more will offer the adventurous reader a Phaiakian archipelago of insight and conversations. The volume at hand intends to be but a small stop on the journey.

Turning to orality from the point of view of folklore studies, we would like to add some further introductory notes. In the theoretical framework of the movement of New Perspectives in American Folkloristics, Dan Ben-Amos's famous definition of folklore as artistic communication in small groups surprisingly does not include the term *orality*. Until the publication of his article "Toward a Definition of Folklore in Context" in 1971, orality was the most persistent element in many definitions of folklore.[1] The oral nature of folklore was considered one of its main attributes. Nevertheless, as Ben-Amos un-

1 Ben-Amos 1971.

derlines, this standard, among others, should not have been a defining term for the substance of folklore since such a definition imposes on it a preconceived framework. In his definition, folklore is not conceived as a closed system. As much as folkloric themes and forms permeate literature through the historical transition to literacy, so do themes, figures, and specific subjects and texts of literature and popular culture filter into oral expressions.

The recognition that oral transmission, albeit important in transmitting folklore, is not considered a *sine qua non* among the criteria for defining it, is aligned with the shift from defining the folk as the peasants, the illiterate in a literate society, to defining it as a variety of diverse groups, both rural and urban, in Alan Dundes's terms,[2] and to studying folklore as the creative response of people to the modern world of technology, in Hermann Bausinger's pioneering work *Folk Culture in a World of Technology*.[3]

This methodological trend of re-integrating the 'folk' into 'folklore' set the scholarly focus on singers and narrators and other individual performers who, in addition to standing out as individuals, would still be recognized as being members of a given social group. Contrary to the romantic devolutionary premise in folklore, the procedure of reappropriation is considered central to the creation of folklore.

The theoretical framework provided by the discipline of folkloristics for the study of orality accentuates the collective aspect, which characterizes oral discourses. As underlined by Ülo Valk, the folklorist's object of research is not the text as a singular unit but its relationships with the rich phenomena beyond its written form, such as the generic, situational, cultural, and performative contexts.[4] In *The Storyteller*, Walter Benjamin writes "The storyteller takes what he tells from experience – his own or that reported by others. And he in turn makes it the experience of those who are listening to his tale".[5]

Accordingly, another central aspect of oral narratives is their variability. Unlike other disciplines, which underline the relation of orality with culture, folklore theory focuses on questions of transmission, variation, and performance. In the process of oral transmission, as Nicole Belmont writes, "the same story will never be narrated in the same way, neither by the one who has already narrated it nor by others who equally know it".[6] As a consequence, the products of orality are not static but dynamically re-worked. Max Lüthi emphasizes that "the *homo narrans* is really in many cases not only a *homo conservans* but also a *homo ludens*".[7] Thus, oral narration depends not only on the shared cultural past and diachronic ideas and values of a given folk group but also on specific narrators, audiences, and the opportunities they have to narrate.

It is its focusing on variation in situated practices that contextualizes folklore as a basically democratic process, in the words of Michèle Simonsen,[8] or, as Frog delineates it, as knowledge and forms of expression, which are socially mediated and negotiated within social groups, rather than having hegemonic standards maintained by an impersonal institution.[9] Folklorist Vassilis Nitsiakos highlights that folklore does not merely constitute a mechanism of ideological inscription of the social norms upon the individual because through everyday practices, but also that individuals, as well as social groups, can transform these norms.[10]

---

2 Dundes 1999, vii–x.

3 Bausinger 1990. The Greek translation of this book from the German edition appeared in 2009.

4 Valk 2003, 139.

5 Benjamin 2006.

6 Belmont 2014.

7 Lüthi 1975, 90.

8 Simonsen 2014, 107-18.

9 Frog 2018, 1-39

10 Nitsiakos 1999, 180. For the relation of folk narratives (especially legends) with the socio-cultural norms of a community see Avdikos 2013.

As early as 1929, Roman Jakobson and Petr Bogatyrev questioned the romantic thesis that only a folk not stratified into classes – a sort of collective personality with a single soul and a single worldview – could create folklore and be the agent of communal creation.[11] According to them, the unchallenged dominance of collective mentality is by no means a necessary condition for communal creation, even if such a mentality does offer an especially favorable ground for its most complete realization. Nor is communal creativity by any means foreign even to a culture that is permeated by individualism.

Oral artistic communication is not a unified entity but is distinguished in specific genres. Each genre transforms personal concerns and emotions into a collectively accepted symbolic narrative code, ruled by specific aesthetic principles. In the words of Ray Cashman, "folklorists have understood that people accomplish different social work through different genres. […] We might assume, then, that a person's desire to assert a certain pre-existing ideological stance emerges in a given situational context, then that person employs a particular genre to express that stance. In other words, we might view different genres as specialized rhetorical tools, and speakers as pragmatically minded social actors who search through their toolkit of genres for the one communicative framework that is most appropriate to their needs in a given situational context.".[12] We should recognize here a process of contextualization where oral narratives are made available to adapt in differentiated circumstances and therefore influence them, according to the wishes and assumptions of the individual who expresses him- or herself in a collectively accepted symbolic way. Here, according to Katharine Galloway Young, the narrative discourse creates an enclave within the realm of the occasion on which the story is told.[13] Following the analysis of Pertti J. Anttonen, phenomenological hermeneutics based on the Bakhtinian term *dialogism* can be juxtaposed with Aristotelian rhetoric, which emphasizes how *logos* (text) never receives its meanings independently, that is, in abstraction, but as situated knowledge created by *ethos* and *pathos*; *ethos* denoting how the speaker makes him- or herself authoritative and persuasive, and *pathos*, how the speaker adopts particular ways to speak to a particular audience.[14]

The term *homo narrans*, coined by Kurt Ranke, refers to the universal distribution of the categories of folk prose, conceived as an anthropological problem.[15] Thus, while the notion of folklore is potentially universal, its applications are bound by the system of communication of each society. Artistic performances occur within frames that have temporal, spatial, and social boundaries. When narrative messages shift frames, a change in meaning occurs.[16]

The problem of continuity and change in orality draws further attention to the creative individual and their audience during performance. As suggested in the structural analysis by William Hansen, individual creativity challenges the generic norms as early as in the Homeric heroic epics.[17] In his study of *Märchen*-telling in the Appalachian Mountains, Carl Lindahl analyses the interplay between "the forestory (the pool of previous images, tellers, and stories that frame the tale), the performance (the tale itself in the moment of oral creation), and the understory (the tale as re-created simultaneously and lived inside the listener)".[18] In his ethno-poetic analysis of oral narratives, Dell Hymes writes: "To say that stories exist only in performance is to say that between performances narrators do not think. That they are prisoners of the presence of an audience. That they

11 Jakobson & Bogatyrev 1966, I-15
12 Cashman 2016, 398

13 Young 1984, 239-259
14 Anttonen 2005, 21.
15 Ranke 1981, 11.
16 Ben-Amos 1981, 32-33.
17 Hansen 2011, 287-302.
18 Lindahl 2010, 251.

go about in their daily lives, encountering nothing that makes them remember a story. Or think of how a story might or ought to have gone. That the stories they know never pose them problems, from perceived incompleteness to contradictions, with one another or with their own experience".[19]

The collective nature of oral communication also involves an aspect of emotional connectedness, which addresses the concept of *empathy*, that is the idea of understanding suffering from the sufferer's point of view, in the definition of the term by Amy Shuman.[20] Michalis G. Meraklis uses the term *sympathy* to describe the mimetic aspect of customary healing practices, that is the *pathos* we invest in our trial to reach the impossible. "*Hypocrisis*", Meraklis writes, "this voluntary irrationality, stems from a rational basis, the principle of similarity or of analogy, based in turn on the old cosmological idea of the sympathy among all things".[21]

Research on orality requires special ethnographic attention regarding situational factors and expressive means used by each narrator, the dialectical relation of the individual narrator with the group of his audience, as well as a comparative perspective on different narrative performances in changing ethnographic contexts. The framework of orality and the oral texts recorded in early collections of folk literature provide direct access to the voices of people representing the lower social groups. As underlined by historian David Hopkin, the works of 19th-century folktale collectors like Emmanuel Cosquin, Paul Sebillot, Jean-François Bladé, or Félix Arnaudin, are valuable historical sources for understanding the ideas, emotions, and meaning invested in these tales by their narrators, who were mostly female servants of the local rural nobility.[22] Following David Hopkin's folkloric turn in history, we may consider, in the framework of his approach, whether the *homo narrans* can use forms of discourse and symbols of fantasy to convey his own experiences and autobiography.

The expression "*littérature orale*" was introduced by George Sand as early as 1858 and was later established by Paul Sébillot in 1886.[23] Even though folklorists have recognized since the late nineteenth century that oral performances are artistic events, which draw on the talents of gifted individuals, elitist approaches did not consider stories transmitted orally to be literary works. On these grounds, written art was defined as creative, varied, fluid, and individualistic while folklore was seen as uninventive, repetitious, static, and communal. By questioning these criteria, which drew a sharp distinction between written and oral art, Carl Lindahl accentuates the interactional aspect of oral art: "the oral performance is a highly structured phenomenon in which the teller, if he wishes to be heard at all, must adopt the stylistic devices of his society to lead his audience on a fictional voyage, which they have charted for him. Though the most gifted narrators put much of themselves into their tales by universalizing their own feelings, they can only be sure they have made themselves understood insofar as they share the general values of the society. The situation is interactive, but the nature of the interaction is stylized and impersonal".[24]

Vernacular orality and literacy have continually coexisted and merged in history, as in the case of the emergence of the literary fairy tale in Italy during the 16th and the 17th centuries.[25] Writers and poets not only drew upon oral narratives but also recreated their telling contexts in situations of *fictive orality* (according to the term used by Ben-Amos)

19 Hymes 2000, 11.
20 Shuman 2017, 92.
21 Meraklis 2011, 113-14.
22 Hopkin 2018, 557-91

23 Belmont 2014.
24 Lindahl 1978, 94-123.
25 Ben-Amos 2010, 426-46.

in which they imagined occasions for storytelling and had tales embedded in their literary works.[26]

The intersection of folklore and literature has been studied in a more general framework by Bakhtin, Burke, Hansen, Velay-Vallantin, Ben-Amos, and Asplund Ingemark, to name but a few, while in Greek scholarship, leading essays were produced by Meraklis, Kechagioglou, and Puchner. In pre-industrial Europe, the continual cultural exchanges among the upper and the lower classes is evident in the celebrations, the festivals, and the appropriation of songs, legends, and folktales. The ambivalent attitude towards orality by the literate classes is evident during the European Enlightenment where, on the one hand, oral culture was rejected, but, on the other, the various collecting and theorizing activities that the term 'folklore' encompassed coincided, according to David Hopkin, with the broader, general revolutionary shock of that historical period to established sources of political legitimacy.[27]

Oral texts, their recording in the framework of ethnographic research, and their transcription in written form have also been part of a long methodological debate. The historical and comparative background of orality, as well as the large amounts of archival materials in many countries, nourished theory and methodology, as in the Oral-Formulaic theory, the Historical-Geographic method, and the compilation of *The Types of International Folktales* by Hans-Jörg Uther (based on the system of Aarne-Thompson in its latest edition by the FFC) and the *Enzyklopädie des Märchens*.

As a concept and a tool of research, orality appears early in Greek Folkloristics in the general context of the relation between the official and the unofficial (folk) culture as is evident in the essays of Nikolaos Politis. Exchanges and dependencies between written and oral tradition in the long term are studied in the whole range of Greek literature, as seen in the Byzantine epos, the late Byzantine romances, the Cretan literature and the "chapbooks" of the Ottoman period. According to Ioannis Konstantakos, "it seems in certain times, that written literary stories, pass into folk oral tradition, transform themselves into folktales and thus begin a new life in the mouth of the simple people. They are orally transmitted, and they have a wide diffusion. This does not occur randomly but with those stories which themselves use characteristic motifs and narrative schemata from folktales, that is they draw on material from folk tradition, thus, as if to repay their debt to the folk narrative background they exploited, they eventually return and are themselves integrated into orality".[28]

Nevertheless, in our digital age, orality, especially as relates to folk or popular culture, really does seem like a foggy day. Today's Information and Communication Technology (ICT) dominates the methods, applications, and products that serve the collection and digital encoding, processing, classification, retrieval, circulation, and dissemination of any textual, auditory, visual, or other type of information. It is now considered a given that innovative ICT does not come into conflict with the phenomena studied by Folklore Studies or with the concept of tradition. Additionally, these technologies seem to structurally influence culture, becoming important carriers of both traditional and innovative expressions of popular culture. As for the question of whether the new phenomena generated and circulated through ICT belong to Folklore or not, it has been satisfactorily answered both at a theoretical level and in practice – placing electronic communication between written and oral, closer to the latter. At least for those familiar with digital technology, these phenomena are part of everyday life.

Resonating with Walter Ong's pioneering work on the transformative nature of communication and the dichotomy between oral traditions, based

26 *Ben-Amos 2017*, 89-90.

27 Hopkin 2012, 371

28 Konstantakos 2008.

on communal storytelling and mnemonic devices, and literate cultures, emphasizing textual permanence, it stands in a place in between, exhibiting traces and traits of both of them. Ong's insights into technology's impact on human cognition shed light on the resurgence of orality in the digital era. The convergence of oral and written attributes on digital platforms highlights an adaptability of oral traditions to new technological forms, forming in essence a secondary, meta-orality, demonstrating both orality's fluidity and literacy's permanence.

Furthermore, many scholars, such as Bronner and Blank, have significantly advanced our understanding of digital orality and its impact on cultural dynamics. Especially since the 1990s, now that the internet no longer only concerns essentially specialized categories of professionals dealing with computers and businesses utilizing it as a tool, the enrichment of interfaces with graphics, the proliferation of available applications, and the freedom of expression offered by virtual culture has allowed an increasingly large portion of the general population to approach it with a familiarity that easily resembles everyday oral communication. Soon, the advances of mobile internet and Web 3.0 (Semantic Web) will allow digital technology to integrate even more extensively into everyday life and communication.

However, as every medium influences the message it conveys, information recorded or circulated on the internet is inevitably influenced by the mode of transmission, and this should not be ignored. Folkloric material undergoes a qualitative transformation and is shaped in its social dimension in a way that users, who retrieve it, may not be aware of. It is similar to what happened when the technology of printing converted studies and collections to an enduring paper format, reinforcing oral tradition.

Folkloric material encountered on the internet may initially constitute an evolution of some existing expression of popular culture, such as rumors, conspiracy theories, fake news, proverbs, rhyming couplets, jokes (textual, virtual, and multimedia), urban legends, and folk wisdom. However, there are also phenomena that give the impression of being born exclusively on the internet, such as trolling, virtual world ethnography (usually related to digital games), and memes, which involve the humorous editing of photos, works of art, historical representations, or movie scenes in combination with original text, aiming at cultural expression, entertainment, social criticism, etc.

For these and many other similar genres that "live" on the internet today, even if traditionally based on oral transmission for their survival, interaction with technology is not unidirectional, given that in most of the aforementioned types, for example, a transition could take place from oral to digital (that is, communicated through writing) speech/articulation and then back to oral communication. Digital orality seems to be a child of both spoken words and written text but with a unique ability to constantly move between these two, gaining other traits in the process, such as sounds, images, even moving ones, essentially forming a new kind of everyday, technology-based communication that is surely here to stay.

The contributions to this volume

The papers of the volume – apart from the first – are organized in a chronological order, covering different periods and offering multiple perspectives on the subject of orality.

Michalis Meraklis's comprehensive introductory address to the conference, entitled "From Homer to Hatzi-Yavrouda – and to Vontorini", offers most valuable insights into the very concept of orality. Through questioning the long-established vertical distinction between "oral" and "written" language, Meraklis instead places emphasis on their interdependence. Using data from ancient Greek language and poetry – phrases from the Iliad, the prosodic (and therefore musical) pronunciation of ancient Greek speech, and the role of the *aoidoi* (singers) – and bringing in examples from other cultures, Meraklis considers that the time of birth of these two languages is the same while including a third, that of body language. The dialectical relation between orality and literacy, handed down by tradition, runs, according to Meraklis, through the history of the Greek language and Greek literature, right up to the folk poetry of the 20th century. By focusing on the rural community of Apeiranthos on the island of Naxos, and especially on the poetry of one of its inhabitants, the female narrator Irene I. Markou or Vontorini, Meraklis places this community at the crossroads between a non-literate and a literate society. Finally, he accentuates the key factor of memory – the ancient Mnemosyne as the mother of all the Muses – and relates this concept to the works of Parry and Lord about the "formulaic" character of the Homeric and other epics and those of the Finnish folklorist Lauri Honko on oral composition.

The two papers that follow take us to the roots of the subject matter of this volume. Read together, they provide a remarkable introduction to oral composition and narrative in Archaic Greece, with inventive thought- and research-provoking propositions. In "Homer the storyteller", **Minna Skafte Jensen** discusses stories and storytelling in the Homeric poems, sung or told by narrators across the whole scale of the Homeric world, be they professionals or amateurs, of noble or low status. She demonstrates how their content ranges from the meritorious to the common, from the divine or the heroic to the private sphere and the autobiographic, from truth to falsehood (Jensen gives a thorough presentation of the art of telling lies, as demonstrated in the Homeric hymn to Aphrodite). The paper then focuses on stories told within a story, namely on the long story that Nestor tells Patroclus in *Iliad* XI. From its analysis, Jensen concludes that its structure, rhythm, and aesthetic norms are similar to those applied not only in Homer but also in oral epics in recent times. It is on the basis of such similarities, including a reading of Odysseus's variations of his lying stories in the *Odyssey*, that Jensen introduces the work of the Finnish folklorist Lauri Honko on oral epics in Karnataka in India as an essential approach to shedding new light on our understanding of the mental process of composition-in-performance in epic poetry, as established in Milman Parry's and Albert Lord's oral-formulaic theory. Honko's model highlights the "mental" text of the narrator, his own peculiar repertoire of songs, which he works on throughout his life, drawing in each new narrative setting on his inventory of multiforms, phrases, formulas, and so on, until he reaches a form that pleases him.

The breadth of the epic singer's conversation with the rich and widespread traditions of oral storytelling in the archaic world is the subject of **Ioannis Konstantakos**'s "Homeric epic and Ionian novella". Konstantakos traces in Homer's epics resonances from the thriving repertoire of Ionian novellas, in particular from the "dramatic novella" genre, best preserved in Herodotus's later work. He demonstrates how Homer drew on and adapted to his epic narrative requirements story patterns and plots from those darkly emotional – if not shocking – stories of highly dramatic content. He meticulously discusses two such examples from the *Iliad* – Bellerophon's life-story (6.155-205) and Phoenix's brief autobiography (9.438-495) – and reveals a whole network of cross-narrative and cross-generic connections, from the Ionian novellas to the early literatures of the Near East and the later romances of the Greco-Roman world. Bellerophon's heroic deeds that are sung of in the *Iliad*, Konstantakos argues, stem from stories of erotic intrigue that were popular in the Ancient Orient (for example, "Potiphar's wife", "Uriah's letter"). In comparison, in Phoenix's account, Homer adapts in epic mode and context more piquant motifs, of a rather comic essence, from the scabrous erotic novella, including the motif of the hero's sexual impotence. Both tales indicate the epic processing of a narrative material so rich in dramatic details and qualities that it may reflect a more expanded Ionian oral tradition.

Christos Zafiropoulos's "'ἐκ ταυτησὶ δὴ τῆς ἐξετάσεως πολλαὶ ἀπέχθειαί μοι γεγόνασι' (Pl. *Ap.*22e6-23a1): Plato's Socrates and Performing Philosophy in the Oral Culture of Athens" is perhaps more restricted in scope, yet it contributes to a fresh trend in scholarship on ancient Greek philosophy and orality. Zafiropoulos focuses on orality in the context of daily interaction and philosophical discourse in Classical Athens, as displayed in Plato's dialogues, namely from the many references to and descriptions of emotional reactions to Socrates's elenchus. In particular, the dialogues contain many vivid scenes of Socrates defaming his interlocutors in public or in front of many others, and they in turn react emotionally in defense. Apart from their dramatic, narrative, and discursive place and significance in each given dialogue, these and such passages are also allusions and testimonies – from the philosopher's defensive and critical standpoint – to the exposure and practice of philosophy under the conditions for public exchange in the predominantly oral societies of Classical poleis. Zafiropoulos argues that these narrative details enrich our picture of the oral framework, as they do the direct and physical, for conversation, one that Plato's intended readership and audience were familiar with. He concludes that by these episodes Plato indicated not only the unphilosophical life and ethos led by the many, but also the need to safeguard philosophical discourse and life from the hindrances that the social and the political presented in fifth- and fourth-century Athens.

In "Oral narrations and Roman imperial history", **Sophia Papaioannou** masterfully unravels a web of historical recordings interwoven with oral traditions that points out the blending of literacy, orality, and propagandistic policies in Imperial Rome. The point of departure and the concluding line of her tracking of sources in Latin and Greek from different periods is an episode of Vespasian's miraculous therapy of a blind man in Egypt, documented in variants by Tacitus, Suetonius, and Dio Cassius. Papaioannou traces three different streams of traditional storytelling behind these accounts: Augustus's self-promoting policies, that were constitutive for Roman politics, as the new Alexander the Great; the association of Vespasian to both Asklepios and Serapis; and the tradition of miraculous healing powers attributed to Alexander, and to Jesus Christ in the gospel of St Mark. She points to Tiberius Alexander, then governor of Egypt, as the masterminding compiler of these traditions of Vespasian's propagandist portraiture, to strengthen his popularity and claim to Rome's throne. Papaioannou's paper presents an impressive (and perhaps also quite instructive as regards our modern mediated sources of information) case of narratives being reframed in written form and then orally circulated, in an ideological capitalization of the complexity and flexibility of intercultural tradition that addressed and politically homogenized a culturally diversified audience.

Nicolette Trahoulia, in her paper "Looking for Traces of Orality in Byzantine Illustrated Manuscripts", examines various manifestations of oral performance within a curated selection of Byzantine illustrated manuscripts, encompassing genres such as gospel books, secular romance, and lectionaries. One novel dimension she introduces pertains to visuality, elucidated through a variety of illustrations. These illustrations suggest a nuanced interplay between oral, textual, and visual modes of expression, presenting users with a multifaceted experiential framework that extends beyond mere oral narration. Notably, this aspect becomes increasingly pronounced in subsequent years, particularly in the 20th century and onward, within the context of visual performance.

In a different perspective, **Andrew Walker White's** "Thoughts on the dramatic *scholia* as *Regiebuch*" should be read as a work in progress that seeks to challenge our certainties on the disciplines of our literary sources and text traditions. Bringing together Greek education practices as performative and *viva voce*, with a look at Byzantine commentaries (*scholia*) on ancient plays that focus on the very form of their recording in the manuscripts, he puts forward the unconventional yet intriguing suggestion that these dramatic *scholia* were actually designed as a means to support the performances of the plays concerned. That is, he argues that these *scholia* were not intended solely for a silent reading process, similar to our philological readings of them, but as guidelines for performance, and as such they addressed a live interpreter of their content. Accordingly, it is in the same context that they should also be regarded and interpreted, by scholars and actors, as prompts to dramatic performance. In this respect, these *scholia* resemble our modern theatrical *Regiebuch*, or "production book". White's subsequent reading of the *scholia* on the first lines of Aphrodite's prologue in Euripides's *Hippolytus*, though limited in extent, substantiates his hypothesis and showcases a promising scope for future research.

The problems concerning the analysis of the narrative art of certain master narrators based exclusively on textual information is touched upon in **Birgit Olsen**'s paper entitled "Hatzi-Yavrouda of Kos and the craft of storytelling". Olsen procedes to an elegant study of the narrative art of Hatzi-Yavrouda, probably a woman of the lower social classes who lived on the island of Kos in the beginning of the 20th century and, it is argued, the source for several of the most complex stories in the collection of Dodecanesian folktales compiled by the local historian Iakovos Zarraftis in the same period. This enigmatic figure is but a scarce allusion made by Zarraftis himself, but Olsen takes into consideration linguistic and stylistic aspects of Hatzi-Yavrouda's tales, conventions of content incorporating other narrative genres like myths and ballads, as well as stylistic and thematic elements taken from written sources to conceptualize Hatzi-Yavrouda's unique performances, surrounding reality, and her tales' conditions of situated use. The focus of the study is on two long tales, "Myrmidonia and Pharaonia" and "Yavrouda". For the latter (where the heroine bears the narrator's own name) Olsen reassesses Bengt Holbek's valuable insights about the tellers' and audience's identification with the hero(in)es of the tales.

Marianthi Kaplanoglou's paper "To give or not to give? Addressing community and poverty through oral narration in a Greek island village" combines folk narrative theory with the concept of moral economy (derived from the works of historian E.P. Thompson) and the concept of the "subsistence ethic" (developed by James C. Scott). She therefore offers a new approach to meaning-making on the part of the individual narrator who, through the poetic performance, negotiates traditional value systems of community relations in times of economic and social transition. Kaplanoglou concentrates on a particular folktale transmitted orally from a father, a landless peasant, to his two daughters who lived on the island of Rhodes in the pre-war years. By comparing the versions of the tale narrated in later decades by the two sisters with the local, national, and international articulation of the same tale, and also the versions of the sisters themselves, Kaplanoglou demonstrates that the two sisters (as probably their father before them) restructure an archaic plot in the light of burning social matters and also of their actual lives. In this framework, poverty, the act of giving, generosity, and the reward received were matters of great importance for the community. Thus, the folktale's cyclical plot, bringing forth an analogy between a threatened domestic and an equally threatened social space, rewards the heroine who maintains the traditional value system and with whom the female listeners of the tale could easily identify and whose example they could follow in their own lives.

Stamatis Zochios, in his paper "Legend as Fact in Greek and Eastern European Traditions: Reality Factors and the Example of Visions", undertakes a narratological analysis to investigate the use in legends of visions or dreams – which are essentially accepted as true – with the objective of enhancing the narrative's credibility. The primary goal is to determine whether a legend constructed on the basis of these reality factors is an orally disseminated story akin to fables and tales, or if it represents a documented outcome of the narrativization of folk beliefs transmitted intergenerationally through lived experiences and practices.

Manolis Varvounis and **Georgios Kouzas**, in their paper "Orality in Contemporary Society: Analyzing the Structure of Social Comments (Gossips) in a Modern Greek Community", employ an ethnographic methodology to examine the organizational framework underlying the practice of gossip. The authors delve into the nuanced role of gossip within modern oral communication, portraying it not merely as a trivial form of amusement but as a discourse with discernible objectives, notably social control and judgment. Additionally, the study illustrates that gossip adheres to specific organizational patterns, following a predetermined hierarchy rather than occurring randomly. Moreover, the authors highlight the coexistence and interaction of various forms of folk speech within this structured framework.

George Katsadoros and **Ioanna Kafetzidaki**, in their paper "The Mantinades (Couplets) of Karpathos Island on the Internet: Local Students' Views", initially expound on how the distinctive genre of folk song known as *mantinades*, prevalent on the Greek island of Karpathos, serves as a significant mode of communication and expression of emotions. This cultural phenomenon is depicted not merely as a facet of local life for residents but as a pervasive influence extending to individuals with connections to the island, even those at a distance. The advent of modern technological advancements has facilitated the seamless integration of these couplets into the digital realm, permitting them to traverse vast distances rapidly and without cost, transcending spatial and temporal boundaries. It seems that the traditionally oral nature of this folk literature genre has demonstrated remarkable adaptability in the online environment. The study also discusses the perceptions and utilization of *mantinades* by the younger generation, revealing that these poetic expressions from Karpathos have discovered a fertile cyber space where they can take root and flourish. In this digital milieu, the *mantinades* serve as a bridge between the old and the new, embodying a contemporary form of digital orality.

During the editing process of this volume, a ring composition was decided on. Namely, Meraklis's address was to be read as an introduction and **Carl Lindahl's** paper as an epilogue to provide the theoretical framework and the connecting thread among the varied theoretical views on the concept of orality addressed in this volume. Lindahl's demanding paper "Your Tale, My Life: Trading Selves in Story" draws on a broad range of central concepts in folklore studies, including narrator, listeners, story, performance, and narrative genre (tale, legend), in order to provide an innovative approach to narration. Lindahl defines a great story, like the *Iliad* and the *Gilgamesh,* as a process where narrators exchange identities with their audience and can create the closest correspondence in role, situation, and emotional state between the narrated character and the living listener. Lindahl takes as a point of departure two contrasting episodes from the Iliad: Phoenix, who in a speech fails to convince Achilles to rejoin the attack on Troy, and Priam, who comes to ask for the body of his son, Hector, and succeeds in moving Achilles to fully share his pain, by imploring Achilles to think of his own old father. By using criteria both external and internal, Lindahl offers a complex analysis of how narrators shape their audiences by making the story fit both the narrator's purpose *and* the expectations of the listeners. Drawing attention to the concept of narrative disguise, Lindahl shows that master Märchen-narrators of the mid-twentieth century, like Alfred Anderson, a sharecropper on a Louisiana plantation, and the Appalachian storyteller Sidney Farmer Muncy, and later her granddaughter Jane Muncy, engaged their listeners by actively involving them in the creation of the story. By juxtaposing contrasting contexts of narration, Lindahl accentuates that the narrator's transformative art can only happen in the realm of the storytelling community. The healing impact of sharing stories in the framework of community cultures guided Lindahl himself when he decided to use a folklorist's skills to respond to the disaster that Hurricane Katrina brought on Louisiana in August 2005, when thousands of survivors were displaced to Houston. "Surviving Katrina and Rita in Houston" became the world's first project in which the survivors themselves took the lead in documenting their experience. Through their heroic paradigm, survivors like Sidney and Charles surrender, in their stories, all claims to heroism and self-importance, thus allowing storytelling to heal them and the whole community like Achilles did thousands of years ago.

The volume at hand originated from live presences, *viva voce* presentations, discussions, and friendly gatherings to become written words. We hope that the pioneering aspirations of this particular collective endeavor to bring back together long-neighboring disciplines in the research of a literary tradition stretching back almost three millennia will provide the inspiration for further thought, fresh exchanges, and collaborations.

Bibliography

ANTTONEN P. 2005
Tradition through Modernity. Postmodernism and the Nation-State in Folklore Scholarship, Helsinki.

AVDIKOS E. 2013
'Vampire Stories in Greece and the Reinforcement of Socio-Cultural Norms', Folklore 124. 3, 307-326.

BELMONT N. 2014
'Couvrez ce conte que je ne saurais voir', *Cahiers de littérature orale,* vol. 75-76 (online)

BAUSINGER H. 1990
Folk Culture in a World of Technology, Bloomington.

BEN-AMOS D. 1971
'Toward a Definition of Folklore in Context', *The Journal of American Folklore* (Toward New Perspectives in Folklore), 84/331, 3-15.

BEN-AMOS D. 1981
'The Cultural Mediators of Folklore', *Croatian Journal of Ethnology and Folklore Research*, special issue vol. 1, 32-33.

BEN-AMOS D. 2010
'Straparola: The Revolution That Was Not', *Journal of American Folklore* 123/490, 426-46.

BEN-AMOS D. 2017
'The Brothers Grimm: Then and Now', in *The tale. From the Brothers Grimm to our times. Diffusion and study*, M. G. Meraklis, G. Papantonakis, C. Zafiropoulos, M. Kaplanoglou, & G. Katsadoros (eds.) Athens, 83-121.

BENJAMIN W. 2006
"The Storyteller", in *The Novel: An Anthology of Criticism and Theory 1900-2000,* D. J. Hale (ed.). Malden, Mass.

CASHMAN R. 2016
'Genre as Ideology-Shaping Form. Storytelling and Parading in Northern Ireland', in *Genre-Text-Interpretation. Multidisciplinary Perspectives on Folklore and Beyond*, K. Koski, Frog, & U. Savolainen (eds.), Helsinki, 387-402.

DUNDES A. 1999
'Preface' in *International Folkloristics. Classic Contributions by the Founders of Folklore*, A. Dundes (ed.), vii–x.

FROG M. 2018
'Myth', *Humanities* 7/1, 1-39.

HANSEN W. 2011
'On Middle-Range Structures in Heroic Epic', in *The Individual and Tradition. Folkloristic Perspectives*, R. Cashman, T. Mould, & P. Shukla (eds.), Bloomington & Indianapolis, 287-302.

HOPKIN D. 2012
'Folklore beyond Nationalism: Identity Politics and Scientific Cultures in a New Discipline', in *Folklore and Nationalism in Europe during the long Nineteenth Century,* T. Baycroft & D. Hopkin (eds.). Leiden, 371-401.

HOPKIN D. 2018
'Intimacies and Intimations: Storytelling between Servants and Masters in Nineteenth-Century France', *Journal of Social History* 51/3, 557-591.

HYMES D. 2000
'Survivors and Renewers', *Folklore Forum* 31/1, 3-16.

JAKOBSON R. & P. BOGATYREV 1966
'Folklore as a special form of creation' in *Selected Writings,* Roman Jakobson. Vol. IV. The Hague 1966: I-15

KONSTANTAKOS I. M. 2008
Response to a lecture by Prof. Gregory Sifakis on Orality and Literacy: Collaboration or conflict? Hellenic Humanistic Society

LINDAHL C. 1978
'On the borders of oral and written art', *Folklore Forum* 11/2, 94-123.

LINDAHL C. 2010
'Leonard Roberts, the Farmer-Lewis-Muncy Family, and the Magic Circle of the Mountain Märchen', *Journal of American Folklore* 123/489, 251-275.

LÜTHI M. 1975
Das Volksmärchen als Dichtung. Ästhetik und Anthropologie, Düsseldorf/Köln

MEGAS G. A., A. ANGELOPOULOS, A. BROUSKOU, M. KAPLANOGLOU & E. KATRINAKI 2012
Catalogue of Greek Magic Folktales, Helsinki.

MÉLÉTINSKY, E. M. 1970
'Problème de la morphologie historique du conte populaire', *Semiotica* 2, 128-34.

MERAKLIS M. G. 2011
Greek Folkloristics (in Greek), Athens.

NITSIAKOS V. 1999
'Love in traditional society' (in Greek), *Dodoni* 28, 171-182.

RANKE K. 1981
'Problems of Categories in Folk Prose' (transl. by C. Lindahl), *Folklore Forum* 14/1, 1-25.

SHUMAN A. 2017
'Empathy and Speaking Out', *Fabula* vol. 58, issues 1-2, 90-104.

SIMONSEN M. 2014
'Danish Folkloristics: between Philology and Ethnology', *Estudis de Literatura Oral Popular / Studies in Oral Folk Literature* 3, 107-118.

VALK Ü. 2003
'Oral Tradition and Folkloristics' *Oral Tradition* 18/1, 139-141.

From Homer to Hatzi-Yavrouda – and to Vontorini

M.G. Meraklis

Abstract

In the first part of this paper, the dialectic interconnection of orality and literacy in Greek tradition is addressed, with emphasis given to the Homeric epics. The Greek example is studied in relation with questions about the "language of the body" (an issue studied more thoroughly in Michalis Meraklis's recent book Tragedy and folk culture in ancient Athens*), the prosodic pronunciation of the language, and the role of the* aoidoi *(singers) and of the memory (Mnemosyne was called in mythology the mother of the nine* Muses*).*

*The second part of the paper discusses the art of the female narrator Irini I. Markou (Vontorini). Markou (1917-2011) was born in the village of Apeiranthos (Naxos, Cyclades), an agrarian community where a special form of poetry was created among its inhabitants. Thus we can speak about a community on the borders between non-Literate and Literate Society. The paper focuses on one of her poems entitled "*Ψάχω να δω μέσ' στ' άθωρο*" ("I search to see in the Unseen"), consisting of 4672 lines. It mainly focuses on the inclusion of some particularly rich material deriving from images of nature where unexpected connections among unrelated concepts and things occur, and the interrelation between oral and written speech and the role of memory.*

The concluding remarks refer to the examples mentioned above in connection with the studies of Milman Parry, A.B. Lord, and the Finnish folklorist Lauri Honko about the composition of the great epics.

I begin with an observation about the established terms "orality" and "oral", which characterize a particular culture in general, and in particular poetry, history, and so on.

The terms are clear, but I have some reservation as to whether they are comprehensive, or at least fully accurate. Oral communication has certainly always existed, and – most importantly – it will continue to exist in the future, alongside the written word and written culture. Besides, the written word, in my opinion, has always existed in some form; it is a primary human inclination. Even if prehistoric peoples did not know writing in the modern sense right from the beginning, nevertheless they knew, that is they had the impulse, to draw their activities, the expectations of fulfilling a task, as they did with hunting.

Such information is provided by those magical paintings in prehistoric caves. These paintings were essentially practical narratives. I will come to specific examples in due course. However, it may be indicative that in Greek Antiquity the main meaning of the word "writing" (*graphe*) was "painting".

In his article on body language, "*Η γλώσσα του σώματος. Χειρονομίες, επικοινωνίες, υβριστικά σχήματα*" ('Body Language, Gestures, Communication, Abusive Forms'), Walter Puchner makes the following observation: "In the so-called 'primitive' people and cultures the non-verbal forms and aspects of communication are quite developed, whereas in the so-called 'civilized' or 'historical' people and cultures they are displaced or constrained by oral speech and soon after from the written word too, although they do not disappear altogether."[1] I would argue, therefore, that no form of language disappears altogether and certainly oral speech does not disappear despite the prevalence of written discourse (which, as mentioned earlier, appears in the Archaic period). In other words, no vertical distinction can be drawn between "oral" and "written" language. It is perhaps more appropriate to accept an inherent agreement between them, including body language. The time of birth of these three languages, but also the time of their death, one may say, is the same. They have the same rights.

I can also present evidence of indigenous people's inclination towards written language given by one of the top ethnologists dealing with this issue. Referring to the inhabitants of North Ghana, Jack Goody writes that "scraps of writing are used as magic amulets, (...) but they also can be valued simply because of the wonderful permanence they confer on words". And furthermore, "writing is often regarded at first as an instrument of secret and magic power".[2] In addition, as Walter Ong points out, Goody and others "made little use of the distinction" between spoken and written language.[3]

Together with these two forms of language, I have already mentioned a third one, with which Greek culture was expressed: "body language" (in my book *Tragedy and Popular Culture in Ancient Athens* I make extensive reference to "gestures" in the Athenian drama).[4]

The question of oral and written language was first addressed by philologists (around the Hellenistic period), and then by other scholars, such as ethnologists, linguists, those who studied the Homeric Epics.

It was triggered by a two-word phrase from the *Iliad*, much older than the *Odyssey*: "*σήματα λυγρά*", "mournful tokens" (*Iliad* 6.168), from a versicle embedded in the main narrative, a brief love epic in the sixth rhapsody (*Il.* 6.155-203). Here, Bellerophon, a young man of divine beauty and male charm, did not give in to the desire of the king's wife, who was mad about him, and wanted him to sleep with her. To get back at him, she told the king that Bellerophon had attempted to rape her – and she asked him to kill him. The king was very angry, but he felt sorry for Bellerophon. So instead, he sent Bellerophon to his father-in-law (i.e. the father of the king's wife), carrying a folded writing tablet with the "mournful tokens" written in it, meaning that by that message he assigned his father-in-law to execute such a horrible task (i.e. to kill his daughter's attempted rapist, yet his own guest, his *xenos*), which he did not do either.

In Ancient Greek, the word "*σῆμα*" [*sēma*] has many meanings; it could indicate a "letter", possibly drawn in the form of some shape. According to some views, these epics were created during a stage when orality met with writing, albeit in a rudimentary form, in contrast with the view of the great German philologist Friedrich Wolf, who maintained that writing was still unknown at the time. Ultimately, however, it was the opposite that prevailed among scholars, and with certainty. For example, from 776 BC the Elians kept written records of all the Olympic champions.

Another great classicist, Ulrich von Wilamowitz-Moellendorff, also German, claimed that around 700 BC it was indeed possible to write extensive texts. However, alongside written texts or poems there was of course the oral tradition, with all the consequences of such co-existence, since the Greek

1 Puchner 2010, 294.
2 Ong 2012[3], 92.
3 *Ibid.*[3], 17.
4 Meraklis 2017.

people enjoyed literature mostly with the ear and not by reading.[5]

This observation induces me to say, thinking especially of poetry, that orality prompted one to sing, given that ancient Greek speech was prosodic, and therefore musical. Later on, grammarians tried to retain that prosody (musicality) of oral Greek, because the Greek language had extensively spread all over the then-known world – "And our Common Greek Language / we carried as far as Bactria, as far as the Indians", writes Cavafy, in his strange style, where it is often difficult to understand whether he speaks seriously or ironically – but with this spread the language was losing its musicality, and gradually changed towards the dominance of the dynamic stress: the stress fell only on one syllable.[6]

It was the grammarians who thus devised the series of *accents* that still exist in modern Greek (yet are inert) and that, to be precise, were musical notations: "strong" *vareia* (i.e. bass), "acute" *okseia* (i.e. high-pitched), and *perispomeni*, which was pronounced with the circumflex. The quantities of vowels or syllables were termed "long" and "short". The vowels were either aspirated (*daseia*, the *spiritus asper*, no longer used in Modern Greek, yet still in use in other languages, such as German or French, the *h* in l'homme, le héros) or unaspirated (*psile*).

"The bards (*aoidoi*) of the Homeric epics", wrote Wilamowitz-Moellendorff, "are inseparable from the muse who inspired them and strengthened their *memory*" (my emphasis). Mnemosyne was the name of the mother of the Muses in myth. And "the inviolable rule, any time that they are mentioned, is that the *phorminx* (*φόρμιγξ*)", an instrument like the harp, "or the *cithara* (*κίθαρις*) and the art of song (*ἀοιδή*) are inseparable" (as in *Iliad* 13.731; *Odyssey* 1.159, 21.406).[7] It is worth mentioning another phrase from the *Odyssey*: "Among all men that are upon the earth, minstrels win honour and reverence" (8.480).

From what I have said, using the Greek paradigm, I think the cordial relationship of oral and written speech in the earliest time becomes obvious.

Nowadays, however, it is the fashion to misuse the terms "oral" and "orality", a fashion that tends to divide something that is unified, something that is indeed in a dialectical relation, from the beginning. This is a symptom of theoretical exaggerations, which, instead of bringing something new, as it is thought, actually destroy and devalue the essence of solutions handed down by tradition. All focus now falls upon "orality", for no reason. In our superficial era, one finds many theoretical "innovations" that prove to be vain endeavours.

In a "mixed yet legitimate" manner, folk poetry went further. I cite the erotic historical novels in Byzantium of the 14th century, sometimes based on Western originals, but re-shaped in a flexible Greek language *(Kallimachos and Chrysorroe, Belthandros and Chrysantza, Livestros and Rodamne)* in Greek fifteen-syllable ('decapentasyllabic verse'). I might also mention the masterpieces of the Cretan School of the 17th century *(Erotokritos, Erofili)*. Cretan men and women recited whole sections of *Erofili* in particular by heart. *Erotokritos* has a known French model, but still it is in itself one of the masterpieces of our literature.

A milestone on this long, beautiful, poetic road is Hatzi-Yavrouda, who will be discussed in a subsequent chapter.[8] For now, I will turn briefly to a female narrator, Irene I. Markou from Naxos (Vontarini, as she was known in her village). She was born in Apeiranthos in 1917 and died in 2011.

A tourist guide from 1947 noted that "poetry is an inherent inclination of the inhabitants" (of this particular village). The well-known scholar, Antonis F. Katsouros, born in Apeiranthos, published an interesting book in 1974 entitled *Ένα χωριό που*

5 Handelis 1938, 289.

6 C. P. Cavafy "Στα 200 π.Χ." ("In the Year 200 BC").

7 Handelis 1938, 114-15.

8 See Birgit Olsen's contribution in this volume.

στιχουργεί (*A village that makes verses*). This is not right time to explain where this special gift of the inhabitants of Apeiranthos may stem from, an interpretation of which I attempted in the introduction to the book I published in 1984, a first volume of Markou's poetic work, which, I hasten to make clear, has no relation to the "*ποιητάρηδες*" of Crete and Cyprus, nor with the "poetry of the newspaper", as one could call it, of Karpathos.[9] Generally, in Apeiranthos there were never "*ποιητάρηδες*" of the type of the two aforementioned larger islands. In Apeiranthos, a kind of song was cultivated, formed in distichs but not related to Markou's epic creations.

Concluding "the question of the poetic praxis of Apeiranthos" I pointed out that "this is a peculiar case of a rural community, located at the crossroads between a non-Literate and a Literate Society where Oral and Written Tradition fight each other",[10] referring also to Jack Goody's *Literacy in Traditional Societies*.[11] Now, I would no longer use the term "fight each other"; instead I speak of a dialectical relation between oral and written language (and by extension, culture).

Irene Markou was a particularly bright child. But her parents, by necessity, did not let her go beyond the elementary school. She also had to work, "in the pots, in the shrubs, in the balm, in our vines" ("στα ποτιστικά, στα λιαζώματα, βαλανομαζώματα, στα ζωντόβολά μας"), as she told me. She married at 16 and had 8 children: four boys and four girls. At the age of ten she became a "day water-miller" ("νερομυλωνάς της μέρας"). For fifteen years she was also a midwife. She said to me, "As long as I have my eyesight, I will keep on writing."[12]

I choose as the title for her 4672-verse poem "*Ψάχω να 'δω μεσ' στ' άθωρο*" ("I am looking to see what is not seen"), referring to the mysterious depth of nature that she sought to study. She also said to me, "Since my parents did not let me study further, I was trying to educate myself from nature and from what I saw" ("...προσπαθούσα να σπουδαστώ στη φύση, κι ό,τι έβλεπα και αντίκριζα, το παρατήρου και πάσχιζα να γνωριστώ μαζί του").[13]

She believed that every living thing is alive in its own right, an intact nature in miniature. Asking a thorn about its secrets, she asks nature as a whole:

σ' ένα κορμί, σ' όποιο κορμί, ό,τι κορμί κι αν είναι,
όλη η φύση δένεται κι απάνω ντού 'ναι κι είναι

in a body, any body, be it whatever body
the whole of nature is bound up in it and lies there

The "body" here is that of the thorn. And she insists on thorns, more precisely on dry thorns, because in that way she emphasizes the democracy that rules in nature; there is wholeness and integrity in all things of nature.

What she knows well is the many forms, the diversity of nature, the immense diversity of the *one*, which is also *everything* in the physical world. The latter she knows and describes accordingly. As a result, the single poem of this first volume is also a poetic phytology that at the same time is a didactic epos. Here it is the thorn that speaks to Vondorini:

πολλά στα πολλολόισα, μα 'πρεπε να τα μάθεις,
'ιατί, πού ξέρεις το, μπορεί στη ζευγοσύνη νά 'ρθεις,
να ξέρεις να τα καλαντράς, τα πάσα τω ζευγάδω.

I told you far too many things, but you had to learn 'em
'cos, you never know, you might be asked to plow,
then you'll know how to drive the plough, all the plower's art

9 Meraklis 1984, 11-19.
10 Meraklis 1984, 23-24.
11 Goody 1968.
12 Meraklis 1984, 25-27.
13 *Ibid.*, 25.

And then it speaks to her didactically, on how to build up a good and beautiful life:

Δωσ' την ψυχή σου στη ζωή επά να παραδείσει,
άφησ' επά το χούι σου επά να καταλύσει
διδάξου στα διδάγματα του φύτρου και του φύλλου.

Let go your soul, it says, to the life of a paradise, in an earthy
heavenly way to shape your character, after you have learnt
how plants and trees grow and make leaves, steadily, normally,
following the law of nature.

And it says it again, in a more generalizing way:

Έμπα στη φύση να τα δεις, σωύρι και ξωύρι,
μοναχικά σου να τα δεις, μοναχικά να μάθεις
να ξέρεις, να μην αρωτάς σ' ό,τι κι α 'δεις κι αν πάθεις·
α' δεν ιδού τα μάθια σου, δεν πιάνει το μυαλό σου

Enter nature to see 'em, from inside and outside,
to see 'em for yourself, to learn for yourself
so that you'll know and won't ask, whatever you may see or go through;
what your eyes do not see, your mind cannot grasp

So here the thorn – and, in other passages, other physical elements – becomes the poet's teacher, her professor:

Εγώ τη πόρτα σου 'νοιξα και συ α θες εμπάσου
κι άνοιξε φυλλοΰρισε βιβλία και διαβάσου.
Κανένας δε θα σ' αμποδά, τ' ενούς δε θα 'χεις χρεία·
χαρισιμιά κι ελεύτερα τση φύσης τα βιβλία.

I opened the door for you and you may enter if you wish
open and browse books and learn.
Noone shall impede you, no one shall you need;
a gift they are, for free are the books of nature.

I wrote back then in my edition of Vodorini's work that, beside the low moments that this poetic endeavour experiences, which is inevitable in such an abundance of verses, every now and then it gets electrified by explosions of images, with unexpected couplings of incompatible concepts and things.[14]

Wheat, to give an example, complains because people are leaving the village. It has not seen, it says, in its eight-month life of fruitfulness, a single woman gathering greens, not even the shadow of a woman coming to collect greens. People have abandoned nature, and in turn nature has changed. They observed nature, and it changed just as the sun that shifted in the west, as if the tamed animals of the earth turned back into the wilderness:

κι ελλάχτη σαν π' αλλάζεται ο νήλιος μεσ' στη δύση·
σαν τ' άγρια 'γριεύτησα τση 'ης τα μερεμένα.

And the ground, she adds, "got its skin dried" just like the "*νεκρό βαβούνι*" (the dead weevil).

To return to the observation I made about the relation of oral and written speech regarding the Homeric epics, Markou *wrote* her poems. And I can imagine, that one thought or other that she had set in motion her inner voice first, which revealed itself first orally and, right after, in writing. Regarding this first act of enunciation, I would like to mention the following event: compatriots of the poet's from Apeiranthos (and from Naxos more generally) organized an event in her honor, of which I was informed by my postgraduate student Georgia Mylonakou, whose doctoral dissertation related to Markou.[15] I went to the event, saw her sitting there, and greeted her warmly since I had not seen her in a long time. I was left with the impression that she probably did not recognize me, although for a full semester – when I had leave of absence (I taught at the Faculty of Humanities

14 Meraklis 1984, 38.
15 Mylonakou 1993.

at the University of Ioannina) – she visited me at the Office of the Hellenic Folklore Society in order for me to familiarize myself with the heavy dialect of Apeiranthos, which her own creative linguistic innovations made even more inaccessible. I also said a few words about her work at the event, and I began to read some extracts. Suddenly, I received a big surprise because, upon hearing the first verse of hers that I read, she began to recite the rest by heart, effortlessly. There I had in front of me an extremely impressive example of an organic meeting between spoken and written word.

Besides, this incident recalled the major factor of memory. We saw in the case of ancient Greek mythology, which, as in popular mythologies everywhere, reflected reality – at least symbolically, the high position that memory held in the field of Poetry, the realm of the Muses, daughters of Mnemosyne.

It is on memory that some scholars built their arguments for an oral creation of the *Iliad* and the *Odyssey*, the most eminent of them being Friedrich Wolf, whom I have already mentioned, with his famous *Prolegomena ad Homerum* (1795), where he claimed that writing was still unknown or not particularly widespread during the time of Homer.

However, as we said, the view that prevailed was that of the epics being written down, without, however, neglecting the existence of smaller poems, *epyllia*, that the *rhapsodes* assembled, or "pieced together" [*rhaptein*, "to stitch"].

The issue of orality was returned to before the Second World War when Milman Parry (1928) was studying the texts of the *Iliad* and the *Odyssey*.[16] Later, Albert B. Lord, following Parry and also examining Yugoslav epic poems, ended up developing the "oral-formulaic" system or the logotype of creating verses in the epics in question. Both of them ended up supporting the oral origin of the epics. Both are examined in detail, alongside others, in Ong's *Orality and Literacy. The Technologizing of the Word*.[17]

Ong, however, does not mention the Finnish folklorist Lauri Honko, whose contribution to supporting the oral composition of the great epics with live examples was presented by Walter Puchner. Honko followed Parry and Lord in their argument for the "formulaic" character of the Homeric and other epics, expressing the belief that it was an oral composition by "one and only one rhapsode".[18] This certainty faced the doubt as to whether one single poet actually had the mnemonic ability to "store and recall such a large volume of linguistic and factual material".[19] Such a hypothesis was proved by Honko's research with a programme of the Finnish Academy of Sciences in southwestern India, where six whole epics were identified. One of these, the *Siri-epos* recorded in 1990, amounts to 15,685 verses, losing only by five verses to the *Iliad*. This epic is not heroic; it is the utterance of a religious cult. In total, twelve extensive epics from the oral tradition from around the world have been recorded during field research. That is, to introduce in the study of oral tradition the great potential of these extensive world epic oral narratives that have been recorded from Honko onwards, would open up a highway for future research.

M.G. Meraklis
National and Kapodistrian University of Athens & University of Ioannina
laographiki@gmail.com

Bibliography

GOODY, J. 1968
Literacy in Traditional Societies, Cambridge.

16 See Parry 1928.

17 Ong 2012³.

18 Puchner 2004-6, 951.

19 *Ibid.*, 952.

HANDELIS, J. 1938
Συμβολή εις την διδασκαλίαν των αρχαίων ελληνικών και λατινικών, vol. 2, Athens.

MERAKLIS, M. 1984
Ψάχω να δω μες στ' άθωρο, Athens.

MERAKLIS, M. 2017
Τραγωδία και λαϊκός πολιτισμός στην αρχαία Αθήνα, Athens.

MYLONAKOU G. 1993
Λαϊκή ποιητική δημιουργία σήμερα. Η μορφολογική προσέγγιση του έργου της λαϊκής ποιήτριας Ειρήνης Μάρκου από την Απείρανθο Νάξου, Ph.D. Thesis, Athens.

ONG, W. J. 2012
Orality and Literacy. The Technologizing of the Word, London & New York.

PARRY, M. 1928
L'Epithète traditionelle dans Homère, Paris.

PUCHNER, W. 2004-6
"Review of L. Honko *The Siri Epic as Performed by Gopala Naika*", *Laografia* 40, 951-58.

PUCHNER, W. 2010
Κοινωνιολογική Λαογραφία. Ρόλοι – Συμπεριφορές – Αισθήματα, Athens, 290-314.

Homer the Storyteller*

Minna Skafte Jensen

Abstract

In this paper I offer an analysis of the story-within-the-story in Homer's works, taking as my point of departure Nestor's long story to Patroclus in Iliad *XI. My purpose is twofold: to describe the characteristics of these stories, and to argue that the storytelling can teach us something about the composition of the Homeric poems.*

The Homeric corpus teems with situations in which somebody tells a story to somebody, and both the stories and their contexts are highly patterned. In this, the world of the epics differs from the real world. However, the structure and rhythm of Nestor's story is closely similar to the way the Iliad *and the* Odyssey *are composed, and it is obvious that Nestor shares aesthetic norms with the poets. These norms are similar to aesthetic norms in oral epics in recent times. In particular, the paper introduces the Finnish folklorist Lauri Honko's studies of oral epics in Karnataka in India and his way of understanding the mental process of composition-in-performance.*

Ever since Milman Parry and Albert B. Lord established their oral-formulaic theory, the flexibility of the Homeric poems has been discussed. The argument was that the cause of Homer's formulaic diction was that the poet was a singer, and the two scholars coined the term "composition-in-performance" to describe how singers of epics recompose their poems with every new performance. However, the Homeric poems have each survived in only one exemplar and so we cannot document their flexibility by comparing different versions, as Parry and Lord did in their fieldwork in Yugoslavia. There are, however, quite a few examples of stories-within-the-story being told more than once, in which we as the readers can experience the flexibility of the stories and their adaptation to specific narratees. Besides, in the second half of the Odyssey *the hero tells a series of lies. The paper analyses these lying stories as variations of one basic model, varied according to the person Odysseus is lying to. In both cases, narrators retelling the "same" story or composing a series of similar lies reveal a model that Honko would call their "mental text".*

Finally, the paper looks closer at the art of telling lies, especially as demonstrated by Aphrodite in her Homeric hymn.

Introduction

In an Athenian volume on oral narration through the millennia, a paper on Homer must almost necessarily treat the subject of storytelling in the poems. Homer often describes situations in which somebody tells a story to somebody; in the *Odyssey*, an important part of the main narrative is such a sto-

* I am grateful to Marianne Pade for having read and commented upon an early version of this paper, to the two anonymous peer reviewers for valuable suggestions, and to Angelos Sakkopoulos for revising my English.

ry-within-the-story told by a second-level narrator. However, the main plots are also stories, and even the first-level narrators may tell stories that are not immediately parts of the plot, so Homer's poems consist of storytelling on more than one level.[1]

Scholars normally interpret the singers who are represented in the poems as mirrors of the poet himself, a view I embrace but with a proviso: like everything else in the Homeric poems, things were better in the old days, heroes stronger, and singers more respected than what the poet himself experienced; their patrons were more generous, and they had audiences that were almost always attentive. In the poems, Homer did not paint images of his own historical surroundings; he described the world as he believed it to have been at the time of the heroes, long ago.

Nevertheless, I shall argue that second-level performance in either prose or song is an important key to understanding the poets' own views of narrative technique and aesthetic. I shall concentrate on storytelling, offering an analysis of its characteristics, functions, and craftsmanship. Unlike the poems themselves, the stories exist in a context containing both narrator and narratee, enabling the modern reader to see how the narrator adapts his/her story to the narratee. Adaptation is an important aspect of the flexibility characteristic of oral poetry, and experience from modern fieldwork offers means to better understand the techniques. Lying stories are especially demanding of the narrators' talents in this field.

Some basic statements about origins and context

Homeric scholarship offers no single, uniform idea of the sources and emergence of the *Iliad* and the *Odyssey* or their place in ancient Greek society and poetry. I shall therefore give a brief sketch of my own opinions on these questions.[2] My approach has as its starting point the theory of oral-formulaic poetry as established by Milman Parry and Albert B. Lord almost a century ago.

Their point of departure was Parry's analysis of Homeric formulaic diction. Next, he and Lord studied the similarities between this and what they found in a tradition of oral epic in former Yugoslavia. They were fascinated to observe how the texts changed from one performance to another, depending on factors such as who was present and how much time was available. They coined the term

1 Homeric scholarship has a long history and is still going strong. Homeric storytelling, too, is a well-known and much discussed theme. Two modern classics call for special attention: Genette [1972] 1980 and de Jong 2001. Genette's book is a general study of narrative, but of special interest to Homeric scholarship because the *Odyssey* is one of the texts he analyses in order to demonstrate his points. De Jong's study is *A Narratological Commentary on the Odyssey*, and a solid help. However, absolutely central to the present paper are two monographs on para-narratives by Maureen Alden, 2000 and 2017. To define para-narratives, Alden writes: "Alongside the main plot and amplifying it in a number of ways are the para-narratives which are my concern. These could be omitted without disturbing the course of the primary narrative: their function is artistic" (2000, 13). Alden's overall thesis is that, even though such para-narratives are not part of the main plot, they are all related to it and thus contribute to how the audience receives the texts. Typically, they repeat in a minor key the elements of major events within the main narrative (2000, 15). Alden is very knowledgeable in mythology and her studies are conducted in a careful and learned dialogue with previous research. They are heavy reading but immensely helpful. These four books are central for the present paper, combined with the folkloristic approach which is my main inspiration. In the present paper I diverge from Genette's terminology in a central point. He distinguishes between "story" and "narrative" so that "narrative" is what is told, and "story" what is told of (Genette [1972] 1980, 25-27). But since the word "story" is in general use in connection with storytellers and storytelling I use that, not "narrative".

2 For sources and argumentation see Jensen 2011.

"composition-in-performance" to describe the fact that the singer of an oral epic must recompose his text face to face with every new audience, and they saw this as the key to understanding the formulaic diction: the formulae are there to help the singer in the difficult task of expressing himself in verse in the heat of performance.

Parry and Lord did their fieldwork in Yugoslavia in the decades just before and after the Second World War, and it took some time before its impact made itself felt; but from around 1960 and onwards an enthusiastic trend of studies in oral epic traditions developed, including exciting new fieldwork.[3] Over the years this led to a comprehensive demonstration that great traditions of oral epic still exist in many parts of the world, with impressive texts gradually being registered, translated, and described for all students of comparative epic to read. In building up an image of epic traditions in archaic Greece, I depend on such fieldwork to try to learn what is normal and what is not in oral epic. In Homeric studies we have the wonderful poems, but very little about their *Sitz im Leben*, the surroundings in which they were composed and performed.

Some biographies of Homer from the early centuries AD have survived, more than half a millennium after the time when the *Iliad* and the *Odyssey* were composed. Even though these biographies differ considerably from each other in detail they agree on describing the poet as a rhapsode. The word *ῥαψωιδός* is a compound consisting of *rhaps-* and *-aoidos*, the second half meaning "singer". The first half refers either to a staff, *rhabdos*, or to the verb *rhaptein*, to sew. Modern etymologists go for the second alternative, but in our connection here it is more interesting that both interpretations existed in antiquity. The *rhabdos*-idea was understood to describe the itinerant epic singer leaning on his staff, whereas the sewing characterized him as a person who added hexameters to each other. Rhapsodes are relatively well known from both literature and images, from c. 450 BC.

The biographies of Homer used to be dismissed by scholars as irrelevant for the Homeric Question. In a thought-provoking book from 2002, however, Barbara Graziosi drew attention to them and to the paradox that "in contemporary scholarship Homer is the poet of kings and aristocrats, whereas in the ancient biographical tradition he is a poor wanderer who pleases powerless people, fishermen, shoemakers, old men in the gathering places of harbour towns".[4] She underlined that what she investigated was not the historical Homer, but a person of fiction, mainly as a way to understand early interpretations of the poems. To me it is important that in Greek imagination the great poet was such a rhapsode since it makes him fit into a setting similar to how great epic traditions documented in our days work.

My view of the history of the Homeric epic is modelled over such oral epic as is known today. The tradition begins in prehistoric times, as it was argued by the linguist Antoine Meillet, who pointed out that the Greek language and hexameter do not fit together. Many normal Greek words or forms of them are not acceptable in the meter, he observed, a fact which compelled the epic poets to either find synonyms or maltreat the words, for instance by lengthening vowels or adding unusual endings, in order to make the hexameter work. Accordingly, he thought that when the Greeks arrived in pre-historic times, they learned this meter from the original inhabitants.[5] The content of such early hexameter epics is, of course, unknown.

When we begin to hear of epics or find traces of them, the subjects are the Trojan War, the Theban War, the expedition of the Argonauts, Heracles's exploits, and the Calydonian boar-hunt, to mention only the best known. Such tales are known to us from

3 Cf. Jensen 2017.

4 Graziosi 2002, 252.

5 Meillet 1923, 58-63.

surviving images and literary texts, especially epics, lyric poetry, Attic tragedy, and later mythographers. Besides, early narrative images contain many scenes representing myths unknown to us. Consider the large vases from the 7th century BC in the museums of Tinos and Mykonos. One of them, a relief amphora from a grave in Mykonos from c. 640 BC, unmistakably shows the Trojan Horse and also a scene that probably illustrates Menelaus threatening Helen with his sword; but besides that, they feature a large number of pictures that do not match any of the surviving myths, reminding us of what seems to have been an overwhelming amount of mythic tales now lost to us. Another witness to the richness of archaic myth is the famous Attic François Vase in the Archaeological Museum of Firenze from c. 565 BC. Many well-known mythic scenes are represented: the Calydonian boar-hunt, Theseus and the young Athenians, the chariot-race at the funeral games for Patroclus, the fight between the Lapiths and Centaurs, the death of Troilos, the return of Hephaestus, Aias carrying the dead Achilles, and the Muses arriving at the wedding of Peleus and Thetis. The painter has added names to the figures – gods, humans, and dogs – and the list runs to 130 labels, a number of individual participants in the events that is much greater than what we know from literature.[6] Early Greece seems to have been teeming with mythic tales.

If we consider these facts in the light of what is known from oral epic traditions in the 20th–21st centuries, it is likely that they were organized as cycles consisting of episodes. For a given performance, a rhapsode would choose an episode or two, depending on the situation, the time available, or the interests of the audience; often listeners would ask for a specific story as Odysseus does when attending the singer Demodocus in Phaeacia. The rhapsodes would agree roughly on the chronological sequence of episodes. Cycles might be connected with each other; for instance, the Theban War featured heroes whose sons fought at Troy, and the father of old Nestor in the *Iliad* fought against Heracles. Homer was considered to have been the first poet to sing about all of this, and rhapsodes did not consider themselves authors of their songs. They would insist that what they performed was Homer's epics. However much they changed their story from one performance to another they would feel that they were always performing the same poem, exactly as they had learned it, and when the listeners were moved, they felt that what engaged them was the truth of the song.

Accordingly, I consider "Homer" the name of the whole complex of epic traditions: both what has survived and what was lost.[7] That is how the name was actually used by the Greeks themselves in the few early mentions of him that we know of; only from c. 350 BC did he become the poet of the *Iliad* and the *Odyssey* exclusively.[8] Similarly, I consider "Hesiod" the name of a related oral tradition of didactic hexameter poetry, with the *Theogony*, the *Works and Days*, the *Shield*, and the fragments as the surviving manifestations. This is a standpoint close to that of the great James A. Notopoulos.[9]

The surviving Homeric texts – the *Iliad*, the *Odyssey*, and the *Hymns* – are individual manifestations of the tradition and were recorded in writing by rhapsodes dictating to professional scribes, a process that began in Athens during the last years of the Pisistratid tyranny. I think the writing of the *Iliad* and the *Odyssey* can be dated to 522 BC with Hipparchus as patron.[10]

6 Wachter 1991.

7 Except *Hom Hymn* 8 and *Batr.*

8 In his *Histories* c. 430 BC (2.116-7), Herodotus argues that the *Iliad*, the *Odyssey*, and the *Cypria* cannot all have the same author, the first mention of the poems' titles and the earliest example of this type of question. Xenophon and Plato are the first to use *Iliad*, *Odyssey*, and Homer as synonymous.

9 Notopoulos 1964.

10 Jensen 2011, 302-4.

If for instance the two singers emphasized Nestor, the ancestor of the Pisistratids, as I think they did, they acted according to what would have been expected of them by their contemporaries. Nestor was an established figure in myth and allowing him ample space in the *Iliad* or giving him an extra son, called Pisistratus, in the *Odyssey*, was no breach of truth. On the contrary, to emphasize that he was an important participant of the war would be felt to be true by an Athenian audience, confirmed by the importance of the *polis* they lived in and its ruling dynasty.

We hear of Homeric competitions at city-festivals and funeral celebrations, and of traveling rhapsodes. They must have performed more or less formally whenever an interested audience was at hand. Add to this that no two oral performances are alike, and we can begin to establish an impression of a huge tradition manifested in an endless amount of performed texts all over the Greek-speaking area. The great majority of them remained oral without ever being recorded in writing, but the broad variety of images on vases and other forms of decoration with motifs from known and unknown myths confirms their existence. Plutarch has an anecdote about the poet Xenophanes, who lived around 500 BC. He complained to his patron Hieron, tyrant of Syracuse, that he could hardly feed two slaves. The tyrant answered him: But Homer, whom you are all the time criticizing, feeds more than 10,000 even after his death (Plut. *Mor.* 175b–c)! This gives a hint as to how many rhapsodes Plutarch, around 100 AD, imagined to have been active in Xenophanes's time.

Oral hexameter traditions continued undisturbed despite the fact that some texts had been recorded in writing. When gradually a reading public began to develop during the second half of the 5th century BC and writing soon spread like wildfire all over the Greek-speaking world, the written poems achieved a new status. The old manuscripts of the *Iliad* and the *Odyssey* were copied and began a new career as school-texts. They took their place as the oldest and most venerable among the rapidly expanding multitude of books, while the rhapsodes and their performances were losing status. Over the centuries that followed, oral epic was assigned its place among the humbler parts of the city populations and the villagers most remote from intellectual culture, as has happened with most of the great oral epic traditions today. In these surroundings, the Homeric oral epic survived until Byzantine times. What eventually ended the tradition was the change in the Greek language and feeling for rhythm; at a certain point, hexameter was overtaken by the so-called politic 15-syllable verse.[11]

To me as a reader, "Homer" means the accessible poems and all that was lost. When I say "Homer" or "the Homeric poems", it means the tradition as well as the poems that are or were manifestations thereof. Furthermore, when I use the words "poets", "rhapsodes", and "singers" in the plural, they refer to artists inside this tradition. When I use the same words in the singular, I mean the creator of the specific poem in hand. These terms are all concerned with real people, those who are represented by the first-level narrators in the poems. I use the pronoun "he" because both in ancient Greece and in our times epic singers are almost always male. A "text" may be oral or written.

Nestor the storyteller

At the end of Book XI of the *Iliad* there is a passage in which old Nestor acts as a characteristic Homeric storyteller (*Il.* XI.656-803). The Trojans are on the point of defeating the Greeks. Achilles, who does not participate, is standing on the stern of one of his ships from where he observes how matters stand, hoping that the Greeks will soon be so desperate that they will come and entreat him to join battle. When he sees Nestor returning from the battlefield with a

11 Pavese [1998] 2007, 51.

wounded warrior, he calls for his friend Patroclus and sends him off to find out who the wounded man is. When Patroclus arrives at Nestor's tent, the old man invites him in to take his seat, but Patroclus declines; he must report to Achilles quickly, for his friend's temper can be violent.

Patroclus remains standing while Nestor engages in an elaborate speech in which two stories make up the substantial part. In the first one he is himself the protagonist. The point of departure is that if he had had the strength of his youth, he would himself have been able to change the situation. As a very young man he led a cattle-raid on his neighbours in his native Pylos and took enormous booty from the Epeians. The story moves backwards to tell how these Epeians used to harass the Pylians. This was made possible because – with another step backwards – Heracles had wrought havoc on the Pylians, especially on their king Neleus, Nestor's father. Out of his twelve sons only Nestor had survived. Moving forwards again the story explains that the massacre had weakened the Pylians so much that they had been unable to ward off the Epeians, whose king, Augeias, had even stolen four race-horses from Neleus. From there Nestor returns to his youth and his remarkable deeds, told at considerable length, and only then to the actual situation, Nestor speaking to Patroclus.

After a couple of lines Nestor again looks backwards, this time to the period just before the Trojan War when he and Odysseus were touring the Greek lands to engage the various princes in Agamemnon's war. This story includes the narratee, as Nestor reminds Patroclus of the situation when he and Achilles enlisted for the war. Both fathers, his own and Achilles's, had exhorted their sons to be brave, but Patroclus had been especially admonished to look after the younger Achilles and give him good advice. "So spoke your father, but you forget!" (*Il.* XI.790). Having thus reminded Patroclus of his duty, Nestor asks him to use his influence with his friend and convince him to join battle.

Patroclus does not answer but hurries off immediately; the narrator spends a single hexameter on stating that he was moved by Nestor's words. An ancient commentator remarks that Patroclus's patience shows what a nice person he is (*Scholion Townleianum* on *Il.* XI.670), while the narrator of the *Iliad* does not comment on the old man's long-windedness. Actually, the first-level narrator is regularly positive when speaking of Nestor, underlining that he was the warrior whose counsels were always the best.

The narrative order of Nestor's first story, with its rather complicated use of analepses, is characteristic of many other Homeric stories, and of course famously so for the *Iliad* and the *Odyssey* as poetic wholes. The Roman poet Horace praised Homer for not beginning *ab ovo*, from the egg from which Helen had been born, but moving *in medias res*, into the middle of the tale (Hor. *Ars P.* 147-48).

The rhythm of Nestor's story, too, is similar to the way other stories, as well as the full poems, are told: Nestor shifts between briefly told dramatic events and more broadly described scenes. For instance, his killing of the enemy Itymoneus takes up 4 ½ hexameters, whereas the following 31 ½ hexameters are spent on a description of the booty they took and how they shared it. Similarly, in the rhythm of the poem the episode of Nestor, Machaon, and Patroclus comes as a break at the end of a book full of bloody warfare. Even though the situation is sad, Nestor bringing back the wounded Machaon, the peaceful description of how the two men cooled down, how Nestor's horses were taken care of, how afterwards the men sat down in his tent, drinking and talking – *μύθοισιν τέρποντο* (they enjoyed themselves chatting) – the scene with all its details provides relief. We are even told how Nestor had a beautiful female slave, Hecamede, who prepared a very special drink for them, and that this wonderful girl had been his part of the booty from a raid on Tenedos, given to him in recognition of his preeminence as a counsellor. Next follows Nestor's long speech, bringing the action almost to a standstill. Especially during the long descriptions of bloodshed in the middle of the *Iliad*, the rhapsode lets his audience relax now and then by means of such peaceful and/or humorous scenes.

Nestor is telling stories in his speech as a second-level narrator, and what he narrates has himself as the protagonist. Both these traits are typical for Homeric stories. This means that stories are very often part of the Trojan cycle or referring to it, and other epic cycles may be included as well. The first of Nestor's two stories here is intertwined with the Heracles cycle, especially the hero's labour of the stables of Augeias. The elliptical way in which Nestor refers to what is obviously a well-known tale is, again, similar to how the first-level narrator handles his narrative.

The briefer story of how Nestor and Odysseus visited King Peleus in Phthia concentrates on the advice the two old fathers, of Achilles and Patroclus, gave their sons. This tale belongs to the enlisting stage of the Troy cycle, in which scenes with fathers exhorting their sons must have been regular. Better known from this stage, however, are tales about how some of the warriors tried to escape, such as Odysseus feigning madness and Achilles hiding on the island of Scyros. There is no hint in this direction in Nestor's version of the story. Perhaps this part of the tradition did not yet exist or rather, it was left out because it did not fit the purpose of Nestor's speech?

Nestor's narratee is Patroclus; the two stories are there to strengthen the message of the speech, told as rhetorical *exempla*, paradigms. The former is actually meant for Achilles rather than for Patroclus. At the beginning of his speech, Nestor expresses his anger at Achilles for his indifference to the troubles of his comrades, and the moral of his recounting how he himself behaved when he was young and strong is clear enough: I was the Achilles of my generation, and I fulfilled the obligations that came with my strength. A striking aspect of this story is that, while Nestor mentions the names of quite a few enemies, he does not name a single compatriot. His story ends with the remarkable statement: "All glorified Zeus among the gods, but among men Nestor" (*Il.* XI.761). This is followed up with a comparison: unlike me, Achilles prefers to enjoy his valour in loneliness, but he will regret it. The later story ends up in a direct appeal to Patroclus: Take your father's advice!

Nestor as a speaker uses his two paradigms to add weight to his messages. His relations with Achilles, acknowledged as the best of all Greek warriors and known for his violent temper, do not immediately allow him to offer criticism or advice. Instead, he builds up a portrait of himself as a warrior of Achilles's calibre, a worthy rival to his fame. The importance of the events is underlined not only by the way in which he gives the impression that he won the two battles almost alone, but also by the references to the Heracles cycle. The war in which young Nestor excelled was not a small local affair, but an important part of the warfare of his generation. Besides that, he appears in the story as his father's son, a fact all the more evident because nobody else is mentioned as fighting on the Pylian side. He states that, after the first battle, his father Neleus was very proud of him; at the beginning of the second, he actually forbade him to participate among the horsemen, but Nestor managed to get his own horses nevertheless. Speaking to Patroclus, he is in an easier position and can base his order explicitly on the authority of the narratee's father; indirectly, however, by means of the importance given to Neleus in his first story, he also takes the role of Achilles's father.

Nestor telling such stories of his life to Patroclus (and Achilles) resembles the poet. Nestor selects out of a multitude of stories from his long life what he finds relevant for the advice he wants to give, and he arranges the elements of his narrative so as to present the moral with as much authority as possible. In all this he adapts his story to his audience, just as Homeric poets must have adapted their traditional poems to their audiences.

When second-level narrators are speaking to their narratees, the poet is at the same time addressing his audience. Such scenes work in many ways. Here he draws a portrait of Nestor as the typical old man who is always eager to talk of former days, do it in many words, and give himself a prominent place in the narrative. To us as modern readers the picture may be ironic, and even in his contemporary audience the storyteller Nestor called forth a smile, I think, as suggested by the explicit mentions of the hurry Patroclus was in. On the other hand, Nestor is one of the respected protagonists of the *Iliad*, and various aspects of both of his stories and of the context make that clear. In Nestor's first story it is noticeable that the goddess Athena is an energetic helper of the young hero and his fellow Pylians, a fact adding considerable dignity to his person, especially in Athens.

Besides, Nestor's speech turns out to be important for what follows. At the beginning of the episode, when Achilles called for his friend and Patroclus obeyed, the first-level narrator stated: "This was the beginning of his misfortunes" (*Il.* XI.604). Reading along we may almost forget this warning while the events develop, and Nestor speaks and speaks. However, at the end of his speech Nestor implants into Patroclus's mind the idea that if he does not succeed in convincing Achilles to go back to battle, he might, perhaps, get his permission to join battle wearing his friend's suit of armour in order to make the Trojans believe that the great warrior himself is back. This plan will be realized only in Book XVI after many other incidents have taken place, but the attentive listener may have noticed the proleptic signal and felt relieved when eventually this thread was taken up.

Aspects of the second-level narrator's story let us hear the poet's voice. For instance, through the stories from Nestor's youth the singer reminds his audience of how comprehensive these epic cycles are. There was the Trojan War, but the present performance offers only a small part of it; many events preceded the episode of Achilles's anger, and before the fighting over Troy there were other heroic deeds and other epics celebrating them. In this way the poet lets the audience get the feeling of an unlimited mass of epic songs, tying the listeners and their ancestors together in one and the same singing community, and reaching out to coming generations.

Furthermore, the singer may perhaps be showing off: The world is full of tales, and I know them all. Similarly, he may be flattering his audience: Surely you are familiar with the Heracles cycle? The massacre of Neleus and his fellow Pylians, Augeias and his gigantic herds of cattle, and the monstrous twins, the Aktorione-Molione, sons of Poseidon. Nestor even mentions a daughter of Augeias, Agamede, "who knew of all the medicines that are grown on the broad earth" (*Il.* XI.740). Her only relation to the action is that her husband was killed, but the brief mention of her expertise suggests that here, again, is a person of whom stories might be told. Augeias was Helios's son, so Agamede was a cousin of the famous witch Medeia. Considering that *φάρμακον* means both medicine and poison, we may well feel uneasy about what this Agamede was up to in her day.

If we move from the stories to the episode of which they form an important part, we may notice that the poet characterizes not only Nestor but also Patroclus. He is well-behaved and patient, listening to Nestor's speech to its end. He is also kind-hearted; running back from Nestor's tent towards where he and Achilles stayed, he met another wounded warrior, Eurypylos, and took the time to help him to his tent. From then on, three books pass in which Patroclus and Achilles retire to the background of events. Only towards the end of Book XV when he has cleaned and dressed Eurypylos's wound does Patroclus finally return to Achilles.[12]

12 Alden 2002 discusses this story (88-102). As always, she argues clearly and gives a full report of previous scholarship; here, though, I cannot agree with her assertion that young Nestor is compared to Patroclus rather than to Achilles.

In summary, typical characteristics of Nestor's stories, especially the first one, are the narrative order, the rhythm, the elliptical traits, the fact that he has himself as the protagonist, and that his stories work as paradigms in a speech. Most other second-level stories in Homer share these properties, and the poet himself has built his epic in much the same way except for the fact that he is not himself part of the events. Nestor and other second-level storytellers adapt their stories to their narratees, and it is reasonable to deduce that Homeric poets/singers did the same.

The poet uses the Nestor-Patroclus scene to draw a portrait of narrator and narratee, and by means of two prolepses, one at the beginning of the scene and the other inside Nestor's speech, he gives the scene an important place in the main narrative. At the same time the peaceful setting in the middle of dramatic narratives of fighting lets the audience relax for a moment from cruelty and bloodshed.

Storytelling: Patterned multiplicity

Homer describes a world in which storytelling is the main form of entertainment. In noble families, the stories may be poems performed by professional rhapsodes; in humbler connections, they are in prose and told by amateurs. However, amateur storytelling is also prominent in the higher levels of society, as when Nestor tells Patroclus of his youth, or in the *Odyssey* when he tells Telemachus of his homecoming (*Od.* 3.103-200, 254-328).

Since everything in Homer is expressed in hexameters, prose comes out as verse, too. However, it is always carefully stated whether an utterance is sung or spoken, and therefore it is unproblematic to distinguish between the two. Even so, "prose" stories may approach the heroic epic because the second-level narrators are so often epic protagonists; when they tell of their own achievements, their stories become closely similar to the epic the rhapsode is engaged in performing and the border becomes blurred. This is most obvious in the stories told by Nestor, Menelaus (*Od.* 4.333-586), and Odysseus (*Od.* 9.2-11.332, 11.378-12.453) in the *Odyssey*. When at the Phaeacian court Odysseus takes a pause in his storytelling, Queen Arete praises him by comparing him to a singer and suggests that he should be given gifts (*Od.* 11.336-41). I hear the rhapsode give his real-life audience a small hint of how listeners should properly behave when enjoying an excellent performance.

When Patroclus arrived at Nestor's tent, the old man and Machaon had enjoyed a pleasant, quiet rest, and the narrator had spent some hexameters on describing for us how the beautiful Hecamede had poured them an especially refreshing wine. Such a setting is suited for storytelling. When, in the *Odyssey*, Odysseus and Eumaeus spent the evening together, the swineherd first arranged for a good meal and next asked his guest to explain who he was and how he had come. Odysseus answers:

> See, I will accurately answer all that you ask me.
> I only wish there were food enough for the time, for us two,
> and sweet wine for us here inside of the shelter, so that
> we could feast quietly while others tended the work; then
> easily I could go on for the whole of a year, and still not
> finish the story of my heart's tribulations, all that
> hard work I have done in my time, because the gods willed it
> (*Od.* 14.192-8; transl. Lattimore 1965).

This is the ideal setting for storytelling: food, drink, leisure, and plenty of time. One of the reasons why more stories are told in the *Odyssey* than in the *Iliad* may be that the heroes in the latter poem spend so much of the time engaged in warfare.

In another passage, Odysseus describes the ideal situation for epic performance:

> O great Alkinoös, pre-eminent among all people,
> surely indeed it is a good thing to listen to a singer
> such as this one before us, who is like the gods in his singing;
> for I think there is no occasion accomplished that is more pleasant
> than when festivity holds sway among all the populace,
> and the feasters up and down the houses are sitting in order
> and listening to the singer, and beside them the tables are loaded
> with bread and meats, and from the mixing bowl the wine steward
> draws the wine and carries it about and fills the cups. This
> seems to my own mind to be the best of occasions
> (*Od.* 9.2-15; transl. Lattimore 1965).

The description is similar. It contains the same basic elements as the occasion for storytelling: food, drink, and plenty of time; only the need for leisure is absent, significantly enough: Eumaeus has his swine to look after and the kinds of work that involves, whereas in the king's palace in fairyland such worries need not be taken into consideration. The difference is between the economic situation of the hosts rather than between rhapsodic singing and storytelling. Storytelling is for everybody, low and high. Singing is for aristocrats. Not that the singer belongs to high society, however much he is respected among the Phaeacians, but his patron does. Singing demands organization and listeners and somebody to care for them.

A result of what might be called the "hexametrification" of the stories may be found in the fact that normal low-style folk-genres like jokes, riddles, and proverbs are absent. This is actually astonishing considering that the poems are clearly related to international folklore – for instance, the main plot of the *Odyssey* is no. 974 in the Aarne-Thompson-Uther index.[13] There are situations where such humbler genres might have fitted in, especially when Odysseus and Eumaeus were entertaining each other in the swineherd's hut. It is as if the dignified meter has excluded them.

Stories come in many formats. The longest is Odysseus's *apologos* which takes up almost all of Books 9-12. Next come the detailed surveys of the *nostoi*, the stories of how the various Greek warriors reached their homes after the fall of Troy, which Nestor and Menelaus tell in Books 3 and 4 of the *Odyssey*, and after that a whole register of briefer stories such as the two Nestor told Patroclus in the *Iliad*. Some stories are short, such as that of Penelope's weaving which takes up 18 hexameters (*Od.* 2.93-110). Some are elliptical, referred to rather than told. For instance, Penelope mentions Pandareos's daughter lamenting Itylos, and the story is so short that it is barely understandable, since it happens not to be known from other sources (*Od.* 19.518-23).

In a way, you might even call many of the famous epithets micro-stories since they refer to well-known tales. When Odysseus is called *πτολίπορθος*, city-sacking, or *πολύτλας*, much-enduring, the adjectives recall two of the best-known exploits of this hero, that he was the one to design the Trojan Horse and thus conquer the city, and that he survived a troublesome journey home. Epithets such as *πολύμητις*, of many counsels, *πολυμήχανος*, of many resources, *πολύφρων*, of many thoughts, refer to situations in which the hero escaped danger by cunning, as for instance he did when he told the cyclops that his name was Nobody (*Od.* 9.353-414). The very fact that so many of his epithets begin with *πολυ-*, many-, suggests his resourcefulness and narrative manifestations of it. His wife Penelope is *περίφρων*, full of thoughts, which may make us think of how she kept her suitors at bay with her weaving trick, and also how she tested her husband's identity by mentioning their very special marital bed (*Od.*

13 Uther & al. 2004.

23.177-204). There are many similar narrative-like epithets as when for instance the goddess Artemis is called ἰοχέαιρα, arrow-pouring; this may trigger in our heads, stories such as how she and her brother killed Niobe's children (*Il.* XXIV.602-17).

The first-level narrators, too, have a broad register of stories. They may contain detailed biographies similar to the many homodiegetic stories we have considered as when in the *Odyssey* Telemachus, on his way back to Ithaca, meets a prophet, Theoclymenos, and his family background is recounted (*Od.* 15.223-56). Very often the first-level narrators provide subordinate characters with life stories. In the *Iliad* it may be a warrior who, at the moment of his death, is given identity by means of a brief story of his background, or we may think of the sweet Hecamede. In the *Odyssey* there are snapshot-like characterizations of persons such as a certain Elpenor. He was part of Odysseus's crew, but the young man was given to drink, and one night in Circe's house he "forgot" to use the ladder when descending from an upper floor terrace so that he fell down and broke his neck (*Od.* 10.552-60). Or the first-level narrator tells of a slave woman grinding wheat in Odysseus's household who cursed the suitors loudly and wished that their coming meal would be their last. She was smaller and weaker than the rest and had to work late into the night in order to fulfil her task (*Od.* 20.105-19). Even objects such as a cup or a chair may have their stories as, for example, the couch on which Penelope sits down when she meets her disguised husband late in the evening. We are told not only how rich it was, decorated with ivory and silver, but even the name of the carpenter who made it (*Od.* 19.57).

A special group of stories told by the first-level narrators differ from those told by characters. They occur typically in the similes when events in the main narratives are compared to mythical or fabulous creatures, such as lions or gods, or to everyday experience. The huge shield that the god Hephaestus forged for Achilles develops into a whole series of narratives, far beyond what would be understood from representation in pictures (*Il.* XIIX.478-608).

Homer conveys to his audiences the impression that the world is old and huge and full of stories, and that besides the story being told an unending mass of other stories are found which could also be told.

What we may overlook when reading Homer is how patterned this omnipresent storytelling is. For instance, the pleasant occasion for storytelling for which Odysseus was quoted above is rare; instead, many of the most important autobiographical stories are told by unknown guests on arrival and have the function of making the guest acceptable to his host. Polite hosts take care of their guests before asking about their identity, and in that way the storytelling may end up in surroundings like those Odysseus praised, but it is not necessarily so. Odysseus tells a false life story to Athena on the beach, and Menelaus relates his long *nostos*-performance to Telemachus in the morning at the young man's bedside (*Od.* 4.306-14). Even the battlefield may provide the setting for a story. In *Iliad* VI, the young Greek hero Diomedes had been wreaking havoc on the Trojans when he met an enemy he had not noticed before. He asked him who he was and how he dared approach him, and his adversary Glaukos answered with yet another life story. This one, however, referenced his ancestors, emphasizing his grandfather Bellerophon and his adventurous life; in this case, only the frame story is homodiegetic (*Il.* VI.145-211).

Unimportant storytelling such as anecdotes or gossip or just small talk as a pleasant means of entertainment does not occur very often. An example is when, in Eumaeus's steading, Odysseus tells the swineherd Eumaeus an anecdote from the Trojan War; even here, the first-level narrator tells us that the hero was freezing, and told his story in order to borrow a cloak (*Od.* 14.457-522). The story functions as a kind of payment: I entertain you, and you help me. The fact that Eumaeus, too, tells his life story to his guest (*Od.* 403-84) may be seen as one more expression of the swineherd's generosity. On a grander level, the story Odysseus told the Phaeacians was his payment for being brought home. While he was still in the middle of the performance, his story was felt by Queen Arete to be a gift deserving a gift in return, and she urged those present to give Odysseus a reward for his exciting storytelling. Similarly, an audience may ask for a special story, accompanying the request with a gift, as Odysseus did when the singer Demodocus was performing at the same party in Phaeacia (*Od.* 8.471-98). When the beggar and Penelope met and talked late in the evening and he told her a story containing the news that her husband would soon be back, she answered with a reward: he would be treated with a bath, a decent bed, and next morning a place next to Telemachus at breakfast (*Od.* 19.317-22). Telling stories just for the fun of it is conspicuously absent.

I see the fact that so many of the important stories are biographical as an example of the patterning that works at all levels of the Homeric narrative. Nestor repeatedly tells stories from his long life; similarly, another old man, Phoinix, tells of his tragic life in a speech to Achilles (*Il.* IX.447-84), and even the first-level narrator tells such a story about Theoclymenos, as we saw. People could have told stories of so many other things, but life stories and especially those that are homodiegetic prevail.

Two of the most important female characters are both unusual storytellers: Helen and her cousin Penelope. Telemachus and Nestor's son Pisistratus visit Sparta in Book 4. Menelaus and Helen are generous hosts, and the evening ends in an atmosphere of common relaxation and storytelling that so rarely happens. The king and queen each tell the two young men a story about the brave deeds Telemachus's father performed at Troy. Helen tells of how he once disguised himself as a beggar and entered the city in order to spy. She was the only one who recognized him, and she did not tell; but he revealed to her the plans the Greeks had. Menelaus tells of the Wooden Horse – how he and Odysseus and many others were hiding inside it when Helen and her new husband Deïphobos came near. Helen began to circle around the horse and imitate the voices of the wives of the Greek heroes who were hiding. Only because Odysseus was alert did the Greeks not disclose themselves (*Od.* 4.240-64; 4.269-89).

These are really strange anecdotes to tell to these narratees: Helen paints Odysseus as a traitor and/or a fool since he gave her information concerning the Greeks' plans, and Menelaus likewise describes Helen as a traitor whose behaviour could have meant death to both himself and the other Greek warriors. It is clear that it is not by thoughtlessness that the narrator lets them tell such stories because we are told that Helen had doctored the wine before serving it. She had a wonderful drug she had brought from Egypt.

> Whoever had drunk it down once it had been mixed in the wine bowl,
> for the day that he drank it would have no tear roll down his face,
> not if his mother died and his father died, not if men
> murdered a brother or a beloved son in his presence
> with the bronze, and he with his own eyes saw it. Such were
> the subtle medicines Zeus' daughter had in her possessions
> (*Od.* 4.222-27; transl. Lattimore 1965).

Penelope tells two stories to beggar-Odysseus at their late-night meeting. The first is the one about the weaving trick. The other is about a dream she had. In the palace she had twenty geese and was fond of them, but an eagle came from the sky, killed them all, and left. She cried, and neighbouring women came by to console her. Then the eagle returned and explained to her that this was an omen: the geese were the suitors and the bird himself Odysseus, and it was not really a dream, but rather a vision. When she woke up, she saw her geese were still alive (*Od.* 19.139-56; 535-53).

This is in all respects odd. For one thing, Homeric dreams are usually messages from the gods, whereas this is more like the dreams people may have in real life. Next, as a story it is unlike normal Homeric stories telling autobiographies. Finally, as part of the portrait of the virtuous wife we may speculate why Penelope underlines so much that she was fond of the geese and very unhappy when they were killed. Immediately before recounting the dream, she compares herself to the nightingale: she has difficulties falling asleep because she is thinking of her relationship with her son and wailing just like the bird who had killed her son in a moment of insanity.

Scholars have, of course, commented eagerly on these stories and offered various interpretations.[14] My point in relating them here is to consider them as portraits that show how mysterious these two ladies are. What was Helen's purpose in revisiting scenes from Troy that were so unpleasant? Why did the death of the geese break Penelope's heart? And why did speculations about her adult son make her compare herself to a murderous mother? The stories reveal both women as potentially dangerous, and just under the surface churns the sea of other, similar stories. Both scenes, in Sparta and in Ithaca, develop peacefully, but we feel the parallel stories as threatening potentialities.[15]

The very patterning of the stories and the contexts in which they are told should caution us against reading the world of the poems as an image of the real world of poets and audiences. Besides, the similarity in narrative order between storytellers in the poems and the poets themselves is an argument that the art of varying and adapting is shared by poets and storytellers.

The flexible oral narrative

The Finnish scholar Lauri Honko (1932-2002) was a professor of folkloristics and comparative religion at the University of Turku, but during the last decades of his life he engaged in the study of the national epic *Kalevala* in a comparative setting. His knowledge of epic traditions worldwide was remarkable. In Karnataka in India, he found a vibrant epic tradition among speakers of the language Tulu in South Kanara. In 1989 he met a farmer, priest, and epic singer called Gopala Naika, who agreed to let him attend his performances, even though they were made at various cult events. Honko established a research team with a Finnish colleague and two Indian scholars who were specialists on Tulu religion and were also willing to work as interpreters. In December 1990, Gopala Naika sang to the recording apparatus his longest epic, celebrating the heroine Siri. The performance took six days and ran to 15,683 verse lines; the total singing time was 26 hours and 9 minutes, counting only singing proper. Afterwards it took almost eight years before an edition with an English translation and commentary was published.

14 Alden 2017 discusses Helen and Menelaus (157-68) and reads their stories as advice to Telemachus: Helen presents herself as smart, but Menelaus's story, directed at her as an answer, works as a warning to the young man. He should beware of letting his mother be part of whatever plans he may have to get rid of the suitors. Helen was not reliable, nor are other women. Alden comments on the nightingale and the dream (132-47). After considering many possibilities she ends up simplistically: Penelope's words about the nightingale refer to versions of the tale in which Dionysiac madness is front and center and she is afraid of being the victim of such madness. She cried over the geese before hearing the eagle's interpretation; she tells her dream to the stranger in order to hear his opinion; she does not accept his interpretation, but takes his subsequent counsel to put up the bow for the shooting competition.

15 One of my peer reviewers suggests that, in contrast to the *Iliad*, "stories in the *Odyssey* are set in a context of falsehood or trickery, which is a form of riddle set upon their recipient". That may be so, but to me the trickery seems dependent on the individuals rather than a common characteristic of Odyssean stories.

The edition is accompanied by a volume describing the process. To the Homeric scholar, the book is a treasure trove of the kind of information we lack when studying the Homeric texts.

In the present connection I am especially interested in Honko's investigations in the variability of Naika's poems and the singer's techniques. He quotes and/or refers to detailed discussions with Naika on such matters, based on his own folklore experience and theories. He states:

> Folklore has no "master" form; folkloric variation is neither stable nor hierarchic; variation has not one but many forms, some of which create more lasting changes than others; hence the construction of a stemma by comparing variants is futile. The picture of variation based on the available materials is not realistic, because there has been more variation, and its scope has been wider than it is possible to assess on the basis of thin materials.[16]

("Thin materials" are those that consist of texts known in few exemplars or without context information.)

With reference to the classics in the investigation of oral poetry, especially Ruth Finnegan, John Miles Foley, and Paul Zumthor, Honko establishes a set of terms: the singer has his idiolect, his special form of the poetic language. His repertoire of epic songs makes up a pool of tradition, described as his inventory of multiforms, phrases, formulas, and the like. This is his proper share of the common pool of tradition, in which the elements reside to be used in different combinations by different performers.[17] When a singer learns a new song, he works through it until he has found a form that pleases him, a mental text, which is open for endless variation but in itself may remain stable for the rest of the singer's active life.[18]

Such a mental text may be performed in various formats. One of Honko's most startling experiences with Gopala Naika was when, one day in 1995, the singer mentioned that he had recently appeared on All India Radio performing the *Kooti Cennaya epic* in twenty minutes. Three years earlier, Honko and his team had recorded a performance of this same epic in 15 hours of singing, and resulting in approximately 7,000 lines.

> To be able to believe him, I had to ask Gopala Naika to sing Kooti Cennaya once more in twenty minutes, just as he had performed it on the radio. Without hesitation he complied and sang for about 27 minutes. When the performance ended, I told him the time he had taken, to which he remarked, "I must have used more voice this time."[19]

Honko asked Naika many questions about how he had learned the epics that he knew, and summarized his information as follows:

> The idea of the compilation of a large epic out of fully-fledged part-narratives may be more literary than oral and thus misleading. There is some evidence that a whole narrative is occasionally learned from one person but it is by no means the only method. In Gopala Naika's case, he maintains that he learned the Kooti Cennaya epic from Seesamma, and during our fieldwork period he learned a new epic, Koordabbu, from a childhood friend. Yet this method does not apply to the "learning" of the Siri epic, which Gopala Naika heard in bits and pieces from many people, male and female, adjusting the acquired material to his mental text, slowly developed on two levels, that of the whole epic and that of part-narratives. This process also contained rejection of elements offered by other

16 Honko 1998a, 45-6.

17 *Ibid.*, 62-74.

18 *Ibid.*, 92-99.

19 *Ibid.*, 30.

> singers. It also kept alive alternative ways of focusing the plot according to the situation of performance.[20]

I do not think these two processes exclude each other. A mental text may be adjusted over the years, typically when the singer attends performances in which he finds elements that please him. In traditions containing many itinerant singers, learning and adaptation is permanently ongoing.

When, many years ago, Milman Parry had his interpreter interview Yugoslav singers about their art, one of the questions was if they were able to learn a new song by just hearing it once. A detail that intrigued him was that if they answered in the affirmative, they also added that they would need a brief interval before performing the new song, a day or two, or at least an hour. For instance, Sulejman Makic, when asked whether it would not be better to sing it right away than later when he might have forgotten part of it, answered: "It has to come to one. One has to think … how it goes, and then little by little it comes to him, so that he won't leave anything out."[21] Makic's experience fits precisely with what Honko learned from Naika. To my understanding the idea of the mental text helps to explain the paradox between documentations of the huge achievements of memory in oral traditions and the documented ongoing changes; besides, it makes sense that the most important changes in traditions tend to take place when one singer learns a song from another.

For the mental text to work, the singer must decide on a performance strategy. Honko writes:

> The singer mostly thinks he is performing the story in full, regardless of the length of his presentation. The chosen form is always relevant and correct, defensible in the eyes of the singer. This attitude derives from the "truth" (*satya* in Tulu) of his narrative, not to be compromised under any circumstances. Epics are "true stories", their moral grandeur, a characteristic of the genre, is based on this qualitative feature.[22]

Honko was deeply impressed by the ease and fluidity with which Gopala Naika handled his mental text. In normal performance, for instance when Naika was leading the possession cult, he might well begin with one of the last episodes of the storyline; nevertheless, he was able to perform a long, continued narrative when the research team asked for it. This was the text that was eventually published; Honko speaks of the singer's "organised totality of the whole story".[23] Gopala Naika stated that such a performance was something he had never tried before.

When it comes to Homer, we are unable to ask a rhapsode how he has been taught, how many songs he has in his repertoire, from whom he has learned them, what he prefers to perform to whom, or what strategy he has for a performance. Homer is known only in what Honko would call extremely thin materials, and we have to study these "materials" themselves for traces of how the rhapsodes proceeded.

Inserting stories is obviously one of the means of expanding a mental text, and no doubt the poets of the *Iliad* and the *Odyssey* used this strategy. However, in the present paper I prefer to discuss the flexibility as it reveals itself when the "same" stories are told more than once. In general, I agree with Maureen Alden that the poets are highly sophisticated in making their inserted stories fit into the main plots.

There are cases in which stories are repeated verbatim with only the kind of change required when shifting from one narrator to another. For instance, when Odysseus travels to the Underworld his errand is to meet the dead seer Tiresias and hear how he can finish his travels and get back to Ithaca. Among other things the seer tells him that in order to finally find peace he must appease Poseidon's wrath, caused

20 *Ibid.*, 133.

21 Parry & Lord 1954, 266; cf. 240.

22 Honko 1998a, 134.

23 *Ibid.*, 314.

by the hero's blinding of the god's son Polyphemus. Teiresias says, You have to do this and that... At the end of the poem when Odysseus and Penelope are finally reunited in bed and husband and wife each tells what happened during the twenty years that have passed, Odysseus relates the seer's order to his wife. It is repeated in exactly the same words, only here in the form, Teiresias said that I had to do this and that... (11.121-37 = 23.268-84).

Another story that is repeated verbatim is that of Penelope's weaving trick, which occurs thrice. First the suitor Antinous tells of it in a speech at the assembly in Ithaca at the beginning of the *Odyssey*. Next, Penelope herself describes her weaving to her husband without yet knowing his identity, in the intense scene of the late-night talk between the two. The third telling occurs in the odd passage of the last book when the dead suitors' souls arrive in Hades. The shadow of Agamemnon asks them why such a crowd is all of a sudden entering, and the dead soul of Amphimedon answers him (2.94-110 = 19.139-56 = 24.129-46).

Similar repetitions occur on quite a few occasions in both the *Odyssey* and the *Iliad*. I think the rhapsodes performing them were displaying their virtuosity in memorizing and adapting. The procedure must have demanded careful training before it could be accomplished fluently, and I imagine that such training was part of the education of young singers. After all, demonstrating that he was able to perform accurate repetitions a rhapsode implicitly guaranteed the truth of his song to his audience: look how good I am at memorizing. Part I of Jonathan Ready's interesting study of *Orality, Textuality, and the Homeric Epics* (2019) is a detailed study of this process.

A different kind of retelling occurs when poets tell of the same events in various formats such as Gopala Naika did. This procedure exemplifies another very important quality a singer of oral epic must command, and again I imagine that Homeric rhapsodes were carefully trained at an early age in order to master it.

Odysseus's adventures, an important part of the storyline of the *Odyssey*, are told three times and switching between narrator levels. First, in an extremely brief version in the prologue to the poem when the rhapsode asks the Muse to tell him and his audience of the hero's journey home. Here the mental text is abbreviated to a very few facts: the hero's troubles after the fall of Troy, his unsuccessful attempts at saving his crew, and a defence of him: they perished by their own fault. The Muse knows it all and needs only a prompt. Next, a very detailed version is given, taking up Books 5-13, in which the first-level narrator relates the hero's departure from Calypso and arrival in Phaeacia, followed by Odysseus's own storytelling in the king's hall, and finally his arrival in Ithaca, again told by the first-level narrator. In this version, the first-level narrator breaks the chronology by beginning with Calypso, but from the point when Odysseus takes over, the events are related in the order in which they occurred. The *apologos*, the part told by Odysseus to the Phaeacians, generously meets the audience's curiosity and appreciation of good entertainment. Even though they are sailors they live in isolation and may well be curious as to other people's adventures.

The third telling occurs at the end of the poem when Odysseus tells it all to Penelope. The version of the story Odysseus narrates here is short, structured chronologically, told in third person, and adapted to his narratee. Notably, the role of the helpful females is downplayed. Circe is barely mentioned, and Nausicaa has disappeared. About Calypso, Odysseus relates that she wanted him as her husband and offered him immortality, implying the flattering fact that he preferred mortality with Penelope. Here we may note the variation in length, the shift between chronological telling and the more elaborate structure of the longest version, and the adaptation of versions to specific narratees. The three stories are different manifestations of the same mental text.

It is well known how scholars in former times cut up the *Iliad* and the *Odyssey* in bits and pieces, and even today most professional readers expel *Iliad* X from that poem. This is not a symptom of arbitrary whims, but the result of learning and clear judgement. However, from my standpoint this is impossible. A singer learning a new song normally keeps close to his model and retains as much as possible of its wording. If he keeps a song and lets it become a regular part of his repertoire, it will gradually be assimilated to his idiolect. I must emphasize that this does not mean that interpolations cannot have occurred, only that we as readers do not have the tools to discern.

Lies

Of special interest in connection with this analysis are the lies Odysseus tells during his incognito stay in Ithaca.[24] They resemble each other but vary considerably in length and content. In this respect they may be classified as a third category next to the passages repeated verbatim and those that occur as shorter or longer versions of the "same" passage. The lies are told as different stories even though according to Honko's model they are built over one and the same mental text. Odysseus's procedure has been criticized for being inappropriate since a liar had better stay with the same lie in order not to be revealed.[25] However, it seems that this kind of logic did not interest the rhapsode, who instead had his hero vary his story and adapt it to his narratees.

In *Odyssey* 13 Odysseus finally arrives in Ithaca, sleeping. The kind Phaeacians carry him ashore and leave him there with all his belongings. When he wakes up, the goddess Athena arrives in the form of an elegant young shepherd. Odysseus asks her where he is, and even though he is enthusiastic when he hears that he has arrived on his native island, he does not reveal his identity, but tells a story of how he has fled from Crete where he has killed a man. The victim was the son of the famous Idomeneus, and the conflict was over booty from the war of Troy. After the killing he shared his riches with his sons, leaving them one half and carrying the other half with him. He paid Phoenician sailors to bring him to the mainland, but they were brought off course by a storm, and while he was asleep the sailors carried him ashore and left (*Od.* 13.256-86). Athena changes her appearance to her normal female form, pats his arm and says, Well, well, well, among humans you are the smartest liar, while I excel among the gods!

First, we may note the appreciation of a good lie, already expressed by the narrator in the lines that introduce Odysseus's story: he did not speak the truth, but with his usual cunning veiled the story. When Athena then gives her expert's evaluation, this point is clear. Next, the fact that Odysseus is able spontaneously to invent a probable and detailed story is also worthy of admiration.

When we consider the quality of his story it is clear that it meets its most important function, to explain the circumstances of how a man comes to be found alone on the beach surrounded by luxurious

24 Blümlein 1971 is a close reading and comparison of 13 lies, including those that are not narrative. The focus is on the poet: how did he characterize his hero? Blümlein emphasizes Odysseus's words to Amphinomos in which he teaches the suitor of the human condition (*Od.* 18.125-50): "sie scheinen mir eine entsprechend wichtige Bedeutung für das ganze Werk zu besitzen: Nirgends sonst äussert sich der Dichter so grundsätzlich über den Menschen" (I think they [Odysseus's words] are of significant importance also for the work as a whole: nowhere else does the poet express himself so fundamentally about human beings, 74). de Jong 2001 discusses the lies (326-28) and offers a comparative survey (596-97).

25 West 2014, 67. On the other hand, de Jong 2001, 327 underlines how each fictional identity Odysseus takes on is adapted to his narratee; I agree with de Jong. Christensen 2020 analyzes Odysseus's lies as the hero's means to reconstruct his identity after his homecoming, and his focus is on the narrator's psychical development.

goods. Besides, it is adapted to the shepherd, first by opening with a laudation of the island of Ithaca in order to dispose the young man kindly toward the speaker, and next by implicitly stating that even though the stranger is alone, he is strong and would be able to defend himself if necessary. Last, but not least, the story achieves verisimilitude by referring to a famous warrior by name, and by being fitted into the stories of the Trojan War.

We shall find these qualities again in other lies Odysseus tells:

Explanation of the situation.
Flattery of the narratee.
Other forms of adaptation to the narratee.
Establishing verisimilitude by reference to factual details such as names of localities and persons.
Inclusion of elements fetched from Odysseus's actual adventures as related in the overall story.
In some of the stories, Odysseus introduces himself with a false name.
Some of the stories begin with an assertion that he will speak the truth.

In general, the Trojan War is a recurring element in the stories. Besides, the island of Crete is so often mentioned that it has called for comments of various kinds. Some scholars have suggested that the prominence of Crete may be related to a widespread idea documented in later texts, that Cretans were notorious liars. Of special interest to me is the hypothesis discussed by Steve Reece and Christos Tsagalis and further developed by Gregory Nagy, that the significance of this island in Odysseus's lies, and its mention even by Eumaeus (*Od.* 14.382-85), may be evidence of traces of an alternative version of the *Odyssey*. I sympathize with this, but in my understanding of Homeric epic, the *Odyssey* is not the epitome, so to speak, of how Odysseus's homecoming should be described, with a Cretan version as a rival. Traditions do not aim at one, final version, but handle its potential tales as multiforms. The common pool contained these alternatives, and singers had learned one or the other or both. The singer of our *Odyssey* seems to have belonged to this last group: being familiar with both versions he opted for the one that suited him and his audience best, and used elements from the other version as handy material for the hero's lies. In any case it is exciting that the contours of another such version of the tale can be drawn.[26]

During the following books Odysseus, disguised as a beggar, tells seven other untrue stories (*Od.* 14.192-359; 14.462-506; 17.415-44; 18.125-50; 19.71-88; 19.107-22, 165-202, 221-48, 262-307; 24.244-79, 303-14). He tells two to the swineherd Eumaeus, three to two suitors and a slave girl respectively, one to Penelope, and one to his father Laertes. They are all carefully designed to explain the speaker's circumstances, and except for the one to Melantho, the slave girl, they are all introduced with some kind of flattery.

As the stories evolve, particular elements of the mental text are activated, according to the narratee in question. The longest stories are told to Eumaeus and Penelope, and these are also those most filled with wondrous events in far-away places, dangerous encounters, flights, and storms. In these cases, the storyteller not only works to convince his narratees, but also entertains them during pauses of their not very exciting everyday lives. Compared to the portrait Odysseus made of himself to the disguised Athena, to the swineherd he appears as an important man of the world who, son of a slave mother, made his way in life by dedicating himself to war, seafaring, and adventures. Most clearly addressed to narratees who miss Odysseus and hope for his homecoming are the passages in which the beggar tells how he has met Odysseus, in some cases even been his host, or has heard of him from others who could tell that he

26 Reece 1994; Tsagalis 2012; Nagy 2017. Tsagalis 314 n. 19 contains a very rich survey of the variety of views on this matter and the scholars that held them.

was on his way. He tells both Eumaeus and Penelope that he has visited the land of the Thesprotians and heard from them that Odysseus is on his way home. However, the hero first planned a visit to Zeus's oracle in Dodone in order to receive advice on how to proceed on arrival.

The stories told to the suitors are brief, and here the flattery serves the purpose of moralizing and warning: you who are basically good men should act accordingly and mind that fortune is fickle. I am a beggar, but once I was just as rich and happy as you are now. His misfortunes have been a journey to Egypt ending with him being sold into slavery, or simply his own criminal acts. The girl Melantho is outright threatened.

All through the various lies the mental text is recognizable, and closely related to the pattern of Odysseus's *apologos* as well as to the other *nostoi*. The life stories of Eumaeus and the old slave woman Eurycleia, too, are modelled over the same mental text. Their stories did not end with a homecoming, but still the ingredients are the same: pirates, storms, and dangerous sea voyages.

To the mental text may be added elements that are special for the relationship between narrator and narratee. This is the case for the story Odysseus tells Penelope during their late-night talk leading up to the famous scene in which the hero's old nurse washes his feet. Among his lies, this is the masterpiece in which he uses his familiarity with his wife to tell a story that is exactly tailored to move this narratee. The lying story has the character of a conversation rather than a story, being broken up by Penelope's reactions and questions. When he asserts that he hosted Odysseus in Crete many years ago, she tries him out asking what her husband was wearing. He hesitates, pointing to the distance in time, a hesitation that only reinforces the convincing effect of the precise description he then offers. The specially adapted story culminates when he depicts how the Cretan ladies admired the fine fabric of his garments, well knowing that his wife had woven them herself.

> *ἴσκε ψεύδεα πολλὰ λέγων ἐτύμοισιν ὁμοῖα* (*Od.* 19.203).
>
> He knew how to tell many lies resembling realities[27]

is the comment of the first-level narrator with evident appreciation, and Penelope breaks down in tears.

To my analysis the verse is central, for although I allow myself to compare prose stories to epic song it must be underlined that for all the similarities there is an important difference: epic is meant to relate true events from bygone days, while the field of prose stories is less restricted. The rhapsode's claim to truthfulness depends on the Muses; without them as his eyewitnesses he would be unable to practise his profession. However, like other gods they are fickle, and when they met the Hesiodic rhapsode and gave him his staff, they used these very words:

> *ἴδμεν ψεύδεα πολλὰ λέγειν ἐτύμοισιν ὁμοῖα,*
> *ἴδμεν δ', εὖτ' ἐθέλωμεν, ἀληθέα γηρύσασθαι* (Hes. *Theog.* 27-28).
>
> We know how to tell many lies resembling realities,
> and we know, when we want to, how to perform truths.

The first-level narrator of the *Odyssey* knows that the hero is lying, but when it comes to their own art, the rhapsodes can only hope that it pleases the Muses to be truthful.

The verse about lying is common to Homer and Hesiod, connected with each other in the same way as the repeated passages above. Something very similar occurs in still another connection when the dangerous Sirens call out to our hero:

27 This and the following two quotes are my translation.

> *ἴδμεν γάρ τοι πάνθ', ὅσ' ἐνὶ Τροίῃ εὐρείῃ*
> *Ἀργεῖοι Τρῶές τε θεῶν ἰότητι μόγησαν,*
> *ἴδμεν δ' ὅσσα γένηται ἐπὶ χθονὶ πουλυβοτείρῃ* (*Od.* 12.189-91).

> For we know everything that in wide Troy
> the Argives and Trojans suffered through the gods' will,
> and we know everything that happens over all the much-nourishing earth.

Is it not touching that what they tempt him with is knowledge? Even goddesses adapt their stories to their narratee. What interests me here, however, is the fact that Homer's Odysseus, his Sirens, and Hesiod's Muses speak in the same way. Muses and Sirens are only connected by the way in which "we know" is placed markedly at the opening of the two verses, so according to Parry's definition of the formula they do not fit into that category. But just as Michael Nagler once said about some intriguing repetitions that could not be called formulae, I feel like saying, "It is a group of *something*".[28] In Honko's terminology, the phrases belong to the pool of tradition common to Hesiod and Homer.

These three brief passages all suggest that storytelling may be dangerous. The Sirens tempt Odysseus with their knowledge, but if he gives way he will die. The explicit danger of the Muses' knowledge is only that they may be lying, but mortal risk still clings to the phrase; the promise of unlimited information includes arbitrariness. As mortals we are at the gods' mercy, and as listeners at the singer's, just as Penelope was an easy victim to Odysseus's lie.

The storytelling scenes suggest that the qualities most admired are precise memorization, constant variation, adaptation to the narratees, entertainment, spontaneous performance, and clever lying. I transfer this aesthetic from the poems to the real world and assert that except for the last point – the lying – the rhapsodes aimed at displaying such qualities in their own handling of the tradition, and that in this they acted just as singers of oral epic have been doing through history and are still doing.

Gods as liars

In her conversation with Odysseus in Book 13, Athena boasted of being the best liar among the gods, and in Book 1 when she arrived to greet Telemachus disguised as his father's friend Mentes, she told him a lying story resembling those that Odysseus tells later on. She opened with an assurance of the truth of her story, explained what circumstances brought her to Ithaca, and took care to include a fair number of details (*Od.* 1.179-205). Other gods are accomplished liars, too, as we learn from the Homeric hymns. Of the four gods to whom long hymns are preserved, three excel at this art: Demeter, Hermes, and Aphrodite. Hermes is irrelevant for my purpose since his lying is not narrative, whereas the two goddesses perform beautiful lying stories drawing from the same pool of tradition as the *Odyssey*-singer. In a charming scene Demeter, disguised as an elderly, poor woman, meets four young princesses in Eleusis. She sits at the fountain when they arrive to fetch water for their parents, and the poet dwells on their names: Callidice, Cleisidice, Demo, and Callithoe, so that the small list of sweetly sounding names in itself becomes a praise of their beauty. They ask her who she is and suggest that she could be employed to look after their small brother. He is *πολυεύχετος ἀσπάσιός τε*, much prayed for and gladly welcomed; we almost feel the relief of the parents who after four daughters finally had a son! Having assured them that she will speak pure truth, Demeter gives herself a false name and tells them a story of how she was born in Crete, had been abducted by pirates who would sell her as a slave, and brought to Thorikos. She had escaped from them, and that is why she now

28 Nagler 1974, 11.

sits at the fountain hoping to find employment as a nurse or housekeeper. She adds all her best wishes that they find good husbands (*Hom. Hymn Dem.* 96-170).

We recognize the ingredients of Odysseus's lies: the assurance of truth, the false name, the explanation of the situation, flattery of the narratees, the establishment of verisimilitude by reference to place names, in this case Crete and Thorikos, and the role of pirates.

The most elaborate lying story told by a god is, however, the one Aphrodite disguised as a young girl tells the Trojan prince Anchises. It contains most of the elements on the list, although in this case Crete is not involved.[29]

The *Hymn to Aphrodite* is surprising since it celebrates the goddess by telling a story in which she is a victim rather than a heroine. The plot is that Zeus is tired of her power over the other gods – not least himself – and decides that for once she shall be treated with her own medicine. Accordingly, he lets her fall in love with a mortal, the shepherd-prince Anchises, who is tending cattle on the heights of Mount Ida near Troy. This is explicitly a punishment, and Eros is represented as a divine power that attacks and conquers a person, but the narrative leaves no doubt that such an attack has its charming aspects for the parties involved. For instance, it is noticeable that the word for desire, *ἵμερος*, is characterized by the epithet *γλυκύς*, sweet (*Hymn Hom. Ven.* 45, 141).

The passage is a realization of a story pattern known from other parts of the transmitted archaic Greek epic: woman seduces man. The most similar passage is *Iliad* 14.153-351, where Hera seduces Zeus in order to distract him from supporting the Trojans on the battlefield. Just like Aphrodite, Hera prepares herself carefully, washes, puts on perfume, dresses elegantly, and adorns herself with jewellery. When she approaches her husband she gives a small speech, claiming to be on her way to visit her foster parents, a lie meant to put him off guard, and she succeeds. In the Hesiodic corpus, it is told twice how the original woman was created as part of Zeus's revenge on Prometheus for having stolen fire and given it to mankind. In *Works and Days* 42-105 the woman is called Pandora, and she brings her jar from which she spreads evils. In *Theogony* 570-612 she has no name, and the evil is her very existence. In both cases she is prepared by the gods as a beauty, wonderfully dressed and ornamented with jewels, and in *Theogony* 571-84 especially the preparation scene is close to Aphrodite's preparations in the hymn, even in its wording. In *Works and Days* she is not only beautiful and wonderfully adorned, but among the talents given her are *κύνεος νόος*, the mind of a dog, i.e. shamelessness, *ἐπίκλοπον ἦθος*, a thievish character, *ψεύδεα*, lies, and *αἱμύλιοι λόγοι*, wily words (vv. 67 and 78). In both versions it is mentioned that she has a voice, and though she gives no speech it is clear that Pandora is able to cheat men by rhetoric. In *Odyssey* 12.39-46 and 181-94, the Sirens are yet another manifestation of the pattern, and here all the focus is on their treacherous speech. The examples are typical of how patterns work: the manifestations vary in length, detail, and moral according to context, and one does not refer to another. In all cases the women are treacherous liars and succeed with their lies – even Odysseus would have obeyed the Sirens had he not been tied to the mast. In a way, Aphrodite is the most innocent of them. Whereas the others use their sexual appeal to fulfil some mischief, her purpose is what it seems, intercourse, and Anchises survives his mating with the goddess without punishment.

Aphrodite goes to her temple in Paphos to make her toilet; she washes, dresses up, adorns herself with luxurious jewellery, and sets off for Mount Ida.

29 I am much inspired by Bergren 2008. Andrew Faulkner published a new edition and commentary on the *Hymn to Aphrodite* 2008, and has continued his study of hymns; his interests, however, are concentrated on reception history and not immediately relevant for the present paper. Faulkner 2011; Faulkner & Hodkinson 2015.

On her way, her mere presence overwhelms wild animals with desire and makes them slink away to mate in shadowy dens. She changes her stature into that of a mortal girl and finds Anchises left alone in his hut, playing the lyre, while the other shepherds have taken the animals to graze. With all her finery, even though she tries to look human he immediately takes her for a goddess, promises to build her an altar and give her sacrifices, and prays for a long life and high status in society.

Aphrodite answers with a delicious lying story. Like Hera's speech to Zeus it serves the purpose to put the man off guard. Aphrodite claims to be mortal, the virgin daughter of the Phrygian king Otreus and his wife. She was participating in a dance for the goddess Artemis in the company of other young girls when the god Hermes snatched her away and carried her off through the air right up to Anchises, ordering her to become his wedded wife and bear him children. Now she asks him to introduce her to his family, send a message to her parents about her dowry, and arrange for a grand wedding.

Anchises is overwhelmed. After all, it is the very goddess of love who stands before him, and as we saw, her radiance is forceful. He brushes aside all thoughts of a lawful wedding, saying that even if Apollo himself will punish him with death he will make love to her, immediately. He takes her to his bed, takes off her adornments, undresses her slowly, and has intercourse with her. "And then Anchises by divine will and destiny lay with the immortal goddess, the mortal, not knowing the truth of it" states the narrator (*Hymn Hom. Ven.* 166-7).

Later in the afternoon, before the return of Anchises's fellow shepherds, Aphrodite stood up. She took on her full outward appearance as a goddess, her head reaching the ceiling. She woke up Anchises, who was terrified and implored her not to punish him with impotence. The goddess answered with a long speech and reassured him that she would not hurt him. However, she would bear him a son, Aeneas. The child would be reared by mountain nymphs, and when he had grown up, she would bring him to Anchises. However, she forbade him ever to tell anybody that he had slept with Aphrodite.

The hymn might be considered an anti-hymn since the goddess is the victim of Zeus's punishment. And yet, in its own tricky way it still relates a story of Aphrodite's power to which animals and humans alike are subject.

Here we shall concentrate on Aphrodite's lying story:

Ἄγχιση, κύδιστε χαμαιγενέων ἀνθρώπων,
οὔ τίς τοι θεός εἰμι· τί μ' ἀθανάτῃσιν ἐίσκεις;
ἀλλὰ καταθνητή τε, γυνὴ δέ με γείνατο μήτηρ.
Ὀτρεὺς δ' ἐστὶ πατὴρ ὀνομάκλυτος, εἴ που ἀκούεις,
ὃς πάσης Φρυγίης εὐτειχήτοιο ἀνάσσει.
γλῶσσαν δ' ὑμετέρην <τε> καὶ ἡμετέρην σάφα οἶδα·
Τρῳὰς γὰρ μεγάρῳ με τροφὸς τρέφεν ἡδὲ διάπρο
σμικρὴν παῖδ' ἀτίταλλε φίλης παρὰ μητρὸς ἑλοῦσα·
ὣς δή τοι γλῶσσάν γε καὶ ὑμετέρην εὖ οἶδα.
νῦν δέ μ' ἀνήρπαξε χρυσόρραπις Ἀργειφόντης
ἐκ χοροῦ Ἀρτέμιδος χρυσηλακάτου κελαδεινῆς.
πολλαὶ δὲ νύμφαι καὶ παρθένοι ἀλφεσίβοιαι
παίζομεν, ἀμφὶ δ' ὅμιλος ἀπείριτος ἐστεφάνωτο·
ἔνθέν μ' ἥρπαξε χρυσόρραπις Ἀργειφόντης,
πολλὰ δ' ἐπ' ἤγαγεν ἔργα καταθνητῶν ἀνθρώπων,
πολλὴν δ' ἄκληρόν τε καὶ ἄκτιτον, ἣν διὰ θῆρες
ὠμοφάγοι φοιτῶσι κατὰ σκιόεντας ἐναύλους,
οὐδὲ ποσὶ ψαύειν δόκεον φυσιζόου αἴης·
Ἀγχίσεω δέ με φάσκε παραὶ λέχεσιν καλέεσθαι
κουριδίην ἄλοχον, σοὶ δ' ἀγλαὰ τέκνα τεκεῖσθαι.
αὐτὰρ ἐπεὶ δὴ δεῖξε καὶ ἔφρασεν, ἤτοι ὅ γ' αὖτις
ἀθανάτων μετὰ φῦλ' ἀπέβη κρατὺς Ἀργειφόντης·
αὐτὰρ ἐγώ σ' ἱκόμην, κρατερὴ δέ μοι ἔπλετ ἀνάγκη.
ἀλλά σε πρὸς Ζηνὸς γουνάζομαι ἠδὲ τοκήων
ἐσθλῶν οὐ μὲν γάρ κε κακοὶ τοιόνδε τέκοιεν·
ἀδμήτην μ' ἀγαγὼν καὶ ἀπειρήτην φιλότητος
πατρί τε σῶι δεῖξον καὶ μητέρι κεδν' εἰδυίῃ
σοῖς τε κασιγνήτοις, οἵ τοι ὁμόθεν γεγάασιν·
οὔ σφιν ἀεικελίη νυὸς ἔσσομαι, ἀλλ' εἰκυῖα.
πέμψαι δ' ἄγγελον ὦκα μετὰ Φρύγας αἰολοπώλους,
εἰπεῖν πατρί τ' ἐμῶι καὶ μητέρι κηδομένῃ περ·

οἵ δέ κέ <τοι> χρυσόν τε ἅλις ἐσθητά θ' ὑφάντην
πέμψουσιν, σὺ δὲ πολλὰ καὶ ἀγλαὰ δέχται ἄποινα.
ταῦτα δὲ ποιήσας δαίνυ γάμον ἱμερόεντα
τίμιον ἀνθρώποισι καὶ ἀθανάτοισι θεοῖσιν (*Hymn Hom. Ven.* 108-42).

Anchises, most glorious of earthborn men, I am no goddess – why do you compare me with the immortals? – but a mortal, and the mother who bore me was a woman. My father is the famed Otreus, if you have perhaps heard of him, who rules over all of well-walled Phrygia. But I know your language as well as ours, because a Trojan nurse nursed me at home and reared me throughout my childhood, taking me over from my dear mother; so I am well acquainted with your language too. But now the gold-wand Argus-slayer has snatched me up from the dance to Artemis of the gold shafts and the view-halloo. There were many of us dancing, brides and marriageable girls, and a vast crowd ringed us about: from there the gold-wand Argus-slayer snatched me, and brought me over much farmland of mortal men, and much ownerless and uncultivated land where ravening beasts roam about their shadowy haunts; I felt that my feet were not touching the grain-growing earth. He told me I should be known as the young wife of Anchises' bed, and bear you splendid children. After showing me the way and pointing you out, the mighty Argus-slayer went off to rejoin the families of the immortals, while I have come to you, forced by necessity. Now I beseech you by Zeus and your noble parents (no humble people would have produced such a child as you): take me, a virgin with no experience of love, and show me to your father and your dutiful mother, and your brothers born of the same stock; I shall not be an unfitting daughter-in-law for them, but a fit one. And send a messenger quickly to the Phrygians of the darting steeds, to tell my father and my anxious mother. They will send you gold in plenty and woven cloth, and you must accept the many fine dowry gifts. When you have done that, hold a delightful wedding-feast that will impress men and immortal gods (transl. West 2003).

Aphrodite had a difficult job. Her scheme was to seduce Anchises, but in order to achieve that she had to convince him that she was not only mortal, but an inexperienced young virgin, an identity diametrically opposed to her true character. Other Homeric liars disguise themselves and she, too, changed to mortal size, but since she wanted to stay beautiful and attractive, she did not renounce her finery. She therefore failed from the start; he guessed immediately that she was a goddess.

Now her autobiography has to explain the facts of the situation. She has arrived from the middle of nowhere and is standing there at the shepherds' hut, dressed up as if for a ball. She has to lie on more than one level: her divinity, her status as the goddess of sexual love and thus the expert above all experts, and her scheme, to have intercourse with him.

First, she flatters him. Next, she fills her own life story with details. She refers to her father by name, and the fact that he is a king goes part of the way to explain her well-groomed appearance. However, in Phrygia a different language is spoken than in Troy, so how can she speak to him in his own language? Because her nurse was a Trojan! Her elegant dress and luxurious adornments find explanation in the fact that she was dancing in a girls' choir for Artemis when she was snatched away, as was normal for young girls in ancient Greece to participate in such events. It was not normal, of course, to be kidnapped by a god, but in Aphrodite's argumentation this link to the divine sphere adds a touch of truth to the lie, just as we have seen it in other lying stories. As a matter of fact, she had actually been compelled, not by Hermes, though, but by Zeus. Furthermore, she tells how it was to be carried away, describing what she saw, and stating that she felt that she did not even touch the ground with her feet. Just like the detail of the language problem, such a description of a divine kidnapping seen with the victim's eyes is very special. Of course, it makes the unbelievable story more convincing. Finally, she spends many verses on how they can be united in lawful matrimony. Anchises must bring her to his home to introduce her to his parents and brothers, who will accept her since she is certainly a suitable match, and he must send a messenger to her parents so that they can deliver the dowry. The wedding party will be the icing on the cake.

The story moves in the highest spheres among gods, heroes, and royalty, but it is open for recognition by much simpler audiences. Not least the attention to the paraphernalia of the wedding – the dowry, the reactions of parents and brothers, the wonderful wedding party – might invite any young marriageable girl to engage with what is told.

The narrative dwells very much on the virginity and virtue of Anchises's unexpected guest. The festival she was participating in celebrated Artemis, the virgin above all virgins, and no word in the story suggests anything other than wedded love. At the same time, in a way that is difficult to pin down, it builds up an erotic atmosphere full of strength and sweetness, and Anchises reacts exactly as Aphrodite wanted him to.

A further subtlety is the reversal of the traditional gender roles. Normally it would be the young man promising marriage when trying to seduce the young girl. Here the seduction works the other way round, but the rhetoric is the same. Just as in other Homeric poems, the hymns are related to the real life of those involved, rhapsode and audience. In ancient Greece as in the modern world we must conceive of girls sometimes trying to seduce boys.

Conclusion

Homeric stories-within-the-story are in themselves a wonderful display of versatility in the store of epic tradition as well as of creative fantasy. Besides, even though the manifestations of the Homeric tradition surviving to our time do not allow us to compare more than one version of each poem, we can form an idea of how flexibility worked at the level of the real singers. The ease with which the poems let their characters adapt their stories to their narratees is an argument for a similar flexibility in the poetic workshop of the rhapsodes.

Minna Skafte Jensen
University of Southern Denmark
minna.s.j@gmail.com

Bibliography

Editions and translations

LATTIMORE, R. 1965
The Odyssey of Homer, translated with an introduction by R. Lattimore, New York (in one place, *Od.* 12.190-91, I have changed a little in order to bring the translation closer to the original).

VAN THIEL, H. (ED.) 1991
Homeri Odyssea (Bibliotheca Weidmanniana 1), Hildesheim.

VAN THIEL, H. (ED.) 1996
Homeri Ilias (Bibliotheca Weidmanniana 2), Hildesheim.

WEST, M. L. (ED. & TRANSL.) 2003
Homeric Hymns, Homeric Apocrypha, Lives of Homer, Cambridge, Mass.

Secondary literature

ALDEN, M. 2000
Homer Beside Himself: Para-Narratives in the Iliad, Oxford.

ALDEN, M. 2017
Para-Narratives in the Odyssey: *Stories in the Frame*, Oxford.

BERGREN, A. 2008
'Homeric Hymn to Aphrodite, Tradition and rhetoric, praise and blame', in *Weaving Truth: Essays on Language and the Female in Greek Thought*, (Hellenic Studies 19), Cambridge, Mass., 161-212.

BLÜMLEIN, G. 1971
Die Trugreden des Odysseus, Frankfurt am Main.

CHRISTENSEN, J. P. 2020
'Odysseus's lies: Correspondence, coherence, and the narrative agent', in *The Many-Minded Man: The* Odyssey, *Psychology and the Therapy of Epic*, (Myth and Poetics II), Ithaca, New York, 115-47.

DE JONG, I. J. F. 2001
A Narratological Commentary on the Odyssey, Cambridge.

FAULKNER, A. (ED.) 2008
The Homeric Hymn to Aphrodite: Introduction, Text, and Commentary, Oxford.

FAULKNER, A. (ED.) 2011
The Homeric Hymns: Interpretative Essays, Oxford.

FAULKNER, A. & O. HODKINSON (EDS) 2015
Hymnic Narrative and the Narratology of Greek Hymns, (Mnemosyne supplements 384), Leiden.

GENETTE, G. [1972] 1980
Narrative Discourse: An Essay in Method, trans. J. E. Lewin, foreword by J. Culler, Ithaca.

GRAZIOSI, B. 2002
Inventing Homer: The Early Reception of Epic, Cambridge.

HONKO, L. 1998A
Textualising the Siri Epic (FFC 264), Helsinki.

HONKO, L. (ED.) 1998B
The Siri Epic as performed by Gopala Naika, by L. Honko in collaboration with Ch. Gowda, A. Honko & V. Rai, I–II (FFC 265-66), Helsinki.

JENSEN, M. S. 2011
Writing Homer: A Study Based on Results from Modern Fieldwork, Copenhagen.

JENSEN, M. S. 2017
'The challenge of oral epic to Homeric scholarship' in *The Challenge of Folklore*, D. Ben-Amos (ed.) http: // www.mdpi.com / 2076-0787 / 6 / 4 / 97 / pdf.

LORD, A. B. [1960] 2000
The Singer of Tales, 2nd ed., by S. Mitchell & G. Nagy, with audio and video CD, Cambridge, Mass.

MEILLET, A. 1923
Les origines indo-européennes des mètres grecs, Paris.

NAGLER, M. N. 1974
Spontaneity and Tradition: A Study in the Oral Art of Homer, Berkeley.

NAGY, G. 2017
'Diachronic Homer and a Cretan *Odyssey*', *OT* 31, 3-50.

NOTOPOULOS, J. A. 1964
'Studies in early Greek oral poetry', *HSCP* 68, 1-77.

PARRY, M. & A. B. LORD (EDS.) 1954
Serbocroatian Heroic Songs, collected by M. Parry, edited and translated by A.B. Lord, I: Novi Pazar, English translations with musical transcriptions by B. Bartók and prefaces by J. H. Finley, Jr., and R. Jakobson, Cambridge, Mass.

PARRY, M. [1928-35] 1971
The Making of Homeric Verse: The Collected Papers of Milman Parry, edited by A. Parry, Oxford.

PAVESE, C. O. [1998] 2007
'The rhapsodic epic poems as oral and independent poems', *Opuscula selecta*, Padua, 29-52.

READY, J. L. 2019
Orality, Textuality, and the Homeric Epics: An Interdisciplinary Study of Oral Texts, Dictated Texts, and Wild Texts, Oxford.

REECE, S. 1994
'The Cretan Odyssey: A Lie Truer than Truth', *AJP* 115, 157-74.

TSAGALIS, C. C. 2012
'Deauthorizing the epic cycle: Odysseus' false tale to Eumaeus (*Od.* 14.199-359'), in *Homeric Contexts: Neoanalysis and the Interpretation of Oral Poetry*, Montanari, F., A. Rengakos & C. C. Tsagalis (eds.) (Trends in Classics, Suppl. 12), Berlin, 309-45.

UTHER, H.-J. ET AL. 2004
The Types of International Folktales: A Classification and Bibliography, based on the system of A. Aarne and S. Thompson, 1-3, (FFC 284-86), Helsinki.

WACHTER, R. 1991
'The inscriptions on the François vase', *MH* 48, 86-113.

WEST, M. L. 2014
The Making of the Odyssey, Oxford.

Homeric Epic and Ionian Novella

Ioannis M. Konstantakos

Abstract

An important aspect of orality in Homer is the relation of the Homeric corpus to the traditions of oral popular storytelling. Archaic Ionia in particular, the homeland of the Homeric epics, was also the cradle of a thriving production of popular novellas, which were developed and diffused by word of mouth. This narrative tradition is indirectly known through its reflections in the work of Herodotos and other Ionian logographers, as well as through its influence on later literary genres. The Homeric compositions draw story patterns and plotlines from the repertoire of the Ionian novella and adapt them to the epic context by projecting them onto the world of gods and heroes. This paper focuses on two stories of the Iliad *that represent the genre of the dramatic novella, otherwise best exemplified in Herodotos's tales about oriental courts and their intrigues. Narratives of this type are sometimes called "court novellas". They are usually set in the milieu of the palace, involve the members of the royal family and their entourage of courtiers as dramatis personae, and describe the dark passions and tortuous intrigues of the court, which often lead to a sombre outcome. The story of Bellerophon* (Iliad *6.155-206) strings together a series of adventurous and romance-like motifs widespread in the narrative traditions of the ancient Orient: "Potiphar's wife", "Uriah's letter", and the motif of heroic labours which are imposed on the hero as a result of an erotic scandal (a common pattern in Iranian legends, for example in the saga of Gushtasp and the story of Sataspes). In Phoinix's brief autobiography (9.447-95), humorous motifs of the erotic novella are reworked in a more solemn mode. The story begins with a variation on the theme of father and son as rivals in love, a favourite of later domestic comedy. It culminates with the hero's sexual impotence and the concomitant personal and social pressures – another widespread motif of piquant storytelling, from the Hittite* Schwank of Appu *to Encolpius's tribulations in Petronius's* Satyrica.

The novella in the ancient world

The study of orality in the Homeric epics has chiefly concentrated on the oral composition of Archaic epic poetry and the techniques used for the oral production and presentation of the poems. In terms of form, the lion's share is claimed by the investigation of the formulaic ingredients of the Homeric language, from typical epithets and standard hemistichs to stock scenes.[1] With regard to content and narrative material, emphasis has been laid on the relations between the *Iliad*, the *Odyssey*, and the foregoing traditions of epic creation and performance. The school of Neoanalysis, in particular, focuses on the

1 For good surveys of research in this field, see Edwards 1986; 1988; 1992 and 1997; Foley 1997 and 2007; Russo 1997; Friedrich 2011; Finkelberg 2012; Latacz 2015.

reuse and adaptation of story-patterns and episodes taken from an earlier, pre-Homeric repertoire of traditional heroic songs, which constituted the Homeric bard's poetic patrimony and the main source of his materials.[2]

There is another important aspect of oral tradition in the Homeric texts, which has commanded less attention in recent years, although important relevant contributions are not lacking. I refer to the relation of the extant epic corpus to the traditions of oral popular storytelling; in other words, the debt of the epic poems to the rich substratum of folk legends, fairytales, parables, and novellas, which must have been widespread on the lips of the people throughout the communities of Archaic Greece.[3] In this respect, the region traditionally regarded as the homeland of the Homeric epics, that is, the world of Ionia, which extended over the western coast of Asia Minor and the adjacent Aegean islands, is of special interest. This area was apparently endowed with a rich repertoire of popular narratives from early times. Apart from producing the first forms of philosophy, science, and ethnography in western civilization, Archaic Ionia was also the cradle of fictional storytelling for the Greeks.

From among the multifarious genres of folk stories, the novella in particular seems to have greatly flourished in the Ionian tradition. In modern folkloristic and narratological scholarship, the term "novella" is applied to a broad category of traditional tales that mostly consist of realistic action and themes taken from the familiar world of experience.[4] The settings and plots of the novella are characterized by plausibility and verisimilitude; the main personages are ordinary humans and the chain of events generally moves within the limits of the humanly possible. Nonetheless, supernatural and marvellous elements are not entirely excluded. In certain advanced specimens of the genre (such as Herodotean novellas or ancient Egyptian tales, see below), occasional touches of the supernatural may occur in the story: divinities intervene in the development of the action or in the fate of the human characters; paranormal phenomena, such as prophetic oracles and mantic clairvoyance, may influence the course of the plot; magically endowed personages display their wondrous powers. However, these supernatural motifs are kept in check and within moderate proportions; they are not allowed to hold sway over the plot, as is the case with magical fairytales or wondrous travelogues, but are harmoniously blended with a storyline of predominantly realistic conditions and verisimilar character.[5] A novella is always a story about the world of ordinary experience, into which weird elements may sometimes intrude, not about an extravagant fairyland.

The novella focuses *par excellence* on urban and domestic themes, on the adventures and vicissitudes of private life and on sentimental matters. Love and romance are prominent ingredients; the narrative of-

2 For these approaches, see Kullmann 1984; 1991; 2012 and 2015; Willcock 1997; Burgess 2001 and 2006; Finkelberg 2011.

3 Important contributions to this field include Radermacher 1915; Carpenter 1946; Cataudella 1957, 17-38; Reinhardt 1960a, 16-36, 47-124; Page 1973; Hölscher 1978 and 1988; Petersmann 1981; Bertolini 1989; Hansen 1997; Davies 2002; cf. the overview of Heubeck 1974, 118-30, 154-59.

4 On the definition and main traits of the novella, see Cataudella 1957, 10-16, 38-41; Trenkner 1958, xiii–xv, 1-13; Clements & Gibaldi 1977, 1-35; von Wiese 1982, 1-33; Yassif 1984; Aust 1999, 1-52; Gier 2002a and 2002b, 134-36; Shojaei Kawan 2002; Propp 2012, 225-74; Hansen 2017, 28-30.

5 Cf. Trenkner 1958, xiv; Thompson 1977, 8, 152; Aust 1999, 10-11, 25-29; Propp 2012, 227-29, 234-38. It is important to stress this feature, because some definitions of the novella exclude altogether the supernatural from its contents; see e.g. Radermacher 1943, 78; Reinhardt 1960a, 33; Clements & Gibaldi 1977, 16-19; Shojaei Kawan 2002, 126; Müller 2006, 53-54.

ten presents difficult or illicit love affairs, unorthodox erotic passions, and the concomitant schemes of the lovers or of their entourage, which may be treated in either a humorous or an emotional and tragic manner. Cunning, deception, and intrigue are also favourite themes. One of the most emblematic figures of the novella is the clever character, who advances in life by means of his intellectual gifts, demonstrates his wisdom on various occasions, and overcomes obstacles and adversaries thanks to his sharpness of mind and his glib tongue.

The population of Archaic Ionia had a flair for this type of narrative, which clearly appealed to their idiosyncrasy. The leisurely and luxurious temperament of the Ionian people favoured the development of stories about piquant love adventures and clever intrigues. The spirit of Ionian curiosity and enquiry, which would give rise to serious research on physical science, cosmology, and ethnography, was also expressed through the creation of fictional personages characterized by mental agility and resourcefulness. The clever picaroon and the wise counsellor are alternative novellistic reflections of the archetypical Ionian intellectual. The emergence of rationalism and of the scientific mind, as displayed in early Ionian cosmology and natural philosophy, is also perhaps related to the production of realistic fictions about the empirical adventures of ordinary human characters in urban settings.[6]

In all these respects, the cultural climate of Ionia was ideally suited to the formation and enjoyment of novellistic fiction.[7] It may be imagined that the Archaic Ionian world had a narrative repertoire as wide-ranging, rich, and variegated as those of the greatest storytelling cultures of medieval and later times – for example, classical India, with its numerous collections of tales, from the fabulistic *Pañcatantra* and the long-winded Buddhist *Jātakas* to the vast compilation of Somadeva's *Kathāsaritsāgara*; or medieval Islam, with its enormous narrative conglomeration of the *Thousand and One Nights*; or the civilization of Renaissance Italy, the true mother of the *novellistica* in modern European literature, with its overflow of storybooks, from Boccaccio and Sercambi to Bandello, Straparola, and Basile. From these latter civilizations, of course, extensive collections of stories have been preserved in written form; these works, in spite of their literary elaboration, afford a good picture of the flourishing popular narrative corpus which was circulating in the corresponding cultures.[8] The novellas of Archaic Ionia, on the other hand, were not gathered in literary repositories and compilations at such an early age. They can only be known indirectly, through occasional specimens inserted in literary works of different genres, or through the influence they have exercised on the poetic or intellectual compositions of their time.

In the surviving Greek textual sources, the form of the Ionian novella first becomes palpable in the historical oeuvre of Herodotos[9] and in sparse fragments from other writings of Ionian logography, such as the *Lydiaka* of Xanthos, the local history of Charon of Lampsakos, and later the *Persika* of Ktesias.[10] Alongside proper historical accounts and

6 Cf. Aly 1936, 1172-73; Cataudella 1957, 41-42; Trenkner 1958, 3-4, 14-16.

7 On the thriving tradition of the novella in Archaic Ionia, see Erdmannsdörffer 1870; Hausrath 1914; Bolte & Polívka 1930, 115-16; Aly 1936, 1172-78 and 1969, 15-30, 208-63; Cataudella 1957, 7-8, 41-61; Trenkner 1958, 1-13, 168-77.

8 For general surveys of the rich novellistic traditions of these cultures, see Landau 1884; Bolte & Polívka 1930, 127-314, 364-418; Clements & Gibaldi 1977, 36-61; von Wiese 1982, 34-46; Gier 2002a and 2002b; Holm 2013, 60-69.

9 On the wealth of novellas and tales in Herodotos's oeuvre, see most notably Thomson 1935; Cataudella 1957, 47-58; Aly 1969, 1-15, 31-207, 228-301; Erbse 1992, 3-117; Tatum 1997; Maronitis 2001; Gray 2002; Griffiths 2006; Müller 2006, 44-96, 153-335.

10 On the novellistic tales of the Ionian logographers, see Hausrath 1914, 442-46; Cataudella 1957, 39-42, 46-47, 58-60; Trenkner 1958, 24-30; Aly 1969, 29-30, 208-27; Müller 2006, 6-44.

ethnographical discourses, these authors included in their texts several novellistic narratives concerning the private and family affairs, sentimental experiences, clever intrigues, or suspenseful ordeals of known historical figures, such as leaders and potentates of the Greek cities or of their oriental neighbours. In the following periods, up to the Hellenistic and Roman age, the tradition of the novella spread over the entire Hellenic world and infiltrated such diverse literary genres as Attic tragedy, comedy, forensic rhetoric, mime, and above all the ancient novel, in whose formation the genre of the erotic novella may have played a significant role.[11]

Long before these developments, during the Archaic age itself, the settings and story-patterns of the Ionian novella underlie the satirical poems of the early iambos, another characteristically Ionian genre which largely exploited the resources of storytelling and often indulged in poetic narration.[12] The great iambographers, Archilochos, Hipponax, and Semonides of Amorgos, recount in their fragments a variety of ribald episodes, adventurous scenarios, and didactic examples, often in the guise of autobiographical memoirs. The world of these stories recalls the vivacious milieu of the ancient novella, in its multiform aspects. Archilochos's experiences with his comrades at war and with his companions in the symposion sometimes bring to mind the anecdotes and apologues of Herodotos. On the other hand, Archilochos's saucy involvement with Lykambes's daughters and Hipponax's tales about the lowlife demimonde of his city resemble the raucous universe of Petronius and Apuleius.[13]

From these early iambographers it is only a small step backwards to the age of Homer. It may be assumed that around the time of composition of the Homeric poems there was already a thriving production of popular novellas in Archaic Ionia, which would have been created and diffused by word of mouth, parallel to the development of traditional legend and the cultivation of heroic epic. A considerable number of parallels can be detected between the attested Greek novellas and some oriental narratives of great antiquity, which were recorded in various types of text, during the 2nd or at the beginning of the 1st millennium BC, in the neighbouring cultures of the Near East, from Egypt and the Levant to Anatolia and Mesopotamia. Archaic Ionia was territorially close to these areas and kept contact with the great eastern powers of the time, such as the Lydian kingdom, the Neoassyrian Empire, and Saite Egypt. It is likely that the Ionian novellistic tradition received formative influence from oriental storytelling, starting from an early age.[14]

Living and performing in this environment, the Homeric bard must have been familiar with a large corpus of popular novellistic narratives characterized by piquant humour or morbid eroticism, suspenseful intrigues or amusing trickeries, thrilling mysteries and sensational adventures, frissons of horror and roars of laughter. The Homeric compositions draw story patterns, plot sequences, and individual motifs from this narrative repertoire. The poet adapts these borrowed elements to the broader context and plotline of the epic, usually by transforming them into incidental episodes of a particular story arc or into inserted digressive tales. The novellistic stories, of course, undergo significant alterations in order to be assimilated into the mythical and heroic world of the epic. They are detached from their regular

11 See the ample surveys of Cataudella 1957, 16-172 and Trenkner 1958; cf. Hausrath 1914, 446-53; Rohde 1914, 578-601, 606-8; and the brief summary of Aly 1936, 1176-79.

12 On narrative and storytelling in the iambos, see Bowie 2001a and 2001b; Kantzios 2005, 20-29, 34-74; Carey 2008; Alexandrou 2016.

13 See Miralles & Pòrtulas 1988, 71-119; and cf. below regarding the story of Phoinix.

14 Cf. Erdmannsdörffer 1870, 26-35; Aly 1936, 1176 and 1969, 19-24, 252-63; Cataudella 1957, 15-18, 60-61; Trenkner 1958, 2-3.

urban and domestic settings, from the milieu of ordinary society and bourgeois households, and are projected onto the epic universe of gods and heroes. Characters, scenery, and circumstantial details are made to conform to the conditions of the epic battlefield or of the Homeric aristocratic society. I have analyzed this process in another essay, focusing on two risqué Homeric stories of divine adventures: Demodokos's song about the adulterous affair of Ares and Aphrodite (*Odyssey* 8.266-366) and Hera's erotic deception of Zeus (*Iliad* 14.161-351). As argued there, these humorous episodes are apparently inspired by ribald popular novellas of adultery and seduction, which have been epically transplanted to the domain of the Olympian gods.[15]

In the present article, two other specimens of Homeric novella will be examined, which represent a different form of tale: the kind of dramatic and passion-laden novella[16] which is otherwise best exemplified in the narratives of Herodotos and other Ionian logographers, especially in their accounts regarding the royal courts of oriental kingdoms and their intrigues. Because of its court setting, this type of tale is often called by modern experts "court legend", "court tale", or "court novella". These terms were first introduced by Old Testament scholars for the study of ancient Jewish and Aramaic narratives, such as those found in the Biblical books of *Daniel*, *Esther*, *Tobit*, and in the famous *Story of Ahiqar*.[17] Nonetheless, the same terms are applicable to a wide range of ancient storytelling materials, which share the same basic characteristics as the aforementioned Semitic narratives and come from all over the Graeco-Roman and Near-Eastern world.[18]

The court novella is a mainly realistic narrative which fictionalizes the adventures and tribulations of a charismatic protagonist, usually a gifted nobleman or official, in the setting of a royal court full of machinations and intrigues. The milieu of the palace provides the backdrop of the action; the king, the queen, and other members of the royal family, together with their entourage of courtiers and attendants, constitute the *dramatis personae*. True to the generic tradition of the novella, the court narrative favours themes of love, erotic passion, and romance, and privileges complex plots that contain wiles and cunning schemes. The royal and courtly characters of the story are usually enmeshed in dark passions, illicit love affairs, and disturbing emotions of desire, lust, envy, or hatred. As a result of these passions, the personages become involved in complicated guiles and tortuous machinations, which often produce a sombre or tragic outcome.

The narrative form of the court novella is very old and was practised in many civilizations throughout the Near East. Classical Egyptian literature, probably the richest fountainhead of *novellistica* in the ancient world, provides many relevant compositions in various modes of fictional writing, attested in papyri from the 2nd millennium BC to the early Roman period. The Egyptian novellistic corpus includes realistic stories of court conspiracies and adventures, such as the *Story of Sinuhe* and later the frame narrative of the Demotic *Instruction of 'Onchsheshonqy*. There are also pseudo-historical fictions that take place in the royal chancellery of historically attested rulers, for example, the *Quarrel of Apophis and Seqenenre* and the *Stela of Bentresh*. Furthermore, one finds novellettes of ribald humour, such as the *Story of King Neferkare and General Sisenet*, which illustrates a secret homosexual liaison

15 See Konstantakos 2012 and the bibliography cited there.

16 On this type of narrative, cf. Cataudella 1957, 38-41, 55-56, 74-88; Trenkner 1958, 23-30; Aly 1969, 238-40; Murray 2001, 41-42.

17 See Humphreys 1973, 214-20; Collins 1975, 219-28, 234 and 1993, 42-47, 173; Niditch & Doran 1977; Wills 1990, 1-13, 18-24, 32-44, 68, 74-76, 80-87, 112-13, 121, 146-52, 193-204 and 1995, 39, 41-48, 66; Yassif 1999, 59, 68-69, 476; Koch 2005, 21-22, 115-16, 263-64; Holm 2005, 149-50, 163 and 2013, 2-7, 29, 63-64, 97-98, 193-203, 253, 377-87, 485-88.

18 Cf. Murray 2001, 41-44.

between the pharaoh and his general; in the Saite and Persian periods an entire cycle of anecdotes developed around the courtly entertainments and picaresque escapades of the jocular Pharaoh Amasis. Another large category of Egyptian narratives comprises fantastic tales revolving around gifted magicians of the royal court, who impress the Pharaoh with their marvellous exploits and protect him by means of their wondrous powers. This crossbreed of the court novella and the magical Märchen proved to be very fruitful in Egyptian literature of all ages, from the Middle Kingdom stories of the *Papyrus Westcar* to the complex novellas of Merire, Petese, and Setne Khaemwaset in the Late Period.[19]

From among the writings of ancient Israel, a prime example of the sophisticated court novella is the story of Joseph and his brothers in the Pharaoh's court, which is now incorporated in the Biblical book of *Genesis* (37-50). It is widely accepted that this tale goes back to an originally independent literary composition, a kind of short romance with great subtlety in plot and characterization and high artistic quality,[20] perhaps written under the influence of Egyptian narrative art.[21] Some scholars date the prototypical version of this work as early as the reign of Solomon (10th century BC) or his immediate successors, when Israelite culture and *belles lettres* enjoyed their first great acme; other experts place the composition around the Exilic age, in the 7th or 6th century BC.[22] Another elaborate Biblical tale, which similarly unfolds a finely woven fabric of royal passions and conspiracies, is the so-called "Succession Story" or "Court History of King David", which is now partitioned between the second book of *Samuel* (11-20) and the first book of *Kings* (1-2). This includes episodes of refined narrative craft and deep psychological insight, such as David's unlawful passion for Bathsheba, his cunning scheme to dispose of her husband Uriah, the tortuous conflict between David and his son Absalom, and the machinations for the enthronement of Solomon during David's last days.[23] Like Joseph's novella, David's court history may also be based on a novelized historical work of pre-Exilic date.[24] Later, in the Persian and

19 The texts of all these Egyptian fictions can be found in the following editions, anthologies, and collections: Griffith 1900; Lefebvre 1949; Brunner-Traut 1965; Lichtheim 1973-80; Posener 1985; Lalouette 1987; Maspero 2002; Simpson 2003; Bresciani 2007; Agut-Labordère & Chauveau 2011. For general literary-historical surveys of the narrative literature of ancient Egypt, see Bolte & Polívka 1930, 95-101; Pieper 1935; Donadoni 1967, 115-37, 186-203, 235-44, 274-88; Tait 1994; Quirke 1996; Baines 1996; Quack 2005, 16-80; Burkard & Thissen 2008, 7-82 and 2012, 122-33, 158-83, 200-15; Holm 2013, 92-183, 378-87.

20 See Gunkel 1922, lii–lv, 395-401; von Rad 1963, 342-43, 428-34 and 1966, 292-300; Redford 1970, 27, 66-105, 178-86 and 1992, 422-29; Niditch 1987, 71-125; Wills 1990, 52-55 and 1995, 158-63; Goldman 1995, 1-6; Carr 1996, 273-89; Yassif 1999, 27-28, 468-69; Westermann 2002, 18-30, 245-52; Van Seters 2004; Louden 2011, 63-104; Blum & Weingart 2017, 503-10.

21 See Gunkel 1922, lix, 398-401, 421-22, 432-35; von Rad 1966, 299-300; Redford 1970, 67, 92-105, 153-58, 241-43 and 1992, 424-29; Hollis 1989, 34-36; Goldman 1995, 3, 36, 57-69; Carr 1996, 279, 289; Yassif 1999, 468-69; Westermann 2002, 28-30, 64-68, 73-75, 85; cf. Peppermüller 1961, 108-13; Blum & Weingart 2017, 513-16.

22 For various views on the formation and dating of the novella of Joseph, see von Rad 1963, 428-31; Redford 1970, 178-86, 239-53 and 1992, 427-29; Wills 1995, 160-61; Carr 1996, 283-89; Westermann 2002, 19-25, 28-29 (with a masterful recapitulation of earlier research and bibliography); Van Seters 2004, 370-72, 387-88; Holm 2013, 108-9; Blum & Weingart 2017.

23 On the literary artistry and subtlety of the narrative, see Jackson 1965; Flanagan 1972; Gunn 1976 and 1978, 13-16, 29-30, 37-62, 87-111; Rost 1982, 68-115; Wesselius 1990; Ackerman 1990; Keys 1996, 114-55, 174-83; Blum 2000, 17-37; Dietrich 2000.

24 From among the immense bibliography, see most notably von Rad 1966, 176-204; Flanagan 1972; Gunn 1978; Rost 1982; Frei 1993, 50-62; Keys 1996; Seiler 1998; Dietrich 2000; Kaiser 2000; and the surveys of Ackerman 1990, 54-60 and de Pury & Römer 2000.

Hellenistic periods, similar tales of court intrigues will furnish the material for literary novellas and didactic romances, such as *Esther*, *Tobit*, and the narrative portions of *Daniel*.[25]

The Lydians may also have developed a tradition of sensational novellistic narratives, which centred on the private lives and sinister passions of their potentates. Although no narrative texts survive from ancient Lydia, a glimpse into the rich oral tradition of this land is afforded by the Lydian *logos* of Herodotos and the *Lydiaka* of Xanthos, which provided a general account of Lydian history and culture.[26] The reports of these writers about the Lydian kings and court life, from Kambles and Adramytes to Kandaules, Gyges, and Kroisos, are replete with suspenseful storytelling, sexual perversions, bedchamber intrigues, and even motifs of horror and Grand Guignol.

Finally, an ample corpus of court tales was produced in Achaemenid Iran, after the formation of the Persian Empire under Cyrus the Great.[27] This narrative repertoire was formed and circulated purely in oral form, given that the ancient Persians did not develop a written mythopoeic or belletristic literature before the Sasanian age. Nevertheless, the testimonia of extra-Iranian authors and later Iranian textual sources enable us to form an idea of the flourishing tradition of storytelling in Achaemenid Persia. Herodotos's stories about Persian kings and their families are strongly influenced by the world of the Persian court novella and allow a good glimpse into its plots of dense intrigue and pathological *eros*.[28] Herodotos doubtless learned many tales of the Achaemenid court from his informers on Persian matters, who included Persian officials and noblemen, as well as Greek expatriates living in the milieu of the Great King.[29] The Jewish book of *Esther* portrays Persian court life in a very similar way and may also have drawn on the themes and poetics of the Persian novella. Diaspora Jews living under Achaemenid rule could have easily become familiar with this genre.[30]

Elements from the Persian novellistic production have also infiltrated the large body of Iranian myths and national legends, which concern the great heroes of the distant past. The main corpus of these traditions was first collected and written down during the Sasanian period; the mythical stories were compiled into a large prose chronicle, the *Khwadāy-nāmag* (*Book of Kings*, mid-7th century AD), which followed Iranian national history from the beginnings of time to the Sasanian dynasty. The famous accounts of Persian mythology now found in medieval Islamic sources, such as the *Annals* of Tabari, the *History of the Kings of the Persians* by Thaʿalibi, and the vast epic *Shahnameh* of Firdausi, are ultimately derived from this lost Sasanian chronicle. The myths

25 See Bickerman 1967, 51-138, 169-237; Humphreys 1973; Collins 1975; Niditch & Doran 1977; Niditch 1987, 126-45; Wills 1990; 1995, 1-131, 212-44 and 2011; Yassif 1999, 27-29, 40-46, 57-69, 469-78; Johnson 2005.

26 Significantly, both authors were in an ideal position to collect and propagate authentic Lydian legends and lore. Xanthos was a Hellenized native Lydian; Herodotos grew up in a region bordering Lydia and might have listened to local stories since his childhood. On the local narrative traditions reflected in their Lydian tales, see Cataudella 1957, 47-52; Aly 1969, 220-25, 228-30; Drews 1973, 78-79, 100-3, 179; Flusin 1976; Talamo 1985; Wills 1990, 61-68; Erbse 1992, 3-9; Dorati 2009, 41-53; Gazzano 2017.

27 On the Persian court novella and its broad influence on the narrative traditions of the Near East, cf. in general Wills 1990, 40-42, 63, 69-71, 194-95; Holm 2013, 63-64.

28 See Reinhardt 1960b, 133-74; Momigliano 1977, 25-35; Wills 1990, 55-71; Sancisi-Weerdenburg 1993, 27-33; Murray 2001, 35-44; West 2003; Müller 2006, 290-335; Konstantakos 2007 and 2016.

29 On Herodotos's sources and informants about Persia, apart from the works cited in n. 28 above, see the bibliography given in Konstantakos 2007, 237.

30 See Talmon 1963, 449-53; Bickerman 1967, 172-84; Gordis 1981, 375-88; Niditch 1987, 132, 142-44; Wills 1990, 37, 154, 180-85, 188 and 1995, 100, 109-10, 129; Dorothy 1997, 302-13, 339-41; Berlin 2001a, 8-14 and 2001b, xxvii–xliii; Johnson 2005, 576-77, 582-89.

themselves, however, were already created in the first millennium BC. Most of them are mentioned in the *Avesta*, the holy scriptures of the ancient Zoroastrian religion. These mythical narratives would have formed the main material of the oral epic poetry performed by the Iranian bards in the courts of the Achaemenid and Parthian magnates.[31] The Iranian myths often include typical themes of the court novella, such as stories of royal amours, conflicts about succession, and conspiracies at court. The interaction between heroic mythology and the novellistic tradition must have been constant and fruitful in ancient Iran.

Two Homeric novellas of court intrigue and passion

Egypt, Israel, Lydia, Persia – the early Greek world was surrounded by a dense net of novellistic traditions regarding court life and intrigues. In the context of the close connections and cultural exchanges between Archaic Ionia and the East, these oriental traditions left a clear imprint on the production and poetics of the Ionian novella, as exemplified in the court tales of Herodotos, Xanthos, and other logographers. The two Iliadic stories to be discussed below also conform faithfully to the narrative model of the court novella. Both narratives are introduced into the epic poem as incidental retrospective accounts of past events; they are placed on the lips of secondary characters who find occasion, in one phase or another of the Trojan War, to speak about the earlier history of their family, in the time of their illustrious ancestors or of their own youth.

31 On the antiquity and transmission of the Iranian myths found in Firdausi and the other Islamic sources, see Nöldeke 1920, 1-19, 41-42; Christensen 1931 and 1936, 9-43, 107-40; Boyce 1954 and 1955; Rypka 1959, 56-58, 66-67, 152-69; Yarshater 1983; Shahbazi 1990; Skjærvø 1998; Konstantakos 2008, 110-14.

Although it so happens that there are no specific models for these particular Homeric tales among the surviving specimens of the Ionian novellistic production, as preserved in the few available Greek texts surveyed above, this may be no more than an accident of transmission. It is significant that both narratives present distinctive parallels to various specimens of court tales known from other ancient sources, whether from Graeco-Roman writings or from the vast literatures of the Orient. In view of such similarities, it is plausible to assume that related narrative material must have passed from the Near-Eastern world into the storytelling repertoire of Ionia, and would thus have been available to the poet of the *Iliad* as part of the large and variegated novellistic treasure of his homeland and his time. In essence, these Homeric case-studies stem from the same fictional universe as the gloomy and sensational court tales of Herodotos.[32]

The story of Bellerophon (*Iliad* 6.155-206) reads indeed like an anthology of materials drawn from the world of the court novella. The narrative gathers together a cluster of adventurous and romance-like motifs that are characteristic of this genre[33] and prominent in the storytelling traditions of the ancient Orient. Almost all the main incidents find striking parallels in ancient Egyptian, Semitic, and Iranian court stories.[34] It is not fortuitous that the

32 Cf. Wiesmann 1948, 5.

33 On the novellistic materials of the narrative, cf. Radermacher 1943, 97-103; Carpenter 1946, 173; Meraklis 1979; Petersmann 1981, 55; Bertolini 1989, 138-40. Strömberg 1961 speaks more generally of "Märchen".

34 On the multiple parallels between Bellerophon's story and oriental lore, see Schachermeyr 1950, 164, 174-87; Peppermüller 1961, 31-51, 62-65, 72-98, 105-54; Astour 1967, 225-40, 250-71; White 1982; Burkert 1983, 51-53; Frei 1993; Brillante 1996, 42-45; Morris 1997, 619; West 1997, 365-67; Stoevesandt 2008, 60, 65-69; Bachvarova 2016, 378, 423-26. Some scholars have surmised that the entire myth has been transmitted to the Greeks wholesale from the East (Anatolia or the Semitic Levant): see Radermacher 1943, 102-14; Malten 1944; and

entire narrative is placed on the lips of an Asiatic prince, Glaukos of Lykia, a grandson of Bellerophon, who is taking part in the war as an ally of the Trojans. Roaming in the battlefield before the walls of Troy, Glaukos meets with the Achaean hero Diomedes, who prepares to fight a duel with him but asks him first about his identity (6.119-43). Glaukos takes the opportunity to give a long account of his ancestors. They include most prominently a grandfather from the Greek mainland, the valiant Bellerophon, who had emigrated from Argos to Lykia, on the southwest coast of Anatolia, and had married into the local dynastic family. By attributing this narrative to a foreign character from the East, the poet may be implicitly acknowledging the ultimate oriental provenance of most of the story material. The mixed ethnic identity of the narrator Glaukos becomes a poetological metaphor for the substance and the creation of the narrative itself. Like the teller, who is a Lykian prince but has Argive origins and blood, the story is a conglomeration of oriental novellistic elements, which are reworked, however, by a Greek poet and assimilated into a Greek epic.

In post-Homeric Greek tradition, especially in lyric poetry and drama, Bellerophon became a paradigmatically tragic figure, an exemplar of hubris and divine punishment, because of his unhappy end. Incited by pride over his heroic feats, Bellerophon attempted to ride the winged horse Pegasus and meet the gods in heaven; but the horse threw him down and he was crushed. Euripides, in particular, turned Bellerophon into a kind of disillusioned existential hero, who is embittered by the prevalence of evil in human affairs, to the point of doubting the existence of divine justice. He therefore flies on Pegasus in order to confront the gods and question them about the iniquities of the world.[35] In the Homeric account none of these developments is exploited yet. Glaukos only makes a brief reference, at the end of his narrative, to Bellerophon's final misfortunes: the immortals conceived a hatred for the hero, and as a result Bellerophon ended up as an outcast, wandering alone in the plain and bitterly tormented in his heart (6.200-2).

Significantly, Glaukos provides no reason for the gods' displeasure and the hero's miserable destiny, nor does he expressly hold up his grandfather's case as a warning against hubris. These matters are of no interest for Glaukos's account, which concentrates on Bellerophon's rising career, his youthful wanderings and valiant exploits, and only makes a vague reference to the hero's end by way of completion of his biography.[36] In the main bulk of the Homeric story, Bellerophon is treated like the typical adventurous protagonist of the court novella. He is described as a candid youth, endowed with great beauty and manly virtue, a praiseworthy character who becomes enmeshed, against his will, in dangerous relations and secret plots in the infectious environment of two royal establishments. The Homeric Bellerophon is similar, in this respect, to emblematic characters of the oriental novella, such as the Joseph of the *Genesis*, the young Solomon in the first book of *Kings*,

---

the overviews of Peppermüller 1961, 76-85 and Meraklis 1979.

35 On Euripides's *Bellerophon*, see Di Gregorio 1983; Collard et al. 1995, 98-120; Jouan & van Looy 2000, 1-35; Dobrov 2001, 91-97, 189-91; Curnis 2003.

36 Cf. Malten 1944, 5-6; Peppermüller 1961, 54-56; Petersmann 1981, 56-57; Kirk 1990, 184, 186; Brillante 1996, 33. Scholars have often underlined the connection between this significant omission and the broader context of Bellerophon's story in the Homeric narrative. Glaukos creates the impression that Bellerophon's fall was brought about mysteriously and inexplicably, because of a whim of the gods; this illustrates Glaukos's initial remarks about the transitory nature of human existence (6.145-49) and serves as a warning towards the impetuous Diomedes, Glaukos's potential opponent. See Gaisser 1969, 169-74; Scodel 1992, 77-84; Alden 1996, 261-63 and 2000, 25, 112-13, 131-42, 167-68, 305; Assunçâo 1997, 56-66; Stoevesandt 2008, 72, 76-77.

and prince Siyavush in Iranian mythology – all of them virtuous youngsters who are dragged into a sombre milieu of perplexing intrigues.[37]

The Homeric tale begins in a Greek setting, the court of King Proitos, who reigns over the Argives. The handsome young Bellerophon is living in Proitos's palace and becomes the victim of an illicit love intrigue. Anteia, Proitos's lustful wife, conceives a desire for Bellerophon, but the virtuous hero resists her indecent proposals. The depraved woman calumniously tells her husband that Bellerophon attempted to seduce her, and demands the culprit's death. Proitos gullibly believes his wife's lies and is filled with rage (6.160-6). A celebrated story-pattern of the ancient novella, usually called "Potiphar's wife", is instantly recognized in this episode: a married woman attempts to seduce a young man, who refuses her; in return, she calumniates the young man before her husband, who plans to take revenge on the youth.[38] This pattern makes here its first appearance in the Greek tradition, in which it was destined to enjoy a fruitful career, ranging from classic myths (e.g. Phaidra and Hippolytos) to the latest Graeco-Roman novels (Heliodoros, *Aethiopica* 1.9-17; Apuleius, *Metamorphoses* 10.2-12).[39] The roots of the story-pattern can be traced back to novellistic compositions of the ancient Near East. In its full and proper form it first surfaces in an Egyptian literary romance from the New Kingdom (c. 1200 BC), the so-called *Tale of the Two Brothers* – another complex narrative crossbreed, which combines elements of magical Märchen with typical storylines of the court novella in a composite fictional concoction.[40] The most famous occurrence of the pattern is of course the novella of Joseph (*Genesis* 39), which has already been singled out as one of the finest specimens of court tale in antiquity.[41]

More elements of oriental *novellistica* follow. The rancorous Proitos is reluctant to kill Bellerophon outright and devises a wilier scheme; he sends the hero away to Lykia, where Proitos's father-in-law, the father of the faithless Anteia, is king. Bellerophon is ostensibly commissioned to carry a coded document to the Lykian ruler, written in a secret and apparently unintelligible script. The Lykian monarch, however, is able to decipher the script and understand the hidden message, which instructs him to put Bellerophon to death (6.167-78). This is the motif of "Uriah's letter", attested in the Sumerian

37 Many scholars have furthermore noted how the Homeric narrative suppresses some of the more marvellous supernatural motifs, which are known from other versions of Bellerophon's myth (e.g. the hero's use of the winged horse Pegasus), in order to make the story more realistic, credible, and human. See Radermacher 1943, 98-101; Kullmann 1956, 23-25; Peppermüller 1961, 42-47; Petersmann 1981, 55-57; Bertolini 1989, 139-40; Frei 1993, 41; Gantz 1993, 313-14; cf. Carpenter 1946, 70-71; Gaisser 1969, 170. This tendency also brings the Homeric tale of Bellerophon close to the world of the novella, which strives to keep the supernatural in check (see above the first section of this article).

38 See Thompson 1955, 474 (motif K2111); Peppermüller 1961, 105-31; Jesi 1962; Redford 1970, 91-93; Gunkel 1987, 139; Hollis 1989; Reents & Köhler-Zülch 1993; Goldman 1995; Hansen 1997, 451-52 and 2002, 332-52; Zimmerman 2000, 417-32.

39 See Trenkner 1958, 64-66; Peppermüller 1961, 106-7, 115-31; Zimmerman 2000, 417-32; Hansen 2002, 337-52.

40 For the corresponding episode of the ancient Egyptian romance, see Lefebvre 1949, 142-48; Brunner-Traut 1965, 28-33, 258-60; Lichtheim 1973-80, II 203-6; Lalouette 1987, 161-65; Maspero 2002, 3-8; Simpson 2003, 81-85; Bresciani 2007, 376-80; cf. Hollis 1989; Goldman 1995, 32-36; Hansen 2002, 333-34. A rather atypical variant of the story-pattern has been traced in a late Hittite mythical narrative, probably of Semitic-Canaanite origin: see Astour 1967, 258-60; Hoffner 1965 and 1998, 90-92; Haas 2006, 213-16; Bachvarova 2013, 30-33.

41 See Hollis 1989; Goldman 1995, 1-2, 31-36; Hansen 2002, 335-36.

Epic of Sargon (early 2nd millennium BC)[42] but best known from the court history of King David in the second book of *Samuel* (11).[43] As in the story of Bellerophon, in the Biblical novella the motif is woven into a dark plot of illicit erotic passion and malicious intrigues against an innocent character.[44] King David is infatuated with Bathsheba, the wife of Uriah the Hittite, an officer in the Israelite army; he begins an adulterous liaison with her, while Uriah is away on campaign. Eventually, Bathsheba becomes pregnant; her unsuspecting husband is hastily summoned back to Jerusalem but prefers to sleep in the barracks, together with his soldiers, and does not approach his wife. David realizes that he needs to put Uriah out of the way, in order to conceal the scandal. He gives Uriah a sealed letter to carry to his commander Joab in the battle front. The letter secretly orders the commander to place Uriah in the most dangerous position in the front line and leave him there to be killed.

These two parallels between the Homeric story and the Near-Eastern novellistic repertoire have often been pointed out.[45] What has escaped notice is that the following part of Bellerophon's biography also reproduces a characteristic story-pattern of oriental court novella.[46] The Lykian king is reluctant to openly kill the vigorous young hero. Instead, he assigns Bellerophon a series of extremely dangerous tasks ("suicide missions") and expects that the young man will die in the process of attempting them. Initially, Bellerophon is ordered to combat the Chimera, a murderous monster which combines the parts of a lion, a serpent, and a goat, and breathes terrible fire. After he has successfully slain this beast, Bellerophon is sent to fight against the powerful armies of wild tribes, first the valiant Solymoi, then the fierce Amazons. While the hero is returning victorious from these new battles, the king has the bravest men of Lykia lay a trap for him on his way; Bellerophon overcomes these adversaries as well. In the end, after all these ordeals, the Lykian monarch recognizes the hero's worth and rewards him; Bellerophon is offered the king's daughter in marriage, together with rich lands and royal privileges (6.179-95).

The same story arc is traced in Iranian court legends, for example in the saga of King Gushtasp, which is set out in full in Firdausi's *Shahnameh* but, like the other old national legends of Iran, demonstrably stems from mythological lore of the 1st millennium BC. The episodes in question form part of Gushtasp's earlier adventures, while he is living in exile in the kingdom of Rum, before he assumes the

42 See Cooper & Heimpel 1983; Alster 1987; Afanas'eva 1987; Frei 1993, 58-59; Black et al. 2004, 40-44; Noegel 2005, 238.

43 See Thompson 1955, 303, 359, 392, 394, 414 (motifs K511, K978, K1355, K1388, K1612); Peppermüller 1961, 132-44; Gunkel 1987, 145, 194; Naumann 2000, 140-45; Uther 2004, 251, 273, 535, 568 (types ATU 425B, 462, 910K, 930); Shojaei Kawan 2010.

44 Cf. Brown 1995, 49; for a detailed comparison of the two stories, see Frei 1993, 57-62. On the Biblical episode in particular, see Gunn 1978, 46-48, 97-101, 108-11; Stoebe 1986; Luther 1991, 101-4; Keys 1996, 128-33; Seiler 1998, 241-57; Naumann 2000.

45 See Bolte & Polívka 1930, 106; Radermacher 1943, 101-3; Malten 1944, 7; Carpenter 1946, 173; Baumgartner 1959, 162-65; Peppermüller 1961, 62, 65, 87-88, 97-98, 105-44; Strömberg 1961, 2, 4, 13; Astour 1967, 256-61; Thompson 1977, 267, 279; Petersmann 1981, 55; White 1982, 123-24; Burkert 1983, 52; Bertolini 1989, 139; Kullmann 1991, 433; Frei 1993, 39-46, 49-51, 57-62; Brown 1995, 49; Goldman 1995, xii, 32-36; Brillante 1996, 33, 42; Assunçâo 1997, 45; Hansen 1997, 451-52; West 1997, 365-66; Noegel 2005, 238; Stoevesandt 2008, 65, 67; Bachvarova 2016, 424.

46 Morris 1997, 619 only points out that Bellerophon's marriage into the Lykian dynastic family has parallels in historical marriage alliances made by the Hittites; cf. Schachermeyr 1950, 177-78 regarding early Achaean colonists in Asia Minor. A number of scholars trace a general similitude with traditional fairytales or myths about a hero who marries a princess by way of reward for killing a dragon or for accomplishing heroic tasks: see Radermacher 1943, 99-101, 108-10; Carpenter 1946, 173; Peppermüller 1961, 62-64; Strömberg 1961, 4-8; Bertolini 1989, 139; Kirk 1990, 182-83; Brown 1995, 228; Stoevesandt 2008, 70.

throne of Iran.[47] The story-pattern occurs twice in this Iranian saga, in two successive episodes that are clearly doublets. In the first version, Mirin, a rich nobleman and learned scholar, asks to marry the second daughter of the Emperor of Rum. The emperor, however, is much chagrined because his first daughter has left the palace and eloped with Gushtasp, an unknown foreigner without a fortune. The emperor therefore stipulates that his second daughter may only marry someone who has performed a great deed and won fame. As a result, Mirin is ordered to kill a dangerous hybrid monster, which is pestering the forest: a wolf strong and huge as an elephant, with a dragon's body, a boar's tusks, and two horns on its head. Mirin, who is a scholar and not a warrior, does not feel up to this heroic labour but learns from astrology that the valiant Gushtasp is destined to accomplish the deed. He finds Gushtasp in a village and requests his assistance; the Iranian hero accepts, fights, and slays the monster. Mirin presents the carcass to the emperor as his own glorious spoil, and marries the princess. A duplicate version follows. Another nobleman, Ahran, asks for the emperor's third daughter in marriage. The emperor assigns him to slay a dragon that is devastating the mountain with its fiery breath. Ahran, advised by Mirin, also enlists Gushtasp's help. Once again, the Iranian hero fights the dragon and kills it after a long battle. Ahran brings the monster's body to the emperor and gains the royal bride.[48]

In spite of the differences in details, these Iranian legends share a common story-pattern with the tale of Bellerophon. The protagonist is ordered by the king to fight a savage monster (the fire-breathing Chimera in Homer, or analogous hybrid and dragon-like beasts in the Iranian myths), and this dangerous mission is an ordeal imposed in the context of court machinations. In all cases the protagonist has been caught up in a contorted love intrigue in the royal milieu: Bellerophon is unlawfully desired by the lewd queen, while the Persian noblemen wish to gain the hand of the emperor's daughter. By withstanding the ordeal and finding a way to slay the beast, the hero marries the king's daughter and gains considerable advancement in courtly society. Of course, Bellerophon performs the dangerous labour himself, while the Persian suitors secretly employ a champion to kill the monster on their behalf; but this secondary narrative development does not affect the essential common storyline.

Another variant of the story-pattern is found in Herodotos's terse report about the Achaemenid nobleman Sataspes (4.43), a cousin of Xerxes's, which is doubtless based on a historical anecdote of the Persian court. The rash Sataspes raped a maiden from a noble Persian family and was condemned by King Xerxes to death by impalement. Sataspes's mother, however, was a sister of the late King Dareios and interceded to save her son from execution. Thus, instead of suffering death, Sataspes was commanded by the king to sail around the entire continent of Africa, from the Pillars of Herakles to the Arabian Gulf, and collect geographical information. Sataspes began the journey and spent many months at sea, but in the end he was daunted by the length and loneliness of the voyage and returned home without completing the circumnavigation. Upon his return, Sataspes gave an account of the wonderful sights he had experienced in his journey. He reported that in the remotest south he had encountered a tribe of savage men of very small stature, dressed in palm-

47 This part of Gushtasp's saga is indeed considered to be very ancient; it must go back beyond the Sasanian *Khwadāy-nāmag* to the mythical traditions of the 1st millennium BC. Some of its central episodes are reflected in a Median love story transmitted by Chares of Mytilene (*FGrHist* 125 F 5, from Athenaios 13.575a–f), one of the companions of Alexander the Great. See Christensen 1931, 119 and 1936, 136-37; Boyce 1955; Yarshater 1983, 467-69.

48 For these two episodes in Firdausi's epic, see Mohl 1876-78, IV 243-64; Pizzi 1886-88, V 28-51; Warner & Warner 1905-25, IV 333-49.

leaf clothes – presumably a race of Bushmen or Pygmies.[49]

Once more, the protagonist is involved in a sexual scandal at court – although this time he is the assailant in a sexual offence, unlike Bellerophon, who is by contrast the innocent target of illicit erotic aggression. Because of his entanglement in the sexual scandal, the protagonist is assigned a dangerous mission, analogous to the heroic labours imposed on Bellerophon and on the suitors of the Iranian saga. Indeed, Sataspes's mission eventually leads him to confront a weird, monstrous-looking horde of savages, comparable to the fierce Solymoi and Amazons whom Bellerophon is ordered to fight. The outcome of Sataspes's tale is of course different from the happy ending of the other court novellas. Xerxes is not satisfied with the young man's reports and his failure to complete the task and has Sataspes executed. Apart from this final deviation, the basic story-pattern is very similar in all cases. Overall, the Homeric tale of Bellerophon is a chain of interrelated motifs which have been lifted from the repertoire of the oriental court novella and strung together into an adventurous heroic biography.

The second example, Phoinix's autobiographical account (*Iliad* 9.447-95), presents a somewhat different case. Phoinix, Achilles's old mentor, is a member of the embassy sent by Agamemnon to appease Achilles's wrath and persuade him to return to battle. In the beginning of his speech, the old man gives an account of his early life and tribulations, which eventually led him to seek refuge in Peleus's household and become the tutor of Peleus's young son. In this way Phoinix stresses his deep-seated devotion to Peleus's family and to Achilles personally.[50] The action of the story unfolds entirely in mainland Greece, between the seat of Phoinix's family, the court of Amyntor in Thessalian Hellas, and Peleus's palace in Phthia. Connections with oriental novellistic patterns are more remote. What distinguishes Phoinix's autobiography is the adaptation of essentially comic motifs, which would properly pertain to the genre of humorous erotic novella but are reworked here in a dramatic and solemn mode.[51]

The narrative begins with another variety of pathological eroticism in a royal milieu. King Amyntor, Phoinix's father, brings into his palace a young concubine; Amyntor's lawful wedded wife feels dishonoured and dismayed. She entreats her son Phoinix to seduce his father's concubine and sleep with her, so as to separate the girl from the old king. Phoinix complies with his mother's wishes, with disastrous consequences (9.449-53). This weird case of erotic threesome is an elaborate variation of the familiar model of "Potiphar's wife", which is here subjected to a tortuous inversion of the interrelationships among the central trio of characters. In many specimens of "Potiphar's wife" the new wife of an elderly man falls in love with her husband's son from a previous marriage and attempts to seduce him, without success.[52]

49 On this story and its sources, see Wells 1923, 101; Klotz 1937; Hennig 1944, 133-37; Desanges 1978, 29-33; Colin 1990; Asheri et al. 2007, 612-13; Bichler 2011, 319-22. The incident is most probably historical, although the extent of Sataspes's itinerary and the veracity of his reports have been disputed by modern scholars. Nevertheless, the account of the historical facts has been adapted and refashioned according to the familiar pattern of the court novella.

50 Cf. Lohmann 1970, 245-52; Bannert 1981, 71-74; Held 1987, 247-49; Hainsworth 1993, 119.

51 On the novellistic material of the story, cf. Carpenter 1946, 171-72; Wiesmann 1948, 5-8, 27-32, 36-39; Aly 1969, 24-25; West 2001, 4-5.

52 See e.g. the myth of Phaidra and Hippolytos and various other Greek and Roman legends and local stories (Trenkner 1958, 64-66; Peppermüller 1961, 115-22; Hansen 2002, 337-44); Apuleius, *Metamorphoses* 10.2-12; Philostratos, *Vita Apollonii* 6.3; Heliodoros, *Aethiopica* 1.9-17; and the Iranian myth of Siyavush and Sudabeh (Mohl 1876-78, II 158-95; Pizzi 1886-88, II 317-54; Warner & Warner 1905-25, II 195-224). Cf. Rocca 1976; Donnini 1981; Zimmerman 2000, 417-32; Hansen 2002, 344-48.

In Phoinix's story, conversely, it is the son who erotically approaches his old father's new female consort and successfully seduces her.[53] In any case, the son who seduces his father's concubine is an established motif of ancient court novella, familiar from the Biblical stories of David and Jacob.[54]

On the other hand, Phoinix's initiative leads to a situation in which both the father and the son have a sexual relationship with the same young woman.[55] This recalls a favourite theme of the ancient comic tradition, the quarrel between father and son for the favour of the same girl.[56] The situation may have already been explored by Pherekrates, the first poet to develop themes of domestic comedy on the 5th-century Attic stage.[57] Later the erotic rivalry between father and son became a mainstay of New Comedy; it dominates the action in three plays of Plautus (*Casina*, *Mercator*, and *Asinaria*), which are based on Greek models by Diphilos, Philemon, and Demophilos. These comic productions are posterior to Homer, but they reveal the essentially humorous tone of the theme. The father-son rivalry in love is primarily an ingredient of comic narrative, capable of generating bursts of laughter with the ridiculous flirtations of the enamoured old man and the resourceful machinations of his young adversary.

In the Homeric tale, this light-hearted theme acquires a sombre and tragic quality. In the versions of the comic stage, the young son invariably overcomes his elderly rival and gets the girl for himself at the finale. The philandering father is discomfited and turned into a laughing stock for his senseless pursuit of matters unsuitable to his age. In Phoinix's life-story, the young son also succeeds in his love affair, but the outcome is severe and heartbreaking. The wrathful father remains a redoubtable figure and execrates his faithless son with a terrible curse, which destroys the young man's life. The son even contemplates murdering his dreadful father;[58] in the end, he restrains himself and avoids parricide, but he can no longer bear to live in disgrace under his paternal roof and is forced to leave his homeland and embrace a life of exile (9.453-77). The amusing scenario of comedy and ribald novella is turned into a mesh of dire emotional tensions and bitter clashes, a veritable familial tragedy.

Amyntor's curse for his son's sex crime is of a suitably physical nature. The old man, who has been betrayed by his son, wishes that Phoinix may never produce a son of his own (9.453-56). There is a touch of *lex talionis* in the envisaged punishment: because Phoinix has not been a loyal son to his father, he is condemned never to enjoy the pleasures of fatherhood himself.[59] A meaningful statement follows, which has curious implications (9.456-57): "*θεοὶ δ'*

53 On the complex relation between these story-patterns, cf. Sourvinou-Inwood 1991, 252-57; Alden 2012, 123-25. See also the variant of the myth of Phoinix in Apollodoros, *Bibliotheca* 3.13.8: Phthia, Amyntor's mistress, falsely accuses Phoinix of seducing her; Amyntor believes her and blinds Phoinix in punishment. In this version, Phoinix's story is assimilated to the pattern of "Potiphar's wife". See Wiesmann 1948, 25-27; Peppermüller 1961, 114-15; Dundes 1962, 102; Gantz 1993, 618; Hansen 2002, 342-43.

54 See 2 *Samuel* 16.20-23, 20.3; *Genesis* 35.22, 49.4; Wiesmann 1948, 28-29; Baumgartner 1959, 162; Peppermüller 1961, 114; Astour 1967, 144-45; Gunkel 1987, 139; Hainsworth 1993, 122; Brown 1995, 66-70; West 2001, 5.

55 On the erotic rivalry of father and son in Phoinix's story, see Wiesmann 1948, 28-31; Sourvinou-Inwood 1991, 252-60; Alden 2000, 217-22 and 2012, 123-26; Gwara 2007, 308-11.

56 Cf. Aly 1969, 25. On this comic theme, see Wehrli 1936, 22-24, 56-69; Trenkner 1958, 112-20.

57 Pherekrates, *Korianno* fr. 77-79 Kassel-Austin; cf. Aristophanes, *Wasps* 1341-81, which may comically invert and parody such domestic scenarios of Pherekratean comedy. See Wehrli 1936, 22-24, 56; Handley 1985, 391-92; Konstantakos 2002, 152; Henderson 2002, 82; Auhagen 2009, 52.

58 On the authenticity of the verses 9.458-61, which are only transmitted by Plutarch, *De audiendis poetis* 26f, see Lohmann 1970, 269; Scodel 1982, 130; Hainsworth 1993, 123; Janko 1994, 27-29.

59 Cf. Griffin 1995, 129; Hansen 2002, 343.

ἐτέλειον ἐπαράς, Ζεύς τε καταχθόνιος καὶ ἐπαινὴ Περσεφόνεια", the gods, Zeus of the underworld and the honoured Persephone, accomplished the curses. This is not an extra-diegetic comment interpolated by the poet or by an omniscient narrator but part of Phoinix's own autobiographical account. How did Phoinix ascertain that his father's malediction had come true? It might be supposed that the young hero spent some time sleeping with a number of women, failed to sire a child with any one of them, and thus came empirically to the conclusion that he had been rendered sterile. However, this presupposes a far ampler timeline than is the case in the Homeric story, which appears to condense the events of a rather brief and heavily charged period. There is also no reference to Phoinix marrying a proper wife, with whom he might try to produce a rightful son and heir.

It seems therefore that the phrase in question is another example of the familiar Homeric tendency towards euphemism for glossing over matters of aberrant or sordid reality. The experience implied at this point is that Phoinix suddenly started failing to perform the sexual act itself; this persistent failure led him to despair about ever fathering a child. The pattern of symmetrical and retributive punishment, in which the form and operation of the penalty match the substance of the wrongful act, becomes even more pronounced in this case. Phoinix's crime was that he turned his sexual energy towards a forbidden target, his father's mistress. In retribution, the young man is punished with total loss of his sexual energy and power;[60] Phoinix is struck with impotence.[61]

Another distinctive motif of piquant humorous storytelling can be traced at this point, reworked again in a darker mode, so as to produce an effect of pathos. Impotence, the great joke against masculine pride, is appropriate stuff for the ribald novella. In Petronius's *Satyrica*, one of the greatest libertine novels of all time, an attack of impotence afflicts Encolpius, the narrator-protagonist, and becomes the main cause of his tribulations in the last surviving part of the narrative (126-39). The young man suddenly becomes unable to perform, whether he tries to have sex with his boy lover Giton (128-29) or with Circe, a beautiful lady who desires him (128-29, 131-32). Encolpius attempts to cure his affliction with various means, including magical spells, prayers, and rituals in honour of Priapus, the god of erection (130-31, 133-38). These situations

60 See Wiesmann 1948, 29-30; Devereux 1973, 43-44; Scodel 1982, 130, 132. West 2001, 8-13 interprets Amyntor's curse of childlessness as a kind of euphemism for castration; cf. similarly Dundes 1962, 102, 105; Hansen 2002, 351; Alden 2012, 124.

61 In Konstantakos 2018, 100-3, this principle of retaliatory punishment, which can be observed in many Greek myths and legends about great malefactors, is named *ἀντιπεπονθός* or *contrapasso*, according to the terminology used respectively by Aristotle (*Ethica Nicomachea* 1132b21-33) and Dante (*Inferno* 28.118-42). In mythical tradition there are two analogous cases, in which an effective sexual incapacitation (due, however, to forbiddance and restraint, not to impotence) is imposed as a symmetrical retaliatory punishment for a sex-related crime. Pandu, in the Sanskrit epic *Mahabharata*, goes out hunting and shoots with his arrow what he takes from afar to be a deer mating with a doe; but these animals turn out to be a holy sage and his wife, who were making love in the forest. The dying sage curses Pandu to die if he ever makes love with a woman (van Buitenen 1973, 246-50). Because Pandu lethally interrupted the sexual union of a couple, he is condemned never to enjoy sex himself. In Greek myth Laios, while he is a guest in the palace of Pelops at Elis, rapes Pelops's young son Chrysippos, who commits suicide out of shame. Pelops curses Laios, and as a result Laios receives an oracle warning him not to produce a child; otherwise, his child will kill him (see Gantz 1993, 488-91). Because Laios has shown lack of restraint in his abnormal erotic passion for Chrysippos, he is practically ordered to restrain his normal sexual appetite for his wife during the rest of his life. These stories are based on a pattern similar to the one that underlies the Homeric tale of Phoinix: the hero commits a sexual offence and receives some form of life-long negation of sex as a penalty.

produce a series of slapstick scenes. Circe is deeply offended after Encolpius's recurrent failures to satisfy her and has the young man flogged by her slaves (132). Encolpius apostrophizes his inert penis with a torrent of complaints and insults (132). The young man even suffers anal penetration with a dildo as part of a ritual apparently supposed to cure his ailment (138). All these experiences are painful for Encolpius himself, but they are narrated with comic brio and provide much amusement to the readers.[62]

Funny illustrations of male impotence are also found in Roman love elegies and salacious Hellenistic and Roman epigrams – genres that amply accommodate themes from comedy and ribald storytelling. The lover himself may complain about bouts of sexual inertia, which afflict him in spite of the stimulating company of his paramour; he holds himself up as a laughing stock but also as an object of commiseration, usually with a tone of self-conscious irony and light-handed humour.[63] In harsher satirical texts, the poet mocks his enemies for their sexual inability and flaccid genitalia.[64] Ridiculous situations of the same kind may well have been narrated in ribald novellas of the Hellenistic age, such as Aristides's *Milesian Tales*.[65] Even earlier, impotence was represented in a burlesque manner in the iambic poems of Hipponax. In one poem (fr. 78 West) a character tries to overcome impotence by making offerings to the Kabeiroi divinities and by smearing his penis with mulberry juice. In another farcical scene (fr. 92 West) the narrator undergoes a degrading and painful magical rite at the hands of a Lydian woman, apparently for the same purpose. His testicles are thrashed with a big branch and something is inserted into his anus, causing him to defecate. The comic vulgarity of these episodes recalls Encolpius's experiences in the *Satyrica*.[66]

In fact, the theme can be traced back to very ancient specimens of novellistic narrative. The earliest known example is a Hittite apologue, the *Story of Appu*, preserved on tablets from the 13th century BC; the old-fashioned language of the text indicates an even earlier date, around the 16th century BC. The main part of this work consists in a didactic allegorical parable about the conflict of good and evil, but the introduction bears the marks of a humoristic *Schwank*.[67] The title-figure Appu is a rich but childless man, and the narrative divulges from the beginning the reason for his lack of heir: Appu is unable to have sex with his wife. The two of them lie on their bed fully dressed and apparently do not even know how to go about the task. The poor wife falls into despair and loudly wonders whether Appu will ever succeed in having intercourse with her. The verbs used in this passage indicate Appu's inability

62 On this episode, on the whole, see Sullivan 1968, 68-74, 119-24, 216-19; Blickman 1988; Di Simone 1993, 94-108; Panayotakis 1995, 161-82; Conte 1996, 91-103, 107-9; McMahon 1998, 80-86, 94-97, 201-15; Obermayer 1998, 313-30; Courtney 2001, 190-208; Jensson 2004, 161-71, 185-86; Schmeling 2011, 471-539.

63 See e.g. Ovid, *Amores* 3.7; *Anthologia Palatina* 5.47, 11.29, 11.30, 12.11, 12.216, 12.232, 12.240 (epigrams by Roufinos, Automedon, Philodemos, Straton, and Skythinos); Tibullus 1.5.39-44; Martial 6.23.

64 See e.g. Catullus 16.10-11; Martial 3.70, 3.75, 9.66, 10.91, 11.25, 11.46, 12.86. On the literary depictions of impotence, see Baeza Angulo 1989; Richlin 1992, 37, 108-20, 132, 139; McMahon 1998, 19-59, 75-80; Obermayer 1998, 255-330; Höschele 2006, 129-35; McLaren 2007, 1-24; Holzberg 2009; Schmeling 2011, 488-94, 499-501; Gärtner 2011.

65 See Hausrath 1914, 454-55, 458; Lefèvre 1997, 34-42; Benz 2001, 89. Regarding in general the ribald sexual themes of Aristides's *Milesian Tales*, see Cataudella 1957, 90, 131-61; Walsh 1970, 10-18; Anderson 1976, 108-14; Harrison 1998; Benz 2001; Jensson 2004, 258-301; Müller 2006, 336-61; Bowie 2013.

66 See Latte 1929; West 1974, 142-45; Miralles & Pòrtulas 1988, 9-21, 73-76, 84-85, 90-94; Degani 1991, 91-93, 103-6; McMahon 1998, 26-28; Ormand 2015, 60-62; Boedeker 2016, 63-64, 72.

67 For text and translation of the Hittite narrative, see Siegelová 1971, 1-11, 18-23; Bernabé 1979, 217-23; Pecchioli Daddi & Polvani 1990, 163-69; Hoffner 1998, 82-84; Haas 2006, 193-97.

to achieve a dynamic sexual performance.[68] In the end, Appu prays to the Sun God, and the god gives him instructions and grants him the power for coitus. Once again, a typical theme of Graeco-Roman erotic novella finds early parallels in the narrative production of an eastern people, in an area that was geographically close to Ionia.

In Phoinix's narrative this fundamentally ridiculous theme[69] is explored in a more sombre way, which highlights its dismal and depressing aspects. What is a source of comic effect and satirical mockery in the ribald stories now becomes a cause of severe psychological and social strain. When Phoinix realizes the disaster that his father's curse has brought upon him, he is enraged to the point of planning to murder the old man; only the fear for his reputation makes him shrink from this terrible crime (9.456-61). Finally, the pressure from his father's anger and from his own feelings of shame proves to be too great. Phoinix secretly escapes from his paternal palace at night and seeks refuge in Peleus's hospitable home at Phthia (9.462-80). At a stroke he has lost his manliness, his inheritance, and his homeland. The generous Peleus, of course, will grant Phoinix an entirely new life, complete with a foster family, dominion over lands and peoples, and a new purpose – the mentorship of young Achilles (9.480-95). This offer will finally save Phoinix, taking him out of the dark space of the court novella and into the sphere of heroic legend, into the world of the *Iliad*.

Conclusion

The discussion of the two Iliadic court stories has hopefully highlighted the fruitful process of exchange between Homeric narrative and the novellistic traditions of the ancient world, both those of Archaic Ionia and the rich storytelling repositories of its Near-Eastern neighbours. The extant specimens of genuine Ionian storytelling, which have been transmitted in ancient sources, are very few. Therefore, Homeric stories that present typical novellistic motifs and strong parallels with analogous novellistic creations of Near-Eastern peoples or of later Graeco-Roman authors are particularly noteworthy. They may be interpreted as epic reworkings and recastings of popular novellistic material, which must have been circulating in the oral tradition of ancient Ionia at the time of the composition of the Homeric poems, probably under the influence of the neighbouring eastern cultures and their oral narrative repertoires.

Whether stringing together oriental narrative motifs, as in the heroic story of Bellerophon, or reworking humorous material in a more emotional mode, as in Phoinix's dramatic account, Homeric court novella achieves an admirable level of artistry in narrative flow and character portrayal, even though it is usually condensed in the limited space of an intercalated tale. These small narrative gems, which are artfully grafted onto the narrative body of the *Iliad*, represent for us the tangible beginnings of the Ionian storytelling art – the art that would come into full bloom a couple of centuries later in the oeuvre of Herodotos.

Ioannis M. Konstantakos
National and Kapodistrian University of Athens
iokonstan@phil.uoa.gr

Bibliography

ACKERMAN, J. S. 1990
'Knowing good and evil: A literary analysis of the court history in 2 Samuel 9-20 and 1 Kings 1-2', *JBL* 109, 41-60.

68 See Beckman 1983, 2-3; cf. Bernabé 1979, 222; Pecchioli Daddi & Polvani 1990, 168.

69 Cf. Scodel 1982, 132-33.

AFANAS'EVA, V. K. 1987
'Das sumerische Sargon-Epos. Versuch einer Interpretation', *Altorientalische Forschungen* 14, 237-46.

AGUT-LABORDÈRE, D. & M. CHAUVEAU 2011
Héros, magiciens et sages oubliés de l'Égypte ancienne. Une anthologie de la littérature en égyptien démotique, Paris.

ALDEN, M. J. 1996
'Genealogy as paradigm: The example of Bellerophon', *Hermes* 124, 257-63.

ALDEN, M. J. 2000
Homer Beside Himself. Para-Narratives in the Iliad, Oxford.

ALDEN, M. J. 2012
'The despised migrant (*Il.* 9.648 = 16.59)', in *Homeric Contexts. Neoanalysis and the Interpretation of Oral Poetry*, F. Montanari, A. Rengakos & C. C. Tsagalis (eds.), Berlin, 115-31.

ALEXANDROU, M. 2016
'Mythological narratives in Hipponax', in *Iambus and Elegy. New Approaches*, L. Swift & C. Carey (eds.), Oxford, 210-28.

ALSTER, B. 1987
'A note on the Uriah letter in the Sumerian Sargon legend', *ZA* 77, 169-73.

ALY, W. 1936
'Novelle', *RE* XVII.1, 1171-79.

ALY, W. 1969
Volksmärchen, Sage und Novelle bei Herodot und seinen Zeitgenossen (2nd ed.), Göttingen.

ANDERSON, G. 1976
Studies in Lucian's Comic Fiction, Leiden.

ASHERI, D., A. LLOYD & A. CORCELLA 2007
A Commentary on Herodotus Books I-IV, Oxford.

ASSUNÇÂO, T. R. 1997
'Le mythe iliadique de Bellérophon', *Gaia* 1-2, 41-66.

ASTOUR, M. C. 1967
Hellenosemitica. An Ethnic and Cultural Study in West Semitic Impact on Mycenaean Greece, Leiden.

AUHAGEN, U. 2009
Die Hetäre in der griechischen und römischen Komödie, Munich.

AUST, H. 1999
Novelle, Stuttgart.

BACHVAROVA, M. R. 2013
'Adapting Mesopotamian myth in Hurro-Hittite rituals at Hattuša. Ištar, the underworld, and the legendary kings', in *Beyond Hatti. A Tribute to Gary Beckman*, B. J. Collins & P. Michalowski (eds.), Atlanta, 23-44.

BACHVAROVA, M. R. 2016
From Hittite to Homer. The Anatolian Background of Ancient Greek Epic, Cambridge.

BAEZA ANGULO, E. F. 1989
'Ovidio, *Amores* III.7', *Faventia* 11, 25-58.

BAINES, J. 1996
'Myth and literature', in *Ancient Egyptian Literature. History and Forms*, A. Loprieno (ed.), Leiden, 361-77.

BANNERT, H. 1981
'Phoinix' Jugend und der Zorn des Meleagros. Zur Komposition des neunten Buches der Ilias', *WS* 94, 69-94.

BAUMGARTNER, W. 1959
Zum Alten Testament und seiner Umwelt, Leiden.

BECKMAN, G. M. 1983
Hittite Birth Rituals, Wiesbaden.

BENZ, L. 2001
'Die Fabula Milesia und die griechisch-römische Literatur', in *ScriptOralia Romana. Die römische Literatur zwischen Mündlichkeit und Schriftlichkeit*, L. Benz (ed.), Tübingen, 43-137.

BERLIN, A. 2001A
'The Book of Esther and ancient storytelling', *JBL* 120, 3-14.

BERLIN, A. 2001B
The JPS Bible Commentary: Esther, Philadelphia.

BERNABÉ, A. 1979
Textos literarios hetitas, Madrid.

BERTOLINI, F. 1989
'Dal folclore all'epica: esempi di trasformazione e adattamento', in *Il meraviglioso e il verosimile tra antichità e medioevo*, D. Lanza & O. Longo (eds.), Florence, 131-52.

BICHLER, R. 2011
'Die Fahrt zu den Grenzen der Erde. Von Herodot bis zur Alexander-Historiographie', *Gymnasium* 118, 315-44.

BICKERMAN, E. 1967
Four Strange Books of the Bible, New York.

BLACK, J., G. CUNNINGHAM, E. ROBSON & G. ZÓLYOMI 2004
The Literature of Ancient Sumer, Oxford.

BLICKMAN, D. 1988
'The romance of Encolpius and Circe', *AeR* 33, 7-16.

BLUM, E. 2000
'Ein Anfang der Geschichtsschreibung? Anmerkungen zur sog. Thronfolgegeschichte und zum Umgang mit Geschichte im alten Israel', in *Die sogenannte Thronfolgegeschichte Davids. Neue Einsichten und Anfragen*, A. de Pury & T. Römer (eds.), Göttingen, 4-37.

BLUM, E. & K. WEINGART 2017
'The Joseph story: Diaspora novella or North-Israelite narrative?', *ZATW* 129, 501-21.

BOEDEKER, D. 2016
'Coarse poetics: Listening to Hipponax', in *Iambus and Elegy. New Approaches*, L. Swift & C. Carey (eds.), Oxford, 56-73.

BOLTE, J. & G. POLÍVKA 1930
Anmerkungen zu den Kinder- und Hausmärchen der Brüder Grimm IV, Leipzig.

BOWIE, E. L. 2001A
'Ancestors of historiography in early Greek elegiac and iambic poetry?', in *The Historian's Craft in the Age of Herodotus*, N. Luraghi (ed.), Oxford, 45-66.

BOWIE, E. L. 2001B
'Early Greek iambic poetry: The importance of narrative', in *Iambic Ideas. Essays on a Poetic Tradition from Archaic Greece to the Late Roman Empire*, A. Cavarzere, A. Aloni & A. Barchiesi (eds.), Lanham, 1-27.

BOWIE, E. L. 2013
'"Milesian tales"', in *The Romance Between Greece and the East*, T. Whitmarsh & S. Thomson (eds.), Cambridge, 243-57.

BOYCE, M. 1954
'Some remarks on the transmission of the Kayanian heroic cycle', in *Serta Cantabrigiensia viris doctissimis clarissimisque qui ad XXIII congressum internationalem*

rebus litterisque orientalibus dedicatum Cantabrigiam convenerunt donum, Wiesbaden, 45-52.

BOYCE, M. 1955
'Zariadres and Zarēr', *BSOAS* 17, 463-77.

BRESCIANI, E. 2007
Letteratura e poesia dell'antico Egitto. Cultura e società attraverso i testi, Turin.

BRILLANTE, C. 1996
'La scrittura in Omero', *Quaderni Urbinati di Cultura Classica* 52, 31-45.

BROWN, J. P. 1995
Israel and Hellas, Berlin.

BRUNNER-TRAUT, E. 1965
Altägyptische Märchen, Düsseldorf and Cologne.

BURGESS, J. S. 2001
The Tradition of the Trojan War in Homer and the Epic Cycle, Baltimore.

BURGESS, J. S. 2006
'Neoanalysis, orality, and intertextuality: An examination of Homeric motif transference', *Oral Tradition* 21, 148-89.

BURKARD, G. & H. J. THISSEN 2008
Einführung in die altägyptische Literaturgeschichte II: *Neues Reich*, Berlin.

BURKARD, G. & H. J. THISSEN 2012
Einführung in die altägyptische Literaturgeschichte I: *Altes und Mittleres Reich*, Berlin.

BURKERT, W. 1983
'Oriental myth and literature in the Iliad', in *The Greek Renaissance of the Eighth Century B.C.: Tradition and Innovation*, R. Hägg (ed.), Stockholm, 51-56.

CAREY, C. 2008
'Hipponax narrator', *ActaAntHung* 48, 89-102.

CARPENTER, R. 1946
Folk Tale, Fiction and Saga in the Homeric Epics, Berkeley.

CARR, D. M. 1996
Reading the Fractures of Genesis. Historical and Literary Approaches, Louisville.

CATAUDELLA, Q. 1957
La novella greca. Prolegomeni e testi in traduzioni originali, Naples.

CHRISTENSEN, A. 1931
Les Kayanides, Copenhagen.

CHRISTENSEN, A. 1936
Les gestes des rois dans les traditions de l'Iran antique, Paris.

CLEMENTS, R. J. & J. GIBALDI 1977
Anatomy of the Novella. The European Tale Collection from Boccaccio and Chaucer to Cervantes, New York.

COLIN, F. 1990
'Le récit de Sataspès s'inspire-t-il de sources égyptiennes?', *ZPE* 82, 287-96.

COLLARD, C., M. J. CROPP & K. H. LEE 1995
Euripides: Selected Fragmentary Plays I, Warminster.

COLLINS, J. J. 1975
'The court-tales in Daniel and the development of Apocalyptic', *JBL* 94, 218-34.

COLLINS, J. J. 1993
Daniel. A Commentary on the Book of Daniel, Minneapolis.

CONTE, G. B. 1996
The Hidden Author. An Interpretation of Petronius' Satyricon, Berkeley.

COOPER, J. S. & W. HEIMPEL 1983
'The Sumerian Sargon legend', *JAOS* 103, 67-82.

COURTNEY, E. 2001
A Companion to Petronius, Oxford.

CURNIS, M. 2003
Il Bellerofonte di Euripide. Edizione e commento dei frammenti, Alessandria.

DAVIES, M. 2002
'The folk-tale origins of the Iliad and Odyssey', *WS* 115, 5-43.

DEGANI, E. 1991
Hipponactis testimonia et fragmenta, Leipzig.

DE PURY, A. & T. RÖMER 2000
'Einleitung', in *Die sogenannte Thronfolgegeschichte Davids. Neue Einsichten und Anfragen*, A. de Pury & T. Römer (eds.), Göttingen, 1-3.

DESANGES, J. 1978
Recherches sur l'activité des Méditerranéens aux confins de l'Afrique (VIe siècle avant J.-C. – IVe siècle après J.-C.), Paris.

DEVEREUX, G. 1973
'The self-blinding of Oidipous in Sophokles: *Oidipous Tyrannos*', *JHS* 93, 36-49.

DIETRICH, W. 2000
'Das Ende der Thronfolgegeschichte', in *Die sogenannte Thronfolgegeschichte Davids. Neue Einsichten und Anfragen*, A. de Pury & T. Römer (eds.), Göttingen, 38-69.

DI GREGORIO, L. 1983
'Il Bellerofonte di Euripide. I. Dati per una ricostruzione. II. Tentativo di ricostruzione', *Civiltà Classica e Cristiana* 4, 159-214, 365-82.

DI SIMONE, M. 1993
'I fallimenti di Encolpio, tra esemplarità mitica e modelli letterari: una ricostruzione (Sat. 82, 5; 132, 1)', *Materiali e discussioni per l'analisi dei testi classici* 30, 87-108.

DOBROV, G. W. 2001
Figures of Play. Greek Drama and Metafictional Poetics, Oxford.

DONADONI, S. 1967
La letteratura egizia, Milan.

DONNINI, M. 1981
'Apul. *Met.* X, 2-12: analogie e varianti di un racconto', *Materiali e contributi per la storia della narrativa greco-latina* 3, 145-60.

DORATI, M. 2009
'La storia lidia di Nicolao di Damasco', in *Rom und der Osten im 1. Jahrhundert v.Chr. (Akkulturation oder Kampf der Kulturen?)*, H.-J. Gehrke & A. Mastrocinque (eds.), Cosenza, 35-64.

DOROTHY, C. V. 1997
The Books of Esther. Structure, Genre and Textual Integrity, Sheffield.

DREWS, R. 1973
The Greek Accounts of Eastern History, Cambridge MA.

DUNDES, A. 1962
'From etic to emic units in the structural study of folktales', *Journal of American Folklore* 75, 95-105.

EDWARDS, M. W. 1986
'Homer and oral tradition: The formula, part I', *Oral Tradition* 1, 171-230.

EDWARDS, M. W. 1988
'Homer and oral tradition: The formula, part II', *Oral Tradition* 3, 11-60.

EDWARDS, M. W. 1992
'Homer and oral tradition: The type-scene', *Oral Tradition* 7, 284-330.

EDWARDS, M. W. 1997
'Homeric style and oral poetics', in *A New Companion to Homer*, I. Morris & B. Powell (eds.), Leiden, 261-83.

ERBSE, H. 1992
Studien zum Verständnis Herodots, Berlin.

ERDMANNSDÖRFFER, B. 1870
Das Zeitalter der Novelle in Hellas, Berlin.

FINKELBERG, M. 2011
'Homer and his peers: Neoanalysis, oral theory, and the status of Homer', *Trends in Classics* 3, 197-208.

FINKELBERG, M. 2012
'Oral formulaic theory and the individual poet', in *Homeric Contexts. Neoanalysis and the Interpretation of Oral Poetry*, F. Montanari, A. Rengakos & C. C. Tsagalis (eds.), Berlin, 73-82.

FLANAGAN, J. W. 1972
'Court history or succession document? A study of 2 Samuel 9-20 and 1 Kings 1-2', *JBL* 91, 172-81.

FLUSIN, M. 1976
'Deux légendes de l'ancienne Lydie d'après Xanthos le Lydien', *RHist* 256, 3-13.

FOLEY, J. M. 1997
'Oral tradition and its implications', in *A New Companion to Homer*, I. Morris & B. Powell (eds.), Leiden, 146-73.

FOLEY, J. M. 2007
'"Reading" Homer through oral tradition', *College Literature* 34, 1-28.

FREI, P. 1993
'Die Bellerophontessage und das Alte Testament', in *Religionsgeschichtliche Beziehungen zwischen Kleinasien, Nordsyrien und dem Alten Testament*, B. Janowski, K. Koch & G. Wilhelm (eds.), Göttingen, 39-65.

FRIEDRICH, R. 2011
'Formelsprache', in *Homer-Handbuch*, A. Rengakos & B. Zimmermann (eds.), Stuttgart, 45-64.

GAISSER, J. H. 1969
'Adaptation of traditional material in the Glaucus-Diomedes episode', *TAPA* 100, 165-76.

GANTZ, T. 1993
Early Greek Myth. A Guide to Literary and Artistic Sources, Baltimore.

GÄRTNER, T. 2011
'Das Erlebnis der Impotenz. Zur Genese, Struktur und Rezeption von Ov., *am.* III, 7', *Latomus* 70, 103-23.

GAZZANO, F. 2017
'L'Oriente Vicino: le tradizioni sulla Lidia nello specchio di Erodoto', *Erga-Logoi* 5, 35-59.

GIER, A. 2002A
'Novelle', in *Enzyklopädie des Märchens* 10, R. W. Brednich (ed.), Berlin, 120-26.

GIER, A. 2002B
'Novellistik', in *Enzyklopädie des Märchens* 10, R. W. Brednich (ed.), Berlin, 134-48.

GOLDMAN, S. 1995
The Wiles of Women / The Wiles of Men. Joseph and Potiphar's Wife in Ancient Near Eastern, Jewish, and Islamic Folklore, New York.

GORDIS, R. 1981
'Religion, wisdom and history in the Book of Esther – a new solution to an ancient crux', *JBL* 100, 359-88.

GRAY, V. 2002
'Short stories in Herodotus' *Histories*', in *Brill's Companion to Herodotus*, E. J. Bakker, I. J. F. de Jong & H. van Wees (eds.), Leiden, 291-317.

GRIFFIN, J. 1995
Homer: Iliad Book Nine, Oxford.

GRIFFITH, F. L. 1900
Stories of the High Priests of Memphis. The Sethon of Herodotus and the Demotic Tales of Khamuas, Oxford.

GRIFFITHS, A. 2006
'Stories and storytelling in the *Histories*', in *The Cambridge Companion to Herodotus*, C. Dewald & J. Marincola (eds.), Cambridge, 130-44.

GUNKEL, H. 1922
Genesis, Göttingen.

GUNKEL, H. 1987
The Folktale in the Old Testament, translated by M. D. Rutter, Sheffield.

GUNN, D. M. 1976
'Traditional composition in the "Succession Narrative"', *Vetus Testamentum* 26, 214-29.

GUNN, D. M. 1978
The Story of King David. Genre and Interpretation, Sheffield.

GWARA, S. 2007
'Misprision in the para-narratives of *Iliad* 9', *Arethusa* 40, 303-36.

HAAS, V. 2006
Die hethitische Literatur. Texte, Stilistik, Motive, Berlin.

HAINSWORTH, B. 1993
The Iliad: A Commentary III: *Books 9-12*, Cambridge.

HANDLEY, E. W. 1985
'Comedy', in *The Cambridge History of Classical Literature* I: *Greek Literature*, P. E. Easterling & B. M. W. Knox (eds.), Cambridge, 355-425.

HANSEN, W. 1997
'Homer and the folktale', in *A New Companion to Homer*, I. Morris & B. Powell (eds.), Leiden, 442-62.

HANSEN, W. 2002
Ariadne's Thread. A Guide to International Tales Found in Classical Literature, Ithaca.

HANSEN, W. 2017
The Book of Greek & Roman Folktales, Legends, & Myths, Princeton.

HARRISON, S. J. 1998
'The Milesian tales and the Roman novel', *Groningen Colloquia on the Novel* 9, 61-73.

HAUSRATH, A. 1914
'Die ionische Novellistik', *NJbb* 33, 441-61.

HELD, G. F. 1987
'Phoinix, Agamemnon and Achilleus: Parables and paradeigmata', *CQ* 37, 245-61.

HENDERSON, J. 2002
'Strumpets on stage: The early comic hetaera', *Dioniso* n.s. 1, 78-87.

HENNIG, R. 1944
Terrae incognitae. Eine Zusammenstellung und kritische Bewertung der wichtigsten vorcolumbischen Entdeckungsreisen an Hand der darüber vorliegenden Originalberichte I, Leiden.

HEUBECK, A. 1974
Die Homerische Frage. Ein Bericht über die Forschung der letzten Jahrzehnte, Darmstadt.

HOFFNER, H. A. 1965
'The Elkunirsa myth reconsidered', *RHA* 76, 5-16.

HOFFNER, H. A. 1998
Hittite Myths, Atlanta.

HOLLIS, S. T. 1989
'The woman in ancient examples of the Potiphar's wife motif, K2111', in *Gender and Difference in Ancient Israel*, P. L. Day (ed.), Minneapolis, 28-42.

HOLM, T. L. 2005
'Daniel 1-6: A Biblical story-collection', in *Ancient Fiction. The Matrix of Early Christian and Jewish Narrative*, J. A. Brant, C. W. Hedrick & C. Shea (eds.), Atlanta, 149-66.

HOLM, T. L. 2013
Of Courtiers and Kings. The Biblical Daniel Narratives and Ancient Story-Collections, Winona Lake.

HÖLSCHER, U. 1978
'The transformation from folk-tale to epic', in *Homer. Tradition and Invention*, B. C. Fenik (ed.), Leiden, 51-67.

HÖLSCHER, U. 1988
Die Odyssee. Epos zwischen Märchen und Roman, Munich.

HOLZBERG, N. 2009
'Ovid, *Amores* 3,7: A poem between two genres', *Latomus* 68, 933-40.

HÖSCHELE, R. 2006
Verrückt nach Frauen. Der Epigrammatiker Rufin, Tübingen.

HUMPHREYS, W. L. 1973
'A life-style for Diaspora: A study of the tales of Esther and Daniel', *JBL* 92, 211-23.

JACKSON, J. J. 1965
'David's throne: Patterns in the Succession Story', *Canadian Journal of Theology* 11, 183-95.

JANKO, R. 1994
The Iliad: A Commentary IV: *Books 13-16*, Cambridge.

JENSSON, G. 2004
The Recollections of Encolpius. The Satyrica of Petronius as Milesian Fiction, Groningen.

JESI, F. 1962
'Il tentato adulterio mitico in Grecia e in Egitto', *Aegyptus* 42, 276-96.

JOHNSON, S. R. 2005
'Novelistic elements in Esther: Persian or Hellenistic, Jewish or Greek?', *The Catholic Biblical Quarterly* 67, 571-89.

JOUAN, F. & H. VAN LOOY 2000
Euripide VIII/2: *Fragments. Bellérophon - Protésilas*, Paris.

KAISER, O. 2000
'Das Verhältnis der Erzählung vom König David zum sogenannten Deuteronomistischen Geschichtswerk', in *Die sogenannte Thronfolgegeschichte Davids. Neue Einsichten und Anfragen*, A. de Pury & T. Römer (eds.), Göttingen, 94-122.

KANTZIOS, I. 2005
The Trajectory of Archaic Greek Trimeters, Leiden.

KEYS, G. 1996
The Wages of Sin. A Reappraisal of the "Succession Narrative", Sheffield.

KIRK, G. S. 1990
The Iliad: A Commentary II: *Books 5-8*, Cambridge.

KLOTZ, A. 1937
'Die Fahrt des Persers Sataspes an der Westküste Afrikas', *Klio* 30, 343-46.

KOCH, K. 2005
Daniel, Neukirchen and Vluyn.

KONSTANTAKOS, I. M. 2002
'Towards a literary history of comic love', *ClMed* 53, 141-71.

KONSTANTAKOS, I. M. 2007
'The warlike and the wary: The council of Xerxes in Hdt. VII 8-11 and some Near Eastern tales', *Eikasmos* 18, 219-44.

KONSTANTAKOS, I. M. 2008
Ἀκίχαρος. Ἡ Διήγηση τοῦ Ἀχικὰρ στὴν ἀρχαία Ἑλλάδα II, Athens.

KONSTANTAKOS, I. M. 2012
'Divine comedy: Demodocus' song of Ares and Aphrodite and the mythicization of an adultery tale', *Maia* 64, 12-34.

KONSTANTAKOS, I. M. 2016
'Cambyses and the sacred bull (Herodotus 3.27-29 and 3.64): History and legend', in *The Art of History. Literary Perspectives on Greek and Roman Historiography*, V. Liotsakis & S. Farrington (eds.), Berlin, 37-72.

KONSTANTAKOS, I. M. 2018
'Time, thy pyramids: The *novella* of Mycerinus (Herodotus 2.129-134)', in *Herodotus: Narrator, Scientist, Historian*, E. Bowie (ed.), Berlin, 77-107.

KULLMANN, W. 1956
Das Wirken der Götter in der Ilias. Untersuchungen zur Frage der Entstehung des homerischen "Götterapparats", Berlin.

KULLMANN, W. 1984
'Oral poetry theory and Neoanalysis in Homeric research', *GRBS* 25, 307-23.

KULLMANN, W. 1991
'Ergebnisse der motivgeschichtlichen Forschung zu Homer (Neoanalyse)', in *Zweihundert Jahre Homer-Forschung. Rückblick und Ausblick*, J. Latacz (ed.), Stuttgart, 425-55.

KULLMANN, W. 2012
'Neoanalysis between orality and literacy: Some remarks concerning the development of Greek myths including the legend of the capture of Troy', in *Homeric Contexts. Neoanalysis and the Interpretation of Oral Poetry*, F. Montanari, A. Rengakos & C. C. Tsagalis (eds.), Berlin, 13-25.

KULLMANN, W. 2015
'Motif and source research: Neoanalysis, Homer, and Cyclic epic', in *The Greek Epic Cycle and Its Ancient Reception. A Companion*, M. Fantuzzi & C. C. Tsagalis (eds.), Cambridge, 108-25.

LALOUETTE, C. 1987
Textes sacrés et textes profanes de l'ancienne Égypte II: *Mythes, contes et poésie*, Paris.

LANDAU, M. 1884
Die Quellen des Dekameron, Stuttgart.

LATACZ, J. 2015
'Formularity and orality', in *Homer's Iliad. The Basel Commentary. Prolegomena*, A. Bierl & J. Latacz (eds.), translated by B. W. Millis & S. Strack, Berlin, 39-64.

LATTE, K. 1929
'Hipponacteum', *Hermes* 64, 385-88.

LEFEBVRE, G. 1949
Romans et contes égyptiens de l'époque pharaonique, Paris.

LEFÈVRE, E. 1997
Studien zur Struktur der "Milesischen" Novelle bei Petron und Apuleius, Stuttgart.

LICHTHEIM, M. 1973-80
Ancient Egyptian Literature. A Book of Readings I-III, Berkeley.

LOHMANN, D. 1970
Die Komposition der Reden in der Ilias, Berlin.

LOUDEN, B. 2011
Homer's Odyssey and the Near East, Cambridge.

LUTHER, B. 1991
'The novella of Judah and Tamar and other Israelite novellas', in *Narrative and Novella in Samuel*, D. M. Gunn (ed.), Sheffield, 89-118.

MALTEN, L. 1944
'Homer und die lykischen Fürsten', *Hermes* 79, 1-12.

MARONITIS, D. N. 2001
Ηρόδοτος. Οκτώ νουβέλες και τέσσερα ανέκδοτα, Athens.

MASPERO, G. 2002
Popular Stories of Ancient Egypt, edited by H. El-Shamy, Santa Barbara.

MCLAREN, A. 2007
Impotence. A Cultural History, Chicago.

MCMAHON, J. M. 1998
Paralysin cave. Impotence, Perception, and Text in the Satyrica of Petronius, Leiden.

MERAKLIS, M. 1979
'Bellerophon', in *Enzyklopädie des Märchens* 2, K. Ranke (ed.), Berlin, 91-92.

MIRALLES, C. & J. PÒRTULAS 1988
The Poetry of Hipponax, Rome.

MOHL, J. 1876-78
Le Livre des Rois par Abou'lkasim Firdousi I-VII, Paris.

MOMIGLIANO, A. 1977
Essays in Ancient and Modern Historiography, Oxford.

MORRIS, S. 1997
'Homer and the Near East', in *A New Companion to Homer*, I. Morris & B. Powell (eds.), Leiden, 599-623.

MÜLLER, C. W. 2006
Legende – Novelle – Roman. Dreizehn Kapitel zur erzählenden Prosaliteratur der Antike, Göttingen.

MURRAY, O. 2001
'Herodotus and oral history', in *The Historian's Craft in the Age of Herodotus*, N. Luraghi (ed.), Oxford, 16-44.

NAUMANN, T. 2000
'David als exemplarischer König. Der Fall Urijas (2 Sam 11) vor dem Hintergrund altorientalischer Erzähltraditionen', in *Die sogenannte Thronfolgegeschichte Davids. Neue Einsichten und Anfragen*, A. de Pury & T. Römer (eds.), Göttingen, 136-67.

NIDITCH, S. 1987
A Prelude to Biblical Folklore. Underdogs and Tricksters, Urbana.

NIDITCH, S. & R. DORAN 1977
'The success story of the wise courtier: A formal approach', *JBL* 96, 179-93.

NOEGEL, S. B. 2005
'Mesopotamian epic', in *A Companion to Ancient Epic*, J. M. Foley (ed.), Oxford, 233-45.

NÖLDEKE, T. 1920
Das iranische Nationalepos, Berlin.

OBERMAYER, H. P. 1998
Martial und der Diskurs über männliche "Homosexualität" in der Literatur der frühen Kaiserzeit, Tübingen.

ORMAND, K. 2015
'Toward iambic obscenity', in *Ancient Obscenities. Their Nature and Use in the Ancient Greek and Roman Worlds*, D. Dutsch & A. Suter (eds.), Ann Arbor, 44-70.

PAGE, D. L. 1973
Folktales in Homer's Odyssey, Cambridge MA.

PANAYOTAKIS, C. 1995
Theatrum Arbitri. Theatrical Elements in the Satyrica of Petronius, Leiden.

PECCHIOLI DADDI, F. & A. M. POLVANI 1990
La mitologia ittita, Brescia.

PEPPERMÜLLER, R. 1961
Die Bellerophontessage. Ihre Herkunft und Geschichte, Ph.D. Dissertation, Eberhard-Karls-Universität, Tübingen.

PETERSMANN, H. 1981
'Homer und das Märchen', *WS* 94, 43-68.

PIEPER, M. 1935
Das ägyptische Märchen. Ursprung und Nachwirkung ältester Märchendichtung bis zur Gegenwart, Leipzig.

PIZZI, I. 1886-88
Firdusi, Il libro dei re. Poema epico recato dal persiano in versi italiani I-VIII, Turin.

POSENER, G. 1985
Le Papyrus Vandier, Cairo.

PROPP, V. Y. 2012
The Russian Folktale, translated by S. Forrester, Detroit.

QUACK, J. F. 2005
Einführung in die altägyptische Literaturgeschichte III: *Die demotische und gräko-ägyptische Literatur*, Münster.

QUIRKE, S. G. 1996
'Narrative literature', in *Ancient Egyptian Literature. History and Forms*, A. Loprieno (ed.), Leiden, 263-76.

RADERMACHER, L. 1915
Die Erzählungen der Odyssee (Sitzungsberichte der Kaiserlichen Akademie der Wissenschaften in Wien, philosophisch-historische Klasse, 178.1), Vienna.

RADERMACHER, L. 1943
Mythos und Sage bei den Griechen, Vienna.

REDFORD, D. B. 1970
A Study of the Biblical Story of Joseph (Genesis 37-50), Leiden.

REDFORD, D. B. 1992
Egypt, Canaan, and Israel in Ancient Times, Princeton.

REENTS, C. & I. KÖHLER-ZÜLCH 1993
'Joseph: Der keusche J.', in *Enzyklopädie des Märchens* 7, R. W. Brednich (ed.), Berlin, 640-48.

REINHARDT, K. 1960A
Tradition und Geist. Gesammelte Essays zur Dichtung, Göttingen.

REINHARDT, K. 1960B
Vermächtnis der Antike. Gesammelte Essays zur Philosophie und Geschichtsschreibung, Göttingen.

RICHLIN, A. 1992
The Garden of Priapus. Sexuality and Aggression in Roman Humor, New York.

ROCCA, R. 1976
'Eliodoro e i due "Ippoliti" euripidei', *Materiali e contributi per la storia della narrativa greco-latina* 1, 23-31.

ROHDE, E. 1914
Der griechische Roman und seine Vorläufer, Leipzig.

ROST, L. 1982
The Succession to the Throne of David, translated by M. D. Rutter & D. M. Gunn, Sheffield.

RUSSO, J. 1997
'The formula', in *A New Companion to Homer*, I. Morris & B. Powell (eds.), Leiden, 238-60.

RYPKA, J. 1959
Iranische Literaturgeschichte, Leipzig.

SANCISI-WEERDENBURG, H. 1993
'Exit Atossa: Images of women in Greek historiography on Persia', in *Images of Women in Antiquity*, A. Cameron & A. Kuhrt (eds.), London, 20-33.

SCHACHERMEYR, F. 1950
Poseidon und die Entstehung des griechischen Götterglaubens, Munich.

SCHMELING, G. 2011
A Commentary on the Satyrica of Petronius, Oxford.

SCODEL, R. 1982
'The autobiography of Phoenix: *Iliad* 9.444-95', *AJP* 103, 128-36.

SCODEL, R. 1992
'The wits of Glaucus', *TAPA* 122, 73-84.

SEILER, S. 1998
Die Geschichte von der Thronfolge Davids (2 Sam 9-20; 1 Kön 1-2). Untersuchungen zur Literarkritik und Tendenz, Berlin.

SHAHBAZI, A. S. 1990
'On the *X^wadāy-nāmag*', in *Iranica Varia. Papers in Honor of Professor Ehsan Yarshater*, D. Amin, M. Kasheff & A. S. Shahbazi (eds.), Leiden, 208-29.

SHOJAEI KAWAN, C. 2002
'Novellenmärchen', in *Enzyklopädie des Märchens* 10, R. W. Brednich (ed.), Berlin, 126-29.

SHOJAEI KAWAN, C. 2010
'Uriasbrief', in *Enzyklopädie des Märchens* 13, R. W. Brednich (ed.), Berlin, 1262-67.

SIEGELOVÁ, J. 1971
Appu-Märchen und Ḫedammu-Mythus, Wiesbaden.

SIMPSON, W. K. (ED.) 2003
The Literature of Ancient Egypt. An Anthology of Stories, Instructions, Stelae, Autobiographies, and Poetry, New Haven.

SKJÆRVØ, P. O. 1998
'Eastern Iranian epic traditions II: Rostam and Bhīṣma', *ActaOrHung* 51, 159-70.

SOURVINOU-INWOOD, C. 1991
"Reading" Greek Culture. Texts and Images, Rituals and Myths, Oxford.

STOEBE, H. J. 1986
'David und Uria. Überlegungen zur Überlieferung von 2 Sam 11', *Biblica* 67, 388-96.

STOEVESANDT, M. 2008
Homers Ilias. Gesamtkommentar (Basler Kommentar) IV.2: *Sechster Gesang. Kommentar*, Berlin.

STRÖMBERG, R. 1961
'Die Bellerophontes-Erzählung in der Ilias', *ClMed* 22, 1-15.

SULLIVAN, J. P. 1968
The Satyricon of Petronius. A Literary Study, London.

TAIT, J. 1994
'Egyptian fiction in Demotic and Greek', in *Greek Fiction. The Greek Novel in Context*, J. R. Morgan & R. Stoneman (eds.), London, 203-22.

TALAMO, C. 1985
'Erodoto e le tradizioni sul regno di Lidia', *Storia della Storiografia* 7, 150-61.

TALMON, S. 1963
'"Wisdom" in the Book of Esther', *Vetus Testamentum* 13, 419-55.

TATUM, J. 1997
'Herodotus the fabulist', in *Der antike Roman und seine mittelalterliche Rezeption*, M. Picone & B. Zimmermann (eds.), Basel, 29-48.

THOMPSON, S. 1955
Motif-Index of Folk-Literature IV, Bloomington.

THOMPSON, S. 1977
The Folktale, Berkeley.

THOMSON, J. A. K. 1935
The Art of the Logos, London.

TRENKNER, S. 1958
The Greek Novella in the Classical Period, Cambridge.

UTHER, H.-J. 2004
The Types of International Folktales. A Classification and Bibliography I, Helsinki.

VAN BUITENEN, J. A. B. 1973
The Mahābhārata I: *The Book of the Beginning*, Chicago.

VAN SETERS, J. 2004
'The Joseph story - some basic observations', in *Egypt, Israel, and the Ancient Mediterranean World. Studies in Honor of Donald B. Redford*, G. N. Knoppers & A. Hirsch (eds.), Leiden, 361-88.

VON RAD, G. 1963
Genesis. A Commentary, translated by J. H. Marks, London.

VON RAD, G. 1966
The Problem of the Hexateuch and Other Essays, New York.

VON WIESE, B. 1982
Novelle, Stuttgart.

WALSH, P. G. 1970
The Roman Novel, Cambridge.

WARNER, A. G. & E. WARNER 1905-25
The Sháhnáma of Firdausí I-IX, London.

WEHRLI, F. 1936
Motivstudien zur griechischen Komödie, Zürich.

WELLS, J. 1923
Studies in Herodotus, Oxford.

WESSELIUS, J. W. 1990
'Joab's death and the central theme of the Succession Narrative (2 Samuel IX-1 Kings II)', *Vetus Testamentum* 40, 336-51.

WEST, M. L. 1974
Studies in Greek Elegy and Iambus, Berlin.

WEST, M. L. 1997
The East Face of Helicon. West Asiatic Elements in Greek Poetry and Myth, Oxford.

WEST, S. 2001
'Phoenix's antecedents: A note on *Iliad* 9', *Scripta Classica Israelica* 20, 1-15.

WEST, S. 2003
'Croesus' second reprieve and other tales of the Persian court', *CQ* 53, 416-37.

WESTERMANN, C. 2002
Genesis 37-50. A Continental Commentary, translated by J. J. Scullion, Minneapolis.

WHITE, J. A. 1982
'Bellerophon in the "Land of Nod". Some notes on *Iliad* 6.153-211', *AJP* 103, 119-27.

WIESMANN, P. 1948
Die Phoinix-Novelle. Interpretation von Ilias IX v. 447 und ff., Chur.

WILLCOCK, M. 1997
'Neoanalysis', in *A New Companion to Homer*, I. Morris & B. Powell (eds.), Leiden, 174-89.

WILLS, L. M. 1990
The Jew in the Court of the Foreign King. Ancient Jewish Court Legends, Minneapolis.

WILLS, L. M. 1995
The Jewish Novel in the Ancient World, Ithaca.

WILLS, L. M. 2011
'Jewish novellas in a Greek and Roman age: Fiction and identity', *Journal for the Study of Judaism* 42, 141-65.

YARSHATER, E. 1983
'Iranian historical tradition', in *The Cambridge History of Iran* III: *The Seleucid, Parthian and Sasanian Periods*, E. Yarshater (ed.), Cambridge, 341-477.

YASSIF, E. 1984
'The novella as an ethnopoetic genre', in *Papers II. The Eighth Congress for the International Society for Folk Narrative Research*, Bergen, 283-89.

YASSIF, E. 1999
The Hebrew Folktale: History, Genre, Meaning, translated by J. S. Teitelbaum, Bloomington.

ZIMMERMAN, M. 2000
Apuleius Madaurensis: Metamorphoses. Book X. Text, Introduction and Commentary, Groningen.

"ἐκ ταυτησὶ δὴ τῆς ἐξετάσεως πολλαὶ ἀπέχθειαί μοι γεγόνασι" (Pl. Ap.22e6-23a1): Plato's Socrates and Performing Philosophy in the Oral Culture of Athens

Christos A. Zafiropoulos

Abstract

Plato's dialogues often present descriptions, in vivid imagery, of Socrates's aptitude for shaming and publicly defaming his interlocutors. Such scenes are at times accompanied by expressions of strong, negative emotions, and occasionally bodily manifestations of such emotions. This paper argues that these passages should not be read simply as narrative adornments, but also as testimonies on the practice of philosophy in Classical Athens under the conditions for public discourse in a traditional society and an oral community like that of Athens, alongside the particular framework for the oral articulation of philosophical logos that the dialogues record, one that involved more non-verbal expressions, direct and physical contact during conversation, attended by a similarly "live" audience and spectators, compared to our silent reading and reflection upon a text. This constituted a narrative framework that Plato's intended readers and audience were accustomed to and perhaps anticipated. By these episodes, Plato also sought to underline and warn against the dangers from exposing philosophical discourse and life in the public sphere, which had already led to Socrates's own trial and sentencing to death, and the need for philosophy to enter a new stage, one of contemplative life segregated from the emotional and sociopolitical parameters of public discourse.

It feels quite comfortable, if not rather fitting, to talk about Socrates here, in the heart of the ancient Athenian *asty*, let alone in *Χαιρεφῶντος* street.[1] In particular, in the following pages I will touch upon a peculiar aspect of Plato's presentation of Socrates's life and words, namely Plato's many references to the master's and his interlocutors' gestures, postures, glances, and in general the intrusion in the dialogues of a whole set of non-verbal accompaniments to philosophical discourse. I shall read these exceptions from the core of philosophical argumentation as intertwined with and embedded in the historical conditions for discourse in Athens in general, and in particular for philosophical conversation as a practice enacted in front of an audience and, accordingly, conducted and judged by the standards of interaction in the oral culture of 5th and early 4th century BC Athens.

A few introductory notes are necessary. First and foremost, when discussing orality with respect to Plato's Socratic portraiture, one must always recall a charter paradox in such an endeavor, namely that, contrary to *our* perception of philosophy as the mental work *par excellence*, in a silent and lonely

1 I have kept my text as close as possible to its original style – in line with the title of the present volume – and length. The Conference "From Homer to Hatzi-Yavrouda" was held at the main building of the Danish Institute in Athens (14, Chaerephontos street), close to the South Slope of the Acropolis.

dialogue with texts and arguments, until Plato's time philosophy was principally conducted in face-to-face interaction, in line with the typical educational method and relationship between teacher and pupil, and its teachings were transmitted mainly orally.[2] This has led many scholars to argue that Plato's dialogues, especially his "early ones", like the *Apology*, addressed a public largely accustomed to orality, not yet to literacy, and thus they seem to have been intended in "writing out loud" (as Roland Barthes termed it) for an audience and a readership shaped by oral culture.[3]

After all, the fundamental deficiency and limitations of the written word in the practice of philosophy and the acquisition of knowledge are famously stated in the *Phaedrus* by Socrates – who notably wrote nothing (at least until his imprisonment).[4] The written word seems to him to be static, socially inactive, it fails to create a bond between the souls of author and reader. He argues that this is so because reading lacks the precious social and human context that is involved in live philosophical conversation: there is no communication between friends in reading, but rather a "dead" process that threatens the very skills that are essential in intellectual labor. That is, readers become idle and their memorizing weakens. Besides, the fact that when reading the author is not present to answer those questions a reader may need to ask, leaves no guarantee of understanding and attaining true knowledge.[5]

In addition, scholarship has long pointed out Plato's standing at a period of transition, at an intermediate standpoint between orality and literacy. In his groundbreaking work, Eric Havelock thoroughly argued that Socrates's way of philosophizing in the dialogues must be inscribed in the old, traditional "oral method of instruction, by way of public recitation or private dialogue". However, Plato saw that the need of dialectic for "highly abstract and conceptual thought, for disciplined and coherent argumentation", for self-reflection and personalized consciousness, for judgments based on cause and effect, could be better served by written texts, a task that he undertook for his *philosophia*, at a time that coincided with the "passing of Greek society from a condition of oral to one of literate communication", and in a process that had its peak from the late 5th to the early 4th century, the dramatic dates of many of the dialogues. From then on, literacy steadily proliferated, until it prevailed in the practice of philosophy.[6]

My approach is in consonance with Havelock's historical reading, and it traces a certain aspect of it in some passages of the dialogues that attest to the mindset of an oral culture. More particularly, late 5th and early 4th century Athenian culture remained predominantly embedded in orality, and this affected Plato as regards his intended audience or readership. By this I mean both that his dialogues were intended for collective recitation and for conversation, rath-

2 Cambron-Goulet 2012, 208-9.

3 Cole 1991, 121-32, esp. 122.

4 See *Phd.* 60d–61b.

5 See *Phdr.* 274b–9b. Cf. *Ep.* 7.341b–2a. See also Cambron-Goulet 2012, 207-11; Heath 2005, 206-11; Ong 2002, 23-25, 78-79, 164-65; Thomas 1992, 3-4. A particular interpretative angle of research on the subject has been put forward by the Tübingen School regarding Plato's unwritten doctrines, his *ἄγραφα δόγματα*, which he reportedly expounded orally in the Academy. See, for example, Capra 2015, 11-13. This particular approach, however, goes beyond the questions set here and is not included in my discussion. On orality and the practice of philosophy in the Academy see Capra 2015, 9-12, 15, 177-80. The shared experience of *sumphilosophein* in the study and practice of *philosophia* in the Academy, its openness to the Athenian public, as well as the "poetic" and "musical" aspects of in the composition and the articulation of philosophical *logos*, all these suggest an oral interpersonal performative context. On these aspects see Capra 2015, 15, 45, 97-101, 173.

6 Havelock 1963, esp. 276-305; 1982, 3-38; 1986, 24-29, 79-126. Cf. Lentz 1989, 11-26, 91-108, 175-84; Ong 2002, 23-28, 78-80. For a critique and a constructive refinement of Havelock's thesis see Capra 2015, 15, 181-82 (esp. n. 21) and Nails 1995, 139-91.

er than for exclusively silent, solitary reading and contemplation, as in our reception of philosophical texts, *and* that Plato addressed a still largely oral community of readers and disciples. Hence this whole set of narrative details and focuses that are spread in the dialogues, peripheral to their philosophical core, such as Socrates's or his interlocutors' emotional reactions, exchanges of glances, side looks and so on, which are not simply dramatic decorations, evidence of Plato's authorial skills, as they are usually considered in scholarship. I read them as that minimal, yet very telling information that Plato filled in to help his audience (and readership) figure out and reconstruct the psychodynamics involved in the practice of philosophy, as well as in human interaction in general, articulated in the oral community of Athens at that time. Namely, the very same details that every Athenian would have paid attention to in his daily interaction with his fellow-citizens, would have drawn from them signification and evaluation on the philosophers and their *logos* and, accordingly, would have expected to find reported in a text. And just like the tragic stage and *logos* of the same period that were rather "empty" in their setting, stripped of many props or of detailed descriptions of objects, yet rich in details about the "human-interaction scenery", such as looks, gestures and so on, so too Plato's philosophical stage and *logos* is rather poor in its "physical" scenery and setting, yet with many details on the interaction of its characters, in our view precisely because it stemmed from and addressed the largely oral culture of the Athenian *polis* and the public performance of discourse in front of an audience accustomed, skilled, and in readiness to focus and conjecture on such details.

Furthermore, the practice of philosophy, from the Presocratics onwards (according to later anecdotal biographic material at least), already involved a high degree of exposure and performativity (which was actually the case for all masters of *logos* articulated in front of a public, philosophers, poets, orators and so on), as in the ability to expose one's discourse to the eyes and ears of the many. In addition, public discourse in Athens and daily life in general, were markedly shaped by certain traits of shame ethics that are characteristic of oral cultures and of the Greek *poleis*, like concern for honor and status, and for one's public face in an agonistic approach to social intercourse, where reciprocity regulated relations and hierarchies. This established a social, political, and cultural framework for philosophy as a practice enacted and realized under those psychodynamics that characterize public discourse in oral cultures: it is agonistic, a lived experience embedded in human interaction, that is, it is empathetic and participatory, situational, and dynamic.[7]

These characteristics and dynamics of social interaction in an oral culture provide the background for my reading of Plato's aforementioned narrative digressions, focusing on the *Apology* and the *Phaedo*, his two works that – perhaps due to their highly dramatic context (Socrates's sentencing to death and his last day) – are the richest in such non-verbal material. In other words, I will read such passages with respect to the emotional and sociopolitical parameters of philosophy as a lived, non-mediated experience in the oral culture of classical Athens. These exceptionally detailed references to emotional reactions, looks, and so on between Socrates and his interlocutors may as well indicate the polemics that accompanied and perhaps also affected the practice of philosophy and of public discourse in general in the *polis*. From such a perspective, this reading may enhance our understanding of both the natal chronotope of philosophy and of our academic ancestry as embedded in human interaction, exposed to the eyes, the ears, and the perceptions of the many. And it may further shed light on attitudes and restraints involved in practising philosophy that is so different from our own, right in the beginning of what is generally conceived as the starting point for the long process that led to our

7 Heath 2005, 267-9; Ong 2002, 42-6, 49-57.

disciplines for discourse and to our well established, secluded academic territories for intellectual work (accordingly, it may raise questions, too, on the state of our modern academic *logos* and its dialectics with and exposure to demotic assessment).

To begin with the *Apology*, from its very proem it marks out the provocativeness of Socrates's public presence and *logos* by means of vivid visual and acoustic suggestions. For example, the word *θόρυβος* and its cognates, that suggest noisy reactions by the crowd, judges, and bystanders alike, or even their uproar, feature seven times in Socrates's first and main defense speech, a frequency that is unparalleled in our corpus of Classical orators.[8] Such emphasis was possibly intended by Plato to stress, via highly dramatic and dynamic images, the dire conditions for practicing philosophy in the *polis*, namely the consistent irritation, even the indignation that the *philosophos* and his *logos* and practices evoked and the consequent underlying threat of interruption and the impediments that would possibly face.[9] As Socrates declares, his philosophy is performed at the very center of the *polis*; he converses in the *agora*, in front of many (*ἐὰν διὰ τῶν αὐτῶν λόγων ἀκούητέ μου ἀπολογουμένου δι' ὧνπερ εἴωθα λέγειν καὶ ἐν ἀγορᾷ ἐπὶ τῶν τραπεζῶν, ἵνα ὑμῶν πολλοὶ ἀκηκόασι*).[10] That is, he exposes himself at the epicenter of Athenian public eye and discourse, thus inevitably evoking the complex interpersonal and emotional framework for public discourse, so characteristic of oral cultures as described by Walter Ong.[11] Thereupon, these conditions render philosophical discourse and conversation "open" to parameters that are external to reasoning and argumentation as practiced in the cloistered world of philosophical communities. As a matter of fact, in the dialogues, the many tend to be immune to reason and argumentation – as their verdict in the *Apology* shall verify – and hence they seem to be "naturally" opposed to the *philosophos*; and perhaps this also mirrors Plato's own predisposition to crowds, to *the many*, and accordingly to democracy itself.

Socrates's main defense speech is filled with similar glimpses of his disturbing public presence, to the unease that his *elenchos*, his inquiry caused, and to his interlocutors' discomfort, all of which resulted to his ill-famed reputation, his bad name all over Athens. Indeed, Socrates's interlocutors are often embarrassed or even ridiculed by him in the dialogues. They may be led to self-diminishing silence, magnified in its shaming aftermath when witnessed by many, which is in particular what happens to one of Socrates's accusers, Meletos, during his cross-examination by Socrates in the *Apology*, in a moment of triumph for the philosopher, his disciples, and us, Plato's readers, but probably in real life, proof for most of his judges (ordinary Athenian citizens) of the threat that he constituted for the public face – of major importance in oral cultures – of anyone frequenting the *asty*.[12] Or they may be left in *aporia*, "loss for words and helplessness", the most characteristic state that one experiences when arguing with Socrates and gets exposed to publics, whether of fellow interlocutors or of bystanders. The experience that they all share (i.e. those who fail to pursue the philosophical way of thinking *and* living) is that they find all their certainties, all their beliefs, which in many cases form the very basis of Athens's

8 *Ap.* 17d1, 20e4, 21a5, 27b1, b5, 30c2-3. Cf. Xen. *Ap.* 14.2, 15.2. Such density is comparable only to the use of θόρυβος and θορυβεῖν in Demosthenes (seven in the *Exordia*, five in *De corona* and *De Chersoneso*). See Heath 2005, 304.

9 The philosopher should never be driven away by the uproar of the many (*ἐκπληττόμενον ὑπὸ θορύβου τῶν πολλῶν*), we read in the *Laws* 659a5.

10 *Ap.* 17c7-9 (cf. 19d3).

11 Ong 2002, 31-76.

12 In his main speech, Socrates presents his practice of *philosophia* as a lifelong, omnipresent, persisting, and castigating nuisance to everyone in the *polis*, especially to those at the heart of political life; see most characteristically *Ap.* 29e3-30a4 (cf. 23c, 33b–e). See Heath 2005, 273; Rossetti 2000, 263-65.

system of values, shattered by him. Discontent from conversations with Socrates has been experienced for a long time in Athens, for many years now since he launched his elenctic mission from god (Apollo), right after Chaerephon is said to have received the celebrated Delphic oracle on Socrates' wisdom, starting with exposing the ignorance those at the very top of the ladder of public acclaim.[13]

His public notoriety is substantiated by the fact that, by 423 BC, well into his forties – at the acme of an ancient man's life – and probably well into his meddlesome philosophical "career" in the *polis*, Socrates was already at the focal point of Old Comedy's attention. At the City Dionysia of that year he starred all over the comic stage, both in the air and on the ground, in Aristophanes's *Clouds*, but quite possibly he also featured in Ameipsias's *Konnos*.[14] Such coincidence on the comic stage, all the more so under the scrutiny of Old Comedy, which programmatically exposed and censured all those who stood out in the "panopticon" of the public eye (especially sensitive in the *asty*, Socrates's favourite daily destination), most likely reflects and testifies to Socrates as the focus of public attention. As the *Apology* attests, he could not be perceived just as some local eccentricity; his unique practice of the *elenchos*, that breached and trespassed all boundaries of daily life, had made things get personal, especially so against men "with good reputation" (*οἱ μάλιστα εὐδοκιμοῦντες*, *Ap.* 22a3-4), the city's best.[15]

In response, many Athenians felt irritated, provoked, even threatened by him. They saw their beliefs, their whole substance and reality – social, political, moral – as being under the pursuit of the *elenchos*, for Socrates's unsettling questions could land on anyone, anywhere, anytime, in face-to-face cross-examination. The dialogues abound in snapshots, vivid images, testimonies, and manifestations of Socrates's power in shaming, public defamation, argumentative castigation, and scornful laughter. Subsequently, Athenians got enraged at him, even hated him, or felt envy and resentment. Usually such scenes are joined by expressions of strong, negative emotions, sometimes through their bodily, almost impressionistic manifestations, such as Thrasymachos's blushing in the *Republic*.[16] Loss of face, in public – even worse, in the *asty*, that everyone attended in the heart of the city, and not of *any* city but of democratic Athens, where rumors traveled fast and reputations, especially of those "best" ones, were contested on a daily basis in the public *fora* – *that* was a grave matter and called for reaction. Being considered such a menace in the core of public acclamation, and self-proclaiming as an annoying stinging gadfly, Socrates's trial may not have come as a surprise, nor perhaps his conviction.

In a "foresight" that reads like an ironic cross-reference to the *Apology*, Socrates acknowledges in the *Gorgias* that he himself and the philosopher in general would be totally at a loss in a court, like a doctor being accused by a confectioner and tried before a jury of children.[17] Yet what sets the *philos-*

13 On Socrates' ill fame gained by his long-lasting philosophical way of life, see 18b–d, 22e–23a, 23e, 28a–b. On the importance of one's public reputation in the *polis*, see Ober 1991, 148-51. On the (still uncertain) dating of the oracle, see Guthrie 1971, 85-86.

14 See Carey 2000, 419-23; Zafiropoulos 2015, 63-66, 209-10.

15 Interestingly enough, perhaps in comic reversal of the sociopolitical dimension of Socrates's dialectics, in the *Clouds* it is the Athenian common man who gets enraged by him, not the elites as Socrates claims in the *Apology*.

16 Inimical reactions and negative emotions are notably stressed by Socrates in the *Apology*: 21d–e,22e–3a, 23c–d, 28a–b, 29c–30a, 31a. Cf. *Chrm.* 169c; *La.* 196a–b; *Lys.* 210e; *Prt.* 316c–e, 333e; *Resp.* 336b–7a, 350c–d, 487b–c; *Symp.* 216b–c. See also Bowery 2007, 94-96; Halliwell 2008, 286-93, 298-302; Heath 2005, 271-77, 280-88, 295-300; Miller 2008, 263-66, 287-88; Rossetti 2000; Saxonhouse 2006, 3-6, 74-75.

17 *κρινοῦμαι γὰρ ὡς ἐν παιδίοις ἰατρὸς ἂν κρίνοιτο κατηγο ροῦντος ὀψοποιοῦ*, *Grg.* 521e3-4.

ophos apart from the shame-ethics agenda that his fellow citizens, and an oral community in general, adhere to is that for him such *aporia*, be it the result of defeat in argumentation or even of being laughed at – that is, such a public loss of face as would constitute a major setback in any oral community, if not a traumatic withdrawal from the public sphere – is no true obstacle for the philosopher. It would never result in shame, silence, or resignation, which were indeed the case for many of his own interlocutors. Instead, he sees them as a call for a fresh start in his lifelong search for true knowledge – for the only truly shameful thing for a philosopher would be to cease inquiring.[18]

Apparently, the trademark of Socrates's annoying public persona in the dialogues is his εἰρωνεία, a term that suggests a figure of speech in which what is to be understood is the opposite of what is said, following Quintilian's definition.[19] It upsets the interlocutors, most notably when Socrates disavows any knowledge at all or any expertise, usually uttering his notorious *οὐκ οἶδα*. Irony is seen as a form of trickery in argumentation, a kind of "sly and intentionally deceptive speech or conduct", which seems to have been the popular view of the term in Aristophanes, our first evidence of it in Greek literature.[20] And despite Socrates's repeated denial of any such intentions on his part,[21] if we think of irony in terms of an oral culture, then the protests of his interlocutors against his conversational ethos may gain our sympathy. This is especially so if we take into account that irony, Socrates's stamp upon others, is basically a figure of *speech*, that is, it gains in strength and effectiveness when addressed orally to someone, in real-life conditions, and perhaps witnessed by others, not in a written text; and it is often accompanied by a series of verbal and non-verbal forms of communication, quite prevalent in oral communities and perhaps especially so in the highly competitive public discourse of 5th century Athens (and still so nowadays, in our modern ironic utterances). Socrates could well have used such means to intensify, subvert, or even leave uncertain the sincerity of such an assertion, thus perhaps further irritating his interlocutors. You, reader, could try your own, many and different versions (in front of a mirror or, preferably, an interlocutor) of *οὐκ οἶδα* sounding ironic, using such means as gestures, intonation, facial expressions, like a sideways look to your interlocutor and a knowing half-smile (more or less playful, leaving them increasingly perplexed or irritated).

To amplify my reading of the Platonic portraiture of the public exposure of the proto-philosopher and of his discourse, I will turn to certain details in Plato's narrative that I think may help us further visualize this subtext of orality and interpersonal grounding of conversation in the dialogues. Notably, the dialogues underscore the offense that Socrates generated even by his very presence, let alone in face-to-face interaction and conversation. Alongside

18 On Socrates silencing his interlocutors and leading them to *aporia*, see Heath 2005, 275-80, 299-300. In particular, on the discomfort caused by *aporia* and its experience by Socrates's interlocutors, ibid., 278-80; Miller 2008, 283-84; Saxonhouse 2006, 37, 112-15. See, among many such passages from the dialogues, *Chrm.* 169c3-d1; *La.* 196a7-b2; *Prt.* 333e2-5; *Resp.* 478b1-c4, as well as the "numbing" experience of *aporia* as the result from Socrates's *elenchos* in the *Meno* 80a–b.

19 Quint. *Inst.* 9.22.44. See Vlastos 1991, 21.

20 Aristophanes *Av.* 1211; *Nub.* 449; *Vesp.* 174. See Edmunds 2004, 193; Vlastos 1991, 21-25.

21 See, for example, *Ap.* 38a1. Cf. *Resp.* 337a4-5 (with Thrasymachos's sardonic castigation of Socrates's typical, customary irony, *ἥ εἰωθυῖα εἰρωνεία Σωκράτους*) and *Symp.* 216e4-5 (Alcibiades accuses Socrates of spending his whole life practicing irony and mocking others – *εἰρωνευόμενος δὲ καὶ παίζων πάντα τὸν βίον πρὸς τοὺς ἀνθρώπους διατελεῖ*).

his reported ugliness, looking almost like Silenos,[22] his whole physique and posture, including his bulging eyes that stared at his interlocutors (in *Theaetetus* 209c1 he is *ἐξόφθαλμος*, "with prominent eyes", in addition to Xenophon's note that Socrates's eyes were situated on his head like those of a crab, *Symp.* 5.5.5-7, cf. Pl. *Tht.* 143e9) – and perhaps, as I already speculated, his intonation too, thus rendering him an esthetically strange amalgam of figure, look, and timbre (not to mention his odor, given that Socrates was probably customarily *ἄλουτος*, "unwashed", as inferred from *Symp.* 174a2-3) – all this may well have supported protests against his public appearance and sustained the biased atmosphere around him.

Actually, our first testimonies to Socrates's obnoxious looks and public attitude come from Old Comedy, not from Plato. Such provenance attests to how widespread his notoriety must have been in Athens, given the popularity of the genre that addressed and lectured great numbers of citizens. He wandered around the streets, sang the Chorus of Clouds in Aristophanes's play, stalking like a *βρένθος*, a water-bird, perhaps a pelican or a stork, and casting his eyes from side to side (protruding and crab-like?).[23] The description is repeated in Plato's *Symposium* in an almost verbatim allusion to the *Clouds*, which allows us to suggest the roots of it in Socrates's real-life poses, perhaps with a touch of comic exaggeration.[24] Namely, there Alcibiades recalls Socrates's fearless stance and peculiar gait on the Delion battlefield, where he stepped along in his water-bird way, strutting and casting his eyes sideways, in a posture that his fellow citizens and fellow hoplites may well have perceived as a sign of haughtiness and arrogance.[25] Alcibiades then points out that, in response, Socrates's fellow hoplites looked askance or angrily at him, *ὑπέβλεπον*, in a strongly illustrative description of an exchange of looks that suggests Socrates's whole posture being interpreted as a clear statement that he looked down upon others.[26] Interestingly enough and perhaps not accidentally, the same verb appears at the end of the *Phaedo*, as Socrates is about to drink the hemlock, once again in connection with his strange attitude and glaring, apt to be misjudged by the many, in one of the most memorable passages regarding the Socratic paradigm. He looked up at the administrator of the poison "from under his brows", like a bull, *ταυρηδὸν ὑποβλέψας*, a customary look of his, notes Plato (*ὥσπερ εἰώθει* – a rather alarming, if not scary, gaze given his bulging eyes).[27] Yet immediately it turns out that it was all just irony from him, as usual, and Plato momentarily counterbalances the dramatic tension of the scene with a semi-playful allusion to his audience's acquaintance with his protagonist's

22 As, for example, in his marble bust in Louvre (MA 59), a 1st century AD Roman copy, possibly of Lysippos's original (ca. 318-17 BC). Zanker 1995, 32-39, 57-62 provides a thorough presentation and a thought-provoking analysis of the two types of Socratic portraiture, his offensive, marginalized depiction as Silenos (5th century onwards), yet still indicative of wisdom, and his reformed portrait as a good Athenian citizen from Lysippos onwards.

23 Ar. *Nub.* 362-63: *ὅτι βρενθύει τ' ἐν ταῖσιν ὁδοῖς καὶ τὼ φθαλμὼ παραβάλλεις κἀνυπόδητος κακὰ πόλλ' ἀνέχει κἀφ' ἡμῖν σεμνοπροσωπεῖς.* Socrates's looks and portraiture: Zafiropoulos 2015, 184-96; Zanker 1995, 32-39, 57-62. See also Stavru 2018, 234.

24 Actually, the allusion of the *Symposium* passage to the *Clouds* description is clearly inferred by Alcibiades citing it to Aristophanes as "those words of yours", *Symp.* 221b3-4: *ἔπειτα ἔμοιγ' ἐδόκει, ὦ Ἀριστόφανες, τὸ σὸν δ ὴ τοῦτο, καὶ ἐκεῖ διαπορεύεσθαι ὥσπερ καὶ ἐνθάδε, βρε νθυόμενος καὶ τὼφθαλμὼ παραβάλλων.* See also *Symp.* 220b–c.

25 Edmunds 2004, 194-96. On Socrates's eyes and gaze: Cairns 2005, 126-37; Stavru 2018, 231-35; Zafiropoulos 2015, 188-92.

26 *Symp.* 221b7-c1: *οἱ δὲ στρατιῶται ὑπέβλεπον αὐτὸν ὡ ς καταφρονοῦντα σφῶν.* Halliwell 2008, 282. See also Cairns 2005, 136 on the negative connotations of compounds in *ὑπο-* with a verb of seeing.

27 Pl. *Phd.* 117b5-6 – following Stavru's translation (2018, 233). On the envisaged look, see Halliwell 2008, 282 n. 40; Zafiropoulos 2015, 191-92.

non-verbal eccentricities: Socrates is not at all angry with the man; he just laughs at the whole thing and then cheerfully grasps the cup.[28]

The *Phaedo* contains a "unique concentration" of depictions of Socrates's gazes, which are not just descriptions of his emotional state, however, as Alessandro Stavru interpreted them. In my reading, these passages emerge at crucial stages of Plato's narrative in order to color the moral portrait of the master with touches from his shared image and memory among the Athenians, and probably one that had been shaped by daily interaction with him under the criteria of an oral culture, in which people's public facial and bodily expressions and postures marked them in collective memory.[29] That is, these specifics in Plato's contextualization of the *Phaedo* narrative seek to underline Socrates's exemplary and didactic attitude on the most challenging and crucial day of his life, but they also seek to render it more vivid and more verisimilar on the basis of the stereotyped, yet reality-based image of Socrates, which included his peculiar looks, way of staring, and such idiosyncratic esthetic and behavioral traits that oral cultures and traditional societies apply. Such narrative impressions in Plato's text may enrich our reading, adding a visual and emotional context to philosophical interaction or even to what the jury saw, misunderstood, and condemned in Socrates's speech and attitude at his trial.

To cite a few more such visual illustrations, when his disciples got worried by the argument that the wise should be troubled at the inevitability of death, he gazed attentively *at* them, ἐπι-*βλέψας* (63a2), as a teacher's glance that calls for attention (and maybe for order as well) before the beginning of a lecture; later, when their belief in the afterlife of the soul was threatened by Simmias's objection that the soul simply perishes alongside with the body, Socrates stared at them with eyes wide open, δια-*βλέψας* (86d5), as if to manifest both his surprise at the statement and the seriousness of the moment, but once again he hurried to undermine the impressions from his gaze, with a *μειδίαμα*, a reassuring smile that Simmias's objection is an easy one to answer.

To such impressions in the dialogues, related to Socrates's physical and behavioral features, that seem to draw from and commemorate Athenians' shared empirical recollection of Socrates, a set of animal metaphors could also be added, metaphors that are applied in the dialogues to describe the workings and the effects of Socratic inquiry – from the celebrated image of Socrates as gadfly in the *Apology* (30e), to Socrates as stingray in the *Meno* (80a–b), a bee in the *Phaedo* (91c), or a viper in the *Symposium* (217e–18b). What these metaphors have in common is, first, their grounding not in abstraction or conceptual thinking, but in lived, "situational" experience, one grounded in nature, as is characteristic of oral cultures.[30] Second, they share the popular perception of the *philosophos* as a nuisance to the community, and of the *elenchos*, especially when conducted publicly, as a sudden, violent and painful intrusion on one's entity, an unsettling piercing of one's physical and social being, which I think visualized the threat of a severe blow to a citizen's status and public face that Socrates represented, and a life experience that stuck in memory.[31]

To make matters worse, such threat was increased by the fact that Socrates had devotees who followed him in his wanderings in and around the *asty*. These

28 This particular Socratic gaze (customary, as it seems, in Plato) calls to mind another preceding Aristophanic visualization of intellectuals, this time in the *Frogs*, where contrary to the philosopher's laughing attitude toward mundane concerns or in the face of death, as in Plato, the tragedian Aeschylus turns out to be quite touchy and his taurus-like gaze toward Euripides is a (comic) sign that he is ready to attack. Ar. *Ran.* 804: *ἔβλεψε γοῦν ταυρηδὸν ἐγκύψας κάτω*. See Stavru 2018, 233; Zafiropoulos 2015, 192.

29 See Ong 2002, 46-47.

30 *Ibid.*, 49-57.

31 Heath 2005, 308.

were not just any followers, but the city's young men, and not any young men, but the *crème de la crème* of Athens's youth and hopes for the future. Thus, Socrates seems to have threatened the traditional *agoge* of rich Athenians, whose youth not only left their *oikos*'s guidance to attend his ruinous teachings, but also witnessed his humiliation of Athens's best, apparently of members of their own class. They rejoiced, almost maliciously, at such public spectacle, adding insult to humiliation. Then, having misinterpreted the true objectives of Socratic inquiry and dialectic, they tried to imitate it themselves, thus seemingly spreading both threat and damage.[32] Yet, in a sociopolitical version of Platonic mimetic misprints, in the end these young men only fuel the accumulated rage against the supposed instigator of such almost contagious disruption of order, status, and "normality".[33]

My reading suggests that by means of such passages and narrative details Plato sought to stimulate a twofold response from those reading or listening to his work, grounded upon Socrates's recognized and shared, if not stereotyped, image in the basically oral community of Classical Athens which held and recalled one's public stature and figure on the basis of one's attitude, posture, gaze, and so on. First, a response of smiles and pride by disciples and friends at the memory of the master's familiar image, and by implication of his persistence, determination, seriocomic attitude, his quasi paternal-figure to them, etc. Then, their discomfiting realization of the provocativeness and the danger from the erroneous apprehension of his public image by the many. This further highlights the philosophical heroism of Socrates, couched in his statement during his speech that despite what the many think of the philosophical life, as long as he breathes and is able to go on, he will never give up philosophizing, exhorting whomever he comes upon in the streets of Athens and pointing out the truth to him, conversing with him in his accustomed way.[34] It looks as if Plato thus implied that Socrates's conviction was also the result of his decision to differ from the standards of public posture and attitudes, and to practice the philosophical life exposed to the life-threatening and erroneous opinions of the many that set the conditions and the criteria for public discourse and interaction in the oral culture of 5th century Athens. Consequently, Socrates's end justified Plato's decision to resort to the world of philosophical schools and written words, enclosed and sheltered from Athenian sociopolitical life.

To conclude, I propose a reading of Plato's highly illustrative and dramatic portraiture of his philosophical hero, not only as proof of his literary, nearly dramatic artistry, but also with an eye to the still largely oral culture of late 5th and early 4th century Athens and the constraints, misconceptions, and even the dangers that such a culture, its standards and values, posed to the conduct of philosophical discourse. It was against this culture too (and against the democratic *polis*, for example) that Plato sought, from the *Apology* onwards, to secure those sociopolitical conditions that he deemed vital for the secure and unhindered practice of *philosophia* by him and his fellow Socratics and disciples. That is, he deliberately and strategically situated his protagonist and philosophical hero

32 *Ap*. 23c2-8: *πρὸς δὲ τούτοις οἱ νέοι μοι ἐπακολουθοῦν τες – οἷς μάλιστα σχολή ἐστιν, οἱ τῶν πλουσιωτάτων – αὐτόματοι, χαίρουσιν ἀκούοντες ἐξεταζομένων τῶν ἀνθρώπων, καὶ αὐτοὶ πολλάκις ἐμὲ μιμοῦνται, εἶτα ἐπιχειροῦσιν ἄλλους ἐξετάζειν· κἄπειτα οἶμαι εὑρίσκουσι πολλὴν ἀφθονίαν οἰομένων μὲν εἰδέναι τι ἀνθρώπων, εἰδ ότων δὲ ὀλίγα ἢ οὐδέν. ἐντεῦθεν οὖν οἱ ὑπ' αὐτῶν ἐξεταζ όμενοι ἐμοὶ ὀργίζονται, οὐχ αὑτοῖς* [...]

33 Heath 2005, 307. Compare the envy and the inimical feelings towards those foreigners and masters of words, the sophists, who charm the best of a city's youth and turn them into their followers in *Protagoras* 316c5-e5.

34 *Ap*. 29d4-7: *ἕωσπερ ἂν ἐμπνέω καὶ οἷός τε ὦ, οὐ μὴ παύσωμαι φιλοσοφῶν καὶ ὑμῖν παρακελευόμενός τε καὶ ἐνδεικνύμενος ὅτῳ ἂν ἀεὶ ἐντυγχάνω ὑμῶν, λέγων οἷάπερ εἴωθα* [...]. See also Heath 2005, 281.

and protomartyr, Socrates, and his philosophical reasoning against a noisy, passionate, and emotional background of reactions and false opinions by the non-philosophical many.[35] Such collective animosity was driven by the "polemics" of public discourse that characterized the social and political sphere of daily interaction in Classical Athens, from a standpoint that is so characteristic of oral cultures, namely one that was conservative, cemented on the human lifeworld and experience, agonistic, empathetic, and situational, one where merit and status were measured by public presence and performance, subject to the sinister passions and opinions of the many – a *cause célèbre* being Socrates's conviction. Conversely, Plato's *philosophia* saw conceptualization and abstraction as prerequisites, as well as intellectual experimentation, the disengagement of oneself from mundane concerns and from the limitations and the competition of lived experience, objectivity, and freedom from memory work that would leave space for fresh and continuous speculation and reflection.[36] Therefore, from Socrates's defense speech in the *Apology* onwards, Plato attempted a breach with the certainties, values, and rules shared by the many and tried to shift shame and status away from public discourse and collective arbitration; that is, to pull it out of the chronotope of the democratic *polis*, and to turn it instead into a matter of the moral agent's own contemplation, following Socrates's paradigm, in a lifelong search for truth and true knowledge. At the same time, he aimed to give rise to the intellectual and the *vita contemplativa*, and perhaps also to lay the groundwork for the transition of the practice of philosophy to the new age of literacy, following Eric Havelock's approach. Accordingly (and once again adversely, if not subversively to the ethos of the many), the philosopher has no problem with being laughed at and even mocks himself, because for those truly leading the philosophical life, loss of face, defeat, and failure consist in not succeeding to pursue it till the very end; for, as Socrates declares, the unexamined life is not worth living.[37]

It was to this end, I consider, that Plato inserted in his work a microcosm of hostile sounds, glances, gestures, emotions, and stances, in order to stress how *philosophia* and the *philosophos* were misinterpreted by the many, how dialectics was wrongly seen as a "destructive" force and a threat to established norms, practices, and even structures, which in turn rendered the lifelong practice of philosophy a dangerous task. He did so to highlight the need (for Athenians) not to repeat their crime against philosophy (Socrates's trial and conviction to death) and to safeguard a new framework for the systematic and uninterrupted practice of *philosophia*. A framework that would nurture abstraction and conceptual thought instead of reliance on and restriction to human experience; self-reflection and moral agency, instead of the self-exonerating power of the many; a framework that would shelter the philosopher from the crowded, violent, and disturbing life of the *polis* in order for him to pursue the isolated, peaceful, and "objective" process of contemplation. Nevertheless, such a safe haven was also bonded with the obligation of Plato's

35 This open-to-all practice of philosophy is in sharp contrast with the 'shadowy', as in cryptic and politically suspicious, view of philosophy as conducted by Socrates and his disciples in the *Clouds*.

36 See Ong 2002, 41-56.

37 *Ap*. 38a5-6 and Heath 2005, 302. Cf. *Ap*. 28b3-9. Plato's philosopher is not offended by derisive laughter or loss of public face, and even mocks himself: Halliwell 2008, 291-93, 298-99; Heath 2005, 286-88, 290-91; Patterson 1987, 343-45. He is even ready for the reactions of those hearing his arguments as a "wave of laughter" that will drown him in ridicule and contempt, *εἰ καὶ μέλλει γέλωτί τε ἀτεχνῶς ὥσπερ κῦμα ἐκγελῶν καὶ ἀδοξίᾳ κατακλύσειν*: *Resp*. 473c7-8. Moreover, to get entrapped in the misdeeds of reciprocating envy, anger, hatred and so on, would have been incompatible with the principle of not reciprocating injustice, wrong: see *Cri*. 49b10-d9. On the incompatibility of jealousy with Plato's *philosophia* (as in *Resp*. 500b8-c6; *Symp*. 210d3-6; *Ti*. 29e1-2), see Gregory & Levin 1998.

philosophos to return to societies and to the masses with philosophical "prescriptions" and "dietetics" that would "cure" selves and social bodies alike, following the lifelong paradigm of Socrates's loyalty to the wellbeing of his fellow citizens. By picturing his protagonist's fatal exposure to the dangers of public discourse in Athens (and later by his opening of the Academy), Plato paved the way for the new age of literacy, where the sage of the old became the trained intellectual assigned the task of prearranging the lives of the many, thus inaugurating the world and the long history of scholars and scholarship.

Christos A. Zafiropoulos
University of Patras
czaf@upatras.gr

Bibliography

BOWERY, A.-M. 2007
'Know Thyself: Socrates as Storyteller', in *Philosophy in Dialogue: Plato's Many Devices*, G. A. Scott (ed.), Evaston, IL, 82-110.

CAIRNS, D. 2005
'Bullish Looks and Sidelong Glances: Social Interaction and the Eyes in Ancient Greek Culture', in *Body Language in the Greek and Roman Worlds*, D. Cairns (ed.), Swansea, 123-55.

CAMBRON-GOULET, M. 2012
'The Criticism – and the Practice – of Literacy in the Ancient Philosophical Tradition', in *Orality, Literacy and Performance in the Ancient World*, E. Minchin (ed.), Leiden, 201-26.

CAPRA, A. 2015
Plato's Four Muses. The Phaedrus *and the Poetics of Philosophy*, Cambridge, MA & London.

CAREY, C. 2000
'Old Comedy and the Sophists', in *The Rivals of Aristophanes: Studies in Athenian Old Comedy*, F. D. Harvey & J. Wilkins (eds.), Swansea, 419-36.

COLE, T. 1991
The Origins of Rhetoric in Ancient Greece, Baltimore & London.

EDMUNDS, L. 2004
'The Practical Irony of the Historical Socrates', *Phoenix* 58, 193-207.

GREGORY, J. & S. B. LEVIN 1998
'Φιλοσοφία ἄφθονος (Plato, *Symposium* 210d)', *CQ* 48, 404-10.

GUTHRIE, W. K. C. 1971
Socrates, Cambridge.

HALLIWELL, ST. 2008
Greek Laughter, Cambridge.

HAVELOCK, E. A. 1963
Preface to Plato, Cambridge Mass.

HAVELOCK, E. A. 1982
The Literate Revolution in Greece and Its Cultural Consequences, New Haven.

HAVELOCK, E. A. 1986
The Muse Learns to Write. Reflections on Orality and Literacy from Antiquity to the Present, New Haven.

HEATH, J. 2005
The Talking Greeks: Speech, Animals, and the Other in Homer, Aeschylus, and Plato, Cambridge.

LENTZ, T. M. 1989
Orality and Literacy in Hellenic Greece, Carbondale, IL.

MILLER, M. 2008
'The Pleasures of the Comic and of Socratic Inquiry: Aporetic Reflections on *Philebus* 48a–50b', *Arethusa* 41, 263-89.

NAILS, D. 1995
Agora, Academy, and the Conduct of Philosophy, Dordrecht.

OBER, J. 1991
Mass and Elite in Democratic Athens, Princeton.

ONG, W. J. 2002
Orality and Literacy. The Technologizing of the Word, London & New York.

PATTERSON, R. 1987
'Plato on Philosophic Character', *Journal of the History of Philosophy* 25, 325-50.

ROSSETTI, L. 2000
'Le rire comme arme dans les mains de Socrate et de ses élèves', in *Le rire des Grecs. Anthropologie du rire en Grèce ancienne*, M.-L. Desclos (ed.), Grenoble, 253-68.

SAXONHOUSE, A. W. 2006
Free Speech and Democracy in Ancient Athens, Cambridge.

STAVRU, A. 2018
'Socrates' Physiognomy: Plato and Xenophon in Comparison', in *Plato and Xenophon. Comparative Studies*, G. Danzig, D. Johnson, & D. Morrison (eds.), Leiden, 208-51.

THOMAS, R. 1992
Literacy and Orality in Ancient Greece, Cambridge.

VLASTOS, G. 1991
Socrates. Ironist and moral philosopher, Cambridge.

ZAFIROPOULOS, C. A. 2015
Socrates and Aesop. A Comparative Study of the Introduction of Plato's Phaedo, Sankt Augustin.

ZANKER, P. 1995
The Mask of Socrates. The Image of the Intellectual in Antiquity, Berkeley and Los Angeles & Oxford.

Oral Narrations and Roman Imperial History*

Sophia Papaioannou

Abstract

In late November 69 AD, a few days after the death of the emperor Vitellius at Rome, the newly declared emperor Vespasian entered Alexandria. Shortly after his arrival he performed two healing miracles in public, curing a crippled man and a blind man. The miracles are recorded in two well-known and widely read Roman sources, Tacitus and Suetonius, who were contemporaries but wrote independently of each other. These accounts differ in crucial details. It is my intention to study the dynamics of orality, and in particular the influence of Greek sources, especially Greek traditions of wide circulation, both orally and in writing, that determined the formulation and the propagation of this episode, and propose to interpret it as an elaborate case of imperial ideology crafted by the governor of Egypt, Tiberius Julius Alexander. I argue that Tiberius Alexander, one of the most powerful men in the Roman East in the first century AD, a Hellenized Jew with ties to every Roman emperor since Claudius, and a pivotal supporter of Vespasian in 69 AD, interwove the traditions, including several oral stories, about miracle-working accompanying the cults of Serapis and Asklepios. The two divinities were widely acknowledged as healers and performers of miracles in the Roman Empire, especially in the Eastern part. Vespasian's miracle-worker profile was meant to cast the new emperor in comparable light and fortify his candidacy to the imperial throne at the same time as Vitellius was about to be ousted. Upon becoming emperor, Vespasian sought to advertise his reign as a restitution of the Augustan era. This parallelism to Augustus was revisited and amplified two decades later, by Domitian. It is likely that during the Domitianic era, Vespasian's miracle-working interacted with the popular oral tradition that developed around Augustus: at Rome, Augustus was hailed as a healer of the ailing Roman commonwealth, being the son of Apollo and the brother of Asklepios (Lat. Aesculapius). Finally, the similarity of Vespasian's narrative of miracle-working to the miracles of Jesus Christ may also suggest that Tiberius Alexander might have drawn inspiration from the Gospel of St. Luke, a narrative primarily intended to be disseminated orally and forge a new line of tradition among the Hellenophone population of Egypt's Hellenized Jews.

I. Introduction: Oral Tradition and Historiography

"I very much wish those venerable odes were still extant, which, Cato informs us in his *Origins*, used to be sung by every guest in his turn at the homely feasts of

* Earlier versions of this paper have been delivered to the Classics faculties of the College of William and Mary, and Union College, and have benefited from the discussions following. I would also like to thank the anonymous referees for several valuable comments and suggestions.

our ancestors, many ages before, to commemorate the feats of their heroes." (Cicero, *Brutus* 75)[1]

With the above quotation Cicero refers to the importance of oral tradition for the transmission of ancient Roman history.[2] Yet, in Cato's context, oral stories, usually in verse, also served entertaining purposes, as has typically been the case for oral and folk narration across time. Quite characteristically, the scholiast of Aristophanes's *Ploutos* 177 identifies the earliest professional storyteller/entertainer beyond the Homeric tradition of the epic bards, an Athenian named Philepsios. He was poor and used his talent for devising all sorts of fun stories (*ἱστορίας καὶ μύθους καὶ παίγνια*, "stories and myths and games"), which, like the compositions of the epic bards, "captivated" (*ἔθελγε*) his audiences and "made a living out of it" (*ἐτρέφετο*). It is further recorded that "he was attacked" (*διαβάλλεται*) as "a tall-tale teller and a babbler" (*τερατώδης καὶ λάλος*).[3]

In the Classical world including the early centuries of the Roman imperial era – not by coincidence the period that saw the rise of the genre of the Ancient Novel – the practice of revisiting stories from oral tradition was a typical source of entertainment.[4] Additionally, storytelling in antiquity served the desire to popularize a certain story and eventually to record it in writing (though not necessarily to eliminate variants); and often it became a vehicle for communicating ideas – a point of reference for instructive or interpretative purposes or, more pragmatically, a cornerstone for the formation of identity or for the advancement of a political agenda.[5]

With the arrival of writing and the invention of historiography as a literary genre, oral tradition unmistakably contributed both to the formation of historical consciousness and to the articulation of historical prose, operating without interruption

1 *Atque utinam exstarent illa carmina, quae multis saeclis ante suam aetatem in epulis esse cantitata a singulis convivis de clarorum virorum laudibus in Originibus scriptum reliquit.* Cato (my translation).

2 Other references include *Tusc. Disp.* 1.3; while *De Or.* 3.197 talks about the early songs and the importance of rhythm and music for memorizing and propagating oral compositions; see Goldberg 2005, 103.

3 Scobie 1979, 236; Dübner 1877 (1969), 333, 550; Koster 1960, 56. The motif of connecting famine and marginalization ("abjection") with poetic creativity is firmly present in Greek literature, especially iambic poetry, see Rosen 2007, 65 nn. 55, 56 and 244-45; *id.* 1987, on hunger inspiring Hipponax's poetic genius; Rosen 1987, esp. 421, builds on the connection between laughter and fertility/return-to-life in the encounter between Demeter and the maid Iambe as related in the *Homeric Hymn to Demeter* 206-11; Herodotos, too, notes of the Lydians' invention of games as a resource against their famine (Hdt. 1.94).

4 Storytelling in general in the Roman world, of various themes and not necessarily confined to Roman topics, was a popular mode of entertainment that cut across classes and levels of literacy; the categories of stories manifest considerable variety, and include the more serious traditional credence narratives (myths, hero-legends, aretalogies, etc.), and the popular traditional fiction tales (fables, animal stories, wonders, milesian tales and outright "tall" tales); the terms used in the sources to refer to the storytellers mainly include *fabulator* ("teller of stories") and *aretalogos* (lit. "teller of wonder stories of divine miracles (*aretai*)"). There is ample evidence in the ancient literary sources that describes the phenomenon in the Roman empire from Augustus onwards: the storytellers were performers, frequently dramatizing their stories, and were part of a travelling company of entertainers that included musicians, pantomime dancers and actors; Suetonius mentions storytellers as frequent performers at Augustus's dinner-table, along with actors and street-corner performers from the Circus (Suet. *Aug.* 74); on storytelling in the early Roman empire see Hansen 2017, 1-46; 1988, 1121-30; and Scobie 1979.

5 Kateb 2002 is an important treatment of the interaction of politics and storytelling, articulated as a discussion on Hannah Arendt's book *The Origins of Totalitarianism*. Havelock (1963; 1978) and Svenbro (1976), among others, have argued on the function of the poet in a predominantly oral culture as a medium for the transmission of the collective "wisdom" of the society, as well as ideological factors, embodied in the pleasurable and memorable form of the narrative and other verse forms.

alongside writing, from Herodotos onwards. When Herodotos visited Egypt in the mid-5th century BC, he collected oral stories from the priests, who were also the custodians of the imperial archives (that is, the written version of Egyptian history). In turn, Herodotos, by integrating foreign oral traditions into his history, himself became a practitioner of oral tradition and oral history. The recording of these traditions in writing greatly influenced their transmission, as it hindered uncritical and prompt manipulation of their content, at least in the Greek world. Herodotos's transcript thereof henceforth became the standard reading available of these stories, at the same time as they were becoming accessible to an ever larger number of readers across centuries and cultures. The form and content of these oral stories cannot be challenged due to permanent loss of earlier variants; their contextualization, however, is subject to ongoing negotiation – and this transfers the fluidity of orality from the narrative of the story to its interpretation. Following Herodotos, ancient authors concerned with discovering and recording the past frequently recount or allude to narratives orally developed and received, which subsequently may be framed by the narrator's comments that direct how the audience will receive them in turn; or they may not be followed by comments, and in that case the audience is confronted with the challenge, as well as the responsibility, of contextualizing them.[6] This may be observed in the beginnings of Roman historiography, when the oral traditions of the leading aristocratic families at the time influenced the construction of the Roman past around certain heroes or heroic accounts.[7]

Oral traditions may have a long lineage behind them but individual oral stories may also be inventions of those who narrate them but do not confess to doing so. The oral stories in this second category are firmly contextualized: in many ways they depend on the historical moment that triggered their formulation – they intend to illuminate it, but in doing so they become inextricably and permanently tied to it. These stories are particularly complex. As a result, in order to increase their credibility and power of persuasion, they may feature historical characters or realistic geographical information (the rich tradition of tales that developed around Alexander the Great is an outstanding example), thus combining fiction and history in inventive ways.[8] The type of oral tradition I presently set out to discuss focuses precisely on a story that belongs to this last category. This story developed about miraculous events, the historicity of which is disputed. The miracles, however, happened to historical characters, in a specific place and time. The tradition of these events has survived to this

6 On the integration of oral tradition for the construction of history in Herodotos, the bibliography is ample and growing; reference pieces include Murray 1987 (repr. in Luraghi 2001); and most studies in Luraghi 2001, esp. those by Luraghi himself (= Luraghi 2001a) and Thomas (= Thomas 2001); Fehling 1971; bibliography on the interaction of oral tradition and historical memory in culture beyond Herodotos include Shrimpton 1997; Vansina 1985; Henige 1982. On the transition from oral stories to historiographical narrative in the Roman Republican tradition, see the bibliography cited in n. 7 below.

7 On the process of transition from oral tradition to literacy in the Roman Republican era, see von Ungern-Sternberg 2011 and 1988; Wiseman 1989, 129-37 (esp. 133-37, where Wiseman laments the neglect among classicists of the study of orality in Roman culture and ideology); Timpe 1988. The study of non-literary culture in Roman Republican antiquity is a complex issue, and this complexity is reflected also on the contrasting perspectives of contemporary scholarly approaches: see for instance Horsfall 2003 (an important study in that it focuses on the largely oral/non-literary popular Roman culture, which was ignored by the aristocratic elite that controlled literacy); Purcell 2003; and Wiseman 2004, esp. chapters 2-7.

8 Although not an oral tradition, the treatment of Cato the Younger's suicide by subsequent generations each applying a different interpretation and appropriating it culturally and ideologically, but also adding details and narrative material, is a comparable case; Rauh 2018 is very good on this.

day in a number of written sources, but each source records a different version of the story as regards important details.[9] My intention is not so much to ascertain the historicity of the event, by proving or disproving those details that seem the least believable, but to explore the motives and the sources of inspiration behind the development of a set of the miraculous details that stem from oral tradition. I will additionally illustrate the political outcome following the rendering of this story in writing. In Roman antiquity, especially from Augustus onwards, political propaganda describes not only the official and organized policy in the employment of language and images produced and imposed by the imperial authority, but also, as Zanker, Ando, and others have shown, includes the employment of word (oral tradition and stories, and literature) and vision (art and architecture) in reciprocal and mutual discourse with people of the empire – a discourse created by imperial mandate as well as by kin, friends, and allies of the emperor, both in Rome and in the provinces.[10]

Narrative variants of a story are the norm in an orally communicated version thereof, which is often reflected in the transmission of a story in writing as well. When this incongruity in the details is present in written accounts of the same story, composed by different but contemporary authors who were not aware of each other's treatments – as is the case with Tacitus and Suetonius, the main sources of the events treated in the present study – the discrepancy suggests that each author either embraced a different version of the story or elaborated independently on a common version of the story. These versions, of unknown origin, may have been circulating orally or in writing. The accounts as recorded in the works of Tacitus and Suetonius, despite the several differences in their narratives, visibly follow a common tradition and agree on core themes, because they serve the same mission: to help their audience recall the past in context and make certain associations. The story in question concerns a miraculous cure attributed to the Roman emperor Vespasian; this miracle and the events surrounding it draw on a set of diverse Greek traditions (or rather, a set of traditions very popular in the Greek world)[11] of great influence on Roman culture.

II. Vespasian, the Miracle-Worker

In the second half of the year 69 AD, a series of supernatural events occurred in Egypt, according to the literary sources, revolving around the Roman general Vespasian who at the time was the leader of the Roman legions in Judea. On July 1st, while Vitellius was the emperor at Rome, Vespasian was declared emperor by the governor of Egypt, Tiberius Alexander. Vespasian heard about his proclamation while he was still in Judea and accepted the title a few days later. In the late summer of that year, he crossed over from Judea to Egypt, without entering Alexandria. He did visit the city, however, a few months later, at the end of November,[12] and upon his arrival, several wondrous things reportedly happened to him. The account is recorded in Suetonius, a valuable source of anecdotal information for the first twelve emperors, and with some notable differ-

9 For a recent comprehensive treatment of the phenomenon of the miraculous and the wondrous in the literary sources in Greco-Roman antiquity, see Gerolemou 2018.

10 Zanker 1988; Ando 2000.

11 In Papaioannou 2018, I have published a different treatment of the same episode, examining miracles jointly with omens in the context of Roman historiography, as means that contribute to the construction of authorial identity and rationalize extraordinary actions.

12 On Vespasian's visit to Egypt and Alexandria, the foundational study is Henrichs 1968; on his visit to Egypt in the late summer of 69 AD, see Turner 1954, 61; his arrival to Alexandria is set either in late November or in January following the death of Vitellius; see Henrichs 1968, 54-55; Chilver & Townend 1985, 62; Levick 1999, 68; Wardle 2012, 192-93 with n. 39.

ences from Tacitus, his contemporary. A third, much briefer account is recorded a century later in Cassius Dio who mainly draws on Tacitus. The three texts in question are listed below:

(Suetonius, *Vesp.* 7.1-3) *Suscepto igitur civili bello ac ducibus copiisque in Italiam praemissis, interim Alexandriam transiit, ut claustra Aegypti optineret. E plebe quidam luminibus orbatus, item alius debili crure sedentem pro tribunali pariter adierunt, orantes opem valitudini demonstratam a Serapide per quietem: restituturum oculos, si inspuisset; confirmaturum crus, si dignaretur calce contingere. Cum vix fides esset ullo modo successuram ideoque ne experiri quidem auderet, extremo hortantibus amicis palam pro contione utrumque temptavit; nec eventus defuit.*[13]

(Tacitus, *Hist.* 4.81) *Per eos mensis quibus Vespasianus Alexandriae statos aestivis flatibus dies et certa maris opperiebatur, multa miracula evenere, quis caelestis favor et quaedam in Vespasianum inclinatio numinum ostenderetur. E plebe Alexandrina quidam oculorum tabe notus genua eius advolvitur, remedium caecitatis exposcens gemitu, monitu Serapidis dei, quem dedita superstitionibus gens ante alios colit; precabaturque principem ut genas et oculorum orbis dignaretur respergere oris excremento. Alius manum aeger eodem deo auctore ut pede ac vestigio Caesaris calcaretur orabat. Vespasianus primo inridere, aspernari; atque illis instantibus modo famam vanitatis metuere, modo obsecratione ipsorum et vocibus adulantium in spem induci: postremo aestimari a medicis iubet an talis caecitas ac debilitas ope humana superabiles forent. Medici varie disserere: huic non exesam vim luminis et redituram si pellerentur obstantia; illi elapsos in pravum artus, si salubris vis adhibeatur, posse integrari. Id fortasse cordi deis et divino ministerio principem electum; denique patrati remedii gloriam penes Caesarem, inriti ludibrium penes miseros fore. Igitur Vespasianus cuncta fortunae suae patere ratus nec quicquam ultra incredibile, laeto ipse vultu, erecta quae adstabat multitudine, iussa exequitur. statim conversa ad usum manus, ac caeco reluxit dies. utrumque qui interfuere nunc quoque memorant, postquam nullum mendacio pretium.*[14]

---

13 Therefore, he began a civil war and sent ahead generals with troops to Italy; he crossed meanwhile to Alexandria, to take possession of the key to Egypt. A certain commoner, who was deprived of his sight, and another who was lame, together approached him while he was sitting at the tribunal, imploring him for the cure for their illness that had been shown them by Serapis as they slept, saying that if Vespasian should spit upon the one, his sight would be restored, and if he should deign to touch the other with his heel, his leg would regain strength. Although Vespasian could scarcely believe that it would succeed by any means, to the point that he dare not even try, at last, with his friends urging him on, he made the attempt publicly before the assembled crowd and he was not unsuccessful (translation from Rolfe 1914).

14 During the months while Vespasian was waiting at Alexandria for the regular season of the summer winds and a settled sea, many marvels continued to mark the favor of heaven and a certain partiality of the gods toward him. From among the Alexandrian commoners, a man, well known for his loss of sight, threw himself before Vespasian's knees, praying him with groans to cure his blindness, being so directed by the god Serapis, whom this most superstitious of nations worships before all others. And he prayed that the emperor would moisten his cheeks and eyes with spit from his mouth. Another, whose hand was useless, prompted by the same god, begged Caesar to step and trample on it. Vespasian at first ridiculed these appeals and treated them with scorn; then, when the men persisted, he began at one moment to fear the discredit of failure, at another to be inspired with hopes of success by the appeals of the suppliants and the flattery of his courtiers: finally, he directed the physicians to give their opinion as to whether such blindness and infirmity could be overcome by human aid. Their reply treated the two cases differently: they said that, in the first, the power of sight had not been completely eaten away and it would return if the obstacles were removed; in the other, the joints had slipped and become displaced, but they could be restored if a healing pressure were applied to them. Such perhaps was the wish of the gods, and it might be that the emperor had been chosen for this divine service; in any case, if a cure were obtained, the glory would be Caesar's, but in the event of failure, ridicule would fall only on the poor suppliants. So,

(Cassius Dio 65.8.1) *Οὐεσπασιανοῦ δὲ ἐς τὴν Ἀλεξάνδρειαν ἐσελθόντος ὁ Νεῖλος παλαιστῇ πλέον παρὰ τὸ καθεστηκὸς ἐν μιᾷ ἡμέρᾳ ἐπελάγισεν· ὅπερ οὐπώποτε πλὴν ἅπαξ γεγονέναι ἐλέγετο. Καὶ Οὐεσπασιανὸς δὲ αὐτὸς τυφλόν τέ τινα καὶ ἕτερον οὐκ ἀρτίχειρα, προσελθόντας οἱ ἐξ ὄψεως ὀνειράτων, τοῦ μὲν τὴν χεῖρα πατήσας τοῦ δὲ τοῖν ὀφθαλμοῖν προσπτύσας, ὑγιεῖς ἀπέφηνε.*[15]

As Vespasian was entering the city, two crippled Alexandrians approached and implored him to cure them. Vespasian was reluctant to do so at first, but eventually, after he was reassured that there was no harm in giving it a try, he undertook the task and succeeded.[16]

There is some variance in the three accounts. In Tacitus and Cassius Dio one of the two men is blind and the other has a paralyzed hand. According to Suetonius, the blind man was followed by one with a lame leg. Both Latin authors record that the two men turned to Vespasian at the instruction of Serapis. In all three accounts spittle is the requested means of healing the blind man. As to the second invalid, regardless of his affliction, both Cassius Dio and Suetonius report that Vespasian used his foot or heel to cure the crippled limb. In the more detailed account of Tacitus the invalid men instruct Vespasian on the precise method of cure, for they had received specific directions on this by an epiphany of the god in their sleep (Dio vaguely alludes to this in the phrase *ἐξ ὄψεως ὀνειράτων*, "because of a vision seen in dreams"). Tacitus's account stands apart from the other two versions also on the emphasis he gives to Vespasian's consultation of expert physicians on the matter. The presence of the physicians enhances credibility and the "historical" character of the miracle, which is additionally strengthened by the anatomical details of the therapy prescribed by the divine epiphany. From a complementary angle, the solicitation of the physicians' opinion corroborates Vespasian's imperial claim by projecting his rationalism and reliance on science for decision-making. The political character of the event may endorse yet another reading: Tacitus filters Vespasian's assessment of the situation through the physicians in order to make plain that undertaking in public the performance of a miraculous cure was a political decision, even though a potentially risky one.

The detail that, in the accounts of Suetonius and Tacitus, Vespasian's healing miracle is witnessed by a large crowd should be assessed similarly along the lines of the need to make the extraordinary seem credible, and also to underscore the political capital that the performance of this miracle before a sizeable audience would accrue for the aspiring emperor. Unlike other forms of divine communication, such as the omens, which may appear equally to individuals in private settings and to larger groups, a miracle is always a public spectacle and is performed before a large audience because performance is a prerequisite for the definition of this miracle as such. As in any performance, the impact and importance – the success – of a miracle is contingent on the spectators' reaction, their marveling at the powers of the miracle-worker. The public performance of miracle-

Vespasian, believing that his good fortune was capable of anything and that nothing was any longer incredible, with a smiling countenance, and amid intense excitement on the part of the bystanders, did as he was asked to do. The hand was instantly restored to use, and the day again shone for the blind man. Both facts are told by eye-witnesses even now when falsehood brings no reward (translation from Hadas 1942).

15 Following Vespasian's entry into Alexandria the Nile overflowed, having in one day risen a palm higher than usual; such an occurrence, it was said, had only taken place only once before. Vespasian himself healed two persons, one having a withered hand, the other being blind, who had come to him because of a vision seen in dreams; he cured the one by stepping on his hand and the other by spitting upon his eyes (translation from Cary 1914-28).

16 On Vespasian's miracle-working, including his dealings with the Alexandrian deities, as recorded in Tacitus and Suetonius, see Levick 1999, 68-69 (with notes); Garland 2011, 84-87.

working receives much greater emphasis in Tacitus, for the more details accompany it, the more objective the story, and hence the more credible the historiographical narrative.[17]

Tacitus and Suetonius wrote their works at the same time, but, as noted earlier, they wrote independently, with specialists agreeing that it is unlikely for one to have used or commented on the other's work.[18] Both wrote their accounts of the Vespasianic era at least a generation following the death of Vespasian, and drew on a variety of sources both written and oral. The account of Vespasian's healing miracle does not feature in literary sources prior to Tacitus and Suetonius. Josephus is the earliest and most historically accurate source on Vespasian's eastern campaign, including Vespasian's visit to Egypt.[19] His silence on the miraculous cure is remarkable, even more so because Josephus was both a contemporary and an eye-witness to the events surrounding Vespasian's sojourn, and an admirer of the first Flavian emperor.[20] He endorses Vespasian's divine claim to the throne of Rome and nearly equates Vespasian to the Messiah (*Jewish War* 3.399-404 and 6.310-5). At the same time, Josephus is well known for his readiness to embrace oral traditions, which were later integrated into the rabbinic works, and his selective use of anecdotal accounts insofar as they conformed to the overall purposes of his own narrative.[21]

Josephus's silence may be enlightening: it could be suggested that the Jewish historian may have rejected the historicity of Vespasian's healing miracle, or he may have considered the tradition one of merely local or temporary interest, hence not worth recording, without anticipating its subsequent appeal. Yet Josephus did not shy away from including miraculous narratives, including dreams and visions, in his work, to claim that he himself has received from God the gift of visions and prophetic dreams in order to announce things that are to come, including some about Vespasian himself – he predicted that Vespasian would become emperor (*Jewish War* 3.400-2), and later, after his prophecy came true, Vespasian believed Josephus's gift of prophecy to be divine.[22] Josephus's fascination with prophecies and dreams suggests that, should he have witnessed or even heard of Vespasian's dream, he would probably have recorded it, and we can thereby assume that the story likely developed at a later time, perhaps several years after Josephus's witnessing of Vespasian's campaign, even after Vespasian's death. Evidently, the story of the healing miracle appealed widely, and as a result it became, first, part of Vespasian's story[23]

17 This is especially true of miracles, events that have no rational cause, and therefore may struggle to make their way into the rational, cause-and-effect-seeking narrative of a historian. On the similarities and differences between omens and miracles, see Garland 2011, who accepts that "an overlap, both essential and linguistic, exists between miracles on the one hand, and omens and prodigies on the other" (76).

18 See the discussion in Power 2014, 205-25.

19 Josephus, *JW* 4.656-57.

20 On the relationship between Josephus and Vespasian, see den Hollander 2014, 68-138.

21 Josephus had been strongly influenced by the novelistic tradition, an issue that has been discussed already in Moehring 1957. On manipulation of oral accounts in Josephus, see Niehoff 1996; especially on intentional omissions, see Halpern Amarus 1988; and on additions, see Feldman 1998, 223-89, on Josephus's additions to the tradition on Abraham aiming at aggrandizing the leading Jewish patriarch, and Avioz 2012, where he retells the story of Jonathan by adding material, especially in the construction of the speeches attributed to Jonathan, in order to make him sound more like a Greco-Roman orator, and thus more appealing to his primary audience of Hellenized readers.

22 Josephus actually viewed himself as a dream interpreter, and reports no fewer than thirty-two dreams in his writings, which fall into various categories depending on their function; on Josephus's dreams, see Gnuse 1989 and 1996; Gray 1993; on Josephus's dream about Vespasian's grand destiny and the predestined Roman world conquest, see Gray 1993, 36-38; Gnuse 1996, 136-42.

23 For Luke 2010, 84, this "better represents the kind of material that circulated in the early years of the Flavian dynasty".

and, eventually, a piece of history upon entering the literary tradition in the works of Suetonius and Tacitus,[24] who, writing their works after the death of Domitian, probably detected in this story an excellent case-study for illustrating the complex way in which literary and religious traditions, which were themselves the product of elaborate fashioning, are collected, reworked, and manipulated in order to disseminate dynastic ideology that would appeal to the different convictions of the diverse cultures and peoples of the Roman Empire.

In light of the above, I will introduce three different streams of traditional storytelling that may have inspired the recordings of Vespasian's performance as miracle-worker. I will first explore the way in which the self-promotion of Augustus as the new, Roman version of Alexander the Great, and the rich tradition that developed as a result during the life of Octavian and became part of Augustus's legend after death, may have directed the construction of Vespasian's Alexander-like profile; and how locally developed narratives, masterminded, as I argue, by Tiberius Alexander and represented in our case by the miracles allegedly performed in 69 AD, may have served this mission. I will next examine how the particular stories of miraculous healing encouraged the association of Vespasian at once with Asklepios, the god of medicine, and with Serapis, the Egyptian version of Asklepios. Finally, I would like to entertain the possibility that the thaumaturgical work of Vespasian might have been inspired by a similar tradition about Alexander's healing powers, and the account of the miracles attributed to Jesus Christ in the gospel of St. Mark.

24 Luke 2010, 81.

III. Vespasian, Augustus, and Alexander

According to Tacitus and Suetonius (respectively, *Hist.* 4.82 and *Vesp.* 7.1), Vespasian miraculously healed the two men and subsequently entered, unaccompanied, the temple of Serapis, eager to consult the god about the stability of his position. Having performed the due rites to Serapis, he turned around and saw the priest Basilides, whom he knew to be far from Alexandria at that time, presenting him, the newly proclaimed emperor, with garlands and other offerings following the local custom. This vision, according to Tacitus, in connection with the significant name Basilides (*basileus*, royal), was regarded by Vespasian as a favourable answer from the god. Suetonius does not play upon the priest's name, but instead stresses the efficiency of the oracle by adding that almost immediately afterwards (*statim*) a message arrived announcing the defeat and death of Vitellius. Modern criticism has deemed the word *statim* as "suspect enough to prevent us from taking the statement at its face value. The swiftness with which a miracle is brought about is a recurrent theme in the terminology of ancient thaumaturgical literature".[25] At the time Vespasian likely ignored the whereabouts of Vitellius, who had been murdered a few days earlier, for the news of the death could not have reached Egypt in such a short time.

As noted earlier, Vespasian arrived in Egypt in the late summer of 69 AD but he did not enter Alexandria until late 69 or early 70 AD. This must have been general knowledge. Tacitus and Suetonius identify the visit to Egypt with that to Alexandria in order to date the miraculous work of Vespasian simultaneously with the death of Vitellius, which in turn happened only a few days after the proclamation of Vespasian as emperor in Alexandria. This slight manipulation of time and place denotes the

25 Henricks 1968, 55 (whence the quotation and the discussion of *statim*).

significance of Alexandria in the Roman narratives, on account of Serapis and the Serapeion.

To several modern critics, the healing powers of Vespasian and the visitation in the Serapeion stress the new emperor's association, in the pattern of the Ptolemaic rulers, with the Egyptian god Serapis, who traditionally performed therapeutic miracles. At the same time, it has also been properly noted that "it is doubtful that the approval of Serapis in Alexandria would have had much immediate impact on the political situation in Rome, a fact that raises questions about the nature and extent of the wonders' reportage in the direct aftermath of their occurrence".[26] The same doubt suggests that it would make better sense to accept that the miracle story either had been invented to address momentum and appeal locally, or had been a later creation, attributed to Domitian, who solidified his imperial rule by tending to the imperial memory of his brother and father. Among Domitian's first acts as an emperor was to support his brother's deification and to finish the triumphal arch honoring Titus's victory in Judaea.[27] Along the same line, he would project himself as the son of a ruler favored by gods, a quasi-*divi filius*, comparable to Alexander and Augustus. Vespasian's consultation and the acclaimed endorsement of Serapis could strengthen his imperial imagery because they drew the Flavian ruler next to Augustus's great exemplar, Alexander the Great. Four hundred years earlier, Alexander, a few months after his triumphant arrival in Egypt, was officially welcomed as liberator from the Persians. His reception is echoed in the one that Vespasian received in Alexandria. The crafty recollection of this legendary, widely known tradition in the miraculous events that distinguished Vespasian's sojourn may be attributed to the political acumen of the Egyptian governor, Tiberius Alexander, who intended to contextualize the visit of his Roman friend in distinct details of the Alexander-legend, in order to bolster Vespasian's popularity and imperial candidacy.

Indeed, the next steps in Vespasian's story very closely trace Alexander's own. Following the reception, Alexander visited the oracle of Zeus Ammon at the desert of Siwah; there, unaccompanied, he entered the temple of the great Egyptian god (Strabon, *Geography* 17.1.43 = Callisthenes *FGrHist* 124 F 14a; Plutarch, *Life of Alexander* 27.5-9), and upon encountering the chief priest he inquired about his paternity. He was reportedly told that he was the son of Zeus/Ammon. This event became for Alexander, according to the sources, the first step on the road to deification.

At least as early as Sulla,[28] the leaders of Rome were fascinated with Alexander, whose conquests became partly a model, partly a justification for Rome's wars in the East for centuries (all the way through Heraclius).[29] In Vespasian's case, time and circumstances favored the association with Alexander strongly: both Alexander and Vespasian had arrived at Egypt coming from Syria via Gaza in the summer; they were both facing a decisive confrontation with their opponents, Darius of Persia and Vitellius respectively. Even the literary form of Tacitus's account seems to have been modeled upon the tradition about Alexander's expedition to the Ammonium. The primary sources concerning Alexander, principally the works of Callisthenes, Aristoboulos, Ptolemy, and Clitarchos, are lost, so the information available comes from secondary sources, specifically Arrian, Quintus Curtius, Strabon, and Plutarch.

26 Luke 2010, 80.

27 The deified Titus was repeatedly commemorated by Domitian, in the *Templum Gentis Flauiae*, in the *Arcus Divi Titi*, in the *Templum Vespasiani* et *Titi*, and in an *aedes* of the *Porticus Divorum*. See Anderson 1983, 95-97; Padcker 2003, 174; Tuck 2016, 118-22.

28 And likely even earlier, in the time of Scipio; see Ogden 2009.

29 Barnett 2017; on Rome and Alexander generally see Spencer 2002; on Caesar and Alexander see Green 1978, 1-5; on Pompey, Caesar, and Alexander, see Welch and Mitchell 2013.

After the death of Alexander, his life story, including the events that took place during his visit to Egypt, was taken over by oral tradition at the same time it was recorded in writing. Oral stories and official records fueled two different strands of Alexander's biography, at times independently developing, at times intertwining. They were communicated in this way not only to Tacitus and Suetonius, who had before them the texts of the historians of Alexander and used their information (according to Henrichs 1968, who has detected many similarities in the Roman accounts of Suetonius and Tacitus, and the Greek historians of Alexander), but also to the people of Rome more broadly. The latter would evoke them upon receiving the story about Vespasian's arrival to Egypt and his encounters with the divine during his visit to the temple of Serapis.

Prior to Vespasian, Augustus had employed images, themes, and artifacts tied to Alexander's legend extensively.[30] The model of Alexander became a powerful and effective tool for the first *princeps* in his effort to impose his rule in Egypt and the East.[31] Once the association with Alexander had been established, Vespasian's association with Augustus would follow.[32] Vespasian's effective miracle-working would bring next a political cure: a new emperor and hope for a conclusion to the year-long civil strife across the empire following the murder of Nero, replicating Augustus in 31 BC, when he "restituted" the republic (*Res Gestae* 1.1).[33] The ties to Augustus would become deeper and stronger during Vespasian's reign, and they would receive even more sustained and emphatic treatment in the era of Domitian.[34] By the time Tacitus and Suetonius recorded their accounts of the Vespasianic era, the miraculous events at Alexandria in 69 AD were part of official imperial history.

The circulation of the oral stories about these miracles and Vespasian's visit to Serapis were of limited popularity beyond Egypt during the summer of 69 AD, and likely during the time of Vespasian as well. This suggests that the mastermind behind them might have been a local agent, with close ties to the Roman elite: a prime candidate is Governor Tiberius Julius Alexander. A member of the Alexandrian elite, of a prominent family of Hellenized Jews but also Roman citizens, a very wealthy man, well connected, probably well educated (he was the nephew of the Jewish philosopher Philo), and a keen politician, Tiberius Alexander had had a remarkable equestrian career in Roman public life, which lasted for at least three decades and under several emperors. As soon as Claudius came to power, Tiberius Alexander was appointed chief political administrator of the Thebaid; four years later (in 46 AD), he was promoted to procurator of Judaea. Following another successful tenure he was appointed, by Nero this time, to the

30 On Augustus and Alexander, Kienast 1969 is still the reference study; see also Weippert 1972, 214-23; and more recently, Gruen 1998; Malloch 2001; Kühnen 2005; Imrie 2018, 99-113.

31 Critics have identified a long series of initiatives immediately after Actium through which Octavian projected himself in light of Alexander in the eastern part of the empire; Gruen 1998, 190-91; Weippert 1972, 214-19. To establish his ties to Alexander, Augustus upon entering Alexandria visited Alexander's tomb (Cass. Dio 51.16.3-5; Suet. *Aug.* 18.1; Plut. *Ant.* 80.1).

32 As noted by Levick (1999, 73), "[...] new emperors routinely made reference to the Founder [...]" (i.e., Augustus), and scholars generally agree that the Flavians actively sought to illustrate their proximity to Augustus in order to legitimize their rule; the bibliography is large and growing; see Isager 1976, 64-71; Boyle 2003, 4-14; Zimmermann 2003, 317-48; Heslin 2007, 16-18; on Vespasian's employing not just the power of images but the very images of Augustus on his coinage, see Rosso 2009; Winkler-Horaček 2010. Egypt has played a particularly important role in this ideological juxtaposition: the coinage of Vespasian celebrated both the centenary of the Battle of Actium (in 70 AD) and that of the annexation of Egypt (in 71 AD); Grant 1950, 88-98, 179-80 (Appendix III); Hannestad 1988, 121-22.

33 Like Augustus, Vespasian's first undertaking upon becoming emperor was the restitution of the Republic; see Suet. *Vesp.* 8.1; also *Vesp.* 6.4, 16.3.

34 Luke 2010.

staff of the Roman general Corbulo and served with distinction in Corbulo's campaigns against the Parthians. Then, in 66 AD, at Corbulo's recommendation, Nero appointed Tiberius Alexander governor of Egypt. According to Josephus, during the turbulent year following the death of Nero, Tiberius Alexander, who sensed the great potential of Vespasian, then the general of the Roman legions in the Judean war, became the first provincial governor to endorse openly his imperial candidacy. On July 1, 69 AD, Tiberius Alexander and his legions took the oath of allegiance to Vespasian as Emperor. In Josephus's account, the most detailed ancient source on Tiberius Alexander, his lead was followed by legions throughout the eastern Empire, and the anniversary of Vespasian's accession was later celebrated on this date (*Jewish War* 4.616-17).[35]

Tiberius Alexander could not have realized the significance the appropriation of the Alexander/Augustus model would have for Vespasian in the political semiotics of Rome. Besides, Augustus is never reported to have healed people. This is not the case with Alexander the Great: the latter is mentioned in the ancient sources not only as expressing, likely under the influence of his teacher Aristotle, great interest in Hippocratic medicine and pursuing medical knowledge, even recommending a particular treatment or a drug (Plut. *Alex.* 8.1; also Diod. Sic. 17.31.6; Plut. *Alex.* 19), but also as receiving therapeutic guidance in visions and dreams (Plut. *Alex.* 41.3; a typical case of an *incubatio*, such as those associated with the Asklepian *iamata* discussed below, is recorded in Curtius Rufus 9.8.27 and Diod. Sic. 17.103.5; in the latter case Alexander wakes up and searches himself for the healing plant, and when he finds it, he applies the cure himself).[36] Critics have interpreted Alexander's ties to medicine as part of the sustained effort of Alexander's dynasty, the Argeads, to associate themselves with the cult of Asklepios. The treatment and healing of Perdiccas II by Hippocrates prefigures Asklepios, and Alexander's father, Philip II, had showed a strong interest in the Macedonian cult of Asklepios;[37] Alexander himself, according to Pausanias (8.28.1), dedicated his spear to the sanctuary of Asklepios in Gortyna (Arcadia).[38] No less popular and widespread was the reputation of Asklepios, the healing god, known and worshiped by people all over the Roman world, including Egypt. I argue that the ideological provenance of Vespasian's miracles should be sought in the tradition of Asklepios's healing miracles, which determined the fashioning of the Egyptian Serapis.

IV. Vespasian and Asklepios

Asklepios (Lat. Aesculapius) enters our story via Serapis (popular tradition anachronistically connected Alexander the Great with Serapis, as well[39]). Serapis was a very popular deity in Egypt, especially among the Greek population, and his cult had been tied to the ruler cult since Ptolemy II.[40] Serapis was the Egyptian version of Asklepios, according to Plu-

35 On the biography and impressive career of Tiberius Alexander, one of the most loyal supporters of Vespasian and his son Titus, see Honigman 2013, 3547-48; earlier studies include Burr 1955; Turner 1954.

36 On the association of Alexander with medicine, see details in Antela-Bernárdez & Sierra Martín 2018.

37 The specific ties of the Argeads to Asclepius are discussed in Antela-Bernárdez & Sierra Martín 2018, 48-49; the study notes in particular that Philip "conceded eponymity to the priests of Asclepius" in certain cities of Macedonia, and emphasizes the amplitude of epigraphic material throughout Macedonia referring to Asklepios, and the dedications of Macedonians to Epidaurus that date from Philip's times.

38 Antela-Bernárdez & Sierra Martín 2018, referring to further discussion in Gabaldón 2004, 65-66.

39 P. Mil. 21 with the restorations of Merkelbach 1960, 108-9.

40 When Ptolemy III built the great Serapeion, the ruler cult was performed inside the shrine and colossal statues of the Ptolemies stood next to those of Serapis; Pfeiffer 2008, 401.

tarch.[41] Tacitus, too, notes that many identified Serapis with Asklepios due to their striking resemblance in iconography (*Hist.* 4.84.5).

Serapis was a medicine god in Egypt, healing both crippled men and blind men. Nile water and incubation is thought to have been used by the priests of the cult to cure devotees.[42] Famously, Serapis had restored the eyesight of Demetrios of Phaleron, the Athenian politician,[43] man of letters and later advisor of Ptolemy I. This is the first of Serapis's miracles that we know of. Demetrios thanked the god in a way that was proper to his genius: he composed paeans in praise of Serapis, and thus created the first aretalogy for the new god – and, in turn, a tradition of orally performed stories of miraculous cures,[44] particularly popular in Egypt. The content of these hymns, the miraculous deeds of the gods, evidently inspired the composition of popular stories that circulated as a form of entertainment under the same term. Aretalogies of this type were known to Augustus, who, according to Suetonius, was very fond of inviting *aretalogoi* to perform their marvelous tales at his dinner banquets.[45]

At the same time, the miraculous cures of Serapis called to mind the miracles of Asklepios. The recollection applied to the same audience of Egyptian Greeks and the eastern inhabitants of the empire, but also to the people at Rome who would later hear about these miracles. The way the two crippled men are instructed by a visitation by Serapis in their sleep to seek their healing, the nature of their afflictions, their appeal to Vespasian, Vespasian's initial hesitation, and ultimately the concession and the healing, follow closely the wording of the Asklepian cure inscriptions (*iamata*)[46] from Epidaurus, a body of written evidence preserved on four stelai dating to the second half of the 4th century BC.[47] These inscriptions record the experiences of ailing people who came to sleep in the sanctuary in hopes of a cure, and they were visited in their sleep by Asklepios who cured their ailment.[48] Cures of ailments concerning body parts and blindness are quite frequent in these inscriptions. A typical such *iama* is the following:

> Ambrosia from Athens, blind in one eye. She came as a suppliant to the god. As she walked around the sanctuary, she laughed at some of the cures as unbelievable and impossible, that the lame and the blind should become well through merely seeing a dream. In her sleep she saw a vision. It seemed to her that the god stood by her and said he would cure her, but that he would ask her in exchange to dedicate to the sanctu-

41 Because his image, like that of Asklepios, combined both the dog and the snake; *De Iside et Osiride* 28.

42 See Wild 1981, 2-4, 29-31, and 167-68 for a discussion on the connection between water, architecture, and the cult. See Brady 1935, 12 and McKenzie, Gibson, and Reyes 2004 on the healing aspects of Serapis and insights gained from architecture.

43 Diog. Laert. 5.76; Ash 1999, 135 n. 26.

44 On the Hellenistic literary phenomenon of *aretalogies*, see Jördens 2013, 143-76.

45 As noted in n. 4 above, in Suet. *Aug.* 74, Suetonius employs the Greek term *aretalogos* (literally: "teller of wonder stories of divine miracles (*aretai*)"; according to Wardle 2014, 463, performers of light entertainment, "spinners of yarns and fanciful tales") to describe these storytellers, thus offering important indirect information on the content of these stories.

46 Luke 2010, 81, discusses the closeness in the language of the miraculous cure and that of the Asklepian *iamata*. Further, Vespasian's therapeutic act calls to mind the therapeutic practices at the Asklepieia (use of water and paeans to the gods); see Renberg 2017, I, ch. 3.

47 Authentic records of Serapis's miraculous cures have not survived, but a few have been reported by Artemidoros (*Oneir.* 2.44); on the association of Asklepios to Serapis in Egypt (and before that to the Egyptian healing god Amenhotep-Amenotes) see Alvar 2008, 329-30.

48 Inscriptions from Delos mention a certain Ptolemaios, who was an *aretalogos* and also a dream interpreter. Even though there is no evidence that *aretalogoi* were not necessarily associated with religious duties or offices, the link between telling tales of divine miracles and cures, and interpreting dreams evokes Asklepios and his administering of cures by dream visitations; see Jördens 2013, 146.

> ary a silver pig as a memorial of her ignorance. After saying this, he cut her diseased eyeball and poured in some medicine. When day came she walked out healthy.[49]

The *iamata* further attest to the widespread reputation of the temple of Asklepios at Epidaurus all over the Greek world.[50] In the course of the Hellenistic era, Asklepios's reputation spread throughout the Mediterranean. About 200 Asklepeia were built on the Greek mainland, and hundreds of temples were devoted to the god beyond.[51] Literary and archaeological sources record Asklepeia in Bithynia, Mysia, Lydia, Caria, Cilicia, Media and Scythia, Phoenicia in Berytus, and Sidon. In the early 3rd century BC, Asklepios was invited to Rome in order to cure a plague that had befallen the city at the time, leading to the establishment of the first cult location of Aesculapius in the Urbs (cf. Livy 10.47.6-7). By the 1st century AD, temples of Aesculapius are attested in several places in Italy, in Latin Gaul, and in North Africa.

The recollection of Asklepios naturally leads to Augustus,[52] for the concept of the emperor as healer of the ailing *Respublica* featured prominently in the biography of Augustus, although he himself capitalized on a political idea well developed in Late Republican thought (prominently discussed in Cicero's treatises).[53] The Jewish philosopher Philo notably reports (*Embassy* 144-45) that Augustus had the ability not only to "calm the torrential storm on every side" but also to "heal plagues that afflicted both the Greeks and the barbarians",[54] a phrase that evokes the circumstances of Asklepios's arrival at Rome. In his account of the Epidaurian god's migration at Rome, Ovid in *Metamorphoses* 15.622-744 places the episode at the beginning of the historical era of Rome, right before he moves on to narrate the catasterism of Julius Caesar and prophesy the apotheosis of Augustus – thus making the connec-

49 Herzog 1931, 11, miracle 4; translation from Edelstein & Edelstein 1998, 230 with modifications.

50 The inscriptions dated from the early 4th century BC record patients who travelled from Aigina, Argos, Halieis, Epeiros, Messene, Sparta, Herakleia, Hermione, Kaphyiai, Keos, Kirrha, Pherai, Thebes, and Troezen, and from more distant places (Chios, Knidos, Lampsakos, Mytilene, Thasos, and Torone) to Epidaurus, reflecting the pan-Hellenic reputation of the sanctuary; Dillon 1994, 243; 1997, 73-80; Wickkiser 2008, 41; on the inscriptions recording the Macedonian dedications, see n. 37 above.

51 Riethmüller 2005, II, 9-315 estimates that 171 Asklepeia were built on the Greek mainland during that period; the same historian records 732 temples built beyond the Greek mainland and provides relevant bibliographical and literary references.

52 In turn, Augustus might have drawn inspiration from the set of miracle-working in the biography of Alexander, starting with the taming of Boukephalas while Alexander was still a child (Arrian, *Anab.* 27.3, Plutarch, *De Alexandri magni fortuna* 2.9, 10, 13); on Alexander's special childhood deeds, see Stadter 1996.

53 Miller 2009, 176-78, Papaioannou 2018, 106-7; the political leader as the healer of a suffering constitution is established in Roman political literature in Cicero, who likens the ideal politician to a physician (*medicus*); Cicero specifically calls on Pompey and Caesar to cure the Republic: Cic. *De Rep.* 1.62, *Pro Marc.* 24, *Pro Mil.* 68; with Tempest 2013, 274-75.

54 Garland 2011, 84; miracle-working was reported also in relation to Emperor Hadrian: when the emperor was sick and wished to kill himself, a certain blind woman came to him. She said that she had been warned in a dream to tell Hadrian to refrain from killing himself, for he was destined to recover entirely, yet she had failed to do this and as a result, she became blind; she had then received a second order to give the same message to Hadrian and to kiss his knees, and was assured of the recovery of her sight if she did so. The woman carried out the command of the dream and received her sight after she had bathed her eyes with the water in the temple from which she had come; see *Historia Augusta* (Aelius Spartianus), *Vita Hadriani* 1.25.1-2.

tion between the migrating healing god and the *princeps* all too explicit.[55]

Most importantly, Augustus is the only emperor prior to Vespasian explicitly associated with Asklepios. According to a tradition recorded in Suetonius, who acknowledged having found it in a work entitled *Theologumena* by Asklepias of Mendes, a female author about whom nothing else is known,[56] Augustus was sired by Apollo in the form of a snake (Suetonius, *Aug.* 94.4), in direct evocation of the serpentine form of the healing god Aesculapius, also a son of Apollo. In fact, Augustus's decision to make Apollo his patron deity may well have been motivated by the fact that, in the Republican era, Apollo was seen in Rome primarily as a healer. Before Augustus, there was only one temple to Apollo in Rome, the Temple of Apollo Medicus, the healer. This Temple of Apollo Medicus was originally dedicated in the mid-5th century BC and was restored in 32 BC. After Actium, Apollo Medicus was appropriated by Augustus,[57] and at the instigation of Augustus, his worship was interfused with the cult of Aesculapius, which had been very popular in Rome since the Middle Republican times.[58] The emphasis on the healing powers of Vespasian, then, cast him not only as a quasi-divine healer but as a healer of the Roman people in the pattern of Augustus, the healer of the Republic, enforcing the Augustus-profile discussed above.

55 In Papaioannou 2005, 32-41, I discuss the ideology surrounding the migration of the therapeutic god Aesculapius in Rome by the Augustan regime.

56 Suetonius does not disclose any other information on the story or the author, including a date or context, while Dio Cassius (45.1.2) reports a similar tale of supernatural birth, but not an identical one, suggesting either the reliance of both authors on a common source which each revised independently. See, for example, Gurval 1998, 100.

57 On the incorporation of the Apollo, "the Healer", into the image of Augustus, and the appropriation of the temple of Apollo Medicus Sosianus, see Miller 2009, 176-78.

58 On the integration of the two cults see Lipka 2009, 77-78; Miller 2009, 365-67; Stok 1992, 178.

V. Vespasian and Jesus

Turning, finally, to the miraculous cures, the question of authenticity is secondary to the fact that the story of the miracle had been transmitted, and since it became part of the Roman historiographical tradition, it was believed. People across the empire believed it, because first Tiberius Alexander (should we accept that he was the instigator of the miraculous narrative) and later Domitian adroitly interwove at least three different trends of oral tradition, which appealed to audiences from different cultural backgrounds. At Rome, Vespasian's miracle-working interacted with the tradition that developed around Augustus; in significance it was a postscript, but nonetheless one that fit in naturally with Vespasian's portrayal as the new Augustus: as mentioned above, Augustus performed miraculous cures, being the son of Apollo and the brother of Aesculapius.

Vespasian's miracle-worker profile was first and foremost intended to impress the Egyptians and create a new biography that would interfuse reality with popular tradition of miracle-working and elevate him to the level of Alexander, and above the very Augustus. The aretalogies of Serapis and the miracles of Asklepios were trailed by a rich tradition for Tiberius Alexander to manipulate. Is it possible, however, to consider that a third tradition originating in the miracle-working of Jesus Christ may have been employed as well? The truth is that the miracles of the cripple and the blind men strongly evoke the miracles of Jesus, especially the spittle employed to cure the blind man, though contrary to Jesus, who performed his miracles in private, Vespasian's miracle was witnessed by a great crowd:

> Mark 8:22-26 (Jesus Heals a Blind Man at Bethsaida)
> 22 They came to Bethsaida, and some people brought a blind man before Him and begged Him to touch the man. 23 He took the blind man by the hand and led him outside the village. When He had spit on the man's eyes and put his hands on him, Jesus asked, "Do

you see anything?" 24 The man looked up and said, "I see people; they look like trees walking around". 25 Once again Jesus put his hands on the man's eyes. Then his eyes were opened, his sight was restored, and he saw everybody clearly. 26 Jesus sent him home, saying, "Don't even go into the village and don't say anything to anybody in the village". (English Standard Version).[59]

Mark 10:46-52 (Blind Bartimaeus Receives His Sight)
46 Then they came to Jericho. As Jesus and his disciples, together with a large crowd, were leaving the city, a blind man, Bartimaeus (the son of Timaeus), was sitting by the roadside begging. 47 When he heard that it was Jesus of Nazareth, he began to shout, "Jesus, Son of David, have mercy on me!" 48 Many rebuked him and told him to be quiet, but he shouted all the more, "Son of David, have mercy on me!" 49 Jesus stopped and said, "Call him". So they called the blind man and said to him: "Cheer up! On your feet! He's calling you". 50 The man threw his cloak aside, stood up and came to Jesus. 51 "What do you want me to do for you?" Jesus asked him. The blind man said, "Rabbi, I want to see". 52 "Go", said Jesus, "your faith has healed you". Immediately he received his sight and followed Jesus along the road. (English Standard Version).[60]

The date of composition of the Gospel of Mark is not universally agreed upon in New Testament Studies. To this day scholars are divided between those who argue for an early date in the early 40s AD, those who prefer a middle date in the mid-60s AD, and those who believe that it presupposes the destruction of the temple of Jerusalem by Titus, and so it must have been composed in the early 70s AD.[61] The distinctly oral character of the prose also suggests that it may have been composed and circulated orally before it was rendered in writing. In light of the low percentage of literacy in antiquity, a narrative primarily intended to be circulated widely would logically follow a structure appropriate for oral performance and aural reception.[62] An oral narrative does not have a fixed form but rather is open to ongoing change and embrace of new material, which makes it more relevant as time passes and audience change. Proposing a date in the mid-60s AD for the earliest composition of the gospel, such that it is likely for a version of it to have reached Egypt by 69

59 22 *Καὶ ἔρχονται εἰς Βηθσαϊδάν. Καὶ φέρουσιν αὐτῷ τυφλὸν, καὶ παρακαλοῦσιν αὐτὸν ἵνα αὐτοῦ ἅψηται.* 23 *καὶ ἐπιλαβόμενος τῆς χειρὸς τοῦ τυφλοῦ ἐξήγαγεν αὐτὸν ἔξω τῆς κώμης, καὶ πτύσας εἰς τὰ ὄμματα αὐτοῦ, ἐπιθεὶς τὰς χεῖρας αὐτῷ ἐπηρώτα αὐτόν εἴ τι βλέπει.* 24 *καὶ ἀναβλέψας ἔλεγε· Βλέπω τοὺς ἀνθρώπους ὡς δένδρα περιπατοῦντας.* 25 *εἶτα πάλιν ἐπέθηκε τὰς χεῖρας ἐπὶ τοὺς ὀφθαλμοὺς αὐτοῦ καὶ ἐποίησεν αὐτὸν ἀναβλέψαι, καὶ ἀποκατεστάθη, καὶ ἀνέβλεψε τηλαυγῶς ἅπαντας.* 26 *καὶ ἀπέστειλεν αὐτὸν εἰς οἶκον αὐτοῦ λέγων· Μηδὲ εἰς τὴν κώμην εἰσέλθῃς μηδὲ εἴπῃς τινὶ ἐν τῇ κώμῃ.* (Greek NT: Greek Orthodox Church).

60 46 *Καὶ ἔρχονται εἰς Ἰεριχώ· καὶ ἐκπορευομένου αὐτοῦ ἀπὸ Ἰεριχὼ καὶ τῶν μαθητῶν αὐτοῦ καὶ ὄχλου ἱκανοῦ, ὁ υἱὸς Τιμαίου Βαρτιμαῖος τυφλὸς ἐκάθητο παρὰ τὴν ὁδὸν προσαιτῶν.* 47 *καὶ ἀκούσας ὅτι Ἰησοῦς ὁ Ναζωραῖός ἐστιν, ἤρξατο κράζειν καὶ λέγειν· Υἱὲ Δαυῒδ Ἰησοῦ, ἐλέησόν με.* 48 *καὶ ἐπετίμων αὐτῷ πολλοὶ ἵνα σιωπήσῃ· ὁ δὲ πολλῷ μᾶλλον ἔκραζεν· Υἱὲ Δαυῒδ, ἐλέησόν με.* 49 *καὶ στὰς ὁ Ἰησοῦς εἶπε· Φωνήσατε αὐτόν· καὶ φωνοῦσιν τὸν τυφλὸν λέγοντες αὐτῷ· Θάρσει, ἔγειρε· φωνεῖ σε.* 50 *ὁ δὲ ἀποβαλὼν τὸ ἱμάτιον αὐτοῦ ἀναστὰς ἦλθε πρὸς τὸν Ἰησοῦν.* 51 *καὶ ἀποκριθεὶς λέγει αὐτῷ ὁ Ἰησοῦς· Τί σοι θέλεις ποιήσω; ὁ δὲ τυφλὸς εἶπεν αὐτῷ· Ραββουνί, ἵνα ἀναβλέψω.* 52 *καὶ ὁ Ἰησοῦς εἶπεν αὐτῷ· Ὕπαγε, ἡ πίστις σου σέσωκέ σε. καὶ εὐθέως ἀνέβλεψε, καὶ ἠκολούθει τῷ Ἰησοῦ ἐν τῇ ὁδῷ.* (Greek NT: Greek Orthodox Church).

61 Recent studies arguing for the earlier and the later date include, e.g., Incigneri 2003; Kloppenborg 2005; Roskam 2004, 81-94; Winn 2008, 43-91; Zeichmann 2017 (for a late date: 70-73 AD); Crossley 2004; Ellis 1992; Taylor 1996 (for an early date: 40-41 AD). Most commentators opt for a date in the middle and place the Gospel's composition during Nero's persecution of the Christians at Rome or shortly afterwards (64-69 AD): e.g., Hengel 1985, 1-28; Head 2004, 240-59; Frey 2012, 465-69.

62 A comprehensive treatment of the theme of the oral character of the synoptic gospels and other Christian writings is Mournet 2005; specifically on the oral character of the Gospel of Mark, see, e.g., Dewey 2017; 1989; Botha 1991.

AD and be circulating around the community of the Hellenized Jewish elite, seems both reasonable and plausible – its circulation and popularity expedited no less by the distinctly oral character of its prose.[63] We cannot prove it, but it might be worth speculating that it was known to Tiberius Alexander, the man who, according to the Roman historians, but also to Josephus, was the key figure behind Vespasian's appointment to the imperial throne. Tiberius Alexander was a Hellenized Jew and a member of the aristocratic elite that controlled the politics, economy, and culture of Egypt. He could have heard of, even read, Mark's Gospel and, being the superb political strategist he was, he saw in the miracles of Jesus material that could be used for advancing the popularity of Vespasian and his establishing on the imperial throne.

VI. Conclusion

Roman historiographical narration builds on reappropriating and revising traditional material too often forged to be circulated orally. Oral tradition in our discussion concerns exploits of a man who was held to be special; the transmission of these exploits in writing did not stop variation. On the contrary, the diversity of written versions seems to have inspired literary narratives that were outright political and served specific cultural purposes with the dynamics of oral narration. Thus, apart from serving the politics of the day, the different literary versions of oral stories also simulated the process of propagating an oral narrative, which typically produces variations of an archetypal account.

The story of Vespasian's miracle-working and its impact on enhancing the aspiring emperor's popularity, which impressed both Tacitus and Suetonius enough for them to record it, comprises an intriguing example of a political initiative that capitalized on the complexity and flexibility of intercultural tradition. I have proposed that Vespasian's miracles could have been orchestrated by the Egyptian governor Tiberius Alexander, with the inspiration of interrelating Greek and Egyptian traditions of prophetic visions and miracle-working. The story was first circulated in Egypt and the East in order to bolster the claim of Vespasian to Rome's throne. As a result of its wide appeal, but also the clear association of Vespasian with divine powers that distinguished kindred deities across cultures, the story was likely added at a later time, perhaps by Domitian, to the official imperial portrait of Vespasian, which in turn fed Tacitus's and Suetonius's accounts. At the same time, Vespasian's miracle-working account is a case study of simulated tradition surrounding a deity, in order to ennoble the story, both according to the expectations of the Roman people, who were encouraged to see in Vespasian an Augustus-double, and in agreement with the beliefs of the eastern subjects of the empire, who expected from their rulers to perform miracles. The oral character of these stories served this dual target superbly.

Sophia Papaioannou
National and Kapodistrian University of Athens
spapaioan@phil.uoa.gr

63 A late tradition, which nonetheless was widely received by the intellectuals of the Early Christian Church (specifically Eusebius, *Ecclesiastical History* 2.16, St. Jerome, *De Viris Illustribus* 8, and the *Apostolic Constitutions* 7.46), represents Mark the Evangelist as the founder of the Church of Alexandria, which according to Eusebius took place during the early years of Claudius's rule (print: "41-44 AD"), who later states (*Ecclesiastical History* 2.24) that Mark's first successor, Anianus, succeeded Mark as bishop of Alexandria in the eighth year of Nero's rule (61-62 AD). On the conflation of Mark the Evangelist with the Alexandrian Mark, see most recently Furlong 2020, esp. 23-54, and passim.

Bibliography

ALVAR, J. 2008
Romanising Oriental Gods: Myth, Salvation and Ethics in the Cults of Cybele, Isis and Mithras (trans. & ed. R. Gordon), Leiden.

ANDERSON, J. C. JR. 1983
'A Topographical Tradition in Fourth Century Chronicles: Domitian's Building Program', *Historia* 32, 93-105.

ANDO, C. 2000
Imperial Ideology and Provincial Loyalty in the Roman Empire, Berkeley & Los Angeles.

ANTELA-BERNÁRDEZ, B. & C. SIERRA MARTÍN 2018
'Alexander and the Medicine', *Karanos* 1, 35-54.

ASH, R. 1999
Ordering Anarchy: Armies and Leaders in Tacitus' Histories, London.

AVIOZ, M. 2012
'Josephus' Retelling of the Jonathan Narratives', *Journal of the Study of Pseudepigrapha* 22, 68-86.

BARNETT, G. 2017
Emulating Alexander: How Alexander the Great's Legacy Fuelled Rome's Wars with Persia, Barnsley, South Yorkshire.

BOTHA, P. J. J. 1991
'Mark's Story as an Oral Traditional Literature: Re-thinking the Transmission of Some Traditions about Jesus', *HTS Teologiese Studies / Theological Studies* 47/2, 304-31.

BOYLE, A. A. J. 2003
'Introduction: Reading Flavian Rome', in *Flavian Rome: Culture, Image, Text*, A. A. J. Boyle & W. J. Dominik (eds.), Leiden, 1-67.

BRADY, T.A. 1935
The Reception of the Egyptian Cults by the Greeks (330-30 B.C.), Columbia.

BURR, V. 1955
Tiberius Iulius Alexander, Bonn.

CARY, E. 1914-28
Dio's Roman History in Nine Volumes. Edited with an English Translation (Loeb Classical Library), London & New York.

CHILVER, G. E. F. & G. B. TOWNEND 1985
A Historical Commentary on Tacitus' Histories IV and V, Oxford.

CROSSLEY, J. G. 2004
The Date of Mark's Gospel: Insight from the Law in Early Christianity, London & New York.

DEN HOLLANDER, W. 2014
Josephus, the Emperors, and the City of Rome: From Hostage to Historian, Leiden.

DEWEY, J. 1989
'Oral Methods of Structuring Narrative in Mark', *Interpretation: A Journal of Bible and Theology* 43.1, 32-44.

DEWEY, J. 2017
'The Gospel of Mark as an Oral/Aural Narrative: Implications for Preaching', *Currents in Theology and Mission* 44.4 (October issue), 7-10.

DILLON, M. P. J. 1994
'The Didactic Nature of the Epidaurian iamata', *ZPE* 101, 239-60.

DILLON, M. P. J. 1997
Pilgrims and Pilgrimage in Ancient Greece, London & New York.

DÜBNER, F. 1877 (REPR. 1969)
Scholia Graeca in Aristophanem, Paris (repr. Hildesheim).

EDELSTEIN, E. J. & L. EDELSTEIN 1998
Asclepius: Collection and Interpretation of the Testimonies, Baltimore.

ELLIS, E. E. 1992
'The Date and Provenance of Mark's Gospel', in *The Four Gospels, 1992: Festschrift Frans Neirynck*, 3 vols. (BETL 100), F. Van Segbroek, C. M. Tuckett, G. Van Belle & J. Verheyden (eds.), Leuven, 2.801-15.

FEHLING, D. 1971
Die Quellenangaben bei Herodot, Berlin & New York [revised as *Herodotus and his Sources: Citation, Invention and Narrative Art*, trans. J. G. Howie, Leeds 1989].

FELDMAN, L.H. 1998
Josephus's Interpretation of the Bible, Berkeley.

FREY, J. 2012
'Temple and Identity in Early Christianity and in the Johannine Community: Reflections on the 'Parting of the Ways'', in *Was 70 CE a Watershed in Jewish History? On Jews and Judaism before and after the Destruction of the Temple*, D. R. Schwartz & Z. Weiss (eds.) (AJEC 78), Leiden, 447-508.

FURLONG, D. 2020
The John also called Mark: Reception and Transformation in Christian Tradition (Wissenschaftliche Untersuchungen zum Neuen Testament, 2. Reihe), Tübingen.

GABALDÓN, M. M. 2004
Ritos de armas en la Edad del hierro: armamento y lugares de culto en el Mediterráneo y el mundo celta, Madrid.

GARLAND, R. 2011
'Miracles in the Greek and Roman world', in *The Cambridge Companion to Miracles*, G. H. Twelftree (ed.), Cambridge, 75-94.

GEROLEMOU, M. (ED.) 2018
Recognizing Miracles in Antiquity and Beyond (Trends in Classics, Supplementary volumes, 53), Berlin.

GNUSE, R. K. 1989
'Dream Reports in the Writings of Flavius Josephus', Revue Biblique 96, 358-90.

GNUSE, R. K. 1996
Dreams and Dream Reports in the Writings of Josephus: A Traditio-Historical Analysis, Leiden.

GOLDBERG, S. M. 2005
Constructing Literature in the Roman Republic, Cambridge.

GRANT, M. 1950
Roman Anniversary Issues: An Exploratory Study of the Numismatic and Medallic Commemoration of Anniversary Years 49 B.C – A.D. 375, Cambridge.

GRAY, R. 1993
Prophetic Figures in Late Second Temple Jewish Palestine: The Evidence from Josephus, Oxford.

GREEN, P. 1978
'Caesar and Alexander: *Aemulatio, Imitatio, Comparatio*', *AJAH* 3, 1-26.

GRUEN, E. S. 1998
'Rome and the Myth of Alexander', in *Ancient History in a Modern University 1.* E. A. Judge & T. Hillard (eds.), Macquarie, 178-91.

GURVAL, R. 1990
Actium and Augustus: The Politics and Emotions of Civil War, Ann Arbor.

HADAS, M. 1942
Complete Works of Tacitus. Edited with an introduction (Modern Library 222), New York.

HALPERN AMARUS, B. 1988
'Portraits of Biblical Women in Josephus' Antiquities', *JJS* 34, 143-70.

HANNESTAD, N. 1988
Roman Art and Imperial Policy, Aarhus.

HANSEN, W. F. 1988
'Folklore', in *Civilizations of the Ancient Mediterranean: Greece and Rome*, M. Grant & R. Kitzinger (eds.), vol. 2, New York, 1121-30.

HANSEN W. F. (ED.) 2017
The Book of Greek and Roman Folktales, Legends and Myths, Princeton.

HAVELOCK, E. A. 1963
Preface to Plato, Cambridge, MA.

HAVELOCK, E. A. 1978
The Greek Concept of Justice, Cambridge, MA.

HEAD, I. 2004
'Mark as a Roman Document from the Year 69: Testing Martin Hengel's Thesis', *JRH* 28, 240-59.

HENGEL, M. 1985
Studies in the Gospel of Mark, Philadelphia.

HENIGE, D. 1982
Oral Historiography, London.

HENRICHS, A. 1968
'Vespasian's Visit to Alexandria', *ZPE* 3, 51-80.

HERZOG, R. 1931
Die Wunderheilungen von Epidauros: ein Beitrag zur Geschichte der Medizin und der Religion, Leipzig.

HESLIN, P. 2007
'Augustus, Domitian and the So-Called Horologium Augusti', *JRS* 97, 1-20.

HONIGMAN, S. 2013
'Iulius Alexander, Tiberius', in *The Encyclopedia of Ancient History*, R. S. Bagnall, K. Brodersen, C. B. Champion, A. Erskine, & S. R. Huebner (eds.), London, 3547-48.

HORSFALL, N. 2003
The Culture of the Roman Plebs, London.

IMRIE, A. 2018
The Antonine Constitution: An Edict for the Caracallan Empire, Leiden.

INCIGNERI, B.J. 2003
The Gospel to the Romans: The Setting and Rhetoric of Mark's Gospel (BIS 65), Leiden.

ISAGER, J. 1976
'Vespasiano e Augusto', in *Studia Romana in honorem P. Krarup septuagenarii*, K. Ascani (ed.), Odense, 64-71.

JÖRDENS, A. 2013
'Aretalogies', in *Shifting Social Imaginaries in the Hellenistic Period: Narrations, Practices and Images*, E. Stavrianopoulou (ed.), Leiden, 143-76.

KATEB, G. 2002
'Ideology and Storytelling', *Social Research* 69.2, 321-57.

KIENAST, D. 1969
'Augustus und Alexander', *Gymnasium* 76, 430-56.

KLOPPENBORG, J. S. 2005
'*Evocatio Deorum* and the Date of Mark', *JBL* 124, 419-50.

KOSTER, W. J. W. 1960
Scholia in Aristophanem. Pars IV. fasc. I, Amsterdam.

KÜHNEN, A. 2005
Die imitatio Alexandri als politisches Instrument römischer Feldherren und Kaiser in der Zeit von der ausgehenden Republik bis zum Ende des dritten Jahrhunderts n.Chr., Duisburg.

LEVICK, B. 1999
Vespasian, London.

LIPKA, M. 2009
Roman Gods: A Conceptual Approach (Religions of the Greco-Roman World, 167), Leiden.

LUKE, T. 2010
'A Healing Touch for Empire: Vespasian's Wonders in Domitianic Rome', *G&R* 57, 77-106.

LURAGHI, N. (ED.) 2001
The Historian's Craft in the Age of Herodotus, Oxford.

LURAGHI, N. 2001A
'Local Knowledge in Herodotus' *Histories*', in Luraghi 2001, 138-60.

MALLOCH, S. 2001
'Gaius' Bridge at Baiae and Alexander-*Imitatio*', *CQ* 51, 206-17.

MCKENZIE, J., S. GIBSON, & A. T. REYES 2004
'Reconstructing the Serapeum in Alexandria from the Archaeological Evidence', *JRS* 94, 73-121.

MERKELBACH, R. 1960
'Alexander im Serapeum', *Archiv für Papyrusforschungen* 17, 108-9.

MILLER, J. F. 2009
Augustus, Apollo, and the Poets, Cambridge & New York.

MOEHRING, H. R. 1957
Novelistic Elements in the Writings of Flavius Josephus, Ph.D. Dissertation, University of Chicago.

MOURNET, T. C. 2005
Oral Tradition and Literary Dependency: Variability and Stability in the Synoptic Tradition and Q, Tübingen.

MURRAY, O. 1987
'Herodotus and Oral History', in *Achaemenid History, ii. The Great Sources*, H. Sancisi-Weerdenburg & A. Kuhrt (eds.), Leiden, 93-115; repr. in Luraghi 2001, 16-44.

NIEHOFF, M. R. 1996
'Two Examples of Josephus' Narrative Technique in his "Rewritten Bible"', *Journal for the Study of Judaism in the Persian, Hellenistic, and Roman Period* 27, 31-45.

OGDEN, D. 2009
'Alexander, Scipio and Octavian: Serpent-siring in Macedon and Rome', *Syllecta Classica* 20, 31-52.

PADCKER, J. E. 2003
'*Plurima et amplissima opera*: Parsing Flavian Rome', in *Flavian Rome: Culture, Image, Text*, A. A. J. Boyle & W. J. Dominik (eds.), Leiden, 167-98.

PAPAIOANNOU, S. 2005
Epic Succession and Dissention. Ovid, Metamorphoses 13.623-14.582, and the Reinvention of the Aeneid, Berlin.

PAPAIOANNOU, S. 2018
'Omens and Miracles: Interpreting Miraculous Narratives in Roman Historiography', in *Recognizing Miracles in Antiquity and Beyond*, M. Gerolemou (ed.) (Trends in Classics, Supplementary volumes, 53), Berlin, 85-110.

PFEIFFER, S. 2008
'The God Serapis, his Cult and the Beginnings of the Ruler Cult in Ptolemaic Egypt', in *Ptolemy II Philadel-*

phus and his World, P. McKechnie & P. Guillame (eds.) (Mnemosyne Supplements, 300), Leiden & Boston 387-408.

POWER, T. 2014
'Suetonius' Tacitus', *JRS* 104, 205-25.

PURCELL, N. 2003
'Becoming Historical: The Roman Case', in *Myth, History and Culture in Republican Rome*, D. Braund & C. Gill (eds), Exeter, 12-40.

RAUH, S. H. 2018
'Cato at Utica: The Emergence of a Roman Suicide Tradition', *AJP* 139, 59-91.

RENBERG, G. 2017
Where Dreams May Come: Incubation Sanctuaries in the Greco-Roman World, 2 vols. (Religions in the Graeco-Roman World, 184), Leiden & Boston.

RIETHMÜLLER, J. W. 2005
Asklepios: Heiligtümer und Kulte, 2 vols (Studien zu Antiken Heiligtümern), Heidelberg.

ROLFE, J. C. 1914
Suetonius, Lives of the Caesars. Edited with an English Translation, 2 vols. (Loeb Classical Library), London & New York.

ROSEN, R. 1987
Old Comedy and the Iambographic Tradition, Atlanta.

ROSEN, R. 2007
Making Mockery. The Poetics of Ancient Satire, New York & Oxford.

ROSKAM, H. N. 2004
The Purpose of the Gospel of Mark in Its Historical and Social Context (NovTSup, 114), Leiden, 81-94.

ROSSO, E. 2009
'Le thème de la Res publica restituta dans le monnayage de Vespasien: pérennité du "modèle augustéen" entre citations, réinterprétations et dévoiements', in *Res publica restituta. Le pouvoir et ses représentations à Rome sous le principat d'Auguste*, F. Hurlet & B. Mineo (eds.), Rennes, 209-44.

SCOBIE, A. 1979
'Storytellers, Storytelling, and the Novel in Graeco-Roman Antiquity', *RhM* 122, 229-59.

SHRIMPTON, G. 1997
History and Memory in Ancient Greece, Montreal.

SPENCER, D. 2002
The Roman Alexander. Reading a Cultural Myth, Exeter.

STADTER, P. 1995
'Anecdotes and the Thematic Structure of Plutarchean Biography', in *Estudios sobre Plutarco: Aspectos Formales, Actas del IV Simposio Espanol sobre Plutarco, Salamanca, 26 a 28 de mayo de 1994*, I. A. Fernandez Delgado & F. Pordomingo Pardo (eds.), Madrid, 291-303.

STOK, F. 1992
'La rivincita di Esculapio', in *Ovidius παρωδήσας*, G. Brugnoli & F. Stok (eds.), Pisa, 135-80.

SVENBRO, J. 1976
La parole et le marbre. Aux origines de la poétique grecque, Lund.

TAYLOR, N. H. 1996
'Palestinian Christianity and the Caligula Crisis, Part 2: The Markan Eschatological Discourse', *JSNT* 62, 13-41.

TEMPEST, K. 2013
'An Ethos of Sincerity: Echoes of the *De Republica* in Cicero's *Pro Marcello*', *G&R* 60, 262-80.

THOMAS, R. 2001
'Herodotus' *Histories* and the Floating Gap', in Luraghi 2001, 198-210.

TIMPE, D. 1988
'Mündlichkeit und Schriftlichkeit als Basis der frührömischen Überlieferung', in *Vergangenheit in mündlicher Überlieferung*, J. von Ungern-Sternberg & H. Reinau (eds.), Leipzig, 266-88.

TUCK, S. 2016
'Imperial Image-making', in *A Companion to the Flavian Age of Imperial Rome*, A. Zissos (ed.), Malden, MA, 109-28.

TURNER, E. G. 1954
'Tiberius Iulius Alexander', *JRS* 44, 54-64.

VANSINA, J. 1985
Oral Tradition as History, Madison.

VON UNGERN-STERNBERG, J. 1988
'Überlegungen zur frühen römischen Überlieferung im Lichte der Oral-Tradition-Forschung', in *Vergangenheit in mündlicher Überlieferung*, J. von Ungern-Sternberg & H. Reinau (eds.), Leipzig, 237-65.

VON UNGERN-STERNBERG, J. 2011
'The Tradition on Early Rome and Oral History', in *Greek and Roman Historiography. Oxford Readings in Classical Studies*, J. Marincola (ed.), Oxford & New York.

WARDLE, D. 2012
'Suetonius on Vespasianus Religiosus in AD 69-70', *Hermes* 140, 184-201.

WARDLE, D. 2014
Suetonius: Life of Augustus, Oxford.

WEIPPERT, O. 1972
Alexander-Imitatio und römische Politik in republikanischer Zeit, Augsburg.

WELCH, K. & H. MITCHELL 2013
'Revisiting the Roman Alexander', *Antichthon* 47, 80-100.

WICKKISER, B. L. 2008
Asclepios, Medicine and the Politics of Healing in Fifth-Century Greece. Between Craft and Cult, Baltimore.

WILD, R. 1981
Water in the Cultic Worship of Isis and Serapis, Boston.

WINKLER-HORAČEK, L. 2010
'Parthersieg und *cista mystica*. 'Tradition' und 'Reduktion' in Münzbildern unter Vespasian und Titus: Zwei Fallbeispiele', in *Tradition und Erneuerung: 304 Mediale Strategien in der Zeit der Flavier* (Beiträge zur Altertumskunde, 285), N. Kramer & C. Reitz (eds.), Berlin & New York, 457-81.

WINN, A. 2008
The Purpose of Mark's Gospel: An Early Christian Response to Roman Imperial Propaganda, Tübingen.

WISEMAN, T. P. 1989
'Roman Legend and Oral Tradition', *JRS* 79, 129-37 [reprinted in Wiseman, T.P 1994 *Historiography and Imagination: Eight Essays on Roman Culture*, Exeter, 23-36].

WISEMAN, T. P. 2004
The Myths of Rome, Exeter.

ZANKER, P. 1988
The Power of Images in the Age of Augustus (trans. A. Shapiro), Ann Arbor.

ZEICHMANN, C. B. 2017
'The Date of Mark's Gospel apart from the Temple and Rumors of War: The Taxation Episode (12:13-17) as Evidence', *The Catholic Biblical Quarterly* 79.3, 422-37.

ZIMMERMANN, M. 2003
'Der Kaiser als Nil. Zur Kontinuität und Diskontinuität von Repräsentation im frühen Prinzipat', in *Propaganda – Selbstdarstellung – Repräsentation im römischen Kaiserreich des 1. Jhs. n. Chr.* (Historia Einzelschriften, 164), in G. Weber & M. Zimmermann (eds.), Stuttgart, 317-48.

Looking for Traces of Orality in Some Byzantine Illustrated Manuscripts

Nicolette S. Trahoulia

Abstract

This paper briefly explores the different ways in which oral performance may be manifested in a selection of Byzantine illustrated manuscripts. While orality has been examined in the context of Byzantine literary studies, few scholars have taken into account visual material. Nevertheless, it can be argued that the visual material is crucial to a reconstruction of the mixed oral/textual culture of Byzantium. The types of illustrated manuscripts examined here include secular romance, lectionaries, gospel books, collections of sermons, florilegia, and psalters. These manuscripts employ various modes of illustration that suggest a complex interface of the oral, textual, and visual.

Byzantine culture has been classified as a "residually oral" culture, one in which texts and orality intersected in interesting ways.[1] Thus in the Byzantine context, orality can be broadly defined to include recitation from memory as well as reading aloud. Unlike in the West, Guglielmo Cavallo has asserted that silent reading, even in private, was rare in Byzantium – an activity confined to intellectual circles.[2] Herbert Hunger has presented evidence suggesting that reading aloud, whether in public or private, continued into the 14th century.[3] Moreover, Emmanuel Bourbouhakis has more recently asserted that the "better part of the texts which have come down to us…were composed for some form of recital".[4] We

Fig. 1. Frontispiece, *Alexander Romance*, Venice, Istituto Ellenico Codex Gr. 5, Folio 1 recto (Photo taken from Trahoulia 1997)

1 Mullett 1990, 160; Ong 1984, 1-12. For a general discussion of orality and textuality in Byzantium with bibliography, see Messis & Papaioannou 2021, 241-72.

2 Cavallo 2001, 845-55.

3 Hunger 1989, 126. Cavallo 2002, 424-44; Mullett 1990, 159-60.

4 Bourbouhakis 2010, 175.

know that oral performances of various kinds took place in the *theatra* of emperors, empresses, and others.[5] I am interested in how illustrated books may have been used in oral contexts, and how the illustrations can be understood to reflect an oral environment.

One manuscript for which I have reconstructed an oral setting is the Venice edition of the Greek *Alexander Romance*, housed in the Hellenic Institute (Codex Gr. 5).[6] The 14th century manuscript was probably made for the Trapezuntine emperor Alexios III (1349-90), pictured in the manuscript's frontispiece (Fig. 1). In the dedicatory inscription accompanying the emperor's portrait, he addresses Alexander: "O brave emperor Alexander, most excellent of all crowned men and ruler of all the world, having contemplated your great labors and [deeds], and your all-triumphant kingship, I had the desire…" Although the page is torn and the inscription ends abruptly, we can speculate that the emperor's desire, or *πόθος*, was to possess a book containing Alexander's great triumphs and adventures, to which he alludes in the surviving inscription. Evidence suggests that the emperor's portrait originally faced an image of Alexander, now missing, so that the rulers may have been shown as if engaged in dialogue.[7]

Fig. 2. Alexander visiting the sacred cyprus trees, *Alexander Romance*, Venice, Istituto Ellenico Codex Gr. 5, Folio 140 recto (Photo taken from Trahoulia 1997)

I believe the nature of the manuscript's text – secular romance meant to be performed in some manner before an audience – dictated its mode of illustration.[8] The miniatures tend to combine more than one moment in the narrative within a single frame (Fig. 2). While red rubrics accompany the miniatures, they are not always sufficient to understand the often complex and narratively dense images. Presumably, additional information would

5 Ibid., 180-81.

6 Xyngopoulos 1966; Trahoulia 1997; for a detailed discussion of how oral performance may have played a crucial role in the functioning of this manuscript, see Trahoulia 2010, 145-65.

7 The emperor folio has been rebound as a recto, but was originally a verso as is indicated by the wide inner margin with Turkish inscription; on the other folios, the wider margin is the outer one and the Turkish inscription is written on the outer margin. In the original arrangement, this folio would have formed a bifolio with the recto image of Alexander in the familiar diptych arrangement of frontispiece portraits. Confirmation of this is found in the Turkish inscription accompanying the surviving frontispiece. This inscription labels the emperor as Alexander's grandfather, presumably because when the Turkish was written there were two imperial images, Alexander and the emperor. See Trahoulia 1997, 39; Gallagher 1979, 180-85.

8 For references to itinerant poet performers in Trebizond, see the Trapezuntine horoscope of 1336: Lambros 1916, 40, 42, 44, 45, 46.

Fig. 3. Alexios Apokaukos, Works of Hippocrates, Paris, Bibliothèque Nationale de France, codex Gr. 2144, Folio 11 recto (Photo: Paris, Bibliothèque Nationale de France)

be available to the viewer who either has read the text or listens to the narrative while looking at the pictures. Indeed, listening to an oral performance of the story would activate the rather dynamic illustrations, which have an almost cinematic quality. The codex is large enough that, if the book were displayed on a book stand, the mostly full page illustrations would be legible to a group gathered for a performance.[9] In a 14th century edition of the works of Hippocrates made for Alexios Apokaukos (Paris, Bibliothèque Nationale, codex Gr. 2144), we see the grand duke seated with the book of Hippocrates's works on a lectern before him (Fig. 3).[10] A figure (who may double as a personification of medicine) stands by the lectern with her hand on the book, possibly to turn the pages while the book is read aloud. Thus the Trapezuntine emperor, together with his court, could derive pleasure from Codex Gr. 5's illustrations while listening to the narrative read or recited.[11] The latter would seem optimal since the text describing a particular episode and the illustration containing that episode are not always on the same or facing folios. This proposed flexibility in the manner of using the book is precisely the kind of interface between orality and literacy that we find in residually oral societies.

One could rightfully say that the Venice manuscript is a special case. It is the only extensively illustrated copy of the *Alexander Romance* to have survived from Byzantium, and other Byzantine romances do not exist in illustrated codices. So while the romance genre may have been part of an oral storytelling tradition, other illustrated editions of this type of text do not survive. Thus we must look to other types of performed texts to see how their illustrations can embody this interface of oral, textual, and visual.

The most obvious place to start is with liturgical manuscripts designed for oral delivery of the text. Like the Alexander manuscript, these books can be quite large. One example is an 11th century lectionary in the Morgan Library in New York (New York, The Pierpont Morgan Library MS. M. 639) which measures roughly 33 by 25 cm, about the same size as the Alexander manuscript.[12] Its text is written in a careful hand with historiated initials and key phrases written in larger text, which would facilitate reading aloud. On one folio we see the Evangelist John dic-

9 The codex measures 32 by 24 cm. For a discussion of lavish illustrated manuscripts in the Medieval West as intended for display rather than private reading, see Camille 1989, 117.

10 Evans 2004, 26-27 no. 2.

11 Trahoulia 2010, 148-49.

12 Vikan 1973, no. 28.

Fig. 4. Anastasis and John dictating to Prochoros, Lectionary, New York, The Pierpont Morgan Library MS. M. 639, Folio 1 recto (Photo: New York, The Pierpont Morgan Library)

Fig. 5. Nativity, Homilies of Gregory of Nazianzus, Firenze, Biblioteca Medicea Laurenziana, Ms. Pluteus 7.32, Folio 63 recto (Photo: Firenze, Biblioteca Medicea Laurenziana, by permission of MiBAC; any further reproduction by any means is prohibited)

tating his Gospel to his disciple Prochoros, a common type of author portrait for John (Fig. 4). The Anastasis appears next to this image. The text below is the beginning of John's Gospel and, although it does not refer to the Anastasis, it was usually read by the priest before the congregation on Easter Sunday. It can be said that the image of the Anastasis serves as an appropriate visual cue for the oral context in which the text was read.[13]

Also used during the liturgy were collections of sermons. It is interesting that the sermons of Gregory of Nazianzus that are arranged for liturgical use, the so-called liturgical editions, are the editions that are most commonly illustrated. The Byzantines called these liturgical books the "read words".[14] On folio 63r of an 11th century edition of Gregory's sermons in Florence (Florence Biblioteca Medicea Laurenziana, Pluteus 7.32), Gregory of Nazianzus is shown preaching at the beginning of his oration on the birth of Christ (Fig. 5).[15] He stands facing a group on the other side of the text column, an apt way to depict his act of speaking the words on the page. Above this is the visualization of the event. The fact that it is the liturgical editions that most often contain illustrations may be an indication of the important role the Byzantines assigned to images in books intended to be used in an oral/performative context. John Lowden has shown that liturgical books of all types, whether intended to be

13 Dolezal 1996, 55.

14 Brubaker 1999, 13.

15 Galavaris 1969.

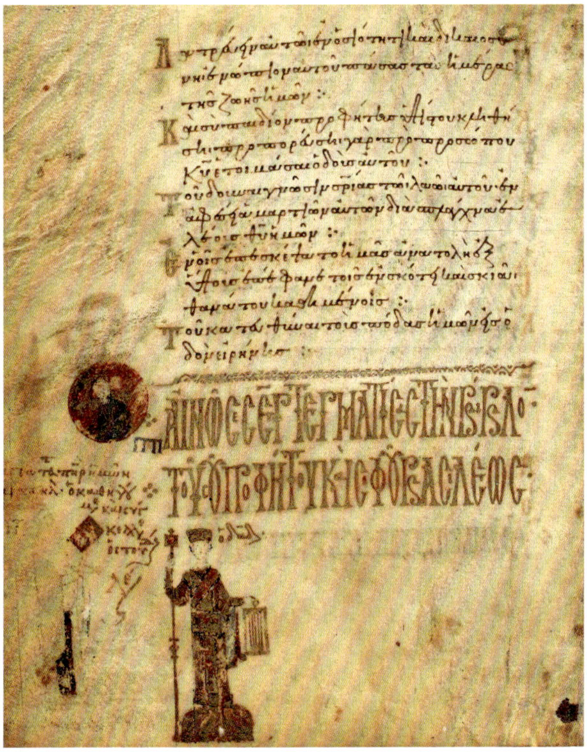

Fig. 6. The Abbot Michael and David, Theodore Psalter, London, British Library Add. 19352, Folio 207 verso (Photo: London, British Library, © The British Library Board)

read or simply displayed during the liturgy, represent the bulk of illustrated manuscripts that have come down to us.[16] Indeed, one could say that the intricate relationship of the spoken word to images is demonstrated by the importance attributed by Byzantine rhetoric to visually evocative literary devices on the part of the orator in order to elicit vivid mental images in his listeners.[17]

Illustrated psalters also bear examining in relation to orality, whether intended for liturgical or private use. The daily recitation of the psalms from memory played a major part in monastic life and could also form part of the daily rituals of lay spirituality. Jeffrey Anderson has noted that in the 9th century Chludov Psalter (Moscow, State Historical Museum MS. D.29), David, Moses, and other figures are depicted next to psalm titles that name them as the speaker. Whereas in the Barberini and Theodore psalters (Rome, Vatican Library Barb. Gr. 372 and London, British Library Add. 19352), both 11th century, saints appear in the margins at the beginning of psalms whose titles or opening lines include words like "prayer", "instruction", "cry out", or "call out".[18] As both Anderson and Charles Barber have pointed out, these saints are shown to speak the words of the psalms, without being the author, and thus demonstrate that the oral performance of the text continues into the present and is indeed a function of the book.[19] On folio 207v, the Abbot of the Stoudios monastery in Constantinople, for whom the book was made, appears beside David (Fig. 6). The inscription above him reads: "Our most holy father Michael, the abbot and synkellos, the Stoudite says:" And to the right we see his prayer in bold gold letters. "Savior, I praise you at the end of the book of your prophet and wise king."[20] Thus while David is shown as author of the psalms and holds the harp to indicate this, Michael is shown as the one who speaks in the present, performing the book.[21]

Overall, in Byzantine manuscripts figures are more frequently pictured orally performing their text as opposed to seated at a desk writing. Those most often shown writing are the Evangelists who, rather than composing a text independently, record that which is divinely inspired. One of the earliest manuscripts to depict authors as performative is the 6th century Rossano Gospels (Rossano, Museo Diocesano di arte sacra Codex 1) in which Old Testament prophets hold scrolls inscribed with their prophetic words, while pointing in a gesture of speech to

16 Lowden 1990, 263-80.

17 James 2003, 61-62.

18 Anderson 2004, 38; for the electronic facsimile see Barber & Lowden 2000.

19 Anderson 2004, 38; Barber 2007, 83-99.

20 Barber 2007, 88-89.

21 *Ibid.*, 92-93.

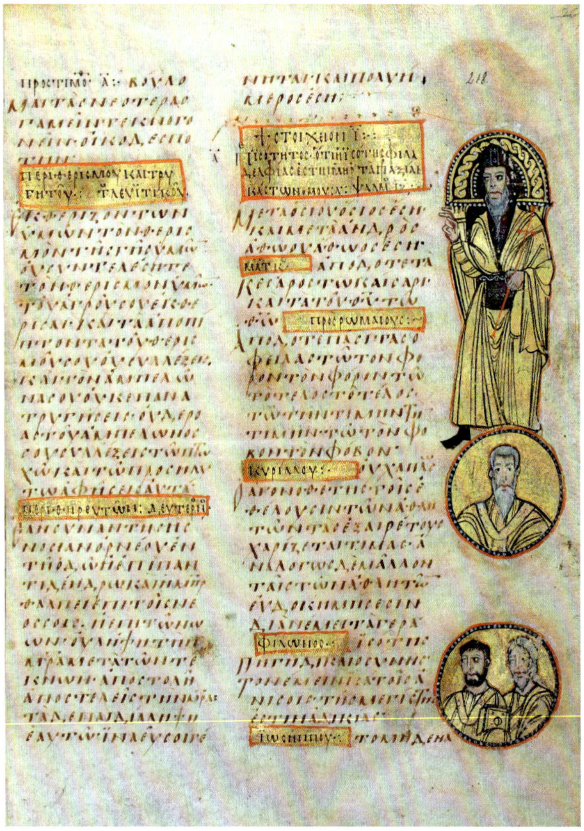

Fig. 7. John of Damascus, *Sacra Parallela*, Paris, Bibliothèque Nationale de France, Par. Gr. 923, Folio 208 recto (Photo: Paris, Bibliothèque Nationale de France)

Fig. 8. Nikephoros Botaneiates and the monk Savas, Homilies of John Chrysostom, Paris, Bibliothèque Nationale de France, Coislin 79, Folio 2bis recto (Photo: Paris, Bibliothèque Nationale de France)

the New Testament scenes above that correspond to their prophecies.[22] In the 9th century *Sacra Parallela* (Paris, Bibliothèque Nationale, Par. Gr. 923), a florilegium of Biblical and patristic texts, figures, such as John of Damascus, are pictured in the margins pointing to their texts, again with a characteristic gesture of speech (Fig. 7).[23] Only rarely are authors in this manuscript depicted in the act of writing.

In certain cases, the complex exegetical nature of a manuscript's illustrations suggests the oral dimension may have been crucial to the functioning of the book. For example, in the famous Paris edition of the complete (rather than liturgical) sermons of Gregory of Nazianzus (Paris, Bibliothèque Nationale gr. 510), quite complex illustrations are accompanied by brief inscriptions and sometimes do not have rubrics at all.[24] The connection between the illustrations and Gregory's sermons is often difficult to make out. One must ask what the process of using the book would have involved. In this particular case we know this manuscript was a gift from the patriarch Photios to the Byzantine emperor Basil I. Leslie Brubaker has demonstrated that the illustrations express ideas particular to Photios's orations.[25] Was it the case, then,

22 Cavallo et al. 1992.
23 Weitzmann 1979.
24 Brubaker 1999.
25 *Ibid.* 1999, 201-38.

that Photios was on hand to explain the miniatures to the emperor? He was, after all, the tutor to Basil's sons. In the Paris edition of the Homilies of John Chrysostom (Paris, Bibliothèque Nationale Coislin 79) we see the emperor Nikephoros Botaneiates enthroned, while a monk identified as Savas reads to him from a book on a lectern and holds a candle to illuminate the page (Fig. 8).[26] His reading of the text could presumably be accompanied by commentary and explanation. It is also possible that exegetical illustrations, like those in the Paris Gregory, would serve as a mnemonic device to trigger the memory of orations heard.

In conclusion, Byzantine illustrated manuscripts must have offered their users a multi-layered experience, an experience that could involve speaking, listening, and looking. In liturgical manuscripts, illustrations often signal the oral embellishment or context of a particular text. Even in manuscripts without a liturgical function, complex exegetical illustrations may have been intended to be legible within an oral environment. Finally, books containing entertaining narratives, which could have been read aloud or recited, seem to have employed the most lively of illustrations, meant to compliment the oral component with an equally rich visual component.

Nicolette S. Trahoulia
Deree – The American College of Greece
trahoulia@acg.edu

Bibliography

ANDERSON, J. C. 2004
'The State of the Walters' Marginal Psalter and Its Implications for Art History', *Journal of the Walters Art Museum* 62, 35-44.

BARBER, C. 2007
'In the Presence of the Text: A Note on Writing, Speaking and Performing in the Theodore Psalter', in *Art and Text in Byzantine Culture*, Liz James (ed.), Cambridge, 83-99.

BARBER, C. & J. LOWDEN (EDS) 2000
Theodore Psalter: Electronic Facsimile, Champaign, Illinois.

BOURBOUHAKIS, E. 2010
'Rhetoric and Performance', in *The Byzantine World*, Paul Stephenson (ed.), London and New York, 175-87.

BRUBAKER, L. 1999
Vision and Meaning in Ninth-Century Byzantium: Image as Exegesis in the Homilies of Gregory Nazianzus, Cambridge.

CAMILLE, M. 1989
'Visual signs of the sacred page: books in the Bible moralisé', *Word and Image* 5, 111-29.

CAVALLO, G. 2001
'Le rossignol et l'hirondelle: Lire et écrire à Byzance, en Occident', *Annales: Histoire et Sciences Sociales* 4, 849-61.

CAVALLO, G. 2002
'Tracce per una storia della lettura à Bisanzio', *ByzZeit* 95, 424-44.

CAVALLO, G., J. GRIBOMONT, & W. C. LOERKE 1992
Codex purpureus Rossanensis (Rossano, Museo dell'Arcivescovado) 2 vols., Rome & Graz.

DOLEZAL, M.-L. 1996
'Illuminating the liturgical word: text and image in a decorated lectionary (Mount Athos, Dionysiou Monastery, cod. 587)', *Word and Image* 12, 23-60.

26 Evans & Wixom 1997, 207-9 no. 143.

EVANS, H.C. (ED.) 2004
Byzantium: Faith and Power (1261-1557), New Haven.

EVANS, H. C. & W. D. WIXOM (EDS.) 1997
The Glory of Byzantium: Art and Culture of the Middle Byzantine Era, AD 843-1261, New York.

GALAVARIS, G. 1969
The Illustrations of the Liturgical Homilies of Gregory Nazianzenus, Princeton.

GALLAGHER, L. 1979
'The Alexander Romance in the Hellenic Institute at Venice. Some notes on the initial miniature', *Thesaurismata* 16, 170-205.

HUNGER, H. 1989
Schreiben und Lesen in Byzanz. Die byzantinische Buchkultur, Munich.

JAMES, L. 2003
'Art and Lies: Text, image and imagination in the medieval world', in *Icon and Word: The Power of Images in Byzantium. Studies Presented to Robin Cormack,* A. Eastmond & L. James (eds.), London, 59-71.

LAMBROS, S. 1916
'Τραπεζουντιακὸν ὡροσκόπιον τοῦ ἔτους 1336', *Νέος Ἑλληνομνήμων* 13, 33-50.

LOWDEN, J. 1990
'Luxury and Liturgy: the Function of Books', in *Church and People in Byzantium*, R. Morris (ed.), Birmingham, 263-80.

MESSIS, C. & S. PAPAIOANNOU 2021
'Orality and Textuality', in *The Oxford Handbook of Byzantine Literature,* S. Papaioannou (ed.), New York, 241-72.

MULLETT, M. 1990
'Writing in early mediaeval Byzantium', in *The Uses of Literacy in Early Mediaeval Europe*, R. McKitterick (ed.), Cambridge, 156-85.

MULLETT, M. 2003
'Rhetoric, theory, and the imperative of performance: Byzantium and now', in *Rhetoric in Byzantium*, E.M. Jeffreys (ed.), Aldershot, 151-70.

ONG, W. J. 1984
'Orality, Literacy, and Medieval Textualization,' *New Literary History* 16, 1-12.

TRAHOULIA, N. S. 1997
The Greek Alexander Romance: Venice Hellenic Institute Codex Gr. 5, Athens.

TRAHOULIA, N. S. 2010
'The Venice *Alexander Romance*: pictorial narrative and the art of telling stories', in *History as Literature in Byzantium,* R. Macrides (ed.), Farnham, 145-65.

VIKAN, G. (ED.) 1973
Greek Manuscripts from American Collections: An Exhibition in Honor of Kurt Weitzmann, Princeton.

WEITZMANN, K. 1979
The Miniatures of the Sacra Parallela, Parisinus graecus 923, Princeton.

XYNGOPOULOS, A. 1966
Les Miniatures du Roman d'Alexandre le Grand dan le Codex de l'Institut Hellénique de Venise, Athens.

Post-classical 'Oraliture': Thoughts on the dramatic scholia as regiebuch

Andrew Walker White

Abstract

It is commonly assumed that drama's primary mode of transmission – and reception – since ancient times has been as text, as 'literature.' But as Dionysius Thrax makes clear, the goal of grammar school education was instruction in the correct mode of dramatic stage performance – καθ'ὑπόκρισιν – not the sedentary analysis of text. This presentation will challenge traditional distinctions between orality and literature and argue for a third path that analyzes Byzantine-era dramatic manuscripts as a means of enhancing and preserving the oral tradition, not objectifying or killing it. Borrowing key concepts from the field of media convergence theory, I will argue that manuscripts were media which, throughout the pre-Gutenberg era, assumed the presence of a live interpreter.

Part 1 – Introduction

One of the most controversial topics in the historiography of Greek theater has been the question of continuity – of whether, and how, the arts of theater and dramatic literature survived in the Greek-speaking world from the Hellenistic through the Early Modern periods. For generations, theatre historians have relied on the cliché narrative sequence of Athens–Rome–Rome's Fall–Dark Ages–Middle Ages–Renaissance. And given the dearth of dramatic output beyond the Early Empire, we have focused almost exclusively on drama in the earlier Graeco-Roman world. In this we have been guided by our colleagues in Classics, who have dutifully produced critically edited texts of the plays, in myriad translations.

Early in the debate, Constantine Sathas[1] and Venetia Cottas[2] posited some form of what we might call absolute continuity – Sathas arguing for continuity in dramatic literature, based on selected evidence in Byzantine-era texts (with a quick leap to Venetian-occupied Crete in the mid-15th century), and Cottas introducing evidence for what she argued was a continuous, living tradition of dance and performances of sacred drama into the early 20th century. Sathas's encyclopedic knowledge of Byzantine texts and Cottas's field work remain valuable early attempts to establish some foundation for further discussion.

Although neither of them was able to support their theories in a proper, diachronic manner,[3] they both made important points that have yet to be reconciled with our generally negative historiography of the Greek performing arts. The questions they raised, and which have yet to receive solid answers, remain:

1 Sathas 1878.

2 Cottas 1931.

3 See especially LaPiana 1936, Sticca 1974, Puchner 2002, and more recently Puchner 2017, 52-111.

if there is no live theatre, why do Greeks continue to use theatrical terms, in both sacred and secular contexts, without any significant gap in usage? If there is no drama, why is the term "drama" applied to genres of performance, and literature, that have no literal theatrical component? Why does the term *theatron* come to signify a circle of elite performers, without any of the trappings of traditional "theater" – i.e., costumes, sets, masks – as we understand it?[4]

Perhaps we have become too distracted by what *disappears*, and should focus more on what *appears* in place of the performance and literary genres we privilege in our own time. Post-Classical and Byzantine Greek culture thrived in its diversity, its inherent orality and performativity, with little need to preserve older traditions that no longer suited the times. Margaret Mullett, looking over the vast repertoire of liturgical and secular performance styles associated with the Byzantine Empire, once discreetly remarked that "we might settle for this society without a drama."[5]". Walter Puchner, one of continuity theory's greatest skeptics, has pointed towards a 'performative turn' in Byzantine studies, one that abandons the search for organized theatre and instead focuses on the rich variety of performing arts that defined the Eastern Empire.[6]

Assumptions that the Greek performing arts never changed, however well intended, are clearly absurd; we don't assume, for example, that composer Wolfgang Amadeus Mozart's career peaked when he was only 10 years old. We aren't shocked to discover that a charming forest sapling has grown into a mature tree. Change in nature is not only natural, it is a necessity: as with nature, so with the artist; and as with the Greek artist, so with the culture of the Greek performing arts.

What I am proposing here is a new mode of theater historiography, focusing on a more abstract conceptual and performative approach to the subject of continuity. Beginning with its roots in Antiquity, we may find it more rewarding to study the ways in which Greek theater and drama developed well beyond the confines of the physical stage and its visual apparatus. For this reason, I propose a performance-based re-examination of the grammatical scholia, for they give us a wealth of information about how dramatic literature was transmitted, taught, and performed, long after the public stages were history.[7]

With regard to the scholia, the irony is that Classicists have been in possession of this precious artifact from the history of Greek theater – or, to be more precise, of post-theatrical dramatic performance – but have left it little explored. With two notable exceptions, the scholia remain uncollated and as a result poorly understood and largely ignored. Always segregated from the plays they were designed to accompany, they have only occasionally been edited.[8]

4 The so-called Byzantine *theatron* has generated great interest in recent years, with an increased emphasis on their role as performance venues for the literate elite. The art of composing and performing letters, for example, seems rooted in the drama-adjacent art of the character monologue, as enshrined in the rhetorical exercise of *ēthopoieia*. See for example Gaul 2020, and for a more complete history see Grünbart 2012.

5 Mullett 2003, 152.

6 Puchner 2017, 53.

7 On Greek education, Marrou remains foundational; For a recent analysis, see Markopoulos 2008. Both Marrou and Markopoulos emphasize the continuity in Greek pedagogical practice from Hellenistic times onward, and this continuity in pedagogy, and in the transmission of Classical dramatic poetry for performance purposes, is fundamental to what I am proposing here. For education in Late Antiquity, see also Cribiore 2001.

8 There has been a renewed interest in critically-edited collections of dramatic *scholia* in recent years—and there is also, finally, movement on their translation as well. For the present essay I will work from Cavarzeran 2016. For a thorough analysis of the history of Euripidean *scholia* in particular, see Mastronarde 2017. Mastronarde, more recently, has spearheaded the first collection of *scholia* to Euripides' *Orestes*, complete with English translation (Mastronarde 2023), which includes text and translations of *scholia* for this tragedy, collated from 136 unique manuscripts.

The scholia served several functions, but here I will demonstrate one vital function that has been neglected, i.e., as documentary evidence of continuity in pre-modern orality, and continuity in a uniquely Greek form of vivid, emotive performativity.

I come from the world of the theater, with many years devoted to solo and ensemble performances onstage; and as academics are beginning to appreciate, performances are a vitally important form of documentation, in our inquiries into pre-Gutenberg orality. I believe firmly that modern performing artists and performance theorists are uniquely positioned to aid classical and Byzantine philologists in the interpretation of the vast body of extant poetic scholia, which were crafted with live performance, not book-learning, as their focus.

The evidence for grammar school education as a school of performance, dramatic poetry included, as I hope to demonstrate, is clear. Yet the scholia as a whole have rarely been analyzed from a performance perspective; they were composed for schools that had living eloquence as their primary aim.[9] The popular, public stages of the post-Classical era, such as they were, were a part of the grammarian's project.

In his analysis of drama, Aristotle makes clear that by his day, for true aficionados, the stage had already become irrelevant. Spectacle, *ὄψις*, was rejected as the least artistic element of tragedy (*ἀτεχνότατος*), and he makes clear that the desired effects of tragedy – pity and fear – should result from the story itself, from recitation, without any reference to the stage whatsoever.[10] This implies that the scroll – one of history's early hand-held recording devices – had already eclipsed the physical theatre as a medium of entertainment by Alexander the Great's time.

It is with the advent of the scroll – and, in Roman times, the codex – as recording devices that the concept of drama as a creature of the page, to be 'played' in private spaces, becomes a commonplace. The dramatic scholia, used in Greek grammar schools throughout the known world, were composed for this specific context. And although there is always the risk for over-interpretation, in the spirit of scientific inquiry I believe that the dramatic scholia, once presented together with their plays as an organic whole, as originally intended, and translated, will enable future generations of scholars to come to their own conclusions about the performance styles cultivated in the grammar school classroom – styles that directly impacted students' later study of rhetorical composition.

Now, a word about orality and performativity: these terms are deliberately generic, because I do not mean to imply that the post-classical uses of drama, particularly in Greek grammar schools, were 'theatrical' in the traditional sense of that word. Although the scholia make passing references to original and/or Hellenistic stage practices,[11] their primary function seems to be to guide solo oral interpretation, and aural reception, of dramatic language. Such interpretation requires no set, no costumes, no actors whatsoever; all it requires is a live interpreter, and the imagination of the audience. The drama has survived, but as a purely aural phenomenon.

9 See for example Mitchell 2015. The awareness of the *scholia*'s function as performance prompts has been around since at least the late nineteenth century. William G. Rutherford pointed out that grammar "laid stress upon the proper management of the voice to convey emotion and sentiment in all their phases, upon the ordering of words as producing a music accommodated to the things with which they dealt." (Rutherford 1905, 15). His failure to grasp the value of training in emotional display, however, is regrettable. Mitchell has argued that in many cases the *scholia* purported to offer a faithful interpretation of the poetry as originally performed. The implication is that grammar students were taught how to perform poetry like the professionals, from an early age.

10 Arist. *Poet.* 1540b16-20 & 1453b1-13.

11 On uses of *scholia* as a record of contemporary/past performance see Falkner 2002.

Grammar constituted a young student's first encounter with the living, oral tradition of Attic Greek, which was designed to inform their oral mode of self-presentation throughout their academic and professional careers, sacred or secular. The ultimate goal of Greek education was the production of highly skilled, eloquent public intellectuals who could speak spontaneously and persuasively in any context. Vivid self-presentation and persuasive advocacy, whatever the topic or issue at hand, was essential; and grammar school performances of ancient drama were a critical first step along that path. Whether written separately (as was done in the Hellenistic era) or included in the margins of the play-text itself (as became common by the Middle Byzantine period), the scholia were designed to inform the live interpretation of the poetry; text and scholia formed an organic whole and remained inseparable for over two millennia.

There are two chief obstacles to appreciating the scholia's value as performance prompts, first being the attention we choose to pay to text-based phenomena like vocabulary and syntax; especially by the Medieval period, Ancient Greek would have been a distinct dialect, whose jargon the average student would have to acquire in much the same way one might acquire fluency in Elizabethan or Middle English. The emphasis placed in our source texts on these matters, as in Dionysius Thrax's Grammar, appeal all the more to modern, Western scholars for whom Ancient Greek is an utterly foreign, and purely textual language.

The second and more subtle obstacle is the modern assumption that the whole package was intended for silent, passive reception. Treating a Byzantine manuscript page as if it were a modern printed text, requiring no vocalization whatsoever, has become so common as to be unremarked and unnoticed. What we are only now beginning to appreciate is the inherent orality of these manuscripts; we have not fully thought through the implications of the diacritical marks, which functioned as a kind of musical notation, indicating rises and falls in pitch, different kinds of pauses of varying lengths[12] and so on – and these markings are only one small part of the matrix of instructions for delivery that the scholia contain.[13]

To explain what I mean by the orality of a manuscript, we need to consider two key concepts from Media Convergence Theory. The first, and most important, is that in order for new media to attain legitimacy they must always contain the protocols of the 'old' media they are replacing. As the theorist Lisa Gitelman points out, "new media are less points of epistemic rupture than they are socially embedded sites for the ongoing negotiation of meaning as such."[14] ". In our case, it means that in order for pre-Gutenberg manuscripts to have validity as vehicles of

12 The question of the inherent orality of Greek manuscripts, and of the need to transcribe all of their notation (or *punctus*) as written, has occupied scholars for some time. For the debate itself see Reinsch 2012 and, Bydén 2012. Bydén cites the printed works of Shakespeare to argue against Reinsch's proposal, not realizing that the same debate was not only engaged but decided in favor of preserving the original *punctus* of both the Quarto and Folio editions of the Bard's work, thanks in large part to the work of artist/scholars like Harley Granville Barker. In fact, it is common for Shakespearian companies to promote their work as coming directly from the original texts (Granville-Barker 1946). Reinsch's efforts have borne fruit in works like Emmanuel Bourbouhakis' critical edition and translation of a funeral oration delivered by Archbishop Eustathios of Thessalonike (Bourbouhakis 2017). He details the complexity of Eustathios' manuscript, argues for the aurality of the text, and goes into some detail about Eustathios' composition methods as well (Bourbouhakis 2017, 125-158).

13 Although Gerard Genette characterizes pre-modern texts as generally "devoid of any formula of presentation," he acknowledges that some form of "oral transcription" may qualify as paratextual, as he defines it (see Genette 1997, 3). I hope to demonstrate here that the Greek-speaking world was one in which Genette's "oral transcription" was actually written down in fine detail. Paratextual discourse was, if anything, a defining element in nearly every Byzantine-era utterance one can find.

14 Gitelman 2006, 6.

meaning, they had to encode the spoken word upon which they were based. This leads to Aristophanes of Byzantium's array of diacritical marks, which assume the presence of a live interpreter, or 'player,' in order for the manuscript to produce any meaningful utterance.

Another key distinction Gitelman makes is between media of transmission and media of representation – in her case, the difference between a telegraph machine (which transmits Morse Code which, in turn, requires interpretation) and a phonograph (which directly conveys sound).[15] For the modern reader, a manuscript page is a medium of representation: we see the image of a speech-act that requires no intermediary. For the Greeks of the pre-Gutenberg era, however, the manuscript page was a medium of transmission. Oral delivery of the text, reading it aloud, was the prevailing assumption behind a manuscript's production and circulation.

Taken as a whole, grammatical scholia played an essential role in preserving and transmitting the most sophisticated oral tradition in the known world for over 2,000 years. Attic Greek remained very much a living language well into the modern era – how enduring was Attic Greek? I summon as my chief witness Panayotis Soutsos, who continually edited his theatrical masterpiece, The Wanderer (*Ο Οδοιπόρος*) in order to make it more classical, and who advocated for Attic Greek as the official language of Modern Greece.[16]

The question for us is: if Attic Greek endured, in some form, as a living language, how did the Greeks transmit this oral tradition down through the ages? What possessed Soutsos to revise a modern drama, in order to align it with an ancient tongue? The answer lies not in our critically-edited poetic ur-texts, but in the dramatic scholia. The life of Attic Greek, the direct link between antiquity and modernity, between Athenian democracy and the modern Greek state, lies quite literally in the margins of our classical texts.

As for the function of these margins, it might help to contemplate the visual code of signification involved. In the Orthodox tradition, sacred images often feature marginal, implicitly narrative panels encircling a central subject – panels depicting the life of the saints, miracles associated with them while alive, miracles associated with their death, even events surrounding the translation of the saint's relics to their current resting place. Everything you need to know – subject, narrative and metanarrative – is presented in the same visual field, and the mind, like the eye, shifts naturally from one level of discourse to the other.[17]

The purpose of these images, moreover, is to bring you into contact with an eternal, living presence; icons are not inert *objets d'art*, they are windows into eternity, calls to prayer and reflection on what will never die. To me, it is hardly coincidental that both kinds of visual fields were constructed by Greek intellectuals; each field is multivalent, and each is in the service of a living tradition. I propose that we see the marginal scholia as they were originally intended: as vital links in the preservation of a living language.

Part 2 – Back To School

To appreciate the proper function of dramatic scholia, we need to go back to school days – Attic Greek grammar school days, to be precise. Dionysius the Thracian, whose work still largely defines our understanding of a child's primary education, states clearly:

15 Gitelman 2006, 4.

16 See for example Puchner 2017, 279-280.

17 See Ševčenko, 1992. Ševčenko identifies the possible roots of these montage-icons in Late Antiquity, although early imperial *sarcophagi* are perhaps the earliest such exemplars.

Γραμματική ἐστιν ἐμπειρία τῶν παρὰ ποιηταῖς τε καὶ συγγραφεῦσιν ὡς ἐπὶ τὸ πολὺ λεγομένων. (Dion. Thrax Tech. Gram. 1 629b2-3)[18]

Emphasis here on the word *ἐμπειρία*, "experience" – young students had the opportunity to experience, directly and actively, the writers who by consensus were the best exemplars of Classical Greek. The grammarian's task, then, was to use these manuscripts as a means of cultivating each student's talents at *ἀνάγνωσις*, a term which is usually rendered as "reading" but which, in the context of an oral culture and especially in the case of dramatic poetry, would be best rendered as "recitation". Dionysius makes clear that the basic contours of poetic performances were laid out specifically from the very beginning:

Ἀνάγνωσίς ἐστι ποιημάτων ἢ συγγραμμάτων ἀδιάπτωτος προφορά. Ἀναγνωστέον δὲ καθ' ὑπόκρισιν, κατὰ προσῳδίαν, κατὰ διαστολήν. (Dion. Thrax Tech. Gram 2 629b13-14).[19]

Note what Dionysius regards as the three keys to recitation: *ὑποκρισία*, *προσῳδία*, and *διαστολή*. Because of its complex connotations, translating *hypokrisia* as "stage technique" is provisional at best; but however we render it, the association of this word with live public performance should remain.

Dionysius makes clear that he wants the entire class to have a visceral, direct feeling for the "glories" (the *ἀρετάς*) of poets like Euripides. This cannot be done just through rote memorization, let alone reading in silence; you must experience Attic Greek as a carefully inflected, musical tongue. For Dionysius, it is through oral transmission that you gain a direct insight into the poet's craft.

Drama, of course, was just one part of a broader program of education; grammar school was, in effect, a master class in a wide range of performing arts, tragedy prominent among them. Each genre, however, demanded its own inflection, its own mode of delivery:

... τὴν μὲν τραγῳδίαν ἡρωϊκῶς ἀναγνῶμεν, τὴν δὲ κωμῳδίαν βιωτικῶς, τὰ δὲ ἐλεγεῖα λιγυρῶς, τὸ δὲ ἔπος εὐτόνως, τὴν δὲ λυρικὴν ποίησιν ἐμμελῶς, τοὺς δὲ οἴκτους ὑφειμένως και γοερῶς. (Dion. Thrax Tech. Gram 2 629b16-21)[20]

Now there may be a moment of cognitive dissonance here, because it is young children who received – in effect – the kind of training we associate today with royal academies and national schools of dramatic arts for adults. But as Raffaele Cribiori points out, children were regarded as miniature adults requiring little more than training in the adult arts.[21] Indeed, when we consider today's intensive training in music or classical ballet from childhood onward, we must acknowledge that an emphasis on rigorous exercises in material associated with mature, adult art forms is taken for granted in other fields, to this very day. This is why these 'little eyases' as Shakespeare might call them[22] were given, in effect, training in mature modes of delivery.

What Dionysius cannot tell you, in the context of a brief grammar manual, are the specifics of how the experience of poetic *ἀρετή* is constructed. A review of the Euripidean scholia indicates that grammar school work on tragedy went well beyond cultivating a generic "voice" for tragedy. There is attention

18 "Grammar is the experience of what is spoken by the poets and prose writers" (This and all following translations are my own). Γραμματική ἐστιν ἐμπειρία τῶν παρὰ ποιηταῖς τε καὶ συγγραφεῦσιν ὡς ἐπὶ τὸ πολὺ λεγομένων (Dion.Thrax *Tech. Gram.* 1 629b2-3).

19 "Recitation is the unwavering delivery of poetry or prose. But one must read with attention to *Stage Technique*, Inflection and Enunciation."

20 "[W]e recite Tragedy heroically, Comedy normally, Elegy sweetly, Epic vigorously, Lyric Poetry tastefully, & Lamentation in a subdued and plaintive tone."

21 Cribiore 2001, 178.

22 See Shakespeare, *Hamlet* 2.2, and the discussion of child actors who have become so popular that they draw audiences away from adult acting companies.

to minute detail, which goes well beyond that outer tragic shell.

Consider the prologue to Euripides's tragedy *Hippolytus*, about the son of King Theseus who worships Artemis and avoids marriage like the plague. As the tragedy opens, we find Aphrodite onstage, ready to give us her side of the story:

> *Πολλὴ μὲν ἐν βροτοῖσι κοὐκ ἀνώνυμος*
> *θεὰ κέκλημαι Κύπρις οὐρανοῦ τ' ἔσω:*
> *ὅσοι τε Πόντου τερμόνων τ' Ἀτλαντικῶν*
> *ναίουσιν εἴσω, φῶς ὁρῶντες ἡλίου,*
> *τοὺς μὲν σέβοντας τἀμὰ πρεσβεύω κράτη,*
> *σφάλλω δ' ὅσοι φρονοῦσιν εἰς ἡμᾶς μέγα.* (Eur. Hipp. 1-6)[23]

Our first note on that first word – it is Aphrodite who strangely refers to herself in a feminine, singular sense of 'many' – comes in the form of a gloss, one of those seemingly trivial notes on the potential meanings of a word. On the page, they don't look like much. But what if these glosses were not meant for the eye? What if they were for the tongue and, equally importantly, for the ear? Here's what our grammarian has to say about the first word alone:

> *Πολλή: δυνατή, θαυμαστή, μεγίστη· Ὅμηρος· πολλὸς γάρ τις ἔκειτο.* (Hipp. Schol. 1 a1)[24]

Remember that, in the grammar school sequence, students had already learned Homer by heart – the *grammatikos*, their teacher, is simply reminding them what they already know. Another scholion explains why there are so many suggested meanings:

> *ἡ διάνοια ἐμφαντικώτερόν τε καὶ ῥητορικώτερον πέφρασται, ἐκ τοῦ ἐναντίου τὸ ἐναντίον παραλαμβάνουσα.* (Hipp. Schol. 1 b)[25]

A silent reader can study this with ease, and move on; but if we see the scholion as one that directs oral interpretation, the student is expected to deliver this word, with a cluster of implied meanings – meanings, moreover, that can be conveyed, hinted at, through the nuances of oral delivery. To illustrate the principle involved, try this oral exercise from where you sit:

> Say "many" with the meaning of "powerful" foremost in your mind.
> Say "many" with the meaning of "miraculous" foremost in your mind.
> Say "many" with the meaning of "divine" foremost in your mind.

Having mastered these, now try this:

> Say "many" in such a way that all three of those meanings are latent in the way you speak it.

"Many" stands alone here because it can mean many specific, yet complementary things.

What is the intended effect? We have a perfectly simple word, requiring no definition whatsoever; but that simple word, the first word, by design, must carry multiple meanings, and those multiple meanings must be implied through the nuances of speech.

23 *"Many among mortals, and not nameless, I am called goddess Kypris, and by heaven am I decked; Both those of the Pontus and those who dwell inside of Atlas' pillars Seeing the light of the sun I support those who revere my powers, But trip up those who think they are as great as we are."* (My own translation).

24 **"*Many* – *Powerful, Miraculous, the Greatest. [As in] Homer: "for he is spoken of as many."* (Cavarzeran 2016, 93).**

25 *"The effect intended is both more forceful and more fitting for oration (ἐμφατικώτερον τε και ῥητορικώτερον) than choosing one as opposed to the other."* (Cavarzeran 2016, 93).

What the *grammatikos* is doing, from the very start, is preparing both the performer and the listener for the creation of multiple meanings, through the medium of the human voice. It was a vital first step in the training of future rhetors – public intellectuals whose ability to perform their visions of the public good relied on a thorough understanding of the uses of poetic delivery, dramatic language being among the most vitally important.

Perhaps one of the main reasons classicists have yet to appreciate the orality inherent in these dramatic scholia is that in our text-bound, Gutenberg world, the only people trained to memorize and perform dramatic texts in this nuanced manner are actors; and up to now, we have only proven useful as performers in stage productions of Greek drama, which we produce in ignorance of the long tradition of directed, well rehearsed delivery found in the scholia. Classicists and actors alike would benefit from sharing each other's crafts, in order to better appreciate what we might call the "original practices" associated with dramatic performance in the post-Classical Greek speaking world.

But we must dispense with the image of mere rote memorization in this grammar school context, just as actors dispense with it the moment they enter the rehearsal room. Mediocre actors, it is said, are delighted if they can simply remember their lines and avoid bumping into the furniture. For them, words are like ammunition to be spewed out as quickly as possible: who cares where or how they tumble out of the mouth?[26] Great actors, on the other hand, plumb the depths of intonation, musicality, gesture, posture, facial expression, etc., in order to convey meanings well beyond the surface of the text. Actors know instinctively, in ways classicists might not yet appreciate, that it is never enough to simply say a word, and give some passing indication to the audience that you know its lexical, dictionary meaning. You have to open the audience's mind to the life and thought of the character, and use whichever words a character speaks to convey everything that is on the character's mind. It is the difference between a word's lexical meaning and its plural, axial meanings. Even a cursory review of a limited number of scholia, as we have here, indicate that grammar school was geared directly towards the axial, and well away from mere lexical usage.

Although instruction in tragic poetry was clearly prescriptive, and designed to establish an authoritative sense of the language, grammarians taught the meanings behind words, and their multiple potential meanings. It is as if, even as the schoolmaster took the rod into his hands, there was still a glimpse of the Bakhtinian Carnival, a site where even the most common word serves as an axis of multiple meanings, which must be implied at the moment of that word's utterance in order to come fully alive in the mind of the audience.

Another common element among dramatic scholia is the paraphrase. Again, let us pause to consider its uses in the context of dramatic performance, the uses any actor would make of it. Consider these for Hippolytus, lines 1-3:

> *τινὲς δὲ τὸ ἑχῆς οὕτως· πολλὴ μὲν ἐν βροτοῖσι θεὰ κέκλημαι. ποίος βροτῶν; ὅσοι καὶ Πόντου ἔσω ναίουσι τερμόνων τ' Ἀτλαντικῶν.* (Hipp. Schol. 1 c).[27]

> *οὐκ ἀνώνυμος μέν τις, ἀλλὰ πολλὴ οὖσα τὴν φήμην ἐν ἀνθρώποις θεὰ κέκλημαι Κύπρις καὶ παρὰ τοῖς ἐν τῷ οὐρανῷ καὶ παρὰ τοῖς ἐν τῷ Πόντου ζῴοις θεὸς νενόμισμαι.* (Hipp. Schol. 1 d1).[28]

26 For an amusing account of theatrical mediocrity see Green 1993.

27 "But others put it this way, as follows: *Many among mortals, I am called goddess*; which mortals? Those of the Pontus, [and] dwelling within the pillars of Atlas." (Cavarzeran 2016, 93).

28 "Not someone anonymous but, being many, the tradition among men is that '*I am called goddess Kypris*,' and among those in heaven and among those living in the Pontus I am regarded a god." (Cavarzeran 2016, 93).

As paraphrases, both are straightforward and, like the glosses, when seen on the page they don't amount to much. But there is an art to paraphrase because, when delivered orally, its purpose is to demonstrate that you have thoroughly immersed yourself in the character's thoughts and understand the meaning, even without the original language to hand.

Professional actors usually devote at least a portion of their rehearsal time developing paraphrases of their characters' lines. Whether in discussing one's role with the director, or rehearsing a scene by means of paraphrases alone, the ability to use your own words is proof that you know the character's thoughts, and the character's situation, quite well. The ability to convey a character's thoughts freely in your own words, in turn, guarantees you can give the actual dialogue its full value.

Beyond glosses and paraphrases, an even more powerful tool for oral interpretation is the provision of subtext. Consider a first scholion for line 3 – and yes, we are still only on line 3 – concerning Aphrodite's reference to the Black Sea:

> *ὅσοι τε Πόντου: ἐπὶ τὸ μέγιστον ηὔξησε τὸ κατηγόρημα τοῦ νεανίου· εἰ γὰρ ἐκεῖνοι θηριώδεις ὄντες τὴν φύσιν καὶ νόμων καὶ γραφῶν ἄπειροι σέβοθσιν ὅμως τὴν θεόν, τὴν φύσιν δεξάμενοι διδάσκαλον, πόσῳ γε μᾶλλον ὁ ἐν μέσῃ τῇ Ἑλλάδι τραφεὶς καὶ μέγιστον ἐπῖ φιλοσοφίᾳ φρονήσας.* (Hipp. Schol. 3a).[29]

Consider that a mediocre actor would be satisfied to remember the line and say "Pontus" as if it were a stop on the Athens Metro. But we know how fond Euripides is of portraying Pontic Greeks as savages (in Iphigeneia in Tauris for example). Never mind that by the time these dramatic manuscripts were prepared, the Pontus had long since been colonized and civilized; this scholion requires an extra twist to the delivery; the performer has to include, while mentioning the Black Sea, a reference to its legendary, prehistoric barbarity.

Here, again, to understand the function of this note – from where you are sitting right now, consider how you might speak the words "those of the Pontus" in such a way that you remind audiences how primitive these people once were, and yet how pious. Then with the second half of line 3, we get what looks to us like a grade-school geography lesson:

> *τερμόνων τ'Ἀτλαντικῶν: τῶν πρὸς Γαδείρος τόπων· ἔστι γὰρ ὄρος Ἄτλας· οὗτος δὲ ἐστὶν ὁ ἄξων (τοῦ ουρανοῦ)· και Ὅμηρος· ἔχει δέ τε κίονας αὐτός.* (Hipp. Schol. 3e).[30]

The world of myth is aligned with the real world; just as it is important to know the ethnography of specific places, it is important to know the mythological associations with those places as well. The performer will speak of Atlas, but must keep in mind the physical landmark to which Aphrodite refers. Also, given that the Pontus and Atlas's Pillars refer to the ends of the earth, it confirms the universality of Aphrodite's cult – which, again, must be expressed in speech.

The goddess shifts now to talk of her followers; but here the scholia make unexpected demands on the performer:

29 "*[T]hose of the Pontus* …she has just strengthened the biggest accusation against the young man [i.e., Hippolytus]; for even those savages, ignorant by nature of both laws and letters, nevertheless worship the goddess, they are receivers of Nature's teaching, greater in quantity than what you find in mainland Greece and, the greatest in terms of philosophy…" (Cavarzeran 2016, 94).

30 "*And Atlas' Pillars*" – those places by Gibraltar: for Atlas' landmark is there; and this is the axis [of the heavens]. And [as] Homer [says]: "Yet he also holds the pillars." (Cavarzeran 2016, 95).

> *φῶς ὁρῶντες Ἡλίου: πάσαις ταῖς ἀπὸ Ἡλίου ἐγκότως διάκειται Ἀφροδίτη διὰ τὸν ἔλεγχον τῆς μοιχείας Ἄρεως.* (Hipp. Schol. 4).[31]

Now we may be shocked to realize that pre-pubescent grammar school students, were routinely exposed to the topic of sex, let alone sex of the extra-marital variety. But as sixth century rhetor Choricius of Gaza confirms in his Defense of the Mimes, even good Christian schoolboys were whipped if they failed to recount, from their own mouths, the sexual misdeeds of mythology.[32] Aphrodite's antics were required performances, not just required reading.

This being Aphrodite, the goddess has a very specific demand of her followers; a demand that might elicit giggles from your average schoolboy or schoolgirl. Here's the next scholion, in case there is any doubt:

> *τοὺς μὲν σέβοντας: τὸ ἑξῆς τῆς διανοίας· προαποδειχθέντος τοῦ μεγάλην μέ τινα εἶναι καὶ ἐπίσημον παρὰ τοῖς ἀνθρώποις, τοιαύτη τις εἰμὶ τὴν φύσιν ὡς τοὺς μὲν σέβοντας με τιμᾶν, τοὺς δὲ ἀποσειομένους τὴν εἰς ἐμὲ εὐσέβειαν καταβάλλειν.* (Hipp. Schol. 5a).[33]

By *ἐπίσημον*, "sign," it is pretty clear what we're talking about; and not to put too fine a point on it, it is Hippolytus's status as a confirmed bachelor that is the issue here.

I will conclude my analysis here with two scholia for line 6, which concludes the prologue's first sentence. For the verb *σφάλλω*, a verb with several shades of meaning, the scholiast is crystal clear which one to keep in mind, and to realize on the tongue:

> *[σφάλλω] βλάπτω, καταβάλλω, σφάλλεσθαι ποιῶ.* (Hipp. Schol 6a).[34]

The verb *σφάλλω* needs to be interpreted as strongly as possible. The function of this gloss is to direct the speaker to shade the word's delivery in a very specific way. So once again, from where you are sitting, say "I trip up" with the meaning specified above.

The last scholion I will introduce here is a paraphrase which, like the gloss, suggests a deeper meaning:

> *[εἰς ἡμᾶς] ἀντὶ τοῦ καθ'ἡμῶν.* (Hipp. Schol. 6c).[35]

Again, the meaning must be specific, and must be spoken in such a way as to leave no doubt in the audience's mind: Aphrodite is not treating Hippolytus as mere competition, she regards him as an enemy.

So to sum up: through glosses we have been introduced to the concept of a word's axial meanings, but also its often dire and specific meanings. We have been given brief lessons in geography and prehistoric ethnography, paraphrases independent of the tragic language itself, and specific ideas behind just about every line in the prologue's earliest lines. The results, in performance, would be a good bit more nuanced than the rote memorization which is the bane of any student to this day.

31 "*Seeing the light of the sun*" – Aphrodite is disposed grudgingly towards all things of the sun because of the disgrace of her adultery with Ares." (Cavarzeran 2016, 96).

32 Chor. *Apol. Mim.* 36: "How many cases of adultery, do you think, we expect our young men to recite? Helen, who took married the brother of the Greeks' great leader; Klytemnestra, whom the king of the Greeks married, Pasiphae, Helios's daughter, whom Minos carried off for himself, who was seduced by the bull."

33 "*Those who worship*" – her next thought: having already demonstrated my greatness there is a sign as well, by which all may see who I am by nature, so that those who worship me honor me, but others throwing off their reverence cast me away." (Cavarzeran 2016, 96).

34 ["*I trip up*"] – "I cripple, I throw down, I force to be overthrown." (Cavarzeran 2016, 96).

35 "[*Those who think themselves as great] as we are.*" – "[those] who are against us." (Cavarzeran 2016, 97)..

Conclusion

The present paper is, of course, a preliminary report and largely experimental. Nobody, to my knowledge, has attempted an interpretation of the scholia as prompts for live performance. But I hope I have demonstrated the value of explorations like this for all who are serious about the study of pre-modern orality, as well as the history of the performing arts in the Greek-speaking world.

Greek grammarians, from the Hellenistic age through the Byzantine millennium and beyond, would be utterly bewildered by our attitude towards their carefully assembled notes; the scholia were not irrelevant to the drama, they were integral – because they were integral to their performance. Every single Byzantine manuscript assumed memorization, assumed a live interpreter, and not one word's delivery could be left to chance.

Cribiore points out that, throughout their academic careers, students would revisit these classic texts in order to gain a deeper understanding of their worth, and their usefulness.[36] The Byzantine-era manuscripts of Hippolytus were not designed as stage plays, even though it is possible that students might have regaled their families with recitations in the evening, over supper. But they were also of great use in acquainting students with the subtleties of emotion and thought required for any public utterance. There is a straight line to be drawn from a pre-pubescent's first efforts at Aphrodite, capturing the subtlety of her speech, and their final efforts in rhetoric class where they were expected to compose and perform, often extempore, similarly subtle speech-acts. The uses of rhetorical and grammatical training in public life were understood; successful careers in both the sacred and secular spheres were rooted in just the sort of training addressed here.

As I have pointed out in publications elsewhere,[37] we also need to appreciate that the manuscript was a peculiar kind of recording device; the scholia rendered it, in effect, a high-fidelity recording, but only if you played it on the proper equipment, and only if the "equipment" – i.e., the performer – had been properly "tuned". The degree of a manuscript's fidelity was based not on the dramatic text itself, but on a vast matrix of instructions delivered live, directly from grammarian to student.

Today the arduous task of preserving the dramatic oral tradition, that direct link to the orality of our ancestors, has been delegated to that most eccentric cultural figure, the actor. It is our job to memorize and perform, as vividly and as faithfully as possible, the exemplary writings of dramatists past and present.

Today's actors rely on a small phalanx of specialists in rehearsal, including a dramaturg, a dialect coach, a movement coach, a choreographer, a music director, etc., all of whom answer to our platoon leader, the director. The record of this process is known as the *Regiebuch*, the production book. Today's *Regiebucher* of course include technical details – blocking, light cues, etc. – which were deemed irrelevant in Attic Greek grammar schools. What "theatre" there was existed in the imagination of the young audience's fertile mind. But the care with which the language of the drama was curated through these scholia, the specificity with which each word's meaning is delineated, constitutes its own kind of *Regiebuch*. We would do well to explore the scholia further.

Andrew Walker White
George Mason University
awhite58@verizon.net

36 Cribiore 2001, 179.

37 See White 2010.

Bibliography

ARISTOTLE 1995
Poetics, S. Halliwell (trans.), (Loeb Classical Library 199) (2nd ed.) Cambridge MA, 28-141.

BIEN, P. 1972
Kazantzakis and Linguistic Revolution in Greek Literature, Princeton, NJ.

CAVARZERAN, J. 2016
Scholia in Euripidis Hippolytum: edizione critica, introduzione, indici, Berlin.

CHORICIUS OF GAZA 1972
Choricii Gazeii Opera, R. Foerster & E. Richtsteig (eds.), (2nd ed.) (reprint), Stuttgart.

CRIBIORE, R. 2001
Gymnastics of the Mind: Greek Education in Hellenistic and Roman Egypt, Princeton, NJ.

FALKNER, T. 2002
'Scholars versus actors: text and performance in the Greek tragic scholia', in *Greek and Roman Actors: Aspects of an Ancient Profession*, P. Easterling & E. Hall (eds.), Cambridge, 342-61.

GITELMAN, L. 2006
Always Already New: Media, History, and the Data of Culture, Cambridge, MA.

GREEN, M. 1981
The Art of Coarse Acting (Reprint), New York.

MASTRONARDE, D. M. 2017
Preliminary Studies on the Scholia to Euripides (California Classical Studies No. 6), Berkeley, CA.

MITCHELL, J. 2015
'Literary Performance in the Imperial Schoolroom as Historical Reënactment: The Evidence of the Colloquia, Scholia to Canonical Works, and Scholia to the Techne of Dionysius Thrax', *AJP* 136(3), 469-502

PUCHNER, W. 2017
Greek Theatre between Antiquity and Independence, Cambridge.

RUTHERFORD, W. G. 1905
A Chapter in the History of Annotation, being Scholia Aristophanica (vol. III), New York.

UHLIG, M. ET AL. 1965
Dionysii Thracis Ars Grammatica Qualem Examplaria Vetustissima Exhibent Subscriptis Discrepantiis Et Testimoniis Quae in Codicibus Recentioribus Scholiis Erotematis Apud Alios Scriptores Interpretem Armenium Reperiuntur. Grammatici Graeci Recogniti Et Apparatu Critico Instructi (Pars 1, Vol. 1), Hildesheim.

WHITE, A. W. 2010
'Adventures in Recording Technology: The Drama-as-Performance in the Greek East', in *Beyond the Fifth Century: Interactions with Greek Tragedy from the Fourth Century BCE to the Middle Ages*, I. Gildenhard & M. Revermann (eds.), Berlin, 371-96.

Hatzi-Yavrouda of Kos and the Craft of Storytelling

Birgit Olsen

Abstract

Hatzi-Yavrouda lived on Kos in the beginning of the 20th century, and she was one of the collector Iakovos Zarraftis's informants. Her tales are long and complex. By analysing in detail two of the tales, the aim of this paper is to show Hatzi-Yavrouda's skills as a gifted narrator.

On an overall level the paper looks into the composition of the tales, i.e. their structure and the various elements of raw material the narrator used to make her tales longer and more interesting, involving for example incorporation of myths and ballads, inspiration from written sources, and the change of a tale's gender. On a detailed level the paper presents Hatzi-Yavrouda's linguistic and stylistic trademarks and points at her tales' relation to the surrounding reality.

The aim of this paper is to present the female storyteller whose name appeared next to that of Homer in the title of the conference and to demonstrate her skills as a gifted narrator. Hatzi-Yavrouda was active on the island of Kos around the turn of the 20th century. She is an interesting figure both because she is one of the few named storytellers we have from this early period and because her tales are of a very high quality. Unfortunately, however, her stories are not widely known probably, because they were published outside Greece, and the edition is now difficult to get hold of. Hatzi-Yavrouda's tales remained unpublished until 1950, when they were included in the British folktale scholar Richard M. Dawkins's bilingual edition *Forty-five Stories from the Dodakanese.*[1]

Hatzi-Yavrouda's stories were originally collected by Iakovos Zarraftis in his home village of Asfendiou on Kos in the beginning of the 1900s. Zarraftis collected various kinds of folklore material from the Dodecanese on behalf of another British scholar, William H. D. Rouse. Rouse paid for this material in order to use it for linguistic studies, and he never published it himself.[2] In the late 1930s, Rouse passed the material on to Dawkins, who by then had become something of an expert on Greek folktales even though – ironically enough – when he himself collected folktales in the Greek-speaking villages of Asia Minor just before World War I, he was only interested in them as samples of language. The content and context of the tales had so little interest for him that he left it to his friend William R. Halliday to write about the subject matter, as he

1 Dawkins 1950.

2 Zarraftis's manuscripts in the form of exercise books are now to be found in the library of the Faculty of Classics at Cambridge University along with his accompanying letters to Rouse.

informs us with regret in his memoirs.[3] Zarraftis provided Rouse with extensive material of high quality, but unfortunately he subscribed to the tradition of 19th century collectors who give no information about their sources or about the circumstances of recording. Only twice does Zarraftis refer to his informants, and in both cases it is the name of Hatzi-Yavrouda he mentions: once in connection with the tale *Myrmidonia and Pharaonia*, no. 33 in Dawkins's edition, and once in connection with a ballad entitled *I Nerazia*.[4] But this is all the information we have about the actual person Hatzi-Yavrouda: that she probably lived in the village of Asfendiou in Kos, where she was Zarraftis's informant, and that he recorded at least one tale and one song from her and sent these to Rouse in 1905 and 1902 respectively.

So, to paint a picture of her craft we must use her stories. Dawkins ascribes five stories from the collection to her, and on a surface level this body of tales may not seem a large one. But we must consider both that the tales are exceptionally long, and that they are composed of several tale types or elements. For the present paper, I shall analyze two of her tales to reveal her narrative techniques: the first and foremost is no. 33, *Myrmidonia and Pharaonia,* both because it is the tale attributed to her by Zarraftis and because from a narrative perspective it presents some interesting features. The second is no. 36, which I have chosen because I am certain that it is also by Hatzi-Yavrouda and because I think it had a special meaning to her – she gave it her own name: *Yavrouda.*

The gifted narrator

Before proceeding to the analysis of Hatzi-Yavrouda's narrative qualities, I would like to specify the characteristics that characterise a gifted narrator. The first collector of Greek folklore material to give some detailed information on the storytelling community, the occasions for narration, and the narrators is Adamantios Adamantiou, who in 1896 published a study based on his own collection from his teaching days on the island of Tinos.[5] This work is often referred to in studies of the Greek folktale because it is all we have from that period and for many years to come. From Adamantiou's information we may deduct that there was a distinction between those who could tell stories and the more skilled narrators, who he names *παραμυθάδες* and *παραμυθούδες*, (respectively male and female narrators of fairy tales). These skilled narrators had a large repertoire. They could tell "the tales of the forty days",[6] i.e. one for each night of Advent. They also knew long tales: sometimes the telling of a single tale could last several evenings.[7] Furthermore, Adamantiou mentions the ability to cut and paste according to the demand of the situation as a characteristic of the gifted storyteller. One of the narrators he met was capable of either finishing the same tale in one hour or extending it to last for three or four hours.[8] Another narrator expressed this ability in the following way: "As soon as I hear a tale, teacher, I take it and if I find it small, I paste something to it, some branches, to make it big."[9] Later, more systematic and detailed studies into the craft of storytelling – also from other parts of Europe – revealed some of the same characteristics of a skilled narrator.[10]

First of all, it is important to differentiate between bearers of tradition and truly skilled storytellers. Or

---

3 Olsen 2004, 115.

4 Olsen 1997, 30.

5 Adamantiou 1896.

6 *Ibid.*

7 *Ibid.*

8 *Ibid.*

9 *Ibid.*, 288; see also note 1 above.

10 I would especially like to highlight Linda Dégh's works, based on research into storytelling communities of Hungary in the middle of the 20th century: Dégh 1989 and 1995. For the Greek area, see e.g. Kaplanoglou 2002.

as the Danish folktale scholar Bengt Holbek expresses it: "The number of people who specialize in the telling of fairy tales is – and probably always has been – strictly limited ... they are told by specialists."[11] However, the skilled narrator is both bearer of the tradition – and is very conscious about this – and at the same time a creative artist in his or her own right. The gifted storyteller has a repertoire of generally at least 40 stories and often many more.[12] This material has been built up over a lifetime. By combining the basic elements learned from tradition, i.e. themes and especially motifs, the narrator has hundreds of possibilities: the tales can be made longer or shorter, two themes combined into one tale, and so on.

The gifted narrators link their stories to the surrounding community, and this is also where they have their greatest freedom: in the way they connect the magical tales to everyday life, in the details concerning reality. We also need to keep in mind that the narrator, as well as the characters of the tales, are rooted in the social reality of the audience. To summarize Holbek:

> Tellers and audience identify with the hero(in)es of the tales. In the beginning of a tale, the social circumstances of the hero(in)es are similar to those of the audience. In traditional communities, fairy tales provided a means of collective daydreaming. They were escape fantasies in which wrongs were righted and the poor and powerless justly recognized for their true worth, and they kept alive a keen sense of justice and fairness and depicted a true world, i.e. the world as it should be.[13]

The Greek collector Eleftherios Ziazopoulos, who worked in Thessaly, commented that the good narrator would be able to keep his audience "with an open mouth", and when the tale had finished, the audience would comment on it, and afterwards they would make comparisons between the tale's characters and their fellow villagers.[14]

As mentioned, the gifted narrators were both bearers of the tradition and creative artists in their own respect. That also means that they would obtain their material from many sources and not necessarily from the oral tradition. It is evident that they would not refrain from extracting material from written books – even if they were not able to read themselves. They would just get somebody to read aloud to them. When a blind storyteller in Finland was interviewed by a scholar, much to the surprise of the interviewer, he said that he obtained a lot of his material from books at the local library. He simply had the children read the books to him.[15] The Greek folklore scholar Manolis Varvounis also had an informant on Samos who obviously drew on written inspiration, but Varvounis deliberately refrained from publishing any of these tales, limiting himself to what he calls folktales (*λαϊκά παραμύθια*) even though he is aware that his informant – and probably no folk narrator – would make such distinction.[16]

Many narrators did not restrict themselves to folktales but had a wider knowledge and repertoire. In an article about storytelling and storytellers, mainly based on previous studies, Dimitrios Oikonomidis adds that his own fieldwork in Ipiros led him to the conclusion that narrators of folktales often knew many verses of folksongs as well as other forms of oral tradition better than other informants.[17]

Even when it comes to the details, it is important to notice how the gifted narrators add their personal imprint. This may be seen in how they actualise the tales and how they perform them. They may colour the stories with their personal touch: some favour a dramatic style, others pay much more attention to

11 Holbek 1987, 405.
12 Dégh 1989, 168-69.
13 Holbek 1987, 406.
14 Ziazopoulos 1951,349.
15 Herranen 1989, 65.
16 Varvounis 1998, 26.
17 Oikonomidis 1978, 38.

narrative details, and yet others may have a more moralistic approach. The final version of a specific tale is created in the moment of performance, and it is very much a result of an interaction between audience and storyteller. The sex of the narrator, the occasion, and the composition of the audience, among other things, are decisive factors in the creation of a folktale.

The narration on a structural level

Some of the elements, mentioned above as characterizing the gifted narrator, we are able to analyze in Hatzi-Yavrouda's tales. Others we must leave out because we lack the required information. This applies especially to the circumstances surrounding the actual performance. We know nothing about how, when, or for whom she performed. But by analyzing the texts of her tales,[18] we may deduce a lot of information about her skills as a storyteller.

The tale *Myrmidonia and Pharaonia*

The first tale to look at in detail is Dawkins's no. 33, *Myrmidonia and Pharaonia:* it is composed of two main parts. The first functions as a very long background story to the second, which is the main fairy tale. The first part is a reworking of the myth about Erysichthon found in Callimachos and Ovid. Erysichthon had committed an offence against the goddess Demeter by cutting down her sacred grove and is punished with a burning hunger that cannot be satiatsfied, and in Ovid's version he ends up eating his own flesh.

The fact that this ancient myth occurs in a modern traditional folktale has puzzled scholars since Dawkins made his edition of *Forty-five Stories.* Dawkins himself, albeit with some reluctance, suggested that this is an example of a real survival from antiquity pre-dating the two classical authors.[19] Later philologists have been divided in embracing and rejecting this hypothesis. Personally, I side with the latter. I believe that Hatzi-Yavrouda must have been influenced by the Ovidian version of the myth. One of the reasons why Dawkins did not believe in the *Metamorphoses* as the inspiration was that "Ovid was of the West and not the East".[20] But as first Edward J. Kenney,[21] and later other scholars, pointed out, Ovid was also of the East from the fourteenth century when Planudis made a prose translation of the *Metamorphoses.* Later translations, followed, and the *Metamorphoses* were read in the Greek secondary school.[22] So, it is possible that the stories were known in one form or the other and found their way into the oral tradition or at least to Hatzi-Yavrouda.

If we compare Ovid's way of treating the myth with Hatzi-Yavrouda's, we will find that there are many similarities in the overall structure as well as in the details.[23] On a structural level: the girl hidden in the tree; the personification of Hunger; the prince sees his punishment in a dream and wakes up extremely hungry, the end by auto-cannibalism. If we look at details: the tree trembles and a moaning is heard; a stream of blood springs from the bark; but the most striking example is the detailed description of Hunger:

18 I must emphasize that we by necessity deal with *texts.*

19 Dawkins 1950, 347-49.

20 *Ibid.*, 348.

21 Kenney 1963, 57.

22 Michalopoulos 2015, 299-301; Zioga 2015, 29-35.

23 See also Fehling 1972, 187.

Ovid	Hatzi-Yavrouda
she had 1) coarse hair and hollow eyes. Her 2) face was pale, her 3) lips were gray with dirt, her throat was lined with scabby sores. She had rough skin, through which 4) one could make out her inner organs. Dry bones protruded from her hollow groin. She had no stomach, just a place for one.... She was so thin her joints appeared enlarged, 5) with puffed up knee caps and huge ankle bones, swollen beyond the normal size	her 1) hair in its filth hung disorderly on her scabby head;... her 3) lips were white and black, covered with slaver... her eyebrows pimples and pustules ... her 2) mug was as yellow as a sulphur candle ... her body was skin and bone; her ribs you could count... 4) inside her you could see her entrails; the bones of her hips in broken array stuck out like dugs; where the joints should fit they were coming apart... 5) the cap-bones seemed to stand out

However, there are also differences. In Hatzi-Yavrouda's version of this myth, the point of departure and thus the reason for the cutting down of the grove has become a rather complicated love story. Demeter has disappeared, but an allusion to her is kept in the name of the young beautiful girl who is in the centre of the story. She is called Dimitroula, a diminutive of Dimitra/Demeter in Modern Greek. In this way the pagan goddess has been eliminated, and the story fits better in a Christian society. It is characteristic for Hatzi-Yavrouda that in general her characters are good Christians, saying their prayers and performing the rituals, and this is one of the means she uses to connect to the surrounding community.

Another major difference in comparison with Ovid is the addition of a detailed description of the food the hungry prince is consuming.

> His shepherds every day used to bring milk, yoghurt, butter, lambs, fresh cheese and other cheeses of all sorts; his butchers every day from his herds of oxen slaughtered the best and sent to him; the poulterers sent fowls, the hunters game of various kinds, the fishermen fish in abundance, the fruiterers fruits of all sorts.

This is obviously an abundance of all the best things a Greek rural mind could imagine, and thus it is once more a way to embed the tale in the audience's world.

As said, the reworking of the myth serves as an introduction to the fairy tale proper. But it is longer than this. The second part of the story is the tale of the children of the hunger-struck prince, and perhaps Hatzi-Yavrouda's way of reworking Ovid's story about Erystichthon's daughter Mestra and her brother, but it is very different from this and much closer to a normal fairy tale. It is built up of many different and well known motifs, and it starts with one that is common in Greek tales. A young prince mocks an old lady who in her turn curses him with the longing for the Thrice-Noble or The Beauty of the World, and therefore he sets out in pursuit of her. This is a classical masculine seeker-type tale,[24] but Hatzi-Yavrouda turns the tale into a feminine one and thus changes the course of events. The heroine, Tartana, is cursed with the longing for the king of Pharaonia, Eptakipis. However, since this is a feminine tale, and women in traditional society had limited mobility, she does not pursue him on her own but sends her brother to do the negotiations. This gets him into capital danger after an Arab, the villain of the tale, questions Tartana's virtue, and a wager is made between the brother and the king. This motif resembles both the Greek ballad *Mavrianos and his Sister* and – perhaps more interestingly – the Ninth Story of the Second Day of Boccaccio's *Decameron*.[25] Like our tale, both these stories are about a man putting a wager on a woman's chastity and losing. In our story, as in that of Zinevra in the *Decameron*, this happens by fraud. Tartana is seen naked in the

24 I.e. with a male protagonist, like the tale-types Propp based his system of functions on, Propp 1968^2.

25 Boccaccio/Rigg 1921 [027].

bath by an informer, and Zinevra is spied upon in her bedchamber, and in both cases a description of some physical characteristics becomes the final proof of her lack of chastity:

Boccaccio	**Hatzi-Yavrouda**
but .... a mole, which she had under the left breast, and which was fringed with a few fair hairs that shone like gold	And so she saw all the marks of her body, two long golden hairs bound round her waist and two others on the mole below her breast

Like the husband of Zinevra, Tartana's brother believes the false accusations. He places her in a chest, and she is thrown into the sea. In the Decameron story, it is the villain who hides himself in a chest in order to spy on Zinevra. Tartana drifts ashore in Pharaonia, and after this point she becomes a persecuted heroine[26] and must fend for herself. She discloses the deceit, saves her brother's life, and gets the king in the end. Both in the ballad of *Mavrianos* and in our story the brother narrowly escapes only by his sister's inventiveness, and in all three cases everything is dramatically disclosed at a public assembly.

I have found this tale in no other version. Neither the combination of the two parts, nor the female adaptation of the second part, is traditional goods. Here we have a combination of a pagan myth with a reshaped tale with biblical allusions: Sussanna in the bath, Moses in the basket, and even the title may be a hint. The names of Myrmidonia and Pharaonia might just mean some strange countries far away in a magical world, but at the same time they allude to the place of Achilles and the land of the Pharaohs. It is also worth mentioning that in the "pagan" part of the tale, words like *έλληνας* (Hellene – the ancient word for a Greek) and *ελληνόπουλα* (diminutive of Hellene) are used in the meaning of a tall lads or "heros of old", as Dawkins so poetically translated it.[27]

The tale *Yavrouda*

The second tale to analyze is no. 36, *Yavrouda*. This tale is a version of the *oikototype* *433B, and unlike *Myrmidonia and Pharaonia* it exists in several other versions: in total, 14 Greek variants are listed in the Tale Type Catalogue.[28] It is therefore possible to compare Hatzi-Yavrouda's version to the others.[29] For the present I shall focus on the narrative aspects of Hatzi-Yavrouda's version.

In short, it is about a girl who kills her own mother in order to make her father marry her embroidery teacher. For this ill deed she is persecuted and must deliver, nurse, marry, and redeem a snake who then turns into a young prince. Afterwards, she is once more persecuted and through misunderstandings thrown out of the castle pregnant. She forms an attachment to another man who is half dead, enchanted by fairies. Her first husband finds her in her new home and claims her back. She is left to choose between her two husbands and chooses the first, the snake.

Hatzi-Yavrouda's version is much longer than any of the others. Right from the start, she makes the opening scene very elaborate. The audience is, without noticing it, brought from a reality-like narrative into the world of the fairy tale by the means of a detailed description of the various embroideries the teacher is working on:

26 Holbek 1987, 433.

27 Dawkins 1950, 336.

28 Angelopoulou & Brouskou 1999, 787-99.

29 See e.g., Olsen 2019.

Πλούμιζε πουκάμισα, πεσκίρια, διψομάντηλα, μαχραμάδες, μαντήλια, σπαρβέρια με τες πόρτες τος, σεντόνια, μαξελάρια, και λοής λοής περλοές πουχικές.	She used to embroider shifts, napkins, face-cloths, veils, kercheifs, bed-tents and their doors, sheets, pillowcases, and all sorts of cloth furnishings.

Embroideries on linen were widely used on the islands and probably surrounded the audience while they were listening to the tale. As Zarraftis informs us in one of his letters to Rouse, the village of Asfendiou, where he collected the tale, had a tradition of fine embroidery.[30] None of the other versions of the tale has this kind of transitory introduction, and I find that it is a good example of Hatzi-Yavrouda's ability as a narrator that she connects at a stroke to the everyday life of the surrounding community *and* makes the smooth transition from reality to fiction. Another lovely example of Hatzi-Yavrouda's using elements from the surrounding reality is the detailed description of Yavrouda's wedding dress and the girls dressing her,[31] and we find this description almost *verbertim* in a ballad, also collected by Zarraftis in Asfendiou:[32]

Tale	**Ballad**
Ηστολίζαν την οι καλές κοπελούδες, εκείνο το ασημένο πουκάμισο, πού'το σαν αφρός κι ολόασπρο σαν ασήμι γυαλλιστερόν, εκείνο το εσθλίκι με τα πολλά χρουσά κουμπιά 'ς το στήθος της, εκείνο το στητό γελέκι το ολόχρουσον, εκείνο το ολοκέντητον ξέρουχον, εκείνο το ολοχλάππωτον τσακκί από καθάριο χρουσάφι 'ς το κεφάλι της, εκείνες οι μαλαματένιες καμπάνες με τα διαμάντια 'ς τ' αυτιά της	Καλές μου κόρες ... Στολίσετε την νύφφημ μας βάρτε της τα ασπόρουχα ... Και τ' ασημοπουκάμισον ... Βάρτε της το εσλίκι της το στενομανικάτον, και το χρυσό γελέκι της ... Βάρτε της το ξέρουχον ... Καρφώσετέ της το τσακκί με τες κομποβολόνες ... Περάστέ της εις τ' αυτιά ... Καμπάνες τες ολόχρουσες με άστρα διαμαντένια

As we know, Hatzi-Yavrouda was his informant for at least one ballad. Whether or not she also gave Zarraftis this one, we cannot say, but she must have known it as part of the village tradition – as must her audience. There are also other examples in the tale of how Hatzi-Yavrouda incorporates elements from the poetic tradition. But more impressively, when the young heroine, Yavrouda, is expelled from the palace and left alone in the mountains, she complains in the form of a lament. The narrator uses the word *μοιρολόγι* (the Greek word for lament) and incorporates the poetic features of the traditional 15-syllable metre and rhyme in the prose narrative:

Αχ, αχ η κακομοίρα 'γω, και η κακογραμμένη!
Εδέ που εκατάντησα να είμαι ξωρισμένη!
Και τώρα εδώ τι να γενώ η κακομοιριασμένη,
Που το ταφιόν της μάνας μου μακρυά 'πο μένα μένει
Αχ, αχ, μανούλα μου γλυκιά, γιατί με καταδιώκει
Ακόμα η κατάρα σου; Πώς τέλος να μη δώκει;
Από τη γένναν μ' έσωσες, από το βύζασμά του,
Κι από το τρισχειρότερον, το νυφφοφάωμά του!
Και πάνω που με έκαμες βασιλοπούλαγ κιόλα,
Μα, μάνα μου συχχώρα μου, αχ, βούθα μου και πάλιν

30 Letter of October 20, 1905. See also Olsen 1999b.

31 Translation: "And the good serving girls were decking the beautiful Yavrouda. There was the silver shift which was like foam and all white as the most shining silver; there was the jacket with its many golden buttons on the breast; there was the beautiful waistcoat all of gold; there was the outer dress all covered with embroidery; there was the cap worked with pure gold on her head; there were golden bells with diamonds hanging from her ears." (Dawkins 1950, 375)

32 Published by Oikonimidis in *Λαογραφία*, Zarraftis 1951, 316-18.

Και μη με αφήκεις να χαθώ 'ς της ερημιάς την ζάλην!
Ναι, βούθα μου! Τί θα γενώ, που είμαι γκαστρωμένη,
Και ίσωστε 'ς τες ώρες μου, η κακομοιριασμένη;
Θηιέ μηιαλοδύναμε, που βοηθάς του κόσμου
Βοήθιαν τώρα 'δω κ' εμέν της κακομοίρας δος μου![33]

The rhyme is not a common feature of the lament or of Greek folksongs in general,[34] but it is commonly used in the written vernacular poetic stories, the so-called *rimades,* often circulating as chapbooks. So, this may be yet another indication of Hatzi-Yavrouda's contact with written literature.[35] I mentioned above that I believe that Hatzi-Yavrouda had a special relationship with this story first of all, because she gave the female heroine her own name. But she also treats her differently from the other narrators of this tale type.[36] I shall give a few examples: firstly, she frees the poor girl entirely from guilt in connection with the killing of her mother. The girl acts as the passive tool for the teacher's ambitions, and neither does the mother blame her. However, in the other versions of the tale the girl plays a much more active role and therefore is also blamed or even cursed by her mother. Secondly, in the central testing scene at the wedding night, where Yavrouda has dressed herself in seven shifts, she responds rather firmly to the snake's demanding her to take off her clothes: "*Γντύσου σκύλλα ... Γντύσου σκυλλί, συ πρώτα*" – "Take off your clothes, you bitch – take off yours first, hound." This exchange of words is repeated seven times, and in the end the snake has no more skins to shed, but Yavrouda still has one more shift, and thus he must admit that she has won. She has redeemed him, and he has become a handsome young man. Apart from making her heroine much more assertive than the other versions', Hatzi-Yavrouda also narrates this scene in a very dramatic and vivid manner. One really feels the power struggle taking place here. My last argument for Hatzi-Yavrouda's special treatment of the heroine Yavrouda is the ending. In almost all versions the heroine dies because she cannot choose between her two husbands; Hatzi-Yavrouda does not let her heroine die but lets her return to the first husband and live happily ever after.

The narration on a linguistic level

Until now my focus has been on Hatzi-Yavrouda's narrative skills on a structural level. In the following I shall look at to her skills on a linguistic level. Some of the linguistic features place her narrative close to the poetic tradition and some show her capacity to connect to the surrounding community.[37]

33 Translation: "Alas, alas! Ill-fated me for whom an evil doom was written! Lo, to this I am come that I am banished. And now here what will become of me and my evil destiny? For my mother's tomb lies far away. Alas, alas, my sweet mother! Why does your curse still hunt me down? Why can it not have an end? When he was born you saved me; and when I had to give him suck; and from that which was thrice as bad, the time when he would devour his bride. And now after making me a princess too you have brought me here to make all these lamentations. But, my mother, pardon me; O, help me once again and do not leave me to perish bewildered in the desert. Nay, help. What will happen to me, who am with child? And perhaps my time has come, to me with my evil fate. O God Almighty, who dost help the world, give me too help, me of evil destiny!".

34 Even though there are exceptions, see Beaton 1980, 148 and Alexiou 2002², 148-49.

35 Hatzi-Yavrouda may e.g., have known the *rimada*-version of the Apollonios story, see Olsen 2002, 62-64.

36 Olsen 2019, 119-23.

37 For convenience, references to the text in question will follow immediately in parenthesis with tale number and page – no. 33 for *Myrmidonia and Pharaonia* and no. 36 for *Yavrouda.*

Poetic features

Firstly, the narrator uses an abundance of compounds – and not just the more common ones beginning with *όλο-*, *κατά-*, *χρυσό-* etc., but also unusual and probably made-up ones, and they belong to all word classes. In the description of Hunger (no. 33, 340) we get a good sample: *καταλερωμένα* (in its filth), *λεπιδοσκουριές* (a scaly rust), *μισομαδιασμένα* (half fallen out), *τα κουκουδοκάρπαθα* (pimples and pustules), *κατακίτρινα* (as yellow as a sulphur candle), *ασπρομελανιασμένα* (white and black), *μαυρομουχλιασμένα* (dirty black), *κατασαπημένα* (all rotten into holes). And I cannot refrain from mentioning the wonderful *νυφοφάωμα* we saw above in the lament (no. 36, 378). Literally it means bride-eating. But notice how many words the translator needs to render this: "when he would devour his bride". Another lovely example from no. 36 is the verb *ξανακαινουργίωσανε* – "began all over again" (no. 36, 376) known from vernacular literature[38] and from a traditional folksong, later set to music by Manos Hatzidakis.[39]

Secondly, Hatzi-Yavrouda uses alliteration and onomatopoeic words: for example, *βιαστικά βιαστικά και δώσαδ δρόμον* (no. 33, 337); *ψευτογογγυσμούς και ψευτονεστεναςμούς* (no. 33, 337); *χυχχειρότερα* (no. 33, 339); *διαταή να διαλλαλήσουν* (no. 36, 371); *βυζάστρες να βυζάξουν* (no. 36, 373); *κουρκούνηξε τα κρουκέλια* (no. 36, 380).

Thirdly, she also uses a lot of reduplication: for example, *γύρου γύρου*; *ψηλά ψηλά*; *βιαστικά βιαστικά*; *βαρύ βαρύ* (all from no. 33, 337); *σιγά σιγά*; *κάπου κάπου* (both from no. 33, 338); *κοντά κοντά* (no. 33, 339); *λογής λογής* (nos. 33, 340); *πωρνόμ πωρνόν* (no. 33, 341); *κομματάκια κομματάκια* (no. 36, 377); *χαδεμένα χαδεμένα* (no. 36, 382). There are even repetitions with emphasis on the second part by use of a compound: *γύρω τριγύρω* (no. 33, 334); *που να σ'έχω και να σε καλώχω* (no. 36, 370); *μάνα, πικρομάνα μου*; *κόρη, πικροκόρη μου* (both from no. 36, 372); *άδικα και παράδικα* (no. 36, 382).

Fourthly, she sometimes uses the technique of *coppia*: for example, *εκαίετο κι ημπυρίζετο* – was burning and on fire (no. 33, 339); *βουβός ... και απολόητος* – dumb and with no answer to make (no. 33, 345); *να μην αθθή και λουλλουδίζη* – that she might never have before her the girl's fair flower and blossom (no. 36, 371); *τα πάθη και τα βάσανά της* – her sufferings and her torments (no. 36, 381); *η κακόμοιρα κι η κακογραμμένη* – ill-fated me for whom an evil doom was written! (no. 36, 378).

Fifthly, our narrator uses many comparisons: for example, *Το ζευγαδόπυλο ήξαπλωσεν κάτω σαν τ' ώμορφο κυπαρίσσι* – The ploughman lay stretched out on the ground like a fair cypress-tree (no. 33, 335); *Τα μμάτια κι οι στόχασες ουλονών σαν αστραπές επαίζαν* – Everyone's eyes and thoughts flickered like lightning (no. 33, 335); *Τα αμίλητα κακόμοιρα δέντρα σαν ώμορφες κοπελούδες και σαν ελληνόπουλα* – The poor silent trees, which stood there like beautiful maidens <and like> children of the heroes of old (no. 33, 336); *Βλέπει ... το παιδί πούτο σαν αγγελάκι* – She sees ... the child who was like a little angel (no. 36, 380); *τα δάκρυά της, άπου τρέχανε σαβ βρύσες* – her tears, which were running like springs of water (no. 36, 383).

References to reality

We have seen how Hatzi-Yavrouda in different ways made her tales come closer to her audience and their reality, through both structure and her use of language. The following examples show her capacity to connect to the surrounding community, also on a linguistic level.

38 Kriaras 1990, 331-32.

39 Ο Μεγάλος Ερωτικός, 1972.

She uses a lot of colloquial or proverbial expressions: for example, *έπεσε μακρύς πλατύς* – he fell on his face (no. 33, 336); *τι να κάμω … ο καϊμένος εγώ* – what am I to do, poor wretch that I am (no. 33, 336); *πετσί και κόκαλο* – skin and bone (no. 33, 339); *το καλό σου βασιλόπουλο* – our good prince (no. 33, 342); *αμέ του κάκου* – but in vain (no. 36, 370); *Δεξιά, ζερβά, βουνά! Ομπρός και πίσω ερημιά!* – To the right, to the left, mountains. In front and behind, a desert! (no. 36, 378).

She familiarizes by comparing to well-known places as e.g., like Alonaki which is a place outside the village (no. 33, 334); products as e.g., walnuts from Zia in Asfendiou (no. 36, 369); institutions as e.g., the Twelve Councilors (no. 33, 345; no. 36, 375); and customs such as when Hunger breathes on the sword three times "like a priest in the ritual" (no. 33, 340). Finally, in no. 36 (*Yavrouda)* the villain speaks the dialect from the neighbouring village of Antimachia (no. 36, 369; 370; 374).

The personal touch

Hatzi-Yavrouda adds a personal touch to her tales. I have mentioned how her characters are good Christians, and she sees no problem in combining Christianity with supernatural elements familiar to the fairy tale. Thus when the young Yavrouda meets her second husband, Neros, who is half-dead, enchanted by fairies or *neraides*, as the most natural thing, he tells her not to be afraid because "God is saving her".[40] Furthermore, we also hear her own voice come through in her asides, which are especially predominant in *Yavrouda*. I shall give just a few examples: *Πάντα με τα όπλα του καλά γιή κακά καθένας πελεμά* – Everyone must always fight with his own weapons, good or bad (no. 36, 369); *Οι μάνες αγαπούν πολύ παιδγιά τος, κι ό τι τος ζητούν, τος το δίνουν* – Mothers love their children much, and what they ask they give them (no. 36, 369); *γιατί 'ς το χάρισμα δα πάντα καθένας φκαριστιέται* – for with presents everyone is always pleased (no. 36 372); *αμ' όταν ένας πόνος γιή φόβος τύχη μηιαλείτερος άλλου, ξεχνάται ο μικρός* – but when one pain or fear is greater than another, then the lesser one is forgotten (no. 36, 380).

Conclusion

I hope to have shown how Hatzi-Yavrouda fits the descriptions of a gifted narrator. We cannot know anything about the size of her repertoire, but her tales are long – longer than other variants, and some of the longest, if not the longest, we have in the editions.[41] For example it would take three hours to read aloud no. 45, *Yannakis* – and maybe more than one evening to perform it.

We saw that her tales may be composed of different types of narration such as myth and traditional wonder tale, and that she skillfully handles various motifs. We also saw how she freely incorporates elements from the poetic tradition into her tales. Finally, we saw that she gets inspiration directly or indirectly from written sources. She connects to the surrounding society both through her language and through allusions to well-known objects, localities, and customs.

We cannot know anything about how she performed or about her interaction with the audience, but she definitely has her own style, comprising very rich and innovative language,

40 That the Christian faith goes hand in hand with the supernatural elements of tales was also an observation that Evald Tang Kristensen made in late 1800s Jutland; see Holbek 1987, 76.

41 We have descriptions of narrators who knew long tales, as we saw e.g. by Adamantiou. He also recorded some long tales (e.g., versions of type 510B and type 531), which run for at least 40 pages, but unfortunately, they remain unpublished. I owe this kind information to Marianthi Kaplonoglou.

detailed descriptions, and dramatic scenes, and she adds her own personal touch to the narration – which I find especially remarkable in her treatment of her female heroines. Even the most persecuted ones are strong and assertive but without transgressing the norms of the surrounding community.

I would like to conclude with an example. The changing of gender in the tale *Mymidonia and Pharaonia* has consequences for the way the heroine can pursue her quest and win her prize. She does this by female cunning. I quote from the end:

> *Η κόρη μεσ' 'ς τηχ χλαμύδα της τηχ χρυσομέταξην τυλιγμένη παρουσιάστη σαν άγγελος εμπροστά 'ς τον αράπη πάλι. Και με τημ παντόφλα 'ς το χέρι της σαν σπαθί της του ξαναλέει αγέρωχα "Πού μούκαμες την άλλημ μου παντόφλα;" Τότες ο αράπης της λέει με απορίαν του μειάλην. "Πού σέδα γω, και πού σε πάντεξα, κυρά μου, και μου γερεύγεις τημ παντόφλα σου;" Μα εκείνη του μεταλέει με περισσότερον της θυμό και αφρόντο "Τημ παντόφλαμ μου πού μού την έκαμες; Γλήγορα να μού τηφ φέρης." Ο αράπης απορούσε, και στρέφει 'ς τηδ δωδεκάδα, και λέει: "Αυτήν εγώ ουδέ την είδα ποτέ μου, ουδέ την ηπάντηξα." Τότες η κόρη ξαναφωνάζει και σιούσε κια τημ παντόφλαντης σα σπαθί "Σαν δεμ μ' είδες ποτέ σου οθδέ μ' απάντηξες, πώς είπες 'ς τομ πολλοχρονομένο βασιλέα σου οτ' είμαι άτιμη κόρη με χίλια δυο σου κακά λόγία;" Ο αραπής ήμεινα βουβός τότε και απολόητος, και καταντροπιασμένος ηγονάτισε μπροστά της και ζητούσε συμπάθιο.*[42]

I find it clever of Hatzi-Yavrouda to exchange the normal male hero's sword for a shoe. What could be more feminine than the very object by which the prince finds his bride-to-be in *Cinderella*? But Tartana in this vivid scene is just as fearsome and effective with her slipper in hand as a male hero would be with his sword. This is Hatzi-Yavrouda at her best, with a dramatic climax to the story where she can let one of her beloved heroines shine and triumph.

Birgit Olsen
Royal Danish Academy of Sciences and Letters (previously: The Danish Institute at Athens)
birgol2016@gmail.com

Bibliography

ADAMANTIOU, A. I. 1896
'Τηνιακά', *Δελτίον της Ιστορικής και Εθνολογικής Εταιρείας της Ελλάδος* 5, 277-326.

ALEXIOU, M. 2002
The Ritual Lament in Greek Tradition, 2nd edition revised by Dimitrios Yatromanolakis and Panagiotis Roilos, Langham, Boulder, New York, Oxford.

ANGELLOPOULOU, A. & E. BROUSKOU 1999
Επεξεργασία Παραμυθιακών Τύπων και Παραλλαγών ΑΤ 300-499 (Α και Β), Γεωργίου Α. Μέγα *Κατάλογος Ελληνικών Παραμυθιών* 3, Athens.

BEATON, R. 1980
Folk Poetry of Modern Greece, Cambridge.

42 Translation: "The girl wrapped in her cloak of gold and silk, again showed herself to the Negro as though she had been an angle of death, and with her slipper in her hand like a sword says to him haughtily: "What have you done to my other slipper?" Then the Negro much at a loss says to her: "Where did I see you, where did I meet you, my lady, that you ask for your slipper?" But she again says to him with still more wrath and defiance: "My slipper, what have you done with it? Bring it to me quickly." The Negro was at a loss and he turns to the Twelve and says: "This girl I have never in my life either seen or met." Then the girl again cries out brandishing the slipper like a sword: "You have never seen or met me! Then how did you come to tell your king – many be his years! – that I am a girl of no honour ..."? The Negro then stood dumb and with no answer to make; utterly put to shame, he knelt down before her and begged her pardon".

BOCCACCIO, G. 1921
The Decameron of Giovanni Boccaccio, translated by J. M. Rigg, London. In the Decameron Web Project: ttps://www.brown.edu/Departments/Italian_Studies/dweb/texts/DecShowText.php?myID=nov0209&lang=eng

DÉGH, L. 1989
Folktales and Society: Story-telling in a Hungarian Peasant Community: Expanded Edition with a New Afterword, Bloomington & Indianapolis.

DÉGH, L. 1995
Narratives in Society: A Performer-Centered Study of Narration, (FF Communications no. *255*), Helsinki.

DAWKINS, R. M. 1950
Forty-Five Stories from the Dodekanese, Cambridge.

FEHLING, D. 1972
'Erysichthon oder das Märchen von der mündlichen Überlieferung', *Rheinisches Museum für Philologie*, 115.2, 173-96.

HERRANEN, G. 1989
'A blind storyteller's repertoire', in *Nordic Folklore. Recent studies,* R. Kvideland & H. K. Sehmsdorf (eds.), Bloomington, 63-69.

HOLBEK, B. 1987
Interpretation of Fairy Tales, (FF Communications vol. CIII no. 239), Helsinki.

KAPLANOGLOU, M. 2002
Παραμύθι και αφήγηση στην Ελλάδα: Μια παλιά τέχνη σε μια νέα εποχή. Το παράδειγμα των αφηγητών από τα νησιά του Αιγαίου και από τις προσφυγικές κοινότητες των Μικρασιατών Ελλήνων, Athens.

KENNEY, E. J. 1963
'Erysichthon on Cos', *Mnemosyne* 16.1, 33-60.

KRIARAS, E. 1990
Λεξικό της μεσαιωνικής ελληνικής δημώδους γραμματείας, vol. 11, Thessaloniki.

MICHALOPOULOS, C. N. 2015
'Literary transfers and cross-cultural exchanges in the Greek speaking world at the turn of the 20th century: the verse translation of Ovid's Metamorphoses by A. S. Kasdaglis (1908)', in *Proceedings of the 5th European Congress of Modern Greek Studies, Continuities, Discontinuities, Ruptures in the Greek World (1204-2014): Economy, Society, History, Literature, Thessaloniki, 2-5 October 2014*, K. A. Dimadis (ed.), vol. 2, Athens, 299-313.

OIKONOMIDIS, D. 1978
'Το παραμύθι και ο παραμυθάς εν Ελλάδι', *Λαογραφία* 31, 29-42.

OLSEN, B. 1997
'Women and Gender Roles in Modern Greek Folk Tales', *Copenhagen Folklore Notes* 3-4, 3-12.

OLSEN, B. 1999A
'Women and Gender Roles in Modern Greek Folk Tales', *Κάμπος: Cambridge Papers in Modern Greek* 7, 21-42.

OLSEN, B. 1999B
'And they embroidered all kinds of embroidery', *Copenhagen Folklore Notes* 4, 1-6.

OLSEN B. 2002
'The exception that proves the rule? A female storyteller from Kos', *Scandinavian Journal of Modern Greek Studies* 1, 61-74.

OLSEN, B. 2004
'R. M. Dawkins and Greece', in *Archaeology, Anthropology and Heritage in the Balkans and Anatolia: The Life and Times of F.W. Hasluck, 1878-1920*, D. Shankland (ed.), vol. 1, Istanbul, 105-20.

OLSEN, B. 2019
'The Snake who became Prince, or The Girl with Two Husbands: An Analysis of the Fairytale (AT *433B) based on Hatzi-Yavrouda's version from Kos', *Proceedings of The Danish Institute at Athens* 9, 115-26.

PROPP, V. 1968
Morphology of the Folktale, 2nd edition, Austin, TX.

VARVOUNIS, M. 1998
Αφήγηση και αφηγητές στα ελληνικά παραμύθια, Athens.

VON HAHN, J. G. 1864
Griechische und albanesische Märchen I–II, Leipzig.

ZARRAFTIS, I. S. 1951
'Λαογραφικά εν Κω. Εκδιδόμενα υπό Δημητρ. Β. Οικονομίδου', *Λαογραφία* 13, 285-339.

ZIAZOPOULOS, E. 1951
'Παραμύθια και παραμυθάδες στα Άγραφα της Θεσσαλίας', *Λαογραφία* 13, 348-50.

ZIOGA, I. 2015
Η διδασκαλία των λατινικών στην μέση εκπαίδευση, Ph.D. thesis, University of Thessaloniki.

To Give or not to Give? Addressing Community and Poverty through Oral Narration in a Greek Island Village

Marianthi Kaplanoglou

Abstract

The present paper focuses on the oral tale The Magic Castle, *(ATU / Megas 545A*). Through the study of variation on a historical, social, generic, and individual level, the present paper a) analyses oral variants and written texts, thus charting the itinerary of the tale and its varied narrative traditions, in the East and in the West, and especially in the Mediterranean, and b) refers to the re-appropriation of the same tale in the framework of a family tradition in an island village of the Dodecanese, where the tale also runs throughout the 20th century. By analyzing the narrator's choices and transformations in regard to the folktale's established storyline, the paper aims to reveal the potency of orality: in this sense it investigates whether the procedure of folktale narration also addresses matters of village life, like community and poverty, articulated in the self-contained aesthetic and poetic language of the genre. Oral narration is thus studied not only as an aggregation of oral texts handed out from the distant past but as a complex social event inaugurated in the period where Greek peasant and maritime communities of the Aegean entered capitalist society.*

Introduction: Theoretical points

The usual confusion made in the public domain between heritage and tradition tends to obscure the basic characteristic of folklore, which is the interplay between stability and variation. On the contrary, folklore research of orality is concerned with questions of transmission, variation, and performance, focusing on the specificity of particular expressions.[1] Members of the folk themselves consider also variation as the main condition for creation: "no two things made by hand are the same", as a local potter from the island of Sifnos told me.

Scholars of folk narrative in different ethnic and social contexts usually stress that folktales, although depicting a fictional world, and thus told as a means of entertainment and instruction, are deeply connected with the changing conditions of peasant life during the 19th and 20th centuries.[2] From this point of view, the psychological tensions of the fairy tale surpass the nuclear family and gender relations in

1 As pointed out by Simonsen (2014, 116): "Lore is any artistic or ritual performance that follows the constraints of traditional poetics as described by Jakobson and Bogatyrev (i.e. the acknowledgment of both pattern and variation). Folklore never occurs when a group operates as a *corporate* group, with one voice, but only when it operates as an *interactive* group, in which all members have their own voice. This is why folklore generates variation".

2 Among other monumental studies see e.g. Dégh 1989; Abrahams 1983; Holbek 1987; Lindahl 1997 and 2011. For a study of narration as an analytical concept in many disciplines see Kakavoulia & Politis 2022.

order to address social matters of class and economy.[3] According to Carl Lindahl, the telling of a story binds together the fore-story (the flow of past souls and stories that precede and frame the telling), the performance (the present, audible, oral creation), and the understory (the tale as visualized within the listener during the performance and held in memory long afterward). Thus, any existing body of collected narratives, even the largest, is not sufficient for the study of folktales in specific situational contexts since the narrative procedure is not confined only to a series of written testimonies, but is an ongoing orality where most narratives are never recorded. In addition, an oral narrative, as existing in individual and collective memory, is never articulated only in expressive terms but mostly consists of unuttered, but operative potentials, as stressed by Dell Hymes.[4]

Folktales were a central part of oral communication among the Greek peasantry long into the 20th century. The great appreciation of this expressive art is attested by the richness and diversity of the material as well as by the opportunities of narration. The complex system of poetic principles, instructive techniques, and linguistic techniques results each time in a different oral narrative, and corresponds to an equally complex nexus of varied situational contexts for its articulation. This desire for tale-telling is accompanied by an acute awareness – shared by both narrators and listeners – that folktales, although apparently connected with entertainment, ancestral wisdom, and wish fulfillment fantasy, were mostly appreciated against the backdrop of their own lives, providing a veiled but powerful value system in everyday life. In the following, I will refer to a tale belonging to the cycle of the animal helper (ATU 545), considering four parameters of variation:

A. The **historical** refers to a tale's existence in the *longue durée*. It unveils the rich, long (even archaic), international narrative tradition of a tale (*the archaeology of a folk narrative*, as Konstantakos called it[5]) resulting in the formation of its dynamic and polyvalent symbolic motifs. The particular tale deals with a poor boy or girl who, guided by a mediating figure (a magic animal, or a supernatural helper, like the Fates), becomes king (or queen) and acquires a palace by defeating its demonic owner who may set him or her tests. I shall briefly state the historical evolution of the tale, especially with regard to its European and Mediterranean traditions.

B. The **social** regards tales as social events, studying their place in active expressive culture, where folktale symbols acquire their specific meanings. On this premise, I will turn to the Greek material of ATU 545, and, more specifically, to a story known in a village on the island of Rhodes that has run in a family repertoire for nearly a century. The tale is then studied in relation to village life and social attitudes towards oral narration as far as matters of social cohesion are concerned.

C. The **generic** refers to the folktale's own esthetic rules which are different or contrasted to those that apply to other genres, for example the legend or the song, all existing in the same community.

D. The **individual** focuses on folktales as personal communicative strategies linking a story to particular narrators (the art of a Greek folk narrator is studied in the paper by Birgit Olsen in the present volume), as well as their audience-response according to their cultural codes. Focus is then on a specific narrator of this Dodecanesian village, her repertoire, choices, performance, and emotions in regard to her story.

3 Noyes 2016, 301.

4 Hymes 2000, 11.

5 Konstantakos 2019.

The boy's tale (ATU 545B)

As a folktale, ATU 545B is almost universally known.[6] The story also offers a typical example of back-and forth transitions between orality and literacy, because of its famous literary retellings corresponding, in their form and theme, to the so-called category of the "rise tale",[7] and addressing the aspirations of a newly rising urban European middle class. The basic theme is developed in two narrative traditions that differ in relation to the animal helper, who may be a cat[8] (in the West) or a fox (in the East).

The western tradition: Puss in Boots

The theme of a cunning cat appeared in the literary tradition of the West during the 16th and 17th centuries. Straparola in his folktale collection *Le piacevoli notti* (11, no. 1), published in Venice in two parts (1550, 1553), writes the story of 'Costantino Fortunato', developed in the framework of sibling rivalry. The poor hero inherits only a cat. The cat, a fairy in disguise, brings to the king a leveret she has caught, as a supposed gift from her master. The cat bade its master to throw himself into the river and afterward explain that some robbers had robbed him of his treasures. The king, believing him to be very rich, gives him his daughter as his bride. On the way home, the cat runs ahead, and threatens the shepherds and finally the guards of the castle that a big army will be coming to kill them, unless they say that they are serving her lord, Costantino. The real lord of the castle, who was absent at the time, dies in an accident on the way, and Costantino Fortunato retains the lordship of the castle and later, after the king's death, becomes King of Bohemia.

The folktale is also included in the Italian collection of Giambattista Basile, *Lo Cunto de li Cunti* (1634-36), known today as the *Pentamerone*, a collection of folktales that Basile had probably heard told in Naples or elsewhere.[9] Thus, in the tale of 'Gagliuso' (Monday, Novel no. 4) a beggar from Naples died so poor that he left only a sieve to his elder son and a cat to his younger. The cat keeps visiting the king, bringing fish and birds, which it says have been sent as gifts by its master, until the king wishes to meet him. The cat returns saying that their servants stole everything, not leaving even a shirt for its master. The king sends expensive clothes. On the

6 It is known from Europe to Indonesia and the Philippines (Köhler-Zülch 1993a). It was also transferred to the American Indians and to Africa.

7 This term, is associated, according to Ruth Bottigheimer, with the Italian author and compiler of modern fairy tales Giovanni Francesco Straparola (c. 1480-c. 1557) who, is thought to express, through his tales, that record the rise of the protagonist from poverty to wealth, the socioeconomic aspirations of an urban artisanal readership. See Bottigheimer 2005. For a critical reappraisal of the term, see Ben-Amos 2010; Vaz da Silva 2010, who convincingly argue that the rags-to-riches plots of the "rise tale" are well known in folktales from earlier times and far more diffused among population different social strata.

8 Narratives about a poor man who inherits or buys a cat that brings him good luck were told in different traditions. One of them refers to a man who becomes rich by selling his cat in a mouse-infested land where cats are unknown (ATU 1651, *Whittington's Cat*). As Ben-Amos points out, in most of these stories, the acquisition of wealth is accomplished through mediation and not directly, since the cat's owner delivers his pet to a merchant or sailor who visits the Land of the Mice, obtains a large sum of money by selling the cat and transfers the amount honestly to the owner (Ben-Amos 2011, 498). This trust resonated with an ancient Persian custom "that when a man undertook a voyage to a distant land, each of his friends entrusted to his care some article of their property, and received its produce on his return" (Keightley 1834, 263, referred to by Ben-Amos 2011, 498). The story has been known in Europe at least from the 13th century and in Asia even earlier (11th century). A similar tradition exists at the end of the 12th century, in the chronicle *Annales* of Albert von Stade, where the story was attached to a historical figure, Richard Whittington (d. 1423), and was further popularized as a chapbook and children's book.

9 Maybe on the Greek island of Crete, then under Venetian Rule. On the relation of the collection of Basile with Cretan folktales, see Puchner 2011, especially 39-41.

way home, the cat goes ahead and intimidates all the shepherds on the way to say that their flocks belong to Gagliuso. Upon learning of all these riches, the king gives him his daughter in marriage. The tale ends with the feigned death of the cat in order to test its master's gratitude.

Perrault's famous reworking of the tale[10] describes the desperate position of the third son of a poor miller who inherits nothing but a cat. The cat visits the king, bringing gifts of small animals, which it has caught. The episode of the fake drowning in the river is also included in this version of the story. Finally the cat devours the ogre (the owner of the castle) who had turned into a mouse in a contest of magical transformations. The miller's son and the cat live happily ever after, in wealth.

The eastern tradition: the fox matchmaker

The other version with the fox as hero is impressively widespread, beginning in Mongolia and ending at the far reaches of Southeastern Europe. In the Central Asian tradition (which includes the Mongolian and the Altai-Turkish versions of the story) a hunter catches a fox that has eaten his prey. In exchange for the hunter's setting her free, the fox promises to make him a khan.[11] The fox presents herself to the khan as a matchmaker and through trickery catches the wild animals the khan had demanded as wedding gifts. She presents the young hero as a rich man who has been robbed along his way. The khan's daughter marries the hero and the fox secures herds of animals and a palace for the hunter by killing their real owner (usually Mangus, the evil demon of Central Asian epics).[12]

In the context of a nomadic herding culture, the theft (acquisition) of animals constituted a very significant event. Thus, if an animal disappeared, it was easily attributed to the activity of some evil demon. The possession and quest for the animals is furthermore incorporated into a ritual framework, the purpose of which was to renew hope for abundance. According to related beliefs in Siberia, the shaman, on the symbolic journey of the quest, encountered the supernatural owner of the animals, the lord of the hunt, and could deceive or compel him to submit, but never kill him.[13]

This theme appears to have passed into the tradition of the folktale early on, in which, however, the acquisition of the bride, the herds, and the wealthy residence is not accomplished by the hero himself, but by a grateful fox.

10 Perrault 1697. Puss in Boots is included in the first edition of Brothers Grimm, *Kinder-und Hausmärchen* (1812-15) under the title "Der gestiefelte Kater". They omitted it from the following editions of the *Märchen* because it bore a close resemblance to the French tale. For the history of the collection see Uther 2017. For the versions of the French Catalogue, see Delarue & Tenèze 1964, 339-46; Bru 2017, 453-56.

11 Lörincz 1979, 40.

12 The fox is linked to Mangus since in the Central Asian epics, he or his relatives can transform themselves into a fox (Uther 1992, 136-44). However, in the heroic epics, in contrast to the tales of magic, the function of the animal as helper is only with difficulty fulfilled by the fox because there it acts as the companion of Mangus, with a clearly negative dimension (Uther 1992, 143). The fox is also known in myths and folktales from China, Korea, and Japan as a mythical and demonic animal (Uther 1987).

13 In contrast, in the mythical cycles that passed through various reworkings by the peoples of Asia and Europe, a mythical hero turns over to man the mastery of animals, slaying their supernatural owners. In the ancient Greek tradition, these stories are included in the mythical cycle of Heracles. The myth of Heracles's labor with the cattle of Geryon comprises the Greek version-adaptation. In order to correlate the stories of Hercules to the Indo-European myth of the cattle raid, see Burkert 1993, 130-59, Lincoln 1976, and Rose 1954 who connect these myths to initiation rituals. For the adaptations of the myth in Greek drama, see Konstantakos 2011.

In the region bounded by the Balkans and Eastern Europe to the West and by Armenia, the Pontus, and the Caucasus to the East, the folktale arrives significantly altered: the hero is usually a miller (for example in Armenian,[14] Kyrgyz,[15] and Turkish[16] versions) or a farmer. In Greek versions a fox (more rarely, a cat or other animal) steals the grapes of a poor villager (or eats a shepherd's animal) and is apprehended.[17] The fox promises him that if he doesn't kill her, she will make him king.

In Greek-Cypriot, Sicilian, and Caucasian versions, the motif of the borrowing of the container for the (presumed) measurement of gold appears to have replaced the Central Asian one of the deception of the wild animals. The final episode of the feigned death of the fox and the proof of the man's ingratitude (as also found in Basile) is a favorite ending in the Armenian, Caucasian, Turkish, and Greek versions.[18]

Erica Taube wondered whether Puss in Boots's ancestor was a fox. She observed that the animal's gratitude, which in these folktales is stereotypically explained as being in return for the hero's unselfish action in sparing the animal's life, is a much more plausible motif, which appeared earlier than the one of the inheritance with which *Puss in Boots* opens. Charting the course the folktale might have followed, Taube believes that even if its native land was India, it spread to Europe through Central Asia, durin the age of Mongol rule (Taube 1978, 473-85). This would confirm the view of Polívka who, as early as 1900, studied the oral versions of the tale and concluded that it came from the East. In his opinion, the animal helper was originally a fox, who was later replaced in Southwestern Europe by a cat. According to Polívka, the Caucasian and Tartar versions show that the folktale took form in the East. Probably under Arabic influence, it arrived in North Africa and Zanzibar and, with Greek mediation through Asia Minor, it arrived in the Balkans and Southern Italy.[19]

We can assume that the tale originated in the Central Asian region where it was already nearly fully formed into a narrative evolving from the existing beliefs of nomadic, livestock-raising peoples such as that of supernatural beings stealing their animals, which could then be found and recovered by the shaman. The story was created around the basic theme of the marriage (in the manner of common tales) between persons of different social position, with certain necessary changes or adaptations to this theme. Thus, the place of the shaman is taken by the crafty fox who acts within the context of grateful animals. The supernatural being also assumes a narrative role, which is sometimes more realistic (the wealthy owner). The tale came to Europe, via the

14 'Conte du renard', in Macler 1911, 85-90.

15 'Le meunier', Dor 1983, 39-40.

16 'Typ. 34 Der Müller und der Fuchs', in Eberhard & Boratav 1953, 49-51.

17 Megas et al. 2012, 215-24. The presence of the fox in Greek tradition is especially common even from the age of the myths of Aesop; indeed, the fox is already playing the role of the crafty animal who is itself deceived in the end. The fox's ability to play dead was also a theme in Byzantine narratives and is noted by Kosmas the Jerusalemite (Koukoules 1955, vol. 6, 318) and in the *Physiologus*. The fox wreaked much damage to village households and was averted either by practical measures or by magical means (Koukoules 1955, vol. 6, 204).

18 The tremendous development of this episode shows that in the Eastern narratives, the narrators felt skepticism about the sudden social ascent of the hero, and thus they altered the central focus of the story. In his analysis of another narrative, the fable of the fox with a cropped tail, of the *Augustana* Collection, Zafiropoulos accentuates the fable's process of internalization of social standards of behaviour as well as the dependence of individual sanctions upon the social (Zafiropoulos 2001, 121).

19 Polívka 1900. Francke, in his collection of a series of tales from Ladakh, also raises the question of whether the ancestor of "Puss in Boots" was in fact a fox.

societies of the "intermediary" geographic regions.[20] In Western Europe, a parallel type was created, in which the fox was replaced by a cat, who had already been promoted to an important role by virtue of its ability to eliminate the scourge of mice.

The girl's tale (ATU 545A / 545A*)

The story of a poor girl who gives her food to an animal (or beggar) divides into a northern type, found mostly in the Scandinavian countries (545A), and a southern type (545A* including the previous type AT 512* *The Sister Driven from Home*), diffused primarily in the Mediterranean (with Sicilian, Greek, Turkish, and Catalan versions), while versions are also known from the Arab world, Libya, and Iraq.[21]

In Northern Europe, the heroine is helped by a cat (or dog) – her sole inheritance – who kills the troll/giant owner of the castle by making him look at the sun.[22] This tale, with mostly Finnish and Russian versions, may be considered as a folk source for the famous literary version by Hans Christian Andersen, *The Princess and the Pea*.[23]

The southern type is known in the Mediterranean where, nevertheless, there is considerable variation. In Sicilian tradition, the story is about a piece of food contested among the female members of a poor family. In two similar versions included in the collection by Gonzenbach,[24] three poor orphan sisters make their living by spinning. They sell their flax in the city, and one day the older decides to buy food and wine there. Returning home, however, a dog grabs the food. The same happens to the second sister. However, the youngest one chases the dog and discovers a palace with wonderful mattresses, food, and treasures. She returns to her sisters and convinces them to move to the palace. At night, the two older sisters get terrified when they hear a strange voice. The younger one discovers that the voice comes from the ghost of a young woman, once a Duchess, who cannot rest until she gets revenge on her lover who unjustly murdered her. The Duchess promises the girl that she may inherit the palace on the condition that she lures the ex-lover, a gentleman, into the palace and kills him. The girl feels pity for the ghost and executes the murder. With the help of her sisters, she buries the man and they inherit the palace.[25]

There is a similar introduction in the Sicilian tale '*Lu Sangunazzu*' (*The blood sausage*), found in Giuseppe Pitrè's collection,[26] while in another tale from the same collection, '*Lu cani 'nfatatu*' ('*The enchanted dog*'),[27] there is a different story: an old

20 Kaplanoglou 1999.

21 Uther 2011, 315-17; Köhler-Zülch 1993b; Oriol & Pujol 2008, 119; Megas et al. 2012, 215-24.

22 ATU 545A, '*The Cat Castle*' (Uther 2011, 315).

23 Kawan 2005.

24 *The Courageous Maiden*, no. 15 in Zipes 2004, corresponding to no. 78 in Gonzenbach 1870, while Gonzenbach included a second version in dialect (no. 94 *The Story of the Three sisters* belonging to AT 512B* *The Ghost is avenged*). At the request of the historian Otto Hartwig, in 1868, Laura Gonzenbach, the daughter of a Swiss consul at Messina, began to collect fairy tales among the peasant women in the eastern provinces of Messina and Catania. The two-volume edition comprised ninety-two of the tales translated into literary German (with two more still in dialect from a Sicilian collaborator).

25 Commenting on the two versions, the one translated in German by Gonzenbach (*The Courageous Maiden*) and the other in Sicilian dialect (*The Story of the Three Sisters*), Zipes notes that, in spite of their similarities, they differ on many points: the hostility among the hungry sisters (in *The Story of the Three Sisters,* the dialect text) is in contrast with the heroines of *The Courageous Maiden* who are more compassionate towards each other. In addition, Gonzenbach informants of *The Courageous Maiden* seem to adhere to a story of revenge, in contrast with the story in Sicilian dialect which seems to reject the actions of the three sisters (Zipes 2013, 106-7).

26 Pitrè (vol. 2) 1875, 101-4 (no. 66); Zipes & Russo 2009, 296-98.

27 Pitrè (vol. 2) 1875, 280-82 (no. 89); Zipes & Russo 2009, 396-98.

woman with a beautiful granddaughter buys a cylinder of grain and sends her granddaughter to the mill to have it ground for baking bread. While the grandmother attends Mass, a dog comes, grabs the bread, and carries it away. The girl chases it and arrives at a palace where a prince proposes marriage to her. The girl accepts but asks for her grandmother to be sent for and join them. Once she has arrived, she keeps asking the girl "what did you do with the bread?" Not enduring this nightmare, the girl has her thrown out of the window, but at the spot where she falls, a vineyard grows. While the heroine is delousing the prince, a branch hits him and she laughs. Her husband wants to know why and threatens to behead her if she does not tell. She answers that she has a box of diamonds more beautiful than his mantle. Her husband wants to see it, and she asks for help from the dog. The dog arrives at an ogre's castle and tells him that the king's army is coming to kill him. They throw the ogre into the well and they find in the castle his treasure chest with the diamonds and all the precious things and take them to the city.

Accordingly, in the narrative tradition of Catalonia, a girl eats all the fish and bread her mother has prepared for her dinner but denies the fact and runs away from home. She meets the king's son and marries him. The mother visits her and again reproaches her for having eaten the fish and bread. The mother dies and from the place she is buried a reed grows, which keeps asking for her piece of bread. The girl laughs and the prince asks her why. She hastily answers that the brooms at her house are better than his beard. The prince wants to see the girl's house and threatens to kill her if he cannot find it. A snake guides the girl to a palace containing these brooms but warns her that she cannot stay there for more than a year. After a year, the snake reappears, but the girl tells the prince that the snake has eaten her parents. They kill the snake, the palace falls down, and the prince and the girl return to their castle.[28]

28 Oriol & Pujol 2008, 119.

The Greek oikotype

This narrative takes another turn in the Greek tradition where the contested food between the girl and her mother is regarded through a different prism: a poor mother is compensated with some food (a fish-head, a loaf of bread, some meat, etc.) or wheat for her labor on other people's properties or the mother begs for food. The mother asks the daughter to guard it until the evening so that they may eat it or make some bread from the wheat, but the girl gives the food or part of it to a beggar (usually Christ transformed into an old man). In other versions an animal (cat) steals the food, like in the Sicilian tales.

The daughter's offering of alms provokes a violent reaction from the mother. She beats her and asks to get back the food. The daughter flees from home and arrives at a palace where she works as a servant but finally marries the king. Her mother reappears asking for her precious food and continues to do so even after having been killed. At the spot where the mother fell, a tree or a reed grows which keeps asking for the fish-head (or other food). The girl laughs (or sheds tears), the king asks her why and as explanation, the heroine hastily responds that his beard resembles the broom in the toilet at her father's palace. The king gets angry and demands to see it, and he threatens to kill her if she does not show him the palace. In her despair, the heroine receives help from the old man to whom she gave the food. He gives her the key to a palace, or the girl is aided by her Fates or a crab, or an ogre (or ogress) appears and gives her the keys to the palace demanding that she return them within 40 days, otherwise (s)he will eat her; but the ogre(ss) gets tangled in some flax and dies, and the heroine keeps the palace.[29]

The final part of this tale bears many resemblances to another development of the story (with a mas-

29 Megas et al. 2012, 213-24.

culine hero): in type 545D* *The Chick-pea King*,[30] a poor man finds a chickpea by accident, and from this calculates he can become rich. Thus he seeks to wed the king's daughter. In order to test him, the king makes him sleep in rags. He stays awake, not of course because the bed bothers him, but because he is looking for his chickpea among the rags. The next night, when they put him to sleep on a soft mattress, he has a restful night. The king is persuaded of his origins and gives him his daughter in marriage. The hero acquires the wealth of an ogre (moor, etc.) by solving the riddle he has put to him. This he does with the help of a magic or divine helper who appears all of a sudden.[31]

Although the basic themes and motifs of this folktale cycle remain throughout its differentiated traditions (animal or supernatural being as mediator-helper against a supernatural, demonic, or monstrous opponent-owner of the flocks and (or) the splendid residence, gratitude and return of favor, rise from rags to riches via a royal marriage, danger of exposure of lies), the pairs of narrative personae have changed. From the boy's tale (545B) to the southern versions of the girl's tale (545A*), especially of the Greek tradition, the story is further distanced from its initial shamanistic-totemic background. Even if narrative actions can be considered symmetrical among the tales, the means of their fulfilment differs. Instead of the man-animal couple who initially struggles over food, a human couple (mother-daughter or sisters) appears, while, instead of the grateful animal, there is a Christian figure in humanized form (old beggar)[32] or other supernatural/divine beings (the Fates).[33] The shamanistic background of the tale remains better preserved in its final part (with the appearance of monstrous animals or beings) but again is subverted by the dramatic conflict between daughter and mother (who, in certain versions, returns as a weeping voice or vampire).

However, the contest for food appears dominant in all forms of the tale, albeit exploited in different ways by different cultures. The older ideas about the relations of conflict and reciprocity among men and supernatural beings over the mastery of flocks, embedded in a shamanistic–religious framework were reworked with the passage of existing beliefs into a secular narrative, like the folktale. According to the pattern of the Aesop fable, the protagonists are a man and a humanized animal[34] (wild or domestic) and their relations are formed on the basis of reciprocity[35] (sharing of food, gratitude, and return of favor), while the supernatural or human owner of the flocks is typically killed. An alternative pattern of dispute over food (or other fortune) is based not on violence but on wit, through deception (like in 545B) or a riddle contest (like in 545D*).[36]

30 This folktale type (Uther 2011, 317-18) is fairly well known in the Greek tradition (especially in Crete), where it is almost always joined in its second part with tale type AT 812, *The Devil's Riddle* (Megas et al. 2012, 215-24).

31 On this riddle and its means of expression, see Kyriakidis 1925.

32 Religious folktales and legends of the orthodox Christian tradition usually include the wanderings of holy people and other supernatural figures in the world of the living, as well as the journeys of the living or dead in the next world. See also Gergatsoulis 2006; Kaliambou 2017; Varvounis 2017.

33 For the role of the Fates in Greek folktales, see Megas 1967.

34 Katsadoros 2019.

35 The important role of the helper (one of Propp's dramatis personae) in folktales is better understood in the framework of these relations of reciprocity (Noyes 2016, 306-7).

36 The stealing of valuable objects (like fire) is a stable attribute of civilizing heroes in many mythologies (Lévi-Strauss 1964; Mélétinsky 1970). On the other hand, disputes about the distribution of food appear in the Aesop fables as well (the lion's share is a well known metaphor referring to an unjust or unequal partnership). The disputed food forms an important part in the relationship between mother and daughter from a psychoanalytical point of view according to Angelopoulou 2017.

In the framework of type 545A* the dispute over food between mother and daughter then transfers an old theme to the field of social relations since, in Greek[37] and Turkish[38] versions, it is typically associated with an act of charity.

Narrating in a village setting: Stamatia's and Marietta's tales

A version of the Greek *oikotype* circulated for over a century among the members of a peasant family in the village of Afandou, on Rhodes. It was attributed to Savvas Drakou, a landless peasant, father of eight children, who, during the 1920s and 1930s (when the Dodecanese islands were under Italian rule), was invited into the households of the village in order to narrate his long, magical tales. At the beginning of the 21st century, two of his daughters, Stamatia (1916-2009) and Marietta (1929-2019), continued to narrate the tales they heard through childhood from their father. I am going to concentrate on Stamatia's tale. Marietta's tale has a similar plot (since they both share the same source) but differs in regard to style, characterization, and worldview.[39] In the framework of this paper, I will consider both narrators, but my textual references are on Stamatia's version.

In their versions of 545A*, the mother is a working woman:

"Once upon a time, there was an old woman. Her husband had died, and she had a daughter. The old woman was a daily laborer in order to earn their living and to do some things. One day, she goes to a man, he gives her two kafizia (type of measuring vessel) of wheat, she took it.

- Let's grind it and then you are going to knead it, my daughter. In the meanwhile, I will go to the daily laboring, and when I will come back, there will be bread ready to eat.

She says:

- Fine.

She grinded it, she brought it back – her mother had already left early in the morning -, the girl takes it, she kneaded it, it was seven kilos, and she made two loafs of bread, she put them in the oven and baked them".

The daughter shows compassion to an old beggar (Christ transformed): "an old man appears: 'Give me, my daughter, alms'. She takes a loaf of bread and gives him (all of it). 'Thank you, my daughter, I wish you well'. He leaves".

But the mother constantly beats her for her kind act, asking for the food back: "May you die, why should you give him the bread?" The girl decides to flee home:

"The girl says:

- I will leave, I will go towards my destiny, I gave the bread to the beggar and she tortures me and she hits me in the face every day. She stood up and left one day, she went to find her destiny, she went, the old man appeared in front of her. He was Christ (transformed into an old man)".

The old man (Christ) gives her a gold thread. Following his advice, she arrives at the palace and asks to become a servant; the girl gives the skein of thread to the king, who searches for a special thread in order to use it for finishing the nuptial dress of his bride, but the skein is always heavier than the coins they

37 Megas et al. 2012, 213-24.

38 Eberhard & Boratav 1953, 181-82 (type 164).

39 For tales narrated by different members of the same family, see Holbek 1987, 173. Licia Masoni, in her field research in the village of Frassinoro, in the Apennines in the North of Italy, studies versions of the same tale narrated by two sisters, through the prism of the interviewees' comments on their tales, in particular those dealing with attitudes towards the uses of traditional narrative (Masoni 2007, 37-47). The folk narrator studied below also forms part of a wider family tradition where the same story was appropriated by a father, his daughters and perhaps other members of the same family. See Kaplanoglou 2022, 321-466.

put on the scale as a compensation; only the king himself weighs the same as the skein, and so the king marries her.

The mother of the pious girl reappears ever asking for her bread; she is thrown down (here it is implied that the mother is killed) by the old man and on that spot a tree grows; a branch hits the heroine on the face, asking for the bread when she is with her husband. A tear falls on her husband's cheek, and he asks her why she is crying; the heroine is taken by surprise and she responds with a lie, by saying that she misses her father's palace, and the king asks to see it. In despair, the heroine meets the old man again. He gives her the key to a palace with many rooms where they arrive and live happily. In order to test their generosity, Christ comes again as a beggar asking for alms. They take care of him and give him a room to sleep in and food to eat:

"When it got dark, Christ went there again and says:
- Do me alms, my boy, who I am a stranger man (he wanted to test the king, see, if he was the same as his wife), give me alms, my child, let me for a night here to sleep, since I don't know where to go, I am an old man and I am feeling cold.

The king says:
- We have rooms, uncle, we have beds, let me put you in a room, to lie down.
- No, he says, my child, I am an old man, my clothes are dirty, I don't want to lie down. If you have a little room apart, I can stay there.

Outside, there, they had a little room, and there was a bed and a fireplace, and he says:
- Here, you can stay, uncle.
- It is fine here, he says, my child, here I will stay.

He went, he sat on the bed, they pleased him so much, they prepared food for him, they put him to eat, when he had eaten, the mother of the girl, goes there".

The heroine's mother arrives again (it is implied that the mother reappears after her death, thus as a kind of a vampire), asking for the bread her daughter had given as alms. The old man (Christ) confronts the mother once again, by transforming her into a piece of wood which he cuts and diamonds are brought out. Then Christ reveals his real identity and reassures the heroine that her mother will never appear to bother her again and that she will live happily ever after.

Stamatia's and Marietta's versions allude to the wider tradition of the tale, but it seems to have gained the coherence, that other Greek versions were striving for, by exploiting alternative forms of established motifs and themes and inducing certain radical changes on the level of the folktale's binary oppositions.

No zoomorphic helper here, the story has moved entirely to the sphere of human relations, opposing a mother to her daughter and to an old beggar, whom only the audience knows is Christ transformed; the characters only realize it at the end. The demonic opponent has also disappeared, along with the archaic contest through riddles (or by deception). The test is a test of giving alms imposed at the beginning on the girl and at the end on both the girl and the prince.

The act of giving and the reward received is thus dominant along the whole tale, developed in a symmetrical way into pairs of actions along the storyline: symmetrical but also antithetical, since certain pairs of these actions follow the fantasy principle (according to the rules of folktale composition) while others, the reality principle (as representations of actual human relations). In the first category belong the actions developed around the offering of alms at the beginning and at the end of the tale. Following the fantasy principle, this pair of actions (charity and reward), corresponding to the schema mérite—récompense by Claude Bremond,[40] is based on the

40 Bremond 1979.

overestimation of the human offer.[41] The reward given by the otherworldly being in return for the loaf of bread surpasses (with magical exaggeration) the initial act of charity: – for a loaf of bread, or for a room reserved for the old beggar, the heroine receives accordingly a skein of gold, a royal marriage, a whole palace, diamonds and florins.

To these, a differentiated pair of repeated actions is contrasted, developed around working relations and based, according to the reality principle, on the underestimation of the offer: the daily work of the mother, as well the service of the daughter in the king's palace are always underpaid (the mother receives for her work some wheat, and the girl in exchange for her work asks for a piece of bread and a piece of cloth).

Accentuating the reality principle, the two basic figures of the folktale (apart from the heroine), the working mother and the old beggar, correspond to actual social groups in the surroundings of the narrator. From this point of view too, elements of social reality pertain to the poetic fabric of the tale.

The seasonal laborers and the daily workers

The organization of the agricultural communities of the Aegean favored in many cases a subsistence economy of small farmers based on mixed agriculture and animal husbandry in a narrow and over-fragmented land-space and with restricted natural resources. Villagers were producing mainly cereals, fodder, and in a lesser amount citrus for their subsistence, while occasional surplus production reached the local markets. They were based on a model of kinship and devolution of property which favored nuclear, matrilineally extended households, thus focusing upon the dowering of daughters (with houses, land, and a trousseau) at marriage in order to set up independent conjugal units.[42] In this sense, each household was economically and residentially autonomous, while the work of all the family members, even of the very young, and the potential co-operation among kin made its survival and reproduction possible.

The status of the worker as described in the tale corresponds to the actual seasonal and daily workers who experienced greater economic and social insecurity, which appears augmented in transitional periods when social inequalities in the Aegean agricultural communities became sharper.

Village life in the Aegean islands was partly based on the model of a closed local economy. Between the late 18th and early 19th century, the agricultural communities of the Aegean were experiencing demographic growth, urbanization, and commodification.[43] The rural population tried to find new sources of complementary revenues through maritime trade and crafting activities. Groups of men from neighboring islands worked together as fishermen, sailors, and sponge-divers. Men also departed from their islands for several months to work as seasonal workers, itinerant professionals (builders), or craftsmen in the dynamic and market-oriented communities of the Greek-Orthodox populations in the surrounding littoral mainland of the west coast of Asia Minor. Accordingly, women from the Aegean islands used to work during their youth as maids or servants in rich Greek households of Constantinople and Smyrna. Dowries were faster monetized than in

41 Thus, the offering of the bread falls under the category of the "unpromising", an important bearer of the basic contrast in folktales between reality and appearance (Lüthi 2017, 73-74).

42 Papataxiarchis & Petmezas 1998, 230.

43 *Ibid.*, 232 and 238; Meraklis 2004, 58.

other regions, and inequalities between offspring's inheritances were sharper.[44]

Landless peasants, both men and women, also became daily workers, mainly during harvest time, in the expanding orchards and vineyards of the islands. In the Dodecanese, under Italian occupation, after 1912, men worked as daily workers in the public construction projects undertaken by the Italian authorities (streets, buildings, irrigation projects, etc.).

Stamatia's and Marietta's family provides a characteristic example of these social transitions. Their father (born during the Ottoman period in the 1880s) was constantly coping with poverty: Deprived of land, he was forced to depart with the groups of seasonal workers at the beginning of summer and worked as a builder and farmer in Asia Minor, to return at the beginning of autumn. Later, when this route to the East was definitively closed, after the great fire of Smyrna of 1922, and the end of the Greek Orthodox communities in Asia Minor, he worked temporarily on his home island, in the construction of roads by the Italians, as well as a daily worker.

Their mother also worked as a daily worker on other people's farms. Stamatia herself left school at the age of six in order to look after their few domestic animals. From the age of ten she worked in the local textile factory, while in the 1930s, after she had turned 15, she worked as a daily worker in local fruit and vegetable production.

Daily workers, as a social group which is formed and augments during the capitalist change of traditional agricultural economy, are personified in the folktale through the mother who receives some wheat in return for her labor, a far from fair compensation.

The beggars

In peasant society, beggars were not a uniform group.[45] Members of a peasant community assumed temporarily the state of a beggar when they were deprived of any other revenue due to some natural or human catastrophe, such as earthquakes or war. A beggar was generally an isolated person, man or woman, an outsider or an insider, a total stranger, a member of the extended community or even of the family group who, because of sickness, old age, or another factor of weakness, could not survive by themselves or be of use to the survival of the family.

With regard to the beggars, narratives not only supported but also modelled a system of mentalities in everyday life. Stories popularized the Orthodox Christian doctrine 'He who shows mercy to the poor, lends to God'; that is, that the alms people gave in this world they will find in the next when they get there.[46] However, giving alms to a beggar was considered reciprocal not only in religious but also in social terms: the beggar who receives help also has something to give: his blessing. Thus the one who does good, will receive good. On the contrary, the one who behaves badly, will receive something bad. Numerous oral tales, proverbs, and similes in local repertoires narrativize social ideas of contact with the underprivileged by projecting these ideas onto a more restricted social space of conflict: the family. Between the tight-fisted mother-in-law and her good-hearted daughter-in-law who secretly gives alms to the poor, or the good woman who turns

44 For the theme of seasonal moving of workers from the islands of the Dodecanese and, more widely the Aegean, to Asia Minor. see Papataxiarchis & Petmezas 1998, 224; Karachristos 2016; Koutelakis 1986-87; Papachristodoulou 1994, 475; Savorianakis 2000.

45 Mendicancy as a social phenomenon in Greece (especially of the urban space) in the framework of the general concept of marginality is studied by Kouzas 2017.

46 For the connection of *philanthropia* with orthodox Christianity in modern Greece, see Kouzas 2017, 285-86 who also cites the relevant bibliography.

into marble; conversely, the woman who gives the old beggar poisoned bread receives her punishment: her son dies, from the accidental consumption of the same bread (ATU 837); or the popular folk legend about the tight-fisted mother of Saint-Phanourios (ATU 804), connected with the relevant custom of *phanouropita*.[47]

The concept of moral economy

It seems that these stories allude to a lurking value-ruling system of obligations and rewards. Even if the family constituted the main economic and social unit in the rural community and, thus, every person was referring to his (or her) own domestic universe, the survival of each household depended on a wider social base. The precarity of peasant life, the poor conditions of a closed economy, and the pressures of the central and local authorities could only be resisted by forms of cooperation and assistance on a communal scale. In the organization of production and labor, there was a kind of mediation between the self-sufficient family and collective life along certain communitarian principles. Not only the family members, then, but the whole community depended on relations of reciprocity, like forms of communal work on an exchange basis. There are different terms describing different types of these non-monetized exchange relations, from more egalitarian ones to more discriminating, depending on the degree of social inequalities inside a community. There is *argatia*, the voluntary collective work for the beneficence of different households in turn; the *nichteri*, the female collective work, like spinning or knitting during the night hours; or the *veggera (*other terms: *geitonema, aposperida, sergianni, rouga),* referring to an unofficial gathering of neighbors or villagers, since communal work also met the needs of sociability and entertainment.

47 Kaplanoglou 2006.

Thus, collective life and economic relations on an exchange basis, rather than being a threat to the peasant household, were a prerequisite for its subsistence. In the precapitalist, traditional system of social and economic organization, family (blood) relations and social relations are formed complementarily.

Additionally, in certain cases, the offering of help inside the community surpasses even the relations of exchange and reciprocity considered on absolute economic grounds and is being conceived on a wider ethical basis.

We may find these traditions relevant to the concept of moral economy (derived from British historian E. P. Thompson's treatment of bread riots in the eighteenth century),[48] which alludes to a deep-rooted pattern of behavior according to which peasant communities share a set of attitudes and norms of justice concerning the social relations and social behaviors that surround the local economy. Thus, the appropriate economic functions of the different social groups inside a community are in accordance with the traditional view of the social rules and obligations.

Of much relevance is also the concept of the 'subsistence ethic' (developed by James C. Scott):[49] it argues that rural communities strategically approved stability rather than maximization of profit, thus relations were structured around the moral principle that profit is less important than survival. The idea that prevails is that local social arrangements should be structured in such a way as to respect the subsistence needs of the rural poor. The subsistence ethic is then a widely shared set of moral values across different traditional peasant societies due to the common existential circumstances of traditional family-based agriculture.

48 Thompson 1963 and 1971.

49 Scott 1976.

Oral narration faced with social transition

The evolution of traditional agricultural economy from subsistence to commercial capitalism exercised new pressure on the underprivileged, as well on the pre-existing system of communitarian principles that ensured their survival. As we have seen, in a more archaic system of social organization, family relations and social relations were formed to a great extent on a complementary basis, due to certain communitarian principles. But as social discrimination deepens, the traditional organization system of the family is also disrupted. Does that mean that the former communitarian principles (such as non-monetized exchange relations conceived on a wider ethical basis) also come to an end?

Researchers, like the Greek folklorist G. A. Megas, who from the 1930s studied the local architecture in the Dodecanese, in relation with the organization of the family and devolution customs, pointed out the dysfunctions of the traditional value system in the new era. Megas had met an 82-year-old Rhodian who had built seven houses for his seven daughters, as customary law for dowries imposed, and 'in the end, he himself remained homeless, staying temporarily with his old wife in the house of one of his daughters, deceased by then, at the tolerance of his grandchildren, who were absent in the Middle East'.[50] As stated by Papachristodoulou in the *History of Rhodes*, village women tried to raise some capital for the dowry of their daughters and also reserve a hoard for their old age. Otherwise they would become a burden for their children who were also poor.[51]

However, those economic and social changes did not immediately destroy the former domestic economy or the traditional value system of community relations, which remained a point of negotiation in everyday communication. Stamatia's and Marietta's tales (reflecting up to a point the tale told by their father) seem then to respond to a burning matter of their time, transferred, through oral narration, to a symbolic level: following a scheme of a cyclical narrative plot, the beggar's (Christ's) last demand for alms from the royal couple (the king and the girl) refers not only to a threatened community space but also to a threatened domestic space: "When it was dusk, Christ, comes back and says: 'Give alms, my son, to me, the stranger. I am an old man, my clothes are dirty and I do not want to stay in your house. Do you have, a separate room, a small room, where I can stay?'" Outside, there was a small room with a bed and a fireplace; they said to him, "Stay here."

Stamatia's folktale in particular offers an impressive analogy of the interconnection between the domestic and the social. The reappearing old beggar behaves not as a social outcast but as an old relative in need. He asks not simply to be hosted but demands that the young couple secures him a small room outside the main house so that he may stay like a parent in the so-called *gerontiko* (the room for old parents).[52]

Conclusion

The versions of the tale studied above differ from the Pan-Hellenic as well as the Mediterranean type of the story, due to the desacralization of the basic thematic core of the magic tale, thus addressing problems of social relations, while they also differ slightly from each other, due to each narrator's choices. This symbolic rearrangement of an archaic plot, on the basis of historically defined value systems and attitudes, is here related to the appreciation of the genre of the folktale by the audiences of a local peasant community, passing through a time of change and

50 Megas 1949, 5.

51 Papachristodoulou 1994, vol. 2 505.

52 The inclusive term used in the Dodecanese, as well as in other parts of Greece is *gerontomoiri* (the old-age share) (Megas 1939, 114; Tsirpanlis 2018, 437-41).

a *disenchantment* process.[53] The folktale seems to imply that as social discrimination dislocates family and kinship relations, community relations (offering of help on an exchange base, giving alms) are also difficult to maintain or are subjected to discriminating procedures. But it is the daughter who, contrary to the will of the mother, keeps maintaining the traditional value system and thus is rewarded in the end. Accordingly, many of my own female informants insisted with hidden pride on the fact that, in spite of the difficulties, they continued to take care of their elderly parents who lived nearby, in the *gerontiko* room. These little one–roomed spaces of elderly women – like the one alluded to in the folktale – were the usual setting where I listened to many of my narrators, including Stamatia, thus elevating reality into folktale fantasy.

Marianthi Kaplanoglou
National and Kapodistrian University of Athens
mkaplanog@phil.uoa.gr

Bibliography

AARNE, A. & S. THOMPSON 1961
The Types of the Folktale: A Classification and Bibliography, Helsinki.

ABRAHAMS, R. D. 1983
African Folktales. Traditional stories of the black world, New York.

ANGELOPOULOU, A. 2017
'Από μάνα σε κόρη, τροφή και κλώσιμο σε τρία μαγικά νεοελληνικά παραμύθια', in *Το παραμύθι. Απο τούς αδελφούς Grimm στην εποχή μας: διάδοση και μελέτη*, M. G. Meraklis, G. Papantonakis, C. Zafiropoulos, M. Kaplanoglou, & G. Katsadoros (eds.), Athens, 205-16.

53 For the range of the term in Folklore Studies, see Radulović & Đorđević Belić 2021.

BEN-AMOS, D. 2011
Folktales of the Jews. Vol. 3: Tales from Arab Lands, Philadelphia.

BEN-AMOS, D. 2010
'Straparola: The Revolution That Was Not', Journal of American Folklore 123/490, 426-46.

BOTTIGHEIMER, R. B. 2005
'France's First Fairy Tales: The Restoration and Rise Narratives of "Les facetieuses nuictz du Seigneur François Straparole"', *Marvels and Tales* 19.1, 17-31.

BREMOND, C. 1979
'Le meccano du conte', *Magazine Littéraire* 150, 13-16.

BRU, J. 2017
Le Conte Populaire Français. Contes merveilleux. Supplément, Toulouse.

BURKERT, W. 1993
Ελληνική Μυθολογία και Τελετουργία. Δομή και Ιστορία [*Structure and History in Greek Mythology and Ritual*, transl. by Ilektra Andreadi], Athens.

DÉGH, L. 1989
Folktales and society: story-telling in a Hungarian Peasant Community, Bloomington & Indianapolis.

DELARUE, P. & M.-L. TENÈZE 1964
Le conte populaire français, tome deuxième, Paris.

DOR, R. 1983
Contes Kirghiz de la Steppe et de la Montagne, Paris.

EBERHARD, W. & P.-N. BORATAV 1953
Typen türkischer Volksmärchen, Wiesbaden.

FRANCKE, A. H. 1925
'Wa-Tsei-Sgruns Fuchsgeschichten erzählt von Dkon-Mchog-Bkrashis, aus Kha-La-Tse', *Asia Major*, 2 408-31.

GERGATSOULIS, V. I. 2006
'Οι θρησκευτικές αντιλήψεις των κατοίκων της Καρπάθου, όπως παρουσιάζονται μέσα στις θρησκευτικές διηγήσεις του νησιού', *Καρπαθιακά* 2, 359-88.

HOLBEK, B. 1987
Interpretation of Fairy Tales. Danish Folklore in a European Perspective, Helsinki.

HYMES, D. 2000
'Survivors and Renewers', *Folklore Forum* 31.1, 3-16.

KAKAVOULIA, M. & P. POLITIS (ED.) 2022
Αφήγηση. Μια πολυεπιστημονική θεώρηση, Athens.

KALIAMBOU, M. 2017
'"Εφυγεν εκεί όπου δεν πεθαίνουν...". Αναπαραστάσεις των νεκρών στα ελληνικά παραμύθια', *Λαογραφία* 43, 177-99.

KAPLANOGLOU, M. 1999
'AT 545B "Puss in Boots" and "The Fox-Matchmaker": From the Central Asian to the European Tradition' *Folklore* 110, 57-62.

KAPLANOGLOU, M. 2006
'The Folk Cult of St Phanourios in Greece and Cyprus, and its Relationship with the International Tale Type 804', *Folklore* 117.1, 54-74.

KAPLANOGLOU, M. 2022
Παραμύθια και Καθημερινή Ζωή. Θεωρητικές και εμπειρικές παράμετροι μιας λαογραφικής έρευνας στη Ρόδο. Athens.

KARACHRISTOS, Y. 2016
'Διασχίζοντας το Αιγαίο: Μεταναστευτικά ρεύματα από το Αιγαίο και τον ελλαδικό χώρο προς τα δυτικά παράλια της Μικράς Ασίας (18ος-αρχές 20ού αιώνα)', *Epetiris tou Laographikou Archeiou* 33/34, 635-65.

KATSADOROS, G. 2019
Αισώπειοι μύθοι. Πρόσληψη και μετάπλαση στη λαϊκή και τη λόγια παράδοση, Athens.

KAWAN, C. S. 2005
'The Princess on the Pea: Andersen, Grimm and the Orient', Fabula 46.1-2, 89-115.

KEIGHTLEY, T. 1834
Tales and popular fictions, their resemblance and transmission from country to country, London.

KÖHLER-ZÜLCH, I. 1993A
'Kater: Der gestiefelte K. (AaTh545B)', *Enzyklopädie des Märchens* 7, 1070-83.

KÖHLER-ZÜLCH, I. 1993B
'Katzenschloß (545A)', *Enzyklopädie des Märchens* 7, 1126-31.

KONSTANTAKOS, I. M. 2011
'Ephippos' Geryones: a comedy between myth and folktale', *Acta Antiqua Academiae Scientiarum Hungaricae* 51, 223-46.

KONSTANTAKOS, I. M. 2019
'The Island that was a Fish: An Ancient Folktale in the *Alexander Romance* and in Other Texts of Late Antiquity', in *Aspects of Orality and Greek Literature in the Roman Empire*, C. Ruiz Montero (ed.), Cambridge, 281-301.

KOUKOULES, P. 1948-55
Βυζαντινών βίος και πολιτισμός, Athens.

KOUTELAKIS, X. 1986-87
'Παρουσία Τηλίων στη Μικρά Ασία: Φιλόπτωχη αδελφότητα Ναζλίου', *Δελτίο Κέντρου Μικρασιατικών Σπουδών* 6, 269-85.

KOUZAS, G. X. 2017
Η επαιτεία στην πόλη. Μορφές οργάνωσης-στρατηγικές επιβίωσης – ταυτότητες. Athens.

KYRIAKIDIS, S. 1925
'Ο Εφταπάρθενος χορός', *Ημερολόγιον της Μεγάλης Ελλάδος* 4, 489-511.

LÉVI-STRAUSS, C. 1964
Le cru et le cuit: Mythologiques 1, Paris.

LINCOLN, A. 1976
'The Indo-European Cattle-Raiding Myth', *History of Religion* 16, 42-65.

LINDAHL, C. 1997
'Introduction', in *Swapping Stories: Folktales from Louisiana*, C. Lindahl, M. Owens, & C. R. Harvison (eds.), Mississippi, 3-29.

LINDAHL, C. 2011
'Female Narrators, Protagonists, and Villains of the American Mountain Märchen', *Fabula* 52.1, 2-16.

LÖRINCZ, L. 1979
Mongolische Märchentypen, Wiesbaden.

LÜTHI, M. 2017
Το λαϊκό παραμύθι ως ποίηση. Αισθητική και Ανθρωπολογία [*Das Volksmärchen als Dichtung: Ästhetik und Anthropologie,* transl. by E. Katrinaki], Athens.

MACLER, F. 1911
Contes et Légendes de l'Arménie, Paris.

MASONI, L. 2007
'Two Different Approaches to the Retelling of Traditional Tales Among 'Non-Storytellers' in a North Italian Village', *Fabula* 48.1-2, 33-49.

MEGAS, G. A. 1939
'Ζητήματα Ελληνικής Λαογραφίας', *Επετηρίς του Λαογραφικού Αρχείου* 1, 99-149.

MEGAS, G. A. 1949
Η λαϊκή οικία της Δωδεκανήσου, Athens.

MEGAS, G. A. 1967
'Die Moiren als funktioneller faktor im Neugriechischen Märchen' *Laographia* 25, 316-32.

MEGAS G. A., A. ANGELOPOULOS, A. BROUSKOU, M. KAPLANOGLOU & E. KATRIANAKI 2012
Catalogue of Greek Magic Folktales, Helsinki.

MÉLÉTINSKY, E. M. 1970
'Problème de la morphologie historique du conte populaire', *Semiotica* 2, 128-34.

MERAKLIS, M. G. 1999
Το λαϊκό παραμύθι. Κείμενα παραμυθολογίας, Athens.

MERAKLIS, M. G. 2004
Ελληνική Λαογραφία: Κοινωνική συγκρότηση – Ήθη και έθιμα – Λαϊκή τέχνη, Athens.

NOYES, D. 2016
Humble Theory: Folklore's Grasp on Social Life, Bloomington & Indianapolis.

OLSEN, B. 2019
"The Snake who Became a Prince, or The Girl with Two Husbands: An Analysis of the Fairytale (AT *433B) Based on Hatzi-Yavrouda's Version from Kos" in *Proceedings of the Danish Institute at Athens* 9, 115-26.

ORIOL, C. & J. M. PUJOL 2008
Index of Catalan Folktales, Helsinki.

PAPACHRISTODOULOU, C. I. 1994
Ιστορία της Ρόδου από τους προϊστορικούς χρόνους έως την ενσωμάτωση της Δωδεκανήσου, Athens.

PAPATAXIARCHIS, E. & S. D. PETMEZAS 1998
'The Devolution of Property and Kinship Practices in Late- and Post-Ottoman Ethnic Greek Societies. Some demo-economic factors of nineteenth and twentieth century transformations', *Mélanges de l'Ecole française de Rome. Italie et Méditerranée* 110.1, 217-41.

PERRAULT, C. 1697
"Le Maitre Chat ou Le Chat Botté", in *Histoires ou contes du temps passé,* Paris.

PITRÈ, G. 1875
Fiabe novelle e racconti popolari siciliani, Palermo.

POLÍVKA, J. 1900
'Le Chat Botté', *Sbornik za Narodni Umotvorenija* 16/17, 782-841.

PUCHNER, W. 2011
Παραμυθολογικές μελέτες Α΄. Η ξεχασμένη νύφη. Από την Ιταλική Αναγέννηση στο Ελληνικό λαϊκό παραμύθι, Athens.

RADULOVIĆ, N. & S. ĐORĐEVIĆ BELIĆ (EDS.) 2021
Disenchantment, Re-enchantment and Folklore Genres, Institute for Literatures and Art, Belgrade.

ROSE, H. J. 1954
'Chthonian Cattle', *Numen* 1, 213-17.

SAVORIANAKIS, P. 2000
'Οικογένεια και γαμήλιες πρακτικές στο νοτιοανατολικό Αιγαίο: η Κως στο 18ο και 19ο αιώνα', *Mnimon* 22, 31-68.

SCOTT, J. C. 1976
The Moral Economy of the Peasant: Rebellion and Subsistence in Southeast Asia, Yale.

SIMONSEN, M. 2014
'Danish Folkloristics: between Philology and Ethnology', *Estudis de Literatura Oral Popular / Studies in Oral Folk Literature* 3, 107-18.

TAUBE E. 1978
'War das Urbild des Gestiefelten Katers ein Fuchs?', in *Proceedings of the Csoma de Körjs Memorial Symbosium,* L. Ligeti (ed.), Budapest, 473-85.

THOMPSON, E. P. 1963
The Making of the English Working Class, New York.

THOMPSON, E. P. 1971
'The Moral Economy of the English Crowd in the Eighteenth Century', *Past and Present* 50.1, 76-136.

TSIRPANLIS, Z. N. 2018
Γαμήλιες συμπεριφορές στο Αιγαίο. Το παράδειγμα της Νισύρου (19ος αι.), Athens.

UTHER, H.- J. 1987
'Fuchs', *Enzyklopädie des Märchens* 5, 447-78.

UTHER, H.- J. 1992
'Der Fuchs als Tierhelfer in Mongolischen Volkserzählungen', in *Fragen der Mongolischen Heidendichtung,* 5, 136-44.

UTHER, H.- J. 2011
The Types of International Folktales. A Classification and Bibliography. Part I–III. Helsinki.

UTHER, H.-J. 2017
'Η ιστορία των Παραμυθιών για τα παιδιά και το σπίτι', in *Το παραμύθι. Απο τούς αδελφούς Grimm στην εποχή μας: διάδοση και μελέτη*, M. G. Meraklis, G. Papantonakis, C. Zafiropoulos, M. Kaplanoglou, & G. Katsadoros (eds.), Athens, 799-844.

VARVOUNIS, M. G. 2017
'Παραμυθιακά στοιχεία σε σύγχρονα αγιολογικά κείμενα γερόντων της ορθόδοξης εκκλησίας', in *Το παραμύθι. Απο τούς αδελφούς Grimm στην εποχή μας: διάδοση και μελέτη*, M. G. Meraklis, G. Papantonakis, C. Zafiropoulos, M. Kaplanoglou, & G. Katsadoros (eds.), Athens, 397-413.

VAZ DA SILVA, F. 2010
'The Invention of Fairy Tales', *Journal of American Folklore* 123/490, 398-425.

ZAFIROPOULOS, C. A. 2001
Ethics in Aesop's Fables: the Augustana Collection, Leiden.

ZIPES, J. (ED.) 2004
Beautiful Angiola: The Great Treasury of Sicilian Folk and Fairy Tales Collected by Laura Gonzenbach, New York.

ZIPES, J. 2013
The Irresistible Fairy Tale: The Cultural and Social History of a Genre, Princeton.

ZIPES, J. & J. RUSSO 2009 (EDS.)
The Collected Sicilian Folk and Fairy Tales of Giuseppe Pitré, New York & London.

Legend as fact in Greek and Eastern European traditions: Reality factors and the example of visions

Stamatis Zochios

Abstract

The present article explores a specific and broad folklore genre, the legend, and its narrative structure given that it is more or less considered as fact. The verisimilitude of the legend is commented through the narratological analysis of the use of the frequently defined temporal and spatial dimensions, its austere, non-literary, informative form, the presence of witnesses that influence the sequence, as well as the narratological use of the so-called reality factors. In this context, the article focuses on the use of a vision or a dream that is commonly believed to be true, in order to give credibility to the narrative. The article's main goal is to answer whether a legend constructed on such reality factors is an orally produced and diffused story similar to fables and tales, or if it is a documented result of the narrativization of the folk beliefs transmitted from generation to generation through lived experience and practice.

I. Defining the main structure: the characteristic of credibility

Four years after *Kinder und Hausmärchen* (*Children's and Household Tales*) was first published in 1812, the Brothers Grimm published a collection of another type of folk narrative entitled *Deutsche Sagen* (*German legends*).[1] The book never became as popular as *Kinder und Hausmärchen*, even if it is one of the first systematic compilations of legends and one of the first attempts to define the genre. Thus, in the introduction, legends are compared to fairy tales:

> The fairy tale is more poetic, the legend is more *historical*;[2] the former exists securely in and of itself in its innate blossoming and consummation. The legend, by contrast, is characterized by a *lesser variety of colors*, yet it represents something special in that it adheres always to that which we are conscious of and know well, such as a locale or a name that has been secured through history. Because of this local confinement, it follows that the legend cannot, like the fairy tale, find its home anywhere. Instead the legend demands certain conditions without which it either cannot exist at all, or can only exist in perfect form.[3]

As we examine this juxtaposition, which could also serve as a definition of this specific genre of folk literature, we read first of all that the legend has a lesser

1 Grimm 1981, 1. According to T. Gunnel, this renowned early definition of the legend might have drawn too distinct a line between the essence of the legend and that of the wonder/fairy tale. Nevertheless, the correlations emphasized by Grimm in this passage between the legend and the temporal and geographical backdrop in which storytellers and their listeners dwell, remain valid (Gunnel 2009a, 13).

2 My emphasis.

3 Ward 1979, 1.

variety of colors. In other terms, it is not so poetic, or at least is less poetic than the fairy tale. Moreover, in the introduction to his emblematic work on German mythology published in 1844, *Deutsche Mythologie*, Jacob Grimm emphasizes that:

> The Fairy-tale (Märchen) is with good reason distinguished from the legend, though by turns they play into one another. Looser, less fettered than legend, the Fairy-tale lacks that local habitation, which hampers legend, but makes it more home-like. The Fairy-tale flies, the legend walks, knocks at your door; the one can draw freely out of the fullness of poetry, the other has almost the authority of history.[4]

In both passages the reason for which the legend is less poetic and finally more historical is its *local confinement,* the fact that it is always connected to some *certain conditions,* and consequently to a specific reality, well-defined by a given community. This sense of reality is significant when we are referring to legends. For Röhrich and Lüthi, the legend attempts to reconstruct reality in a believable way.[5] In other words, the legend narrates a fact, or rather something that is considered as fact, that is believed to be true. This is also stated in Politis's,[6] Megas's,[7] Kyriakides's,[8] Loukatos's,[9] Meraklis's,[10] and Papachristoforou's[11] definitions of *paradóseis* ("traditions"[12]), a word that is used rather indiscriminately as a synonym of *thrýlos,* meaning legend. For that reason, it is necessary for legend to feature a convincing style by presenting witnesses and evidence.[13] The narrated event is believed to be factual, is considered as fact-based,[14] and the narrative has an informative function and utilitarian, direct, almost documentary character, organized according to the narrator's experience.[15]

According to Lüthi, in legend, the experiencer is under the influence of his experience.[16] That is why in most cases a legend is a dry, factual account, narrated in the first person according to the teller's experience.[17] Moreover it is monoepisodic, referring to a single event and may be quite brief as a consequence.[18] It is difficult to imagine a fairy tale of three to five lines while there are many cases of such concise legends. The reason, as Tillhagen and Hand explain, is because "legend does not lead an independent literary existence, as does the *Märchen,* but is a part of folk belief".[19]

This connection between legend and a sense of belief is most crucial in the analysis of the specific genre. Legends primarily revolve around matters of truth and aim to assert the truthfulness of an event;[20] underlying the emphasis on "truth" and "belief" is the key aspect that distinguishes legends from wonder tales: legends are said to have unfolded in the "actual" world we inhabit.[21]

By belief it is not only meant that the narrated event is connected to a personal faith, issued from narrator's individual experience, but on a larger scale that it is also connected to a common folk faith belonging to the community from which the narrator originates. For Dégh and Vazsonyi it is not the narrator's or listener's belief that is important, but a certain belief that makes its presence felt in any

4 Grimm 2012, xv. See also Dégh 1972, 73.
5 Tangherlini 1990, 372.
6 See Politis 1904.
7 Megas 1967, 190-93.
8 Kyriakidis 1965, 168-214.
9 Loukatos 1992, 151-7.
10 Meraklis 1992/1996, 148 and Meraklis 1992, 325-35.
11 Papachristoforou 1999-2003, 148-52.
12 In this case the term is used as a synonym of folk beliefs.

13 Dégh 1972, 74.
14 Ward 1991, 301.
15 Lüthi 1961, 46-48.
16 Dégh 1996, 36.
17 Dégh 1972, 75.
18 Blehr 1978, 707.
19 Tillhagen 1964,13; Hand 1965, 441.
20 Oring 2008, 128.
21 Gunnel 2009a, 14.

kind of legend.[22] In other words, legends are stories about belief. Röhrich called them *fabula credibilis*, opposing them to fairy tales *fabula incredibilis*,[23] while according to Gunnar Cranberg, legends exist because they express the shared beliefs of a specific community or region.[24]

In reality, the relationship between legend and folk belief is particularly complicated and the topic's extensive bibliography demonstrates the existence of different point of views that do not agree on whether the two terms are synonymous or not. For some specialists, legend is identified with folk belief and cannot be considered as separate, while for some others a clear distinction should be made; for this reason a series of alternative names are proposed, such as belief legend, belief story, belief tale, memorate, fabulate, and so on, as well as a distinction between the historical, supernatural, religious, etiological, etc.[25]

Without entering into details about the distinction between legend and folk belief, which is not the key issue of this article, I will schematically consider legend as the narrativization of folk beliefs, the main narrativization of folk beliefs but not the only one, given that they can be channeled through different folk literary genres like incantations, songs, or (more rarely) fairy tales, and above all that it can be closely connected to folk practices and rituals.[26]

II. Objective-subjective evidence, legendry's rhetoric of truth and reality factors

Folk beliefs, like any belief, have an abstract, non-stable, undefined form that does not permit us to derive a specific morphology. They are actually formless. Moreover, folk beliefs constitute an open system, making it almost impossible to categorize or classify them. The latter explains why it is not always easy to classify a narrativized form of a folk belief, in other terms a legend, into a historical, religious, etiological category: some legends can thus be historical, religious, and etiological at the same time, as folk beliefs constitute an open system. Moreover, in this regard, the establishment and application of an Aarne-Thompson-like index of legends is unrealistic, as the genre is shaped by an infinite number of motifs.[27] Any type of categorization is risky and categories are not strictly defined. In most cases, they are fragile, abstract, non-stable, and open, exactly like the folk beliefs on which they are based. For example, a legend about a fairy may represent a fairy with elements adopted by another category of supernatural being: a witch, a mermaid, a white lady, a genius loci, etc.

On the other hand it seems that legend, even if difficult to classify, has a more specific (and in this case narrativized) form and is rather structured. In order to present evidence, and to persuade the audience, according to Dégh, an introduction is often needed.[28] This more or less journalistic introduction

22 Dégh & Vazsonyi 1976, 119.

23 Ward 1991, 297.

24 Granberg 1935, 120-27.

25 Dégh 1996, 43. For a comprehensive overview of the different theories that have been proposed, see Tangherlini 1990.

26 A ritual "performs" and quite often embodies a folk belief. In an example from a Greek village in the Doxario region, a local narrator informs the interviewer that: "Our village is protected by a magic circle. Neither gipsies nor bears are allowed to enter it because were they to do so the protective magic would be dispelled"(Blum 1970, 37). This specific circle that protects the village is a magic one – a sacred space created by practitioners around a person or, on a bigger scale, around a village or even a city. In the above example, the widespread popular belief about a magic circle defining a sacred protective space around a person or a place acquires locality and substance through a ritualistic performance transforming it from faith into practice (Levkievskaja 2002, 27-42).

27 Hand 1965, 444.

28 Dégh 1972, 75.

gives all the preliminary information: hour, day, season, year, i.e. time, and then the exact space. The following example of Russian narration about witches is quite informative, personalized, and adapted to the community's reality:

> Interviewer: Is it true that wizards look into water?
> Informant: Certainly. A glass of water can reveal things. Let's say I'm a wizard and someone has harmed you. The wizard can show you that man in the water. That man will appear in the glass as if in a photograph. The wizards can do something else as well, but only the ones who don't believe in God or the Devil, not in anything. You might ask Uncle Anton to do to that person what he had done to you. For example, you might ask him to knock out an eye. Of course, there would be times when he would not agree, but he might show you the man in the glass and he'd take some object and poke it in the man's eye while he was in there and the eye would pop out. So that man would lose his eye. Oh yes, *that happened here.*[29]

The context is defined according to personal experience (*that happened here*) with the addition of personal details (Uncle Anton). Moreover, the above folk belief is presented in a conversational style as a dialogue between a journalist/interviewer and an informant, which is very frequent in this kind of narrative.

Consequently, a legend is usually structured against a spatiotemporal background, which implies the formation of belief on a realistic basis. Time and space are the two main axes of the fact, something that is explained by von Sydow's important concept of ecotypification,[30] according to which the ecotype, a term from evolutionary biology, denotes a local variation of an international type.[31] There exists an interdependence relationship between the legend, the community, and the place where the community resides. The legend is influenced by the community, its principles, codes, and the landscape in which it is rooted, all of which ultimately shape the axes of a shared truth and the credibility that that preserves its integrity. Legends strive to depict events within a world that closely resembles the external reality experienced by the traditional participants.

As a result, legends often provide intricate details about various aspects of the community (including market towns, mountain dairies, fishing grounds, churches, farming methods, foods, and cultural connections between different countries, counties, and parishes).[32] Logically, different categories of legends reflect different aspects of society. Legends related to religious themes reflect ideas about a common religious ethics and worldview shared by local storytellers within a specific cultural context, and not only provide a narrative backdrop for the landscape but also serve as maps that encompass the geographical, mental, historical, and spiritual dimensions of the community. On a practical level, they serve to familiarize listeners with place names and routes, while also adding historical richness to the area by populating it with memories, spirits, and various supernatural entities. Moreover, these legends function as guides for behavior, emphasizing moral and social values and presenting examples to emulate or avoid. At the same time, they remind individuals of the temporal and physical boundaries of their existence, prompting contemplation of life, death,

29 Warner 1995, 80.

30 Sydow 1948, 16. See also Hasan-Rokem 2016.

31 In ancient Greek mythology, for example, Lamia was a beautiful queen of Libya transformed by Hera into an insomniac vampiric monster who seized children and ate their flesh. The specific supernatural being not only reappears (as a witch, a fairy, or a revenant) in modern Greek folk beliefs – in this case the evolution is vertical while the spatial background is stable – but also in European mythology in general via a horizontal evolution: for example, in Bulgaria it is a dragon, while in western Europe it has appeared since the Middle Ages as a dragon, a child-eating monster, a revenant, a witch, a fairy, a mermaid, a nightmare, etc. See Zochios 2011.

32 Gunnel 2009b, 312.

and transitional periods, as well as highlighting the distinction between insiders and outsiders.[33] In this case, the beliefs, values, and practices that collectively shape a shared and intra-community truth should be understood from an emic point of view.

Change in time and space consecutively transforms community, personal and communal experience and, finally, folk belief: as a result, legend, narrativizing a folk belief, is distinct even if it is based on international motifs and themes. This phenomenon defines whether legend is historical, as the brothers Grimm pointed out, or not, and whether it is characterized by historicity, connected to a specific spatiotemporal frame. In reality, legend is a historicized and not a historical narrative. The point of view is not objective and expanded as in history, and thereby does not permit a historical-objective approach of a fact believed to be true, but rather a perspective limited to the boundaries of the community (the legend in this case can reflect the historical consciousness of a given society)[34] or even of the person.[35] This finite (and in many cases even subjective) perspective is shaped by what Elliott Oring calls legendry's rhetoric of truth.[36]

Starting from the assumption that a legend deals with factual matters and asserts the truth of an event, Oring concludes that legendary storytelling has its own language ("belief language") and vocabulary ("belief vocabulary"), which are specific to particular communities.[37]

This specialized language is used to make the story credible, even if the narrator does not believe in it.[38] Based on this language, a rhetoric is developed to allay doubts and foil challenges,[39] relying on a set of factors that make the legend credible. Such factors include the authority of the source, the distancing (the closer the connection of a narrator to his or her source, the more credible the account is likely to be), the intonation, the framing, the narrative positioning, the existence of witnesses or of secondary legends that support the main one, the narrative strategy, the story logic, and the use of aesthetic effects.

In order, finally, for a legend to be perceived as true, it is more likely to be accepted when it aligns with the cognitive, emotional, and moral expectations of its audience.[40]

Similarly, Dégh argues that credibility is built upon certain reality factors. However, unlike Oring, whose framework is more elaborate and analytical, Dégh's framework is highly schematic and focuses on the issue of verifying the factor of credibility.

According to Dégh, reality factors can be separated into two categories that can mostly be found in the introduction of a legend:[41]

A. The first is "a verifiable fact, commonly known to be true, for it has been experienced or preserved in memory, and may also be supported by physical evidence, by an object that commemorates a past event".[42] In this case the use of the factor is more directed and proceeds from an objectified truth.
B. The second category of reality factors is an illusion, commonly believed to be true.[43] This spe-

33 *Ibid.*, 309.

34 Siikala 2009, 39.

35 The "very serious element of personal experience" in *paradóseis* is pointed out by Meraklis, considering that Politis erroneously omits it from his definition (Meraklis 1992/1996, 148). The specific element of personal experience is later used by Papachristoforou for the definition and classification of *paradóseis* (Papachristoforou 1999-2003, 148-49).

36 Oring 2008.

37 *Ibid.*, 128.

38 As Koski points out the alleged "the alleged belief in legends was later observed to be overestimated. The modified suggestion was that legends involve a claim to be judged as true or false" (Koski 2016, 114).

39 Oring 2008, 129.

40 *Ibid.*, 157.

41 Dégh 1972, 74.

42 *Idem.*

43 Dégh 1972, 74.

cific category is extremely broad and essentially encompasses anything that cannot be verified and therefore falls within the realm of faith: the hoofmark of a horse on a rock where a hero rested, a vision and a hallucination, beliefs in supernatural agencies and witches, etc. This particular distinction is rather problematic because it is overly general. However, it is interesting because it treats visions as a subcategory of legends.

III. The example of visions

This subcategory of reality factors cannot be considered self-evident like the first category, where something is commonly known to be true because it has been experienced or preserved in memory and is often accompanied by tangible proofs. In this case, the corroborating evidence is absent.

In this second case, the reality factor is not objective but subjective, as it is based on the self-evidence of the dream and/or vision, which are purely personal experiences and exclude the existence of an eyewitness or corroborating evidence. Therefore, the way in which the event occurs is different, since the narrator is obliged to insist on the realistic character of his narration in order to persuade his listener. In short, the realism of storytelling in this category is not self-evident, but presupposes what is considered a subjective experience – the dream – to obtain objective and thus proven dimensions. As expected, precisely because the experience is highly personal, the way the narrative and its credibility are constructed is different from cases with verifiable reality factors. This naturally affects the rhetoric of the narrative itself.

Two basic categories of legends that are structured on the reality factor of dreams and visions are those related to a) searching for and finding a treasure (or a miraculous icon), and b) a visionary's soul's journey to the Other World.

A. *The case of the treasure hunt*

The first category of narratives is characterized by the usual simple structure of legends, and is articulated through a rather stable series of motifs: i) the hero, through a dream or vision,[44] is informed about a place where he can find a chest, a grave, a pot, a container with valuables – the hero becomes a treasure hunter; ii) the hero finds the spot and follows the instructions: perform a sacrifice, wizardry, etc.; iii) potentially the hero has to win in a hand-to-hand fight against the treasure guardian; iv) the hero grabs the treasure and according to the successful accomplishment of the instructions and the obligation to keep silent, he finds the valuables (usually gold) or, in the opposite case, coals inside the container.[45]

The most interesting motif for our study is the first, in which the subject is usually informed about the existence of a treasure through a dream or vision. This specific narrative medium, through which a saint, a black man, or another supernatural being informs the subject about the treasure, is developed in the introduction of the narrative; a phenomenon that perfectly agrees with the aforementioned observation of Dégh, according to which reality factors of both categories can mostly be found in the introduction of a legend. The variations are numerous, without transmuting the narrative core. In Greece, for instance, a folk belief with its origins on Milos, an island in the Cyclades, informs us that:

> A saint appears to many people in their sleep and tells them that in this or that place, below a tree or a hedge, a treasure can be found. The one who has such a dream, after waking up in the morning, must take a cock, go the revealed place without saying a word, and when he arrives there, slay the cock; then he must dig

44 The distinction between the two terms is a complex issue, and we do not intend to analyze it in this article. We will adopt Stewart's view, according to which the distinguishing line between dreams and visions in folk narratives is not clear (Stewart 2012, 16).

45 For more details, see Stewart 2012; Zochios 2013.

> and find the treasure. But if he does the foolish thing and lets slip anything about his dream, when he digs for the treasure, he will find a pot full of coals.
>
> Once somebody had a similar dream, and when he woke up in the morning, said nothing to anybody, and ran to the place he dreamt of.[46]

The basic line is common: the hero sees a saint in his dream, which indicates the very spot of the treasure. Next, the hero must find the place, proceed methodically to the necessary sacrifice and finally acquire the valuables. A prerequisite for success is to keep silent; in traditions throughout Europe, the contrary case in which the secret of the treasure is revealed, proves detrimental to the valuable content and it is transformed into worthless matter, usually coals.[47]

Similarly, the narratives of the excavation of an icon are formed. A faithful person receives a command from a saint through a dream or vision to dig at a specific location and uncover an icon, which is usually ancient and miraculous. At the site where the icon is found, a church is built. Everything unfolds in the form of a dream, in a world that does not follow the logical structures of reality. These structures are rearranged as desired, to a point where the fundamental pillars of reality (and the credibility associated with it), such as space and time, are reconfigured. For example, Stewart showed how the division between present, past, and future in dreams is violated and abolished, creating a new perception of time (from which the historical dimension of these vision-dreams ultimately emerges).[48]

As expected, in the case of icons (similar to the dreams of treasure), we continue to speak of personal experiences whose authenticity cannot be verified through objective evidence. They are based, therefore, on self-reported evidence. The fact that their credibility is considered given from the outset is evident in the following claim by Stewart, which he reached during the study of prophetic dreams (mainly concerning the discovery of icons) in Naxos. As he points out, during the initial phase of his research on dreaming, he engaged in inquiries by posing general questions to individuals he encountered. Specifically, he would ask, "Tell me, what do you think about dreams?" and "Have you had any dreams lately, or heard any dreams being discussed?" However, he consistently encountered a response that served as a challenging retort, expressed as follows: "Do you believe in dreams?" This response initially perplexed him, as the occurrence of dreams is an empirically established phenomenon devoid of subjective interpretation. Consequently, the act of believing in dreams appears as an inexorable inevitability. The motivation underlying this line of questioning thus became a subject of intrigue. Partially, his confusion stemmed from an erroneous understanding of the intended connotation behind the verb "believe". Initially, he misconstrued the respondents' inquiry as pertaining to his belief in the existence of dreams, whereas their true intention was to ascertain his conviction in the predictive efficacy of dreams.[49]

Therefore, the self-reported evidence of the narratives and the fact that they are considered true from the outset (the issue of belief in them is not debatable) initially render the described events valid. In a second phase, and this is very significant, they activate their prophetic function and their predictive efficacy.

46 Politis 1904, 229.

47 This conversion can be found in other folk beliefs as well and is primarily linked to the obligation of silence imposed on the subject in initiations, rites of passage, magical practices etc.

48 Stewart 2012, 3.

49 *Ibid.*, 23.

B. The case of travel to the Otherworld

The second example of dreams or visions corresponding to legends, but this time of a more extensive length, are visions – in oral or written form – which describe how the subject, in a state of coma, ecstasy, or temporary death, visits the Otherworld, not in body but in soul, usually accompanied by a supernatural being (an angel, a saint, an ancestor, etc.). This narrative is entirely based on the dream factor. The experience of the subject (that of traveling to the Otherworld) is bounded by the dream: it starts with the vision and ends with the vision, unlike treasure hunt narratives, which start with a dream-vision but end with an act outside the dream, i.e. finding the treasure in a specific place. This individual (and never collective) experience was later associated, mainly by neuroscience, with the Near-Death Experience,[50] an element that intensifies the realistic character of the narrative, as it is considered as an occurrence.

At the same time, this particular category of narratives is more complex since in modern Greek this kind of vision has not been adequately studied and has not been classified in the categories of folk literature; at the same time it has not been treated as apocryphal text, and as a result this narrative category remains on the sidelines. By contrast, Russian folk science, even rather recently, has included this type of text in folk literature. In their 1995 article "On the genre of *obmiranie* (visits to the Otherworld)",[51] ethnolinguists and folklorists Nikita and Svetlana Tolstoy classified visions among the genres of folk literature, considering that it is not difficult to notice that they have much in common with other folk genres, especially with spiritual poems.[52] The relationship of this category with other types of folk literature was then underlined by many scholars, among them Aleksandr Pigin, according to whom modern Russian visions usually retain the canon of the genre and the eschatological theme of old Russian works, adding a number of new features, in particular an abundance of folk elements,[53] and Soboleva, who links visions to fairy tales.[54]

Having determined the place of visions in the system of other folklore genres, Nikita and Svetlana Tolstoy reveal their composition and structural features, highlighting 1) the introduction, 2) the main text, where the journey to the Otherworld is developed, and 3) the ending, including the awakening from sleep and return to life, as well as the didactic message, the moral and the prohibitions connected to what was seen during the journey.[55]

My goal here is not to set out separately and in detail the structure of this kind of text, that displays significant homogeneity in Eastern and South-Eastern Europe, but to focus on the narrative elements that exist for the sake of verity of the described dream and consequently of the whole narrative. The structure itself affects the realism of storytelling, since those elements that emphasize the correspondence of a vision to reality and define the described events as facts are encapsulated in the first part, that is, what the Tolstoys describe as the introduction. This condensation works rhetorically, building an undeniable argument from the very beginning in order to persuade the listener (or the reader if the vision has a written form).[56] As Baun points out in the chapter "Are the visions true?" of her work *Tales from another Byzantium*, byzantine visions, texts of serious religious purpose, would not have been written or copied (and I would add imitated) by later generations unless their teaching

50 For more information, see Lommel 2011.

51 Tolstoy; Tolstaya 1995. In this study we will consider the terms *videniya* and *obmiraniya* as synonymous, despite their slight differences.

52 *Ibid.*, 458.

53 Pigin 1997, 552.

54 Soboleva 2016, 163-64.

55 Tolstoy; Tolstaya 1995, 459.

56 For more details about the rhetorical function of specific narratives, see Zochios 2022.

were not thought in some sense to be "true".[57] Moreover Zaleski insists on the factuality as used by medieval authors of visions, arguing that their texts were presented as recounting genuine experience.[58]

The persuasiveness of this type of narrative is structured gradually and mainly before entering the subjective nature of the dream. Many of the elements that contribute to persuasion precede the dream and relate to objective and unambiguous information (biographical, topographical, chronological, and other elements). At the same time, many of the elements that form the convincing character, through which the vision will be considered as fact, are similar to those encountered in other types of legends.

A. Information about the individuals involved in the narrative: especially about the protagonist (the one who is travelling to the Otherworld) or even about secondary characters (e.g. a doctor, a priest, a member of the family sitting next to the deathbed, etc.). In an example coming from 20th century Russia, Klavdija is a sinful woman who, after her trip to the Otherworld, decides to repent and change her lifestyle, becoming a faithful Christian.[59] The first-person narrative provides us with a lot of information about the protagonist/narrator (that she was born on March 5, 1919 in the village of Yarki in the Novosibirsk Region; that in 1928 she lost her mother and in 1934 her father; that in 1937 she got married; that in 1963-64 she was forced to go to the hospital for an examination and that she had a malignant tumor due to which she died but only temporarily in order to come back after her "journey"). In some parts the narrative provides us with some information about secondary people like her family members or "the renowned professor Israel Isaevich Neimark" (a Jew, as she points out)[60] who operated on her.
B. Information on the place where the subject lives before falling into a coma/ecstasy/temporary death state, or the time at which the trip/dream begins and ends. For example, in Klavdija's story, the place where the events take place is the city Barnaul, in the Altai Krai region of Siberia, and the year is 1964.
C. Information on how the soul leaves the body and the Living World. Klavdija, for example, recounts that "right on the operating table, death came. I didn't feel the process of my soul separating from my body, but suddenly I saw my body from the side, as we see, for example, a thing: a coat, a table, etc. I saw people rushing around my body, trying to bring me back to life. I heard and understood everything they were talking about. I felt worried, but I could not let them know that I was there. Then I flew up. I was very surprised that I was flying over Barnaul, as if on an airplane".[61]
D. Information on how the soul returns to the body and to the Living World, which usually also describe the awakening/end of the dream. Thus, as Klavdija narrates: "I flew to the ground. And I saw cars driving along the ground and people going to work. I saw that I was flying to the area of the new market, I did not land, but I was quietly flying to the place where my body was lying, and I instantly stopped on the ground – it was at 1:30 am. After having visited the Otherworld I did not like the Earth. I went to the hospital. I went to the morgue, went into it, I looked: my body was dead, my head hung down a little and my hand, and the other hand and side were pressed by a dead man. And I didn't know how I entered the body, I just felt the icy cold".[62]

57 Baun 2007, 136-67.
58 Zaleski 1987, 87-89.
59 [Anonymous] 1999, 16-30.
60 *Ibid.*, 29.
61 *Ibid.*, 18.
62 *Ibid.*, 26

E. Use of standard phrases that assure the listener-reader of the narration's plausibility and which are the same as in all types of legends.
F. Linking of the Otherworld and trip's destination with the Living World, which creates immediacy. As mentioned above, Klavdija after having visited the Otherworld did not like the Earth. In another oral narrative from 1995, the informant Vera Stepanova Taranova from a Russian village, aged 79 and illiterate, tells a story in which a neighbor visited the Otherworld in her dream and glimpsed a beautiful, tidy garden with trees and so on that was "just like in our world".[63]

The persuasiveness of the dream gives a convincing character to the narrative itself, which is absolutely necessary in order to achieve the basic purpose of the narration. As we have already pointed out above, the legends perform different purposes according to their category: they can simply act as testimonies that inform or they can also be religious, historical, etiological, etc. sources. In the case of legends/visions describing a journey to the Other World, a narrative can describe a Near-Death Experience but since narrators are members of traditional and thus Christian communities, the function of narratives is mostly didactic and moralizing and aims at the moral education of faithful listeners or readers.[64] The still-alive visionary, through his dream travels to the world of the dead, has to return to the Living World and transfer the messages he has received from his experience.[65] According to Krinichnaia, "it is assumed that a visionary who has visited the Otherworld will be able to concretely explain to his relatives and neighbors with concrete examples that earthly existence is just a preparation for otherness, where everyone will be rewarded according to his deeds".[66] It is understandable, therefore, that those elements that will convince the reader/listener of the truth of the experience are absolutely necessary and exist at the core of the narrative, which in most such narratives is the didactic message.

As we already mentioned, according to Oring, in order for a legend to be perceived as true, it is more likely to be accepted when it aligns with the cognitive, emotional, and moral expectations of its audience. In this particular case, moral expectations prevail over cognitive and emotional ones, since the fundamental purpose of storytelling is ethical formation. The ethical dimension of these expectations is not indefinite but specific, closely linked to Christian, and more specifically Orthodox, teachings.

Conclusion

Belief in legends goes beyond personal faith and is connected to a common folk faith within the community. The relationship between legend and folk belief is complex, with different perspectives on whether they are synonymous or distinct. Legends

63 Wigzell 2005, 346.

64 These particular narratives may have – albeit less often – other functions, for example, justifying a folk belief or explaining a specific ability of the visionary (especially the ability to cure patients) that he acquired during his journey and his contact with the dead. See, Krinichina 2005, who believes that ecstatic/shamanic practices are behind these visionary therapists.

65 The moment of return is functionally crucial for two main reasons. Firstly, it allows the protagonist to act as an eyewitness, describing first-hand what they have seen beyond and offering a rare (miraculous) testimony of the afterlife. This situation is clearly linked to the very nature of the narrative, whose primary purpose is credibility, which is necessary to activate the rhetoric of the text. Secondly, it enables the protagonist to repent, to change their way of thinking and living. In this case, the return serves as a moral dividing line that distinguishes a before and an after, each associated with a different moral state. In this case, the text belongs to the collection of Christian conversion or repentance narratives where the narrator must construct a temporal rupture with their past.

66 See Krinichnaja 2005, 116.

can be seen as the narrativization of folk beliefs, closely connected to folk practices and rituals.

Folk beliefs are abstract and non-stable, making it challenging to categorize or classify them. Legends, on the other hand, can encompass historical, supernatural, religious, etiological, and other categories, often intertwining different aspects. They are structured narratives that provide detailed information about various aspects of the community, such as geography, history, cultural connections, and social values. They serve as guides for behavior and reminders of temporal and physical boundaries, being shaped by the community, its principles, its codes, and the landscape, reflecting shared beliefs and credibility.

Legends employ a rhetoric of truth to make the stories credible, utilizing factors like authority, distancing, intonation, framing, witnesses, narrative strategy, story logic, and aesthetic effects. The audience's cognitive, emotional, and moral expectations also influence the acceptance of legends as true. Reality factors play a role in establishing the credibility of legends, including verifiable facts and illusions commonly believed to be true. The distinction between objective and subjective reality factors is important, as the latter relies on personal experiences like dreams and visions to create a sense of realism in the narrative.

In all types of legends – based on either more secure reality factors (such as a commonly accepted and objective faith) or less secure ones (such as a dream-vision) – it is a necessary condition to prove that the event, on which the narrative is based, is a fact. Credibility is not an end in itself but a necessary means, a starting point from which the narrative must begin. For this reason, the realistic elements are listed without delay and usually placed in the introduction. This principle applies to all categories of legends (and folk beliefs) regardless of their function. Whether the narrative is etiological, religious, or historical, the need for credibility is paramount. Lack of credibility automatically undermines the narrative and hence its basic purpose, which, unlike in fairy tales, is not entertainment. Without the necessary believability, the narration is automatically transformed into *fabula incredibilis*, a tale that is defective and unable to perform its basic functions.

Stamatis Zochios
Hellenic Folklore Research Centre, Academy of Athens
szochios@academyofathens.gr

Bibliography

[ANONYMOUS] 1999
Pravoslavnye chudesa v XX veke: svidetel'tva ochevidcev, Tir.

BAUN, J. 2007
Tales from Another Byzantium: Celestial journey and local community in the Medieval Greek Apocrypha, New York.

BENNETT, G. 1989
'"Belief Stories": The Forgotten Genre', *Western Folklore* 48, no. 4, 289-311.

BLEHR, O. 1978
'A Hypothesis concerning the Relationship between "Verifiable" and "Unverifiable". Folk-Belief Stories in the Context of Storytelling', *The Journal of American Folklore* 91/no.360, 704-8.

BLUM, R. & E. BLUM 1970
The Dangerous Hour: The Lore of Crisis and Mystery in Rural Greece, New York.

DÉGH, L. 1972
'Folk narrative', in *Folklore and Folklife: An Introduction*, R. Dorson (ed.), Chicago, 53-83.

DÉGH, L. 1996
'What Is A Belief Legend?', *Folklore* 107, 33-46.

DÉGH, L. 2001
Legend and Belief: Dialectics of a Folklore Genre, Indiana.

DÉGH, L. & A. VAZSONYI 1973
The Dialectics of the Legend, Bloomington.

DÉGH, L. & A. VAZSONYI 1976
'Legend and Belief', in *Folklore Genres*, D. Ben-Amos (ed.), Austin & London, 93-123.

GRANBERG, G. 1935
'Memorat und Sage, einige methodische Gesichtspunkte', *Saga och sed*, Uppsala, 120-27.

GRIMM, J. 1835 (2012)
Teutonic Mythology, vol. 3, Cambridge.

GRIMM, J. & W. GRIMM 1981
The German Legends, vol. 1, Philadelphia.

GUNNEL, T. 2009A
'Introduction', in *Legends and Landscape: Plenary Papers from the 5th Celtic-Nordic-Baltic Folklore Symposium*, T. Gunnel (ed.), Reykjavik, 13-24.

GUNNEL, T. 2009B
'Legends and Landscape in the Nordic Countries', *Cultural and social history* 6.3, 305-22.

HAND, W. 1965
'Status of European and American Legend Study', *Current Anthropology* 6.4, 439-46.

HASAN-ROKEM, G. 2016
'Ecotypes: Theory of the Lived and Narrated Experience', *Narrative Culture* 3.1, 110-37.

KOSKI, K. 2016
Genre-Text-Interpretation: Multidisciplinary Perspectives on Folklore and Beyond, Helsinki.

KRINICHNAJA, N. 2005
'Legendy o vozvrashhenii iz zagrobnogo mira (po vostochnoslavjanskim materialam)', *Jetnograficheskoe obozrenie* 6, 114-29.

KYRIAKIDIS, S. 1965
Ελληνική Λαογραφία, Athens.

LEVKIEVSKAJA, E. 2002
Slavjanskij obereg. Semantika i struktura, Moscow.

LOMMEL, P. VAN 2011
Consciousness Beyond Life: The Science of the Near-Death Experience, New York.

LOUKATOS, D. 1992.
Εισαγωγή στην ελληνική λαογραφία, Athens.

LÜTHI, M. 1961
Volksmärchen und Volkssage. Zwei Grundformen erzählender Dichtung, Bern.

MEGAS, G. 1967
Εισαγωγή εις την Λαογραφίαν, Athens.

MERAKLIS, M. G. 1992
Λαϊκή τέχνη: Ελληνική Λαογρφία, Athens, 325-35.

MERAKLIS, M. G. 1992/1996
'Παράδοση', *Papiros-Larousse-Britanica* 48, 148.

MULLEN, P. 1971
'The Relationship of Legend and Folk Belief', *The Journal of American Folklore* 84.334, 406-13.

ORING, E. 2008
'Legendry and the Rhetoric of Truth', *The Journal of American Folklore* 121.480, 127-66.

PAPACHRISTOFOROU, M.
'Το ζήτημα της κατάταξης των παραδόσεων και οι παραδόσεις του Λαογραφικού Αρχείου', *Επετηρίδα του Κέντρου Ερεύνης της Ελληνικής Λαογραφίας* 29-30, 147-62.

POLITIS, N. G. 1904
Παραδόσεις. Μελέται περί του βίου και της γλώσσης του ελληνικού λαού, vol. 1, Athens.

PIGIN, A.V. 1997
'Videnija potustoronnego mira v rukopisnoj tradicii XVIII–XX vv.', *TODRL* 50, 551-57.

RÖHRICH, L. 1956
Märchen und Wirklichkeit: eine volkskundliche Untersuchung, Wiesbaden.

SIIKALA A.-L. 2009
'Reproducing social worlds: The practice and ideology of oral legends', in *Legends and Landscape: Plenary Papers from the 5th Celtic-Nordic-Baltic Folklore Symposium*, T. Gunnel (ed.), Reykjavik, 39-68.

SOBOLEVA, A. 2016
'Zhanr videnij v drevnerusskoj literature (na materiale Azbuchnogo paterika)'. Accessible at: http://poetica.pro/files/redaktor_pdf/1429104398.pdf

STEWART, C. 2012
Dreaming and Historical Consciousness in Island Greece, Massachusetts.

STEWART, C. 2003
'Dreams of Treasure: Temporality, Historicization and the Unconscious', *Anthropological Theory* 3.4, 481-500.

SYDOW, C. W. VON 1948
'On the spread of tradition', in *Selected papers on folklore*, C. W. von Sydow (ed.), Copenhagen, 11-43.

TANGHERLINI, T. 1990
'"It Happened Not Too Far from Here...": A Survey of Legend Theory and Characterization', *Western Folklore* 49.4, 371-90.

TILHAGEN, C. H. 1964
'Was ist eine Sage? Eine Definition und ein Vorschlag fur ein europaische Sagensystem', *Acta Ethnographica* 13, 9-17.

TOLSTOY, N. & S. TOLSTAYA 1995
'O zhanre "obmiraniya" (poseshcheniya togo sveta)', in *Yazyk i narodnaya kultura*, Moscow, 458-60.

WARD, D. 1991
'On the Genre Morphology of Legendry: Belief Story versus Belief Legend', *Western Folklore* 50.3, 296-303.

WARNER, E. 1995
'Russian Peasant Beliefs and Practices concerning Death and the Supernatural Collected in Novosokol'niki Region, Pskov Province, Russia, 1995. Part II: Death
in Natural Circumstances', *Folklore* 111.2, 255-81.

WIGZELL, F. 2005
'Reading the Map of Heaven and Hell in Russian Popular Orthodoxy: Examining the Usefulness of the Concepts of Dvoeverie and Binary Oppositions', *Forum for Anthropology and Culture* 2, 346-67.

ZALESKI, C. 1987
Otherworld journeys: Accounts of Near-Death Experience in Medieval and Modern Times, New York.

ZIPES, J. 2002
The Brothers Grimm: from enchanted forests to the modern world, Basingstoke.

ZOCHIOS, S. 2011
'Lamia: A Sorceress, a Fairy or a Revenant?', *Trictrac* 4, 96-112.

ZOCHIOS, S. 2013
'Treasure Spirits and Guardians: between dream and illusion', *Caietele Echinox* 23, 59-68.

ZOCHIOS, S. 2022
Le voyage de l'âme en Russie et en Grèce moderne. Les Expériences de mort imminente à la lumière de la religion, Diplôme postdoctoral at EPHE, Paris.

ZOCHIOS, S. 2022
'Faire un aller-retour édifiant dans l'au-delà: la formation de la rhétorique du jugement et du châtiment *post mortem* dans les visions russes et grecques modernes', dir. Zochios, S., Karamanes, E., *Études balkaniques – Cahiers Pierre Belon* (*L'au-delà en Europe de l'Est et du Sud-Est*), vol. 26, 177-203.

Orality in Contemporary Society: Analyzing the Structure of Social Comments (Gossip) in a Modern Greek Community

Manolis Varvounis and Georgios Kouzas

Abstract

This article investigates how the issues of both public and private life, and public events (even in the micro-level of the neighborhood or the macro-level of the city or the country where we live) pass into the private arena through social comments, i.e. daily gossip.

As well as the dissemination of information, the article focuses on the structure of gossip, a dimension that researchers have neglected. The researchers suggested that gossip has an irregular form because gossipers do not follow a specific structure during their narration. Nevertheless, this is another aspect where stereotypical views with no direct connection with reality have prevailed.

The article is fully based on ethnographic fieldwork research, as a part of a wider research project. It is based on participant observation and semi-structured interviews with both individuals and groups of informants.

Introduction and study goals

Oral communication has always been the leading means of everyday communication. However, as Calvet notes,[1] despite its great importance, oral communication has been neglected by researchers as unequal to written speech for two main reasons. First, speech has been held as ephemeral compared to written communication, which remains eternal and unchanged. Second, it has not been viewed as the discourse of significant literary themes but is instead mainly linked with everyday life and routine needs.

However, as Ong points out,[2] these views are nowadays obsolete. The social approach of speech and the participation of sociology and social anthropology in aspects concerning the analysis of orality offered a solid boost to the social reading of aspects of speech and stressed its communicative dimension. Since the 1950s, as Bausinger argues,[3] emphasis was further put on forms of oral communication that were – incorrectly – considered "subordinate" or "inferior", such as gossip, rumors –widely known as the grapevine – and, of course, urban legends. It gradually became apparent that these forms of speech, apart from the obvious value they have for communication, contributed significantly to promoting social relations and bonding.

The study has two main goals:

Firstly, to illustrate the importance of the topics prevailing during gossip, which is believed to be a type of speech without any meaningful subjects. Nevertheless, as illustrated by the ethnographic field

1 Calvet 1984, 13.

2 Ong 2002², 10-11.

3 Bausinger 1977, 323-24.

research, gossip is organized around specific topics that constantly feed the conversation.

Secondly, the analysis of gossip's content will illustrate that it has a specific structure that contributes to convincing the group members of the importance of what is being said and, most importantly, convincing them that what is being said is true.

Previous research on gossip: Ethnographical and anthropological approaches

Folklorists, sociologists, and social anthropologists in Greece and abroad have conducted wide-ranging research on gossip. Each discipline has studied its nature and social dynamic according to its perspective and interests. Folkloristics was among the first disciplines that turned its attention to gossip. Bausinger's studies,[4] which depicted for the first time the importance of "everyday narrations", have been very representative of such value Folkloristics has been particularly interested in the importance of orality in spreading folk culture topics and the typology of gossip and other types of everyday narrations. Undoubtedly, it is the discipline that deals with artistic folk speech by default and was interested in the comparative examination of gossip and other similar types of speech, such as rumors[5] and urban legends.[6]

Interest in gossip has also been expressed by sociology, particularly the fields of micro-sociology and social anthropology. The first steps are taken by the representatives of the Chicago School. Paul Cressey pointed out the importance of gossip in promoting one's work in the workplace,[7] and Elliot Liebow highlighted the importance of gossip as a way that unemployed and poor Americans used to find work in big cities.[8] In addition, in the 1960s, Goffman's research on the presentation of oneself in everyday life and the stigmatized identity[9] became widely known. In the 1960s and 1970s, various anthropologists published research on the anthropological approach to ephemeral and "unofficial" communication.[10] They focused mainly on the role of gossip in fundamental anthropological contexts, such as family systems, life within a community, and economic life. Furthermore, they were interested in how gossip affected the choices of both professionals and clients.[11]

Last but not least, it would be an omission not to mention the discipline of psychology, which was among the first social sciences to deal with the psychological and social dynamic of gossip.[12] To be more specific, psychology dealt, on the one hand, with the adverse effects of gossip on the psychology of the people concerned, as it is a means of bullying. On the other hand, it examined the psychological stimulation of gossip, as people who generally manipulate situations and influence their interlocutors.

Conducting research on gossip

Research on gossip is not easy for two fundamental reasons: firstly, it concerns private conversations that are challenging for the researcher to penetrate. Secondly, even if the researcher were part of a group of people gossiping, it would not be easy to record on the spot the gossip at the café, the restaurant, the workplace, or wherever they may be.

With this in mind, the research followed a multimethod approach to address these challenge aspects

4 Bausinger 1958, 239-54; Bausinger 1977, 323-30.
5 Allport & Postman 1947, 12-15; Meraklis 1993, 37-38.
6 Shermer 1997, 58-62.
7 Cressey 1932.
8 Liebow 1967.
9 Goffman 1963.
10 Gluckman 1963, 307-16; Paine 1967, 278-85; Abrahams 1970, 290-301; Cox 1970, 88-98; Wilson 1974, 93-102.
11 Hannerz 1967, 35-59; Gilmore 1978, 89-99; Kouzas 2017, 132-35.
12 Stirling 1956, 262-67.

of gossip. Our ethnographic research was conducted in 2017 in a single place, the municipality of Rafina, to develop stable networks of connections with the inhabitants, shopkeepers, and merchants of the area, and moreover, to identify gossip that has a specific origin and dissemination pattern within a limited space. During this research, the methodological tool of participative observation was employed, as the goal was to record the reactions of the people participating in the conversations. On a secondary level, questions and semi-guided questionnaires[13] as well as free conversations[14] with the informants were used to understand the essential topics included in their gossip and explore its structure.

Lastly, for the recording to be as accurate as possible, any gossip heard throughout the research was recorded immediately upon our return home to study it with as much detail as possible.

Gossip's structure

As the famous German folklorist, Bausinger, has highlighted, everyday narrations, just like gossip, did not attract researchers' attention as, on the one hand, they were considered ephemeral types of speech, whose importance lasts for a few minutes – as long as a conversation or a meal lasts. On the other hand, it was considered that these everyday narrations do not have a particular structure, and of course, no traits in common with other types of artistic folk speech. Therefore, Bausinger emphasizes that they were held as unworthy of being studied by the discipline of both philology and folkloristics. However, in the 1950s, Bausinger defended the importance of these types of everyday narrations[15]. In the 1960s, sociological and anthropological studies began to focus on the social dynamic of gossip as a type of oral communication.[16] This drastically affects a neighborhood's audience, a community, or even a city. Thus, it is characterized by temporality linked to society and the economy. If gossip succeeds to have economic and social influence, this implies that it is not a type of speech without any form or structure. On the contrary, as pointed out later on, it is an intentional and purposeful type of speech using specific structures to achieve specific results.

Let us now analyze the basic gossip structures that we identified during the field research. In general, it is a fact that gossip follows certain figures of speech. Interestingly, though, the structure of gossip appears to be closely related to its content, given that the speaker, depending on the topic chosen, follows specific structures in the way they comment on and present the issues.[17] We managed to locate five basic gossip structures, which are presented here with the frequency with which they are found in people's everyday speech:

- Figures of deductive and inductive reasoning (from a general to a specific notion and from a specific to a general notion) [Identified in the biggest proportion of gossip analyzed – 37 out of 70 cases]

  Let us analyze two relevant examples:

  1) From a specific to a general notion (deductive reasoning)

I learned yesterday from Yiannis, who fuels gasoline here at the intersection, that the owner of the gas station adulterates gasoline. This offense takes place during nighttime after midnight. People have seen him many times pouring water in the tank at night. I have not seen it with my own eyes, but at least two other people have told me so [specific conclusion]. Anyway if you see the news on TV, this is a more general prob-

13 Gilmore 1978, 90-91; Kouzas 2017, 218-20.

14 Hannerz 1967, 37-8.

15 Bausinger 1958, 239-54.

16 Rosnow & Fine 1976, 36-37; Bergmann 1993, 21-23.

17 Bausinger 1977, 323-24; Degh 1995.

lem in many areas of Greece, particularly during the summer months [general conclusion].

2) From a general to a specific notion (inductive reasoning)

> It is over; families are not like they used to be. Divorces are increasing, parents live separately, and children grow up by themselves nowadays. This is the common conclusion of any research you may read in the newspapers, i.e. that we now have the dissolution of the traditional Greek family [general conclusion]... Today Mrs. Martha told me that Yiannis and Elena, who got married last year, got divorced, and the main cause was an affair of the husband. And he did not consider that he has a small child. This is why I am telling you that the traditional Greek family does not exist anymore.

Both structures are prevalent in gossip as they satisfy two essential criteria pointed out by Abrahams.[18] First, the criterion of persuasiveness: the gossiper always wishes to persuade the audience of what is being talked about. In order to do so, a standard of comparison with cases of other people is needed. Such stories are presented as similar to the one in the gossip.[19] Second, the criterion of truth through comparison with other valid information.[20] The truth (be it the actual truth or plausibility) also plays an important role, given that it makes gossipers both credible and respected people to the community, in the sense that they convey true and correct information and not false and "constructed" truth, which would render them discreditable people.

- Figures of similarity [Identified in 30 out of 70 cases]

Many gossip examples obey the "figure of similarity"; that is, for their content to be credible, gossipers try to guide the conversation and find a realistic example from everyday life to make their argument stronger. Let us take the following, for example:

> Manolis is a good guy, a real catch for a girl to marry. I believe he would be ideal for your daughter, Eleni. Manolis is smart, very hard-working, and loves family very much. He eminds me of my husband; this is how he was, too, hard-working and a person who wanted to have a family. And I married him, and we lived happily for 40 years together.

Our ethnographic research concludes that there is a slight differentiation regarding the figures of similarity in gossip structure. In other words, when gossip has positive content, speakers tend to identify the gossip's content with examples from their own life. Instead, when gossip is mainly negative, there is a tendency to compare the stories with other people's lives. Nevertheless, why is this happening? The reason behind it is the fact that negative gossip usually touches upon sensitive family (e.g. the breaking-up of a marriage or the having of an affair) and professional matters (e.g. getting fired from a job) that nobody would want to associate with their personal life – possibly due to shame – even if the gossipers themselves have experienced similar issues.[21]

- Figures of dissimilarity [Identified in 28 out of 70 cases]

As the famous anthropologist Hirschon has pointed out, gossip as a process and the person gossiping carry negative associations.[22] There are two main reasons for this, according to her: the first is that, quite often, gossip is held to be a negative activity, most likely related to the slander of and casting as-

18 Abrahams 1970, 290-301.

19 Schoeman 1994, 72-74.

20 Levin & Arluke 1987, 123-25.

21 Rosnow 2001, 204-5.

22 Hirschon 1989, 153.

persions on other people; the second reason is that gossipers are generally considered to be people who do not have any inhibitions and judge everything and everyone.[23] What is more, they could potentially judge their interlocutors and gossip about them so as to be recognized and accepted by others. Gossipers know very well both the negative image that others have about them and their gossiping.[24] Besides, they know that no matter if the broader audience has a negative image about them and the gossip they are spreading, this negative impression does not decrease the interest in negative gossip. Through our research, we realized that gossipers, in order to keep the audience's interest, add to their narrations figures of dissimilarity, i.e. stories from the life of other people with positive content that draw a contrast with the negative stories of the gossipers (which usually refer to negative facts of everyday life, e.g. adultery, divorce, economic fraud cases). This way, gossipers achieve multiple goals: firstly, there is a contrast between negative and positive stories, making the narration more interesting since it is not monotonous. Also, it is crucial for making the content of gossip even more apparent. By contrasting stories in this way, the gossip narrator underlines the dissimilarities, i.e. the main features of the negative narrations, which urges the audience to pay more attention to them. Let us examine a specific example pointing out these contrasts:

> I have learned the worst about Koula and about what she is going through with her husband's problems, he is a gamester and has lost all his money and has closed his business. They are going through a drama. [Here is where the contrast with the previous begins] On the contrary, her sister Tonia lives a wonderful life with her husband and their three children. But this is how life is; unfair, generous to some, and hardship to others. I am sorry for the parents of these two girls; one girl living unhappily, and the other so happily! It is really unfair!

- Figures of comparison and combination with urban legends or grapevine [Identified in 12 out of 70 cases]

Less frequently, the gossipers' narrations include urban legends. Bausinger had included urban legends in these "everyday narrations" (gossip, grapevine, social comments, and urban legends). As far as their form is concerned, they resemble each other and present non stable structure. These four types of speech, as Bausinger points out, not only resemble each other but are often confused since they share common traits.[25] Yet what are urban legends? It is not easy to give a precise definition. Initially, they could be defined as modern and common short stories that either have an accurate historical background and are based on facts or have imaginary content whose creator is, by default, unknown.[26] Some basic characteristics of urban legends, whether purely Greek or originating from abroad, are the vagueness as to the time and place of the narrated facts, fear, the reproduction of older superstitions and old wives' tales, and the focus on known people and facts. Urban legends are disseminated widely via oral means, written texts, or electronic media.

During our ethnographic research, urban legends are included towards either the middle of the gossip or its ending. Their role primarily supports the ideas expressed and the widely known spreading such as a legend. They support conceptually what is being said by the gossiper. Furthermore, they give plausibility and a type of authority to what is being uttered. The following example provides an illustration:

23 Du Boulay 1974, 210-13.

24 Rosenbaum & Subrin 1963, 820-21; Dunbar 2004, 103-7.

25 Bausinger 1977, 324-25.

26 Shermer 1997, 110 12.

> The new fast-food place that opened in the square has only frozen foods and low-quality food in plastic bags. I wonder why children eat these things and why their parents give them to them; it is a huge mistake, as is drinking soft drinks and Coca-Cola all the time. [This is where gossip is combined with the urban legend regarding the composition of Coca-Cola] It is known that no one knows the recipe of Coca-Cola and that it is kept in a secret vault in Switzerland. Don't you wonder why? Because some people say that it is made by human blood and others say that it contains secret preservatives as all the foods sold in those specific stores. Many people say that these things about Coca-Cola are a legend, but I believe them.

- Figures of connection with personal examples or personal stories [Identified in 11 out of 70 cases]

The least common gossip structure is the linking of negatively charged narrations with examples from the gossiper's personal life. The difference compared to the gossip narrations mentioned above lies in the fact that people identify themselves with the "protagonists" of negative aspects of the stories. Let us explore a few specific examples:

> Poor Nitsa's husband has been financially ruined due to the economic crisis, which I, unfortunately, ascertained the other day that I went to their house to give them clothes and food for the children. It is a tough situation since Nitsa has a low salary of 300 Euros. [Here is where the personal story with a similar situation begins] I have experienced similar situations, and I can understand these people, as well as feel for them. Unfortunately, my husband was fired too and remained unemployed for a long time, and I had to go and work when I was 45. Of course, we had small children too [...] In the end, only when you experience similar situations with others do you understand the difficulties that other people are going through.

The reference to common negative points among the gossipers and the people commented on in gossip is undoubtedly unfamiliar and has specific broader extensions, which the narrators themselves point out. Parallelism with their reality without a doubt strengthens their arguments and adds plausibility to their narrations. According to Bertaux,[27] this relation with the truth, featured in all life narrations, even if many subjective elements are included, makes gossip credible to the broader public. Still, this point comes in a different aspect, which could further be characterized as a question of moral nature. By narrating gossip and personal stories that may be equally humiliating for themselves (by referring to failed marriages and relationships, family problems, or workplace problems), they may feel ashamed during narration as well. What happens with other people's emotions? Why do they recount such unpleasant life events without feeling ashamed? An answer may be given by Gilmore's rationale, who researched the social dynamic of gossip within a Spanish community.[28] Gossipers, be they men or women, are usually so devoted to gossiping that they do not hesitate to expose themselves and their personal lives to become likable to their audience and, furthermore, to become credible. Finally, according to Gilmore (and our conclusions from this research), gossip, apart from being a process used to spend one's time pleasantly, is an intentional act, portraying (the commented-on) people positively or negatively. It can affect the audience's thoughts and practices and their future actions, and, at the same time, it adds authority to the gossiper who is deemed one of the people who affect the gossip community's opinion.

27 Bertaux 1981, 2-3.

28 Gilmore 1978, 90-91.

Conclusions

Completing this short exploration of gossip, we may come to certain conclusions regarding our community's structure. First of all, we must focus on gossip's place in modern orality. Using the examples mentioned here, we point out that gossip is not an "indifferent" form of speech, merely existing for entertainment purposes. On the contrary, it is a form of speech with solid intentionality that aims – on various occasions – at social control and judgment.

However, a form of dynamic oral communication, like gossip, has an immediate connection with social emotions. Ethnographic research is most likely the only type of research that may penetrate human reality and give answers to such questions. Our research ascertained that gossip might be linked with positive or negative emotions depending on the people and situations. In particular, from the gossiper's side, gossiping is seen positively, as it offers satisfaction and the feeling that this person holds a central role in information management. Nonetheless, when examined from the side of the "others", i.e. the people being gossiped about, the feeling that they are being unfairly judged and controlled by gossipers is linked with negative emotions. Similar conclusions may also be drawn from anthropologists' work from other countries. It should be noted that for such a subjective and "fluid" process, we may not proceed with classifications based on the generalization of various studies, given that the emotional world of each individual varies, has many aspects, and cannot be standardized.

Moreover, the research illustrates that gossip is a form of speech that is neither without rules nor without structure. On the contrary, it illustrates that gossip follows organizational structures that appear in a specific order of preference and not randomly. So, regarding their frequency, figures of deductive and inductive reasoning are the first to appear, then follow figures of similarity, figures of dissimilarity, the combination of gossip with urban legends, and finally the connection with examples from one's personal life.

The answer to whether the structures identified are created intentionally or non-intentionally may not be absolute. In particular, intentionality in the gossipers' speech (either to convince or to become likable) may be definitely discerned. Still, sometimes – but not always – this intentionality may be part of a broader strategy. Often, we realize that intentionality may be linked with gossiping, which entails the narrator's effort to convince and attract.

What the ethnographic research further confirms is that everyone (both those gossiping and those simply listening to gossip) knows at the end of the day that even if gossip is uttered within a specific circle of people (groups of friends, conversations between couples or colleagues at work), it is broadly disseminated. At the same time, gossip aims at public life, given that it seeks to have a drastic effect on a broader audience.

Last but not least, the interactive relationship between the various types of folk speech (gossip, rumors, grapevine, and urban legends) is interesting. Apart from their similarities (temporality, irregular form, ephemeral content), these types often seem to co-exist and reinforce one another, which has become apparent in the gossip structures analyzed above.

Manolis Varvounis
Democritus University of Thrace
mvarv@otenet.gr

Georgios Kouzas
National and Kapodistrian University of Athens
gkouzas@phil.uoa.gr

Bibliography

ABRAHAMS, R. D. 1970
'A Performance-centered Approach to Gossip', *Man* 5, 290-301.

ALLPORT G. & L. POSTMAN 1947
The Psychology of Rumor, New York.

BAUSINGER, H. 1958
'Strukturen des Alltäglichen Erzählens', *Fabula* 1, 239-54.

BAUSINGER, H. 1977
'Alltäglichen Erzählens', in *Enzyklopädie des Märchens* 1, 323-30.

BERTAUX, D. 1981
'Preface', in *Biography and Society. The Life History Approach in the Social Sciences*, D. Bertaux (ed.), London, 1-3.

BERGMANN, J. R. 1993
Discreet Indiscretions: The Social Organization of Gossip, New York.

CALVET, J.-L. 1984
La Tradition Orale, Paris.

COX, B. A. 1970
'What is Hopi Gossip about? Information Management and Hopi factions', *Man* 5,88-98.

CRESSEY, P. 1932
The Taxi-Dance Hall. A Sociological Study in Commercialized Recreation and City Life, Chicago.

DEGH, L. 1995
Narratives in Society: A Performer-centered Study of Narration, Helsinki.

DU BOULAY, J. 1974
Portrait of a Greek Mountain Village, Oxford.

DUNBAR, R. I. M. 2004
'Gossip in Evolutionary Perspective', *Review of General Psychology* 8, 100-10.

GILMORE, D. 1978
'Varieties of Gossip in a Spanish Rural Community', *Ethnology* 17, 89-99.

GLUCKMAN, M. 1963
'Gossip and Scandal', *Current Anthropology* 4, 307-16.

GOFFMAN, E. 1963
Stigma. Notes on the Management of Spoiled Identity, New York.

HANNERZ, U. 1967
'Gossip Networks and Culture in a Black American Ghetto', *Ethnos* 32, 35-59.

HIRSCHON R. 1989
Heirs of the Greek Catastrophe. The Social Life of Asia Minor Refugees in Piraeus, Oxford.

KOUZAS, G. 2017
The Beggary in modern city. Organization – Survival Strategies – Identities, Athens.

LEVIN, J., & A. ARLUKE 1987
Gossip: The Inside Scoop, New York.

LIEBOW, EL. 1967
Tally's Corner. A Study of Negro Steetcorner Men, Chicago.

MERAKLIS, M. 1993
Έντεχνος λαϊκός λόγος, Athens.

ONG, W. J. 2002[2]
Orality and Literacy: The Technologizing of the Word, New York.

PAINE, R. 1967
'What is Gossip about? An Alternate Hypothesis', *Man* 2, 278-85.

ROSENBAUM, J. B. & M. SUBRIN, M. 1963
'The Psychology of Gossip' *Journal of the American Psychoanalytic Association* 11, 817-831.

ROSNOW, R. L. 2001
'Rumor and Gossip in Interpersonal Interaction and Beyond: A Social Exchange Perspective', in *Behaving Badly: Aversive Behaviors in Interpersonal Relationships*, R. M. Kowalski (ed.), Washington D.C., 203-32.

ROSNOW, R. L. & G. A. FINE 1976
Rumor and Gossip: The Social Psychology of Hearsay, New York.

SCHOEMAN, F. 1994
'Gossip and Privacy', in *Good Gossip*, R. F. Goodman & A. Ben-Ze'ev (eds.), Lawrence, 72-82.

SHERMER, M. 1997
Why People Believe Weird Things. Superstition and Other Confusions of Our Time, New York.

STIRLING, R. B. 1956
'Some Psychological Mechanisms Operative in Gossip', *Social Forces* 34, 262-67.

The *Mantinades* (Couplets) of Karpathos Island on the Internet: Local Students' Views

George Katsadoros and Ioanna Kafetzidaki

Abstract

Mantinades constitute a type of folk song, present on the island of Karpathos for centuries. They are improvised couplets, usually in rhyme and in iambic decapentasyllabic verse. Mantinades exhibit a strong presence in everyday occasions for Karpathians living on the island, but also for others residing elsewhere. In joy and in sorrow, mantinades constitute a major means of communicating and of expressing emotions: a way of life.

Their initially oral transmission led to the creation of many variants, whereas written culture allowed their recording in books. Modern technological developments allowed them to enter the world of the Internet. As happened with many other folkloric genres, the World Wide Web helped mantinades travel further, faster, and at no cost through space and time.

Introduction

Even though much research has recently been conducted on *mantinades*, the specific genre has not been thoroughly examined. In our article we aim to present data and conclusions from research concerning the use of *mantinades* in the everyday lives of young people of Karpathos, their presence and diffusion on the internet, and how they are received and regarded today.

Aiming to highlight the presence and circulation of this initially orally transmitted folk literature genre in our essentially digitalized world, we will present the views of secondary education students in Karpathos, gathered through questionnaires, in regard to their relationship with the mantinades, their everyday use, and their distribution on the Internet.

Mantinades are a means of spontaneous folk expression in many parts of Greece. They fall under the category[1] of folk songs[2] and they are particularly widespread in Crete; they also exist in Karpathos, Kasos, other islands of the Aegean and Ionian Seas Cyprus, and urban environments as well.

1 Folk songs are generally categorized according to their theme, tune, content, form, or the occasion they refer to. A first categorization of folk songs based on their theme was presented by the founder of Greek Folkloristics, Nikolaos Politis (1914); it became a landmark for future researchers, who came up with their own categorizations according to songs' form, tune, content, etc. Puchner (2013, 146) makes a distinction of folk songs in: lengthy ones, with a rhymed narration of an historical event, in *μαντινάδες* and *τσιαττίσματα*, found in the eastern Aegean and in Cyprus. He also mentions the *ριζίτικα*, laments or religious songs, that are performed *a cappella* in western Crete.

2 Greek folk songs originate from antiquity. Only a few of these songs, as well as ones from the Byzantine era, have been written down, through later references, mostly since the development of Folkloristics in Greece.

Definitions and traits of *mantinades*

Under the broad categorization of folk songs, *mantinades* are considered either everyday or love songs.[3] They constitute a subset of folk songs, sharing the characteristics of immediateness, fullness of meaning, and lyric style.[4] These are improvised couplets, usually in rhyme, in iambic fifteen-syllable verse. Their content is usually about love; they can be teasing, sad, or cheerful and they are sometimes accompanied by musical instruments (such as lyre and lute).[5] As a rule, they are adapted depending on circumstances. Their style is poetic and their notion is complete.[6]

According to Alexiadis,[7] *mantinades* are used to express strong emotions and possess a key role in village micro-communities and wherever Karpathians reside; they constitute examples of modern folk creation and are of great interest. These couplets deal with many themes, inspired by everyday life. They are mostly rhymed or comprised of four semi-verses not necessarily rhymed; they include words of a local dialect, of Crete or other locales, wherever they are created. They are an integral part of poetic tradition, as they essentially exhibit verse, rhyme, and, usually, a lyric tone (lament). *Mantinades* are used to demonstrate social life aspects, emotions, or people, or even to convey messages to fellow countrymen.

Some examples of couplets, demonstrating the above:

Πολλά δεν έχω να σας πω, γιατί πολλά δεν ξέρω,
ένα μικρό χαιρετισμό, ήρθα να σας προσφέρω.

Much to say I have not, as much I do not know,
just a small salute, that's all I offer to you.
(Alexiadis 2001, 210)

Να γράψω θέλω σήμερα στον τύπο της Καρπάθου,
ένα πικρό παράπονο, όλοι για να το μάθου(ν).

I want to write something to Karpathos's press,
a bitter complaint, for all to know.
(Alexiadis 2001, 177)

Ο μισεμός είναι καμός, τσε το "'χε 'γεια" 'ναι ζάλη,
τσε το "καλώς ορίσατε" είναι χαρά μι (γ) άλη.

Parting is bitter, and farewell is sad,
and a welcome is a great joy.
(Alexiadis 2001, 27)[8]

Creation and diffusion of mantinades

There have been many opinions and much research concerning the origin,[9] the conditions of creation,

3 See Dimaras 2000, 7-14.
4 See Pavlakis 1994, 8.
5 See Babiniotis 1998, 1052.
6 See Makris 2007, 61. A similar definition is given for *mantinades,* specifically of Crete: Cretan *mantinades* are decapentasyllabic rhymed couplets in the Cretan dialect that present a complete notion and exhibit poetic traits. An exception, as far as their notion is concerned, applies to facing (*αντικριστές*) *mantinades* aiming to reply to other *mantinades* or add to their meaning (Kafkalas 1998, 142).
7 See Alexiadis 2001, 177-79. Also Mirasgezi 2003, 428-29.
8 The first of these couplets comprises a modest salutation to a social event; the second addresses an introduction to a complaint to follow in a Karpathian newspaper; the third expresses the sorrow that separation brings and the joy of the reunion.
9 The word *μαντινάδα* possibly derives from the Greek words *μαντεύω* (to foretell, prophesy) + *άδω* (to sing, chant; connected to the Latin word *ca(n)do*, *candada* or *cantata*). There are various other analyses, such as that it may also be related to the Venetian *matinada* or the Latin words *mano* or *mando* (*mandatum* = message, related to the Greek *μαντάτο*). See Mpampiniotis 1998, 1052. It may instead be connected to the Greek word ομάδιν (= in group) + άδω, as they are performed in group events. See Vasilaras 2008, 216.

and the circumstances of the genre's circulation.[10] In the past, the creation and diffusion of mantinades were based strictly on oral transmission. In this way many variations were produced and the initial author's identity was lost. Literacy, later on, led to the recording of many collections up to the present day. Today, vast and rapid technological developments have permeated people's lives and constitute a part of our everyday routine. In Greece, a computer with internet access can be found in almost every home. This condition has led, among many other things, to the passage of many folk literature genres from oral circulation or written distribution to a new form of diffusion, one that does not require face-to-face contact or the acquisition of texts: the internet.

That is true for the *mantinades* of Karpathos as well,[11] which appear to have found a new "place to live"[12] and a function that is not bound by rules of space or time.

The presence of *mantinades*, especially the ones of Karpathos, on the internet has already been discussed[13], so we will not delve into matters of typology here.

Our research

We shall focus on how young people between the ages of 12-18, all secondary-school students residing on the island of Karpathos, regard this particular genre, whether they utilize it in their everyday communication or general expression, and how it is connected to modern orality; in our opinion, their

10 In 1930, the Swiss musicologist Samuel Baud-Bovy recorded the songs and tunes of Karpathos; this collection remains preserved today. Later, other researchers also included poetic material in their works and thus helped its preservation. See Skevofylaka 2010, 762-63. Since 1952, people of Karpathos of all social classes began publishing *mantinades* or laments in the pages of three newspapers that are still published in Piraeus: "*Καρπαθιακή*", "*Καρπαθιακή ηχώ*" and "*Η φωνή της Ολύμπου*". These newspapers provide a "habitat" for these couplets. They are published in special sections and have become a means for Karpathians to express their emotions. The topics of the couplets cover all the stages of a person's life: birth, christening, engagement, school, economic, professional or academic success, sports, death, etc. See Alexiadis 2008, 130-35.

11 It is difficult to provide a precise chronological placement for the appearance of traditional songs, and by extension *mantinades*, in Karpathos, as the emotional need of people to compose songs has always existed. It is easier for the researcher to find the chronology of historical songs, provided that they are connected to known historical facts or people that can be delimited in time. However, most traditional songs of Karpathos constitute chants about love, faith, infidelity, foreign lands, and the beauty of nature. Their topics alone do not offer enough data for a precise dating. For this reason, researchers emphasized rhyme, form of language, names of things, and the presence of geographic names and cities that can be chronically traced. Minas 2005, 189-90.
Vasilaras (2006, 219, 223) agrees with many other researchers that it is difficult to pinpoint the precise time of the appearance of *mantinades*. It is possible that four to five centuries before they appeared in Karpathos, rhyme and couplets were first established in Crete, before being transmitted to the nearby islands, such as Karpathos, Kasos, and Kythira.

12 Since the old days, efforts have been made to preserve the folk culture of Karpathos and transmit it to new generations. Many people of Karpathos sought a better future abroad and it is estimated that 14,000 individuals travelled seasonally to other islands, cities, and countries for work. Many remained in these places permanently, about 10,000 of these in America. See Alexiadis 2011, 155-58. The need for connection with their place, the traditions, and their culture led to the creation of associations for all people of Karpathos local and abroad, which maintain the bonds and connections between them.

13 A (named) example:
Στο κινητό, στο facebook, μηνύματα σου στέλνω,
Την τόση αδιαφορία σου δεν την καταλαβαίνω.
In your phone, in Facebook, so many messages I sent you,
such indifference I fail to comprehend.
Sophia Pitta-Bra, https://www.facebook.com/profile.php?id=100064379753711, accessed on 13/06/2023).
See also Katsadoros 2016.

responses reveal much about the ongoing development of the genre. Furthermore, as important as it is to theorize about forms of folk expression, it is also essential to listen to what their everyday users have to say.

As already mentioned, the *mantinades* of Karpathos, which rely heavily on improvisation, in the past transitioned from oral form to written records; nowadays, along with ones from other Greek islands, they find their way onto the internet, a means of communication that exhibits many new qualities: it knows no geographical boundaries, no physical or social restrictions. It can be accessed from almost everywhere in the western hemisphere at any time and it presents almost everyone with the opportunity to learn, share, distribute, or even create every kind of information, including various forms of folk or popular culture. Nevertheless, we are very far from accepting every rhyme or couplet found on related webpages, such as cultural associations' websites, or in social networks, such as Facebook or X, formerly called/known as Twitter, as folk material.[14]

Mantinades, mostly from Crete,[15] since the dawn of the new millennium, have not followed the example of other folk literature genres whose dissemination seems somehow diminished in the vast world wide web, but have been, if we may say, reborn and have reached a far wider audience than their initial spatial limits allowed. That is, one no longer has to originate from Crete, Karpathos, or Kasos to engage in using them or even in adapting or creating new ones, according to specific circumstances. Just a recent search for the word in Google yields almost 500,000 results in Greeklish and 2,000,000 for the Greek word. In the above results, several websites dedicated exclusively to *mantinades* are included.[16] In most of them (the majority deals with Crete), community users are able to publish their own and comment on previous ones, just as they would in a circle of friends.

Singing, in all its forms holds a special place in everyday life for the inhabitants of Karpathos.[17]

14 There are of course many, well-deserved, reservations concerning the quality and content of such material circulating on the web, since they clearly do not, as a rule, follow the characteristics of traditional *mantinades*. Furthermore, many of them could be called simply couplets. A similar case is strongly presented for Cretan mantinades in SMS messages by Lenakakis (2011). See also Christodoulou 2014, 153-55; Perraki 2015, 37 and Kafetzidaki 2017, 89.

15 A very interesting and noteworthy relevant case can be traced in the example of the schools in Rethymno and Chania (in Crete): on the occasion of International Safer Internet Day (5/2/2013) and with the aim of informing students and encouraging them to use modern technology in a safe way, a competition to compose relevant *mantinades* was held. Some examples are:
Η κουτσομπόλα τση εποχής που ίντερνετ τη λένε
ότι τση πεις αλλού θα πει κι ύστερα ποιοι θα φταίνε;
The gossip of our time internet is named
whatever you share everyone will know and then who will take the blame?
Το facebook με έκανε να μη ζω τη ζωή μου
αλλά να βλέπω αλλονών απού γελούν μαζί μου.
Facebook made me not live my life
but to watch the lives of others who laugh at my expense.
See http://mantinades4edu.blogspot.com/p/2012-2013.html, accessed on 13/6/2023.

16 The most popular web page seems to be https://www.mantinades.gr/ (accessed on 15/7/2024). It has a vast collection of mantinades (20.171 up to 2024) and over 3,100 registered users, who have the option to upload their own mantinades. The page connects to many social media, such as Facebook, Twitter, Instagram, Google+, Pinterest, and YouTube.

17 This kind of research falls under the category of e-Folklore and Digital Ethnography, dealing with material in its living environment, the digital world. See also Dorst 1990, Miller & Slater 2000, Krawczyk-Wasilewska 2006, Chatterji 2007, Blank 2007 & 2009, Beneito-Montagut 2011, Gasouka & Foulidi 2012, Hallet & Barber 2014. Ethnographers find it difficult to adequately comprehend interpersonal communication without witnessing first-hand non-verbal behavioral patterns; nevertheless, the digital world is in need of modern ethnographic approaches. See Gasouka & Foulidi 2012, 95-109. Kirchenblatt-Gimblett (1998, 284) characterized language used in digital environments as something between the oral and the written, that continuously

Mantinades in particular address all aspects of social life and their creation constitutes a "way of life". They can be found in various websites, including cultural associations' pages, tourist guides, personal blogs, and social media. Many of these sites include collections of mantinades categorized thematically or even encourage the creation and publication of new ones. This strong presence of this specific folk material in the digital world points not only to an effortless and cost-effective means of storage and communication, but for creation as well, as folk culture continuously evolves in its functional and semantic capacity, constantly adapting to new environments and to the needs of each society and its individuals.[18] Related sites can be divided into two categories: those that focus on *mantinades* and those that deal with general matters of Karpathos and include elements of local folk culture. Many aspects of "traditional" orality are preserved in these cases,[19] as digital speech, a secondary orality in its essence, as Ong would put it,[20] has more to share with orality than with written texts: leaving matters of accessibility or diffusion behind, we need only mention how easy it is for every digitally literate person to view, delete, modify, or share all kind of data. This digital orality essentially comprises a new form of communication, combining orality's plasticity and writing's permanency.

The island of Karpathos was chosen for our research, because *mantinades* are still present in everyday life, but in the digital world of Karpathos as well. Questionnaires were administered to all students in secondary education from the areas of Aperi and Pegadia. Our choice was based on the fact that young people living on the island at this age (12-18) are already familiar with mantinades and their performance on various occasions, such as festivities, marriages etc. Moreover, they have free and frequent access on the internet and they have accounts on social media.

Research results

We will present some specific findings from our mainly quantitative research,[21] sometimes mentioning noteworthy differentiations, mainly concerning age or place of birth[22] (of course there were other factors considered as well, such as gender or socioeconomic status but their results need not to be mentioned here).

Starting with the fundamental question, whether they use *mantinades* at all, half of high school students state that they do use *mantinades*, whereas this number rises to two thirds when the same question is addressed to lyceum [high secondary education]

evolves along multimedia advances, shaping a folk culture not of spoken words but of "modem words". Bronner (2009, 29) pinpointed "visibility" as the main factor differentiating digital speech from written: it is oral speech written down that can express the author's notions or emotions utilizing text or images, without the need for further explanation or non-verbal expressions.

18 See Katsadoros 2013, 100.

19 Katsadoros 2016, 516.

20 Communication on the internet exhibits many traits common with orality, forming a "secondary orality", as Ong mentioned, even before the internet as we today experience it. See Ong 1982, 129-36, 170-76. This is so since users exchange information at a great speed, anonymously, ever producing variants that bring to mind the oral stage of traditional society. See also Androutsopoulos 2001 and Katsadoros, 2013 and 2016.

21 See Kafetzidaki 2017.

22 At the time of our research (2016), on the island of Karpathos school units of secondary education are assembled in Aperi and in Pegadia. Students have to travel from neighboring villages by bus. In Aperi there is a high school and the only general lyceum of the island. There were 14 students in high school and 115 in lyceum. In Pegadia there is only a high school with 141 students. Of these 270 students, 169 completed questionnaires.
The majority of students originated from Karpathos (77.5%). The rest came from Albania (10.6%), Athens (1.78%), and other places in Greece or the world. Around one in twenty (5.32%) students chose not to share this personal information.

students.[23] It seems that students become more familiar with *mantinades* as they grow up.

On the same question, over two thirds (69%) of students originating from Karpathos report that they use *mantinades*, whereas fewer than half (48%) of students originating from other parts of Greece or elsewhere in the world do.

It seems that the factor of origin is significant, as students from Karpathos appear to engage with this genre more easily. This outcome seems logical, as they become acquainted with it from a young age, as will be demonstrated.

Regarding the sources from which students learn or encounter *mantinades*, there seems to be a slight differentiation between high school and lyceum: younger people (12-15) hear them mostly from the internet (21%), books (17%), and their family (15%), while lyceum students get them mostly from their friends (26%), their family (26%), and the internet (21%). Other sources for both age groups include television and local festivities. It seems that younger students rely more on the internet and books, whereas older lyceum students use friends and family more.

Looking at students' origins, the ones coming from Karpathos primarily draw *mantinades* from their family members (23.23%), the internet (21.21%), and their friends (20.2%). In contrast, students from outside the island learn them from friends (19%), the internet (17%), television (17%), and books (14%), with only 8% indicating family as a source. As anticipated, in the specific case of *mantinades*, family functions as a source mainly in the case of natives.

Regardless of age or origins, most students (41.58%) favor *mantinades* that express love and other emotional expressions. When asked on what occasions they use them, students indicated that they prefer everyday joyful moments (21.4%), weddings (20.5%), festivities (20.27%), company of friends (19.2%), and other, mostly habituary traditional, occasions.

Another question asked whether they created their own *mantinades*. Again, results were different with respect to age: 39% of high school students and 57% of lyceum students answered positively. As was the case with our first question, age seems to be a significant factor.

With regard to origins, the results were almost equal, with a little "surprise", as a slightly higher percentage (59%) of non-native students provided a positive answer, compared to 53% of natives.

The themes students in general choose when composing *mantinades* are mostly about love (25%), everyday joyful instances (24%), and for fun (20%).

When asked whether they post their own creations on the internet, only one in five students (20%) across all age groups claims to do so. As far as origins are concerned, almost the same percentage (24%) applies to Karpathian natives, but only 3% of non-natives do so. Apparently, as before, young people born into a society where *mantinades* are applied to everyday use seem more inclined not only to create but also to publish on the internet.

For all of the above, students had to choose among some given options. The most intriguing questions for us folklorists, however, were the last two: the first encouraged students to present, in their own words, their opinion about advantages or disadvantages of posting *mantinades* on the internet. The analysis of their responses yielded the following results.

23 Approximately half of the participating high school students (51%) stated that they do not use any kind of *mantinades* at all. Almost a third (31%) use them rarely, 15% use them often, while just 3% claim to make very frequent use of *mantinades*.
Results seem to somehow differ for lyceum students in Aperi, the sole lyceum of Karpathos, as the majority of students (60%) rarely use *mantinades* and almost a quarter of them (23%) do not use them at all. Percentages for frequent or very frequent use more or less follow those of the high school students, 14% and 3% respectively.

Regarding advantages, students believe that posting on the internet allows the continuity of tradition (20%) and its global diffusion (16%). It provides a way to express emotions (15%) and to identify oneself with verses of joy or sorrow (11%). A few others (8%) noted the opportunity the internet provides for everybody to seek and find couplets for every occasion. Fewer (5%) recognized the opportunity the internet presents for a composer to showcase his works in front of a greater audience. Another 5% consider the posting of such material as a source of inspiration for the creation of new ones. Very few, just 1%, came up with an interesting response, that *mantinades* make the internet "a more beautiful place".

According to the above, the young people of Karpathos show an interest in the continuation of local traditional elements and believe that the internet provides a means for that. Furthermore, on a more personal level, the presence of *mantinades* on the internet not only presents them with the opportunity to express themselves, but also to make their creations available to a wider audience than spatial limits allow.

As for disadvantages, nearly one-third of the participants (31%) states that posting *mantinades* on the internet might encourage others to "steal" others' creations and present them as their own. Others (14%) expressed concerns about the possibility of offensive material being created and circulated, or even targeting an individual with a negative sentiment(13%). A few others (7%) believe that many found online are of poor quality, as they do not rhyme and, generally, do not follow the rules of composition. Another few (5%) believe that easily finding them on the internet possibly discourages the creation of new *mantinades*. Other expressed concerns include (2% each) the possibility for posting for selfish reasons, such as personal promotion, the degradation of existing *mantinades* through their digital diffusion, and the presence of traces of localism. Finally, 2% believe that *mantinades*, as part of local tradition, should remain within their geographical limits and should not be distributed elsewhere.

It seems that the majority of students fear the lack of control over published material, which constitutes a main aspect of the internet. They are afraid that they may be stolen, copied, exploited, or degraded in form or content. There are also some concerns regarding issues of local identity.

The final, optional, question invited students to produce a *mantinada* of their own. Three quarters (75%) of students coming from Karpathos produced one, while fewer (62%) of those from elsewhere did the same. As anticipated, many of the *mantinades* created derived from external sources, such as related websites, social media, and friends' creations. Many obviously had little to do with Karpathos, either in form or content, but few were improvised for the occasion.

Some examples:

Θεέ μου βάλε μια φωτιά να κάψει τα βιβλία
που τυραννούν τους μαθητές σε τέθ(τ)οια ηλικία.

Dear God send down a fire to burn books
that tyrannize pupils at such an age.
(Kafetzidaki 2017, 90)

Κάρπαθος όμορφο νησί στο νότιο Αιγαίο,
και από τα Δωδεκάνησα είσαι το πιο ωραίο.

Fair Karpathos in the south Aegean
among the Dodekanese you're the fairest of them all.
(*Ibid.*, 94)

Η αγάπη δεν υπάρχει πια,
την πάτησε το τρένο,
γιατί ο βλάκας οδηγός
δεν πάτησε το φρένο.

Love does not live any more,
She was hit by the train,

> because the stupid driver
> did not hit the brakes.
> (*Ibid.*, 99)
>
> *Μην απορείς που σ' αγαπώ μετά από τόσα λάθη.*
> *Έτσι είναι λέει οι έρωτες και τα μεγάλα πάθη.*
>
> Do not wonder about my love after so many mistakes.
> That's the case with love and passions great.
> (*Ibid.*, 100)

The above constitute part of an ongoing, wider research, concerning the presence of *mantinades* especially on Crete, Karpathos, and Kasos, but on the internet as well. These are some primary results. Our aim for the future is to include not only inhabitants of all these islands but people originating from them even though they now reside elsewhere, in Greece or abroad, or even others just sharing with the aforementioned an interest in this folk genre.

Conclusions

In our present research our aim was not to present a theoretical treatise on *mantinades* or their digital circulation, but to demonstrate how young people of Karpathos, today's learners and tomorrow's bearers of this traditional genre, perceive and utilize them. A mostly oral genre, in their traditional form, *mantinades* of Karpathos were improvised on specific occasions, attributed to their initial composers and safeguarded from being used again or altered.

That does not seem to be the case anymore; as already mentioned, the presence of *mantinades* on the internet is extremely strong. Furthermore, this specific type of folk expression has come to experience wide dissemination since it became known on the internet and through various related websites and social media. What was previously a relatively locally confined aspect of folk expression has now reached people all over the world, regardless of age, origin, or place of residence, factors that previously placed boundaries on their spread.

Another important issue, to be discussed in the future, is whether we can or should characterize all of these couplets circulating in modern media as *mantinades*, since they clearly do not strictly adhere to poetic norms of the past.

What do these conclusions spell for orality today, in our case, for young residents of Karpathos Island, where customary traditional practices still apply? It seems that, according to their answers, most of them have accepted *mantinades* as a means of expression and communication. That is, they readily adopt given material, but try to adapt it to new circumstances.

Nevertheless, at the same time young people are concerned about the uncontrollable diffusion of such folk material on the internet: they see that everybody can find, adjust, and possibly pass off such material as his/her own and that can lead to uses other than the original ones, such as of racist or sexist content, and, finally, to the degradation of *mantinades*.

All of the above attest to *mantinades*' and similar material's adaptivity on the internet. They are regarded more as oral expressions than as written documents. In their digital "travels", *mantinades* seem to exhibit basic traits of folk phenomena: they have existed for many generations. They rely more on spontaneous expression than on logical thought. Their diffusion and circulation demonstrate a mass acceptance. Furthermore, many variants can be found and a *mantinada* can appear anywhere, in any form, constantly acquiring a local character each time.

The way young people receive, perceive, and choose to employ *mantinades* or not is essentially differentiated compared to past practices. It seems that digitally circulated material develops new traits: it is accessible to more people, not locally confined, and offers the opportunity for almost everybody to partake and even create his/her own pieces or variants.

It is evident that users of modern social media have developed a new way of communicating in the digital world. This surely affects the way related material, folk material in its essence, is created, diffused, altered, and forms the basis of a new digital culture. Subsequently, one cannot view and study this material using traditional approaches, as it introduces pure traits of orality into written texts, forming a new kind of orality, a secondary one, according to Ong.

As far as the modern *mantinades* of Karpathos are concerned, they seem to have found fertile ground to take root and flourish on the internet, bridging the old with the new and allowing this traditional genre to thrive, apart from its physical local birthplace, in a global digital home.

George Katsadoros
University of the Aegean
katsadoros@aegean.gr

Ioanna Kafetzidaki
University of the Aegean
joanna5rhodes@hotmail.com

Bibliography

ALEXIADIS, M. A. 2001
Καρπαθιακή Λαογραφία: Όψεις του Λαϊκού Πολιτισμού, Athens.

ALEXIADIS M. A. 2008
Νεωτερική Ελληνική Λαογραφία: Συναγωγή μελετών, Athens.

ALEXIADIS, M. A. 2011
Έντυπα μέσα επικοινωνίας και λαϊκός πολιτισμός. Νεωτερικά λαογραφικά, Athens.

ANDROUTSOPOULOS, Y. 2001
'Η θαυμαστή καινούργια εγγραμματοσύνη', *Η Καθημερινή. Αρχείο Πολιτισμού* (14/10/2001), https://www.kathimerini.gr/102763/article/politismos/arxeio-politismoy/h-8aymasth-kainoyrgia-eggrammatosynh, accessed on 13/06/2023.

BABINIOTIS, G. 1998
Λεξικό της νέας ελληνικής γλώσσας, Athens.

BENEITO-MONTAGUT, R. 2011
'Ethnography goes online: towards a user-centred methodology to research interpersonal communication on the internet', *Qualitative Research* 11 (6), 716-35.

BLANK, T. J. 2007
'Examining the Transmission of Urban Legends: Making the Case for Folklore Fieldwork on the Internet', *Folklore Forum* 37.1, 15-26.

BLANK, T. J. (ED.) 2009
Folklore and the Internet: Vernacular Expression in a Digital World, Utah.

BRONNER, S. J. 2009
'Digitizing and Virtualizing Folklore', in *Folklore and the Internet: Vernacular Expression in a Digital World*, T. J. Blank (ed.), Utah, 21-66.

CHATTERJI, R. 2007
'Orality, Inscription and the Creation of a New Lore', *Cultural Analysis* 6, 72-90.

CHRISTODOULOU, E. 2014
Σύγχρονη λαϊκή λογοτεχνία: Κρητικές μαντινάδες στο διαδίκτυο, M.A. Thesis, Rhodes.

DIMARAS, K. T. 2000
Ιστορία της Νεοελληνικής Λογοτεχνίας – Από τις πρώτες ρίζες ώς την εποχή μας, Athens.

DORST, J. 1990
'Tags and Burners, Cycles and Networks: Folklore in the Telectronic Age', *Journal of Folklore Research* 27 (3), 179-90.

GKASOUKA, M. & X. FOULIDI 2012
Σύγχρονοι Ορίζοντες Λαογραφικών Σπουδών: Εννοιολογικό πλαίσιο, Έρευνα, Φύλο, Διαδίκτυο, Σχολείο, Athens.

HALLET, R. E. & K. BARBER 2014
'Ethnographic Research in a Cyber Era', *Journal of Contemporary Ethnography* 43 (3), 306-30.

KATSADOROS, G. 2013
'Η επιστήμη της τεχνολογίας στη σύγχρονη τεχνολογική εποχή. Η ηλεκτρονική προφορικότητα', in *Επιστήμες της εκπαίδευσης. Από την ασθενή ταξινόμηση της Παιδαγωγικής στη διεπιστημονικότητα και στον επιστημονικό υβριδισμό*, G. Kokkinos & M. Chionidou (eds.), Athens, 99-122.

KATSADOROS, G. 2016
'σύγχρονη λαϊκή λογοτεχνία. Καρπαθιακές μαντινάδες στο διαδίκτυο', in *Κάρπαθος και Λαογραφία: Δ' Διεθνές Συνέδριο Καρπαθιακής Λαογραφίας*, M. A. Alexiadis (ed.), Athens, 505-17.

KAFETZIDAKI, I. 2017
Η παρουσία καρπαθιακών μαντινάδων στο Διαδίκτυο και οι αντιλήψεις μαθητών της Καρπάθου, M.A. Thesis, Rhodes.

KIRCHENBLATT-GIMBLETT, B. 1998
'Folklore's Crisis', *Journal of American Folklore* 111 (441), 281-327.

KRAWCZYK-WASILEWSKA, V. 2006
'e-Folklore in the Age of Globalization', *Fabula* 47, 248-54.

LENAKAKIS, A. 2011
'Ευχετήρια δίστιχα sms: το κύκνειο άσμα της μαντινάδας (;)', *Κρητική Λαογραφία*, http://kritiki-laografia.blogspot.com/2011/07/sms.html, accessed on 13/6/2023.

MAKRIS, M. 2007
Τα παραδοσιακά τραγούδια της Ολύμπου Καρπάθου, Athens.

MICHAEL, G. 2009
'Homo Interneticus ή Λαογραφία και Διαδίκτυο', *Λαογραφία. Δελτίον της Ελληνικής Λαογραφικής Εταιρείας* 41, 291-305.

MILLER, D. & D. SLATER 2000
The Internet. An Ethnographic Approach, Oxford.

MENAS, K. 2005
Ιστορικά, Αρχαιολογικά και Λαογραφικά της Καρπάθου, Athens.

MIRASGEZI, M. D. 2003
'Ο λαϊκός πολιτισμός της Καρπάθου μέσα από τα δημοτικά της τραγούδια', in *Κάρπαθος και Λαογραφία: Β' Διεθνές Συνέδριο Καρπαθιακής Λαογραφίας*, M. A. Alexiadis (ed.), Athens, 427-29.

ONG, W. J. 1997
Orality and Literacy. The Technologizing of the Word, London & New York.

PAVLAKIS, G. 1994
Κρητική Δημοτική Ποίηση: Οι μαντινάδες, Athens.

PERRAKI, A. 2015
Η παρουσία της μαντινάδας στο διαδίκτυο. Οι αντιλήψεις των μαθητών της Κρήτης, M.A. Thesis, Rhodes.

POLITIS N. 1914
Εκλογαί από τα τραγούδια του ελληνικού λαού, Athens.

PUCHNER, W. 2013
Μελέτες για το ελληνικό δημοτικό τραγούδι, Athens.

RAPTIS, A. & A. RAPTIS 2013
Μάθηση και Διδασκαλία στην εποχή της Πληροφορίας, Athens.

SKEVOFYLAKA V. M. 2012
'Μιχάλης Ι. Αναγνωστόπουλος (Υψηλός). Ο χαρισματικός τραγουδιστής από τα Κάτω Χωριά της Καρπάθου', in *Καρπαθιακά: Περιοδική Επιστημονική Έκδοση* 4, 509-62.

VASILARAS, E. E. 2006
'Οι Τρικάντουνες μαντινάδες της Καρπάθου', in *Κάρπαθος και Λαογραφία: Γ' Διεθνές Συνέδριο Καρπαθιακής Λαογραφίας*, M. A. Alexiadis (ed.), Athens, 215-56.

Your Tale, My Life: Trading Selves in Story

Carl Lindahl

Abstract

Abundant evidence of the healing power of storytelling resides in the earliest surviving epics as well as in the personal narratives of twenty-first-century disaster survivors. A narrator's skill in shaping a story to match the personal circumstances and needs of its audience often constitutes the most important facet of a great performance. Master narrators reveal human vulnerabilities in seemingly superhuman characters, thereby enhancing listeners' engagement and capacity to identify themselves with narrative protagonists. Epic singers require such godlike figures as Achilles to "unlearn divinity" before they can attain the quality of heroism that humanity requires; in a parallel manner, on a smaller scale, disaster survivors who relate their lifesaving acts must deny their heroism in order to achieve it. Correspondingly, narrators of folk fiction endow "lowly" and "unpromising" fairy tale heroes with the traits of their listeners to bolster their confidence and induce them to strategize paths to success.

In story after story, in epic, *märchen*, legend, and personal narrative, the most heroic character tends to be the one who seems to surrender and not the one who visibly conquers. It takes a narrator – the narrator *of* the story, or a narrator *within* it – to create a world in which the storied character, or the narrator, or the listener – or all three – become someone else.

To be about oneself, paradoxically, a traditional story often needs to be about someone else. In traditional narratives, the hero of my story will most likely be you only if it is seemingly about me, or vice versa. Narrators create commonality by exchanging identities with their listeners. In narratives as old as *Gilgamesh* and the *Iliad*, stories are told to spur action, and those that most successfully shape audience actions are those that create the closest correspondence in role, situation, and emotional state between the narrated character and the living listener. This elaborate social masquerade often serves to effect social change and emotional healing both inside the story and in the community that performs it.

Both the *Iliad* and *Gilgamesh* begin with part-divine heroes undefeated and apparently undefeatable, and end with those heroes compromised or defeated, diminished by their growing distance from their immortal roots. These stories have now lived for millennia and endured, I think, at least in part because they end at a point where their heroes have shrunk small enough for us to see ourselves in them – allowing other characters and ourselves to share their identities.

The great achievement of these ancient heroes is *the unlearning of divinity*. Gilgamesh is two-thirds god and Achilles semi-divine. They so overmatch the humans who surround them that they render themselves immortally dull. It is far too easy to win when you cannot lose.

In *Iliad* book IX, three of his fellow Achaeans come to Achilles and beg him to rejoin the attack on Troy. One of them is as close as kin: Phoinix, the hero's foster-father. Phoinix essentially tells Achilles, "Put yourself in my shoes: think of what I have done for you, and what you owe me, and how disappointed you would be if I treated you as you had treated me." Achilles will not bend. He refuses to play the role of anyone but himself.

But something transformative has happened to Achilles by book XXIV. Wielding god-forged weapons, he has killed countless Trojans including Hector, his greatest adversary. But looming largest is the loss of his dearest friend Patroclus, a loss that for all Achilles's strength he is powerless to reverse. Now another man comes to him to beg him to act. This is not his foster-father Phoenix, but rather the opposite: King Priam, father of his worst enemy. Priam cannot ask Achilles to remember everything he has done for him – for Priam has never done anything for Achilles. Rather, Priam does the inconceivable. He asks Achilles for the body of own son, Hector, the killer of Patroclus.

Priam succeeds in moving Achilles where Phoinix has failed, in part because of Achilles's experience. He has suffered a loss so great that he no longer sees himself as distant from other mortals. But Priam succeeds at least in part because he pleads in a certain way. He does not say, "Put yourself in my shoes," but rather "put yourself in *your* shoes", imploring Achilles to think of his own father – and what his father means to him.

> Remember your own father, great godlike Achilles—
> as old as *I* am, past the threshold of deadly old age!
> No doubt the country men round about him plague him now,
> with no one there to defend him, beat away disaster.
> No one – but at least he hears you're still alive
> and his old heart rejoices, hopes rising, day by day,
> to see his beloved son come sailing home from Troy.
> (*Il.* 24.570-76; transl. Fagels 1990)

Only after imploring Achilles to feel his own pain for his aged father does the aged king ask Achilles to feel the pain of a father who has lost all his sons.

> But I – dear god, my life so cursed by fate...
> I fathered hero sons in the wide realm of Troy
> and now not a single one is left …
> Fifty sons I had …
> But one, one was left me, to guard my walls, my people –
> the one you killed the other day...
> Revere the gods, Achilles! Pity me in my own right,
> remember your own father! I deserve more pity...
> I have endured what no one on earth has ever done before –
> I put my lips to the hands of the man who killed my son."
> (*Il.* 24.577-91; transl. Fagels 1990)

Priam's speech moves Achilles to fully feel his own pain and to share his sorrow and compassion for a man who just moments ago was his worst enemy:

> Those words stirred within Achilles a deep desire
> to grieve for his own father. Taking the old man's hand
> he gently moved him back. And overpowered by memory
> both men gave way to grief. Priam wept freely
> for man-killing Hector, throbbing, crouching
> before Achilles' feet as Achilles wept himself,
> now for his father, now for Patroclus once again,
> and their sobbing rose and fell throughout the house.
> (*Il.* 24.592-99; transl. Fagels 1990)

Weeping for his own father allows Achilles in turn to put himself in Priam's shoes. The two antagonists are instantly brought together in shared tears for their common condition of utter loss. As the young man wails for his father and the old man weeps for his son, Seth Schein states, "the two enemies virtually adopt one another as father and son".[1] This transcendental relationship has been forged because Achilles, allowed to walk in his own shoes, has become somebody else, somebody whose generosity to his enemy spurs his noblest act. This generosity, Graham Zanker notes, "outstrips even that of the gods themselves, whose immortality debars them from the totality of Achilles' vision".[2] It is through unlearning his divinity, surrendering the immortal within him, that Achilles makes himself a greater man, ironically even greater than the gods who rule his fate. And the instrument of that transformation is Priam's speech. The masquerade of the tale demands that we cannot be ourselves until we have become someone else.

When Achilles discovers his smallness, his quiet, acquiescent acts are instantly infused with giant meaning. His bow to his mortality, his gestures of respect to those once deemed so far beneath him, guarantee the deathlessness of his story. The poets of the *Iliad* tell many stories in book XXIV, and one of them is the story of how to tell a story. The story that a great narrator tells must find a way to work the listener's very being into its plot.

It is a truism that all great novelists write their own, individually personalized and self-reflecting stories; in contrast, all great oral storytellers *tell the story of each individual audience.* Folklorists speak of proverbs as the "social use of metaphor":[3] a proverb remains always *verbatim* the same, but it becomes serious art when applied effectively to the situation immediately at hand. The proverb, states a proverb about the nature of proverbs, constitutes "the wisdom of many", but when used effectively in a social situation, it becomes "the wit of one". Oral prose stories on the lips of master narrators are far more liquid; they are *never* memorized. Narrators must make their stories fit *both* their purposes and the expectations of their listeners. Even faltering narrators know that they must try to retool each of their stories to the occasion at hand. Johannes T. Kakridis has demonstrated that Phoinix, in his failed performance in book IX of the *Iliad*, succeeds at least in changing the details of the tale of Meleagros to fit more closely with the situation that Achilles and his supplicants are facing at that moment. Achilles, and the Homeric audience, would recognize instantly that Phoinix's story is less about Meleagros than about Achilles.

Yet the task of a great narrator does not end with analogy. The greater test is whether the narrator can induce each listener to self-identify as the story's leading character. One great narrator, Joshua Alley of coastal Maine, habitually told tales that tested his listeners' sense of reality. The audiences continually asked Alley if the events recounted in his tales had really taken place. Is this story *true?* He always answered, "I don't believe there ever was a story all true." Yet a good story needed to possess

> … truth enough in it to make it hold together, see? … If you are mixing up something, why, you can put stuff into that that you are mixing, something to make it stick together and hold together. It ain't all the same kind of stuff. And that's the way of my story.[4]

Stories are never all the same stuff. No story is all true and no story is all false. To Joshua Alley, the very definition of story was a speech act that is partly false and yet fundamentally true. And it often happens that the stuff that is least literally true is the truest part of the story. What makes the story most real to us its listeners is its power to make us feel the truth of what it means to us.

1 Schein 1984, 159.
2 Zanker 1994, 125.
3 Seitel 1981.
4 Lindahl 2004, 1, 222.

We now live in a world where people feel increasingly free to say whatever they wish about themselves. But what we narrate is too seldom heard by a small group of people who share the same room. We tell our stories on Facebook, Twitter, Instagram. With no one physically present to rein us in, no one whose sensitivities or approval may affect and inflect what we say, we talk only about ME. Everything I say is MY own story. I speak only to say who I am. My "I" is not someone who is negotiating his relationship to "you", personally, because there are thousands of unknown "you"s listening in. In Facebook-world, my only model for presenting myself is another unseen stranger's narrative, photo, or chat. We compete at baring our souls to people we know only as pixels or soundbites endlessly repeating their own stories, on a rotating wheel of anonymous exhibitionism. We echo one another without ever *talking together,* or *listening together.*

In those parts of the world – and of course there are many of them in Greece – where face-to-face narration continues to dominate as a source of entertainment and learning, anonymous exhibitionism is impossible. In these intimate contexts, the narrator is seldom, if ever, the central figure of his story. Of course, in one way or another, speakers always tell versions of their own stories, but in the story-rich corners of the English-speaking world that I know best – rural Ireland, Scotland, Newfoundland, and Appalachia, for example – narrators very rarely make themselves the center of their stories.[5] Even when narrating local history that they have taken part in, the tellers will not focus on themselves; if they enter the story as a character at all, it is simply to *witness,* to authenticate someone else's story by saying that they were present at the event described.

In these oral communities, narrators most commonly introduce themselves as characters when their stories are pure fictions – and experienced listeners know that they are not speaking literal truth. To be themselves, they are required to wear a mask. In the opening formulas of Newfoundland magic tales, a narrator's self-introduction is a craven falsehood, as when Freeman Bennett opens "Jack and the Three Giants":

> Well once upon a time, in olden times ya know, … perhaps five or six hundred year ago. …I can only just mind [remember] that anyhow! I wasn't very ol', not five or six hundred year ago! But anyhow I can mind a little bit about it. … there was a family living here.[6]

Bennett as much as tells us that it is impossible for him to have witnessed the story, and yet at the story's end he revisits his lie:

> … An' when I left they had three children… An' th' ol' man an' th' ol' woman … was 'bout seventy or eighty year ol'.…[7]

Bennett has presented his act of witness as a physical impossibility. Yet throughout the long narration, he has made it his business to make us feel the story as true. He could claim a certain truth in saying that he was there, because it is his wordplay that has created the imaginative space we inhabited as he spoke, and if we became engaged enough to half-feel that we have actually *been* there, if we half-believe that anyone has ever been there, the storyteller is the most likely candidate. In presenting himself as an emissary from his own creation, is Bennett really lying? It might be fair to say that in such performances the narrator has exchanged himself for his story.

Received folkloristic wisdom has it that the formulaic frame of fairy tales is a verbal stage curtain marking the enclosed story as a fiction utterly divorced from daily reality: we are about to enter a fantasy world that exists far beyond the realm of the

5 Cashman 2008, 139; Glassie 2006, 289; Lindahl 2010, 257.

6 Bennett 2002, 15.

7 Bennett 2002, 23.

possible. Yet master märchen narrators constantly use the frame not to set fantasy apart from everyday reality, but rather to blur the boundaries between truth and falsehood.

One of the great boundary-blurring narrators I have been honored to hear was Alfred Anderson, a Creole (i.e. a French African American) gentleman who grew up sharecropping on a Louisiana plantation in the mid-twentieth century in conditions not far removed from slavery. His storytelling emerged from a tradition that was typically coded, with narrators and characters constantly trading identities. Narrative disguise was sometimes a matter of life and death – because the slaves and sharecroppers who created his tradition had to be able to communicate with one another while under constant surveillance from their white masters and landlords.[8] In Alfred Anderson's community, the narrator was a verbal shapeshifter whose general purpose was to teach *by example* how much truthfulness one can convey without seeming to be speaking truth. His culture had created such tricksters as *Lapin* (Brer Rabbit) to present positive and negative lessons for how to challenge white masters without getting caught.

Alfred's daughter, one of my students, told me about how her father would make his stories simultaneously false and true. He would tell the animal tale known internationally as ATU 123, "The Wolf and the Kids".[9] In most cultures, the story's cast consists entirely of nonhuman characters. For example, in Greece, this plot most often features a wolf and a fox (cf. Megas 1970 and ATU 123A and 123B). But in Alfred Anderson's version the kids are part of a human family that lives by a swamp, and the role of the wolf is played by an alligator. In Greece, such a tale might be perceived as an unbridled fantasy, but in Donaldsonville, Louisiana, alligators were common and it was necessary for parents to warn their young children about them. In Anderson's tale,

> … at a house at the edge of a swamp, a mother needs to leave her three daughters alone while the father is away at work. She tells the children to lock the door and not to open it for anyone except her. She sings to them a string of syllables: *mamalito, tee-tum, tee-tum, tee-tum.* Only when they hear her sing these words should they come to the door and open it. An alligator has listened the mother's song and practices singing it until he believes he can successfully imitate the mother. After the mother leaves, the alligator sings outside the door. The older sisters recognize that the voice does not belong to mother, but the youngest is fooled and before her sisters can stop her, she runs through the door into the beast's jaws. While the family wails for the little girl whom they believe to be dead, the father returns home, kills the alligator with his knife and slashes its belly open to free the child.[10]

Even the most far-fetched elements of this tale were invested with realistic meanings for the sharecroppers who inhabited Donaldsonville Plantation. For example, Alfred used a low-pitched, gravelly voice in performing the chant of the alligator, and his voice evokes the grunting and growling sounds of real-life alligators. One of the important messages of this tale was to teach children to listen carefully for, and learn to distinguish, the sounds that real-life alligators make.

Alfred Anderson typically ended his performance with his personal variation on a closing formula popular in African American narration. The most common form is:

> Stepped on a pin, de pin bent
> And dat's de way de story went.[11]

8 See Lindahl 1982.

9 ATU refers to The Types of International Tales, a 3-volume, classification of widespread folktale plots first published in 1910 and revised and expanded three times since then (Uther 2004).

10 Anderson 1997.

11 Hurston 1990, 123.

Alfred always intruded into this closing rhyme to carry a part of the story out of the frame. When he narrated "The Girls and the Alligator" for Debra, he would sign off with these words:

> I stepped on a wire, and the wire bent—and I got out of there, girl, because that alligator was terrible.[12]

—uttered in a whispery tone that was memorably frightening for Debra. When she heard that whisper, she became confused. The story wasn't supposed to be true, but it felt true when her dad made himself a character in the fiction – so it had to be true in some important way.

By presenting himself as a true witness to the alligator's near-fatal attack, Alfred effectively communicated a lesson in survival. The narrator twisted himself and his moral through the frame to communicate a real danger. The threat of the alligator was the truest part of this fantasy story. In Alfred's world, people simply do not have fantasies about things that don't concern them.

When great narrators *become* their stories, they can literally transform their listeners. And that is exactly what happened to my favorite Appalachian storyteller, Jane Muncy. When she was three years old, her mother disappeared, leaving Jane alone with her father for a year, until the Japanese attack on Pearl Harbor drove him into the military, so at age four Jane was effectively an orphan. She was weak, undergrown, beset with what the doctors now call "failure to thrive". At this point, Sidney Farmer Muncy, her 67-year-old grandmother, entered her life. Sidney took Jane into her mountain home and set about curing her with stories.

> [F]irst time that I remember meeting [my grandmother], I was about four… World War II had just started – the bombing of Pearl Harbor – and my father and mother were getting a divorce. And my father wanted custody and he wrote [my grandmother] a telegram. I saw the telegram when I was just a child, and the telegram said, "MOM, COME AND GET JANE – I'M GOING IN – STOP." And so that she did. She got on a train and she rode … from … Kentucky all the way to … Philadelphia – to pick up little Jane. And, she was a stranger to me, and I was basically a stranger to her. She was sixty-seven and, as far as she knew, I was going to be her charge for a long time, because the war had started, my dad was going in the Marines, and he was going to be far away, and she was going to have me on her own…
>
> She told me many times that I was her salvation, that I kept her young. She slept with me. She cuddled me. She said I was terribly, terribly thin and small, and that she must revive me. She was surprised that I was living, as thin and small as I was, and she could hold me in [the crook of] one arm.
>
> … [O]ur life together alone took on a pattern of creativity on her part … teaching me how to listen to stories, and teaching me how to read the censored letters that came from my father and my Uncle Gill. Uncle Gill was a straightforward kind of guy, who liked to drink a lot, and he would write on and on and on and many times say things that were, disclosing things the war effort people didn't want him to disclose. So his letters would be one or two sentences, and then a whole lot of cut-outs, and one or two sentences, and a whole lot of cut-outs – it was very frustrating to us, as we were trying to figure out where he was, because he couldn't tell us. My dad, however, was more cunning, and he would say things to her like, "Mom, you know that [coral shell] necklace that I sent to Jane? Well, that necklace came from Uncle Sol's store. Remember Uncle Sol? You can remember him, where he lived out on that little place all by himself?" And she would go get the map … and she would say, "Ah, okay, it means he's on the Solomon Islands, it's an island all by itself, and that's the Sol he's talking about and they have shells." And so we, we had like a little war map and flags and his picture nearby. And he was my hero.

12 Anderson 1997, 126.

> And *she* was my comfort. One of the things that she did for me for comfort was I was allowed to sleep with her. … families did sleep together [then]. … [T]he comforting thing we did at night was, we looked at the map one more time, … and then we wound up the clock. … we banked the fire, and we went to bed. But it wasn't the end of the day, because the end of the day involved her telling me at least a couple of stories that she had heard as a child – and then drifting off to sleep. I would always drift off to sleep with my ear at her back, because I liked to hear her heart beat.
>
> So we were, bedtime buddies and bedtime storytellers, … I would [name] a favorite story I wanted to hear, and she would usually tell that and then she would tell me the favorite story she wanted to tell me…[13]

Jane credits Sidney with saving her emotional life – by transforming her into a fairy tale character. Grandmother Sidney's family tale tradition centered on the boy hero Jack, so Sidney set about turning Jack into Jane, and Jane into Jack. Jane listened to her grandmother in the darkness, and Sidney used that darkness and whispered words as a sort of stage for the creation of a new Jane. Listening, Jane would visualize scenes through which she lost her identity and took on the identity of folktale characters.

Sidney's first transformative act was to change the folktale boy-hero's name to create an androgynous figure that a girl could more easily identify with. Jack became Merrywise; like Jane, Merrywise was young and small and physically weak, but strong in his confidence and resourcefulness. But Sidney did not describe how Merrywise looked. She left it up to Jane to visualize the boy, and Jane, of course, saw an image of herself:

> He was … small, smaller than the other boys of course, maybe up to their shoulders. And he wore sort of a knickers kind of clothing, like little boys would wear. He had a little boy haircut that maybe came down over his ears, [a bowl haircut], sort of round, and he had freckles. I had freckles too. [I started out ashamed of them. But my grandmother] always told me that *she* had freckles as a child. "And freckles … made you beautiful." And so, when I pictured Merrywise, I pictured Merrywise as sandy blonde hair and freckles – sort of like me. *Surprise. Surprise.*[14]

The images that Jane's grandmother had planted in her imagination became, in some ways, Jane's second-closest family member, and Jane herself became the co-narrator of Merrywise and his story.

Sidney's stories were so successful in creating a path forward for Jane that they directly influenced her career choice. Jane was not always conscious of how well the stories succeeded in changing her life. When, as an adult, she realized what Sidney's stories had done for her, Jane decided that she, too, would use stories to heal. She became a psychologist and appropriated her grandmother's narrative techniques in shaping tales to help her patients script better lives for themselves.

Jane explained both how, as a young girl, she envisioned this boy, and how she still uses him to create models for grown men suffering from post-traumatic stress:

> I became very acquainted with a little guy named Merrywise. Now, Merrywise was an overcomer. I tell my clients there are two ways to be in the world. One way is to be a mastery person: you do *everything* right all the time. Things come easy. A mastery person doesn't know very well how to deal with failure. Or you can be a coping person. A coping person – and that's the way to be – a coping person has a tool kit and when they come to an obstacle in their road, they will take out something from the tool kit, and use it to chop through, go over, walk around, dig under the obstacle, and get to the other side.

13 Lindahl 2004, 1, 284-86.

14 Fugate 2000.

> Well, Merrywise was very much a coping kind of guy. He was the youngest in his family. He had two brothers. Tom and Bill. And while they were older and stronger and had more experience and people trusted them sometimes, it was always Merrywise, with his smallness and his cunning and his ability to *craft* his way through his world, that got them all out of a big jam.[15]

The Merrywise that Sidney presented to Jane, and the Merrywise that Jane recreates for her patients, are remarkably flexible in nature, developed in various types and degrees of detail in accordance with the message that the teller attempts to impart to the listener.

> When I look at ... Merrywise ... he was not only the hero who was the youngest, but he [...] could figure out things that [others] couldn't figure out. And so, the message to me was, you can be little, and you can be frail, and you can be the youngest, and you can be alone, but you could also be the smartest. And the [name] Merrywise: ... you could be happy. ... and you could be wise and you can overcome. And so I thought of myself as that overcomer.[16]

In very few words, Sidney could change a tale to enhance its healing impact for Jane. When, for example, Merrywise and his brothers are sleeping in a witch's house, he is able to hear her whisper, "I'll get up and whet my knife" while preparing to cut off his brothers' heads. At this point in the story, Sidney would whisper suggestively to Jane, "Merrywise was too small to hurt the witch, so he listened to every sound she made, because that's what he *could* do" – Jane inferred that Merrywise – and, by extension, *she* – possessed the resources to overcome.

Jane did indeed overcome. Jane became Merrywise, and ultimately became her grandmother, as she retooled Sidney's stories to help heal her patients.

Folk narrators can retain power only by sharing it. Their art thrives only insofar as it engages its listeners, and it best does so by actively involving the audience in the creation of the story. A great storyteller does not rob us of our imagination, but rather persuades us to transform their suggestions into *our* thoughts. Great narrators *free us to surrender to their suggestion.*

To experience the narrator's transformative art, one must gain access to the intimate realm of the storytelling community. As Georgios Megas wrote about twentieth-century Greek storytelling, "Only when one is a member of the popular narrator's audience at an evening session is it possible to feel what [the folktale] is in substance".[17] For narrators to change themselves and trade places with you, they first must know who you are.

As an American movie proverb goes, "It's not your word; it's who you give it to".[18] The narrator's relationship with the listener makes the difference between a story without a point and a subtly masterful communication.

I learned this truth on an intimate scale from hearing Debra talk about her father Alfred, and Jane talk about her grandmother Sidney. Their knowledge guided me in August 2005, when Hurricane Katrina landed in Louisiana, killing at least 1800 people, rendering one million instantly homeless, and driving 250,000 of them to shelters in Houston, the city where I work. As this massive migration began, my university's president sent out a call to the

15 Lindahl 2004, 1, 288.
16 Lindahl 2010, 260-61.

17 Megas 1970, pp. xlvii–xlviii.
18 The origin of the quote is the screenplay for the Hollywood Western *The Wild Bunch* (Green & Peckinpah 1969). The proverb condenses the following bit of dialogue from the film:
Pike: "He gave his word." *Dutch*: "He gave his word to a railroad." *Pike*: "It's his word." *Dutch*: "That ain't what counts! It's who you give it to."

whole faculty asking how we, as individuals, could use our professional skills to respond to the disaster.

Above all, folklorists study community culture: the narrative teaching performed by Alfred Anderson and the narrative healing effected by Sidney Farmer Muncy succeeded in large part because of the intimate preexisting relationships between teller and listener. At first glance, an enormous influx of displaced people – comprising thousands upon thousands of mutual strangers – appears to be the opposite of a folk community, and the folklorist seems inadequate to address human suffering of such massive proportions. But, paradoxically, it was the disaster itself that created the community that invested the survivors' stories with healing power, because folkloric communication increases in intensity and importance within an *involuntary frame*. People who are thrown into close interaction and interdependence by outside forces tend to establish tight communities; in fact, they often must do so simply in order to survive. Consequently, soldiers in combat, prisoners, cancer or AIDS patients, stigmatized minorities, or disaster victims will form intense communal bonds, creating a common expressive vocabulary to confront and transcend adversity.[19] I had witnessed such close and rich community interactions in small Cajun communities that had long been separated by language and religion from the mainstream culture surrounding them. But as I began working with the displaced survivors of Hurricane Katrina, I observed a greater degree of community solidarity among participants than I had seen in any earlier context. I witnessed what Rebecca Solnit would later describe as *A Paradise Built in Hell*,[20] as she titles her book about *The Extraordinary Communities That Arise in Disaster*. In studying large-scale disasters, from the 1906 San Francisco Earthquake to Hurricane Katrina, Solnit detected a predictable tendency for cultural outsiders and wealthy insiders to blame the poorest, most vulnerable, most stigmatized victims for the disaster; this is a scenario that has also been long recognized by folklorists and historians.[21] In the media accounts, these poor minorities are typically portrayed as looters, rapists, and murderers, but in fact, at ground zero, in the midst of overwhelming adversity, survivors tend to become *better than themselves*, continually risking their own lives to save others.

The Katrina survivors displaced to Houston had wriggled out of one involuntary frame (the hurricane that threatened their lives and destroyed their neighborhoods) only to find themselves trapped in another (exile, isolation, and stigmatization by the media in Houston). Most had lived in a New Orleans neighborhood where they had seen, daily, hundreds of people they knew by name, but they were now surrounded by strangers and often singled out as loafers and whiners at best or, at worst, as malicious criminals. To a disaster survivor in such an environment, a phone call or knock on the door from a fellow survivor, especially a stranger, was profoundly welcome. The instant trust that developed when one displaced survivor sat down to listen to another survivor's story broke down the inhibiting frames that typically constrain a recorded interview. During the hurricane they had inhabited the "paradise built in hell", and, as the first survivor recorded by our project said, they had experienced "That … one time [when] our town really, really as a community came together, … And everybody chipped in together".[22] Just as survivor narratives document the paradise built in hell, the recording session *recreated*

19 Lindahl 2016.

20 Solnit 2009.

21 Smith 1995; Lindahl 2012.

22 SKRH 2006-9: SKR-CL-SR02. These are the words of interviewer trainee Angela Trahan, who narrated her storm story on the first day of our first training session: 23 January 2006. Much of that first interview is published (Trahan 2013), but the quote presented here is from a follow-up interview that took place at the end of the training session, on January 27. This unpublished interview is archived at the University of Houston under the identifier SKR-CL-SR02.

this paradise: sitting across from one another in the narrator's living room, or at the kitchen table, two strangers broke free of their circumstances of exile and isolation to share their past, the good and the bad, at an uncommon level of intensity and good will.

Surviving Katrina and Rita in Houston – the project that I developed with folklorist Pat Jasper and in coordination with the American Folklife Center at the Library of Congress – became the world's first project in which the survivors themselves took the lead in documenting their experience of disaster. In this project, as survivor-interviewers recorded the narratives of their fellow survivors, their goal was not to extract information by asking questions, but rather to free the narrators to put themselves in their own shoes. The "interviewer" simply listened as the narrator took over. The project became a success among the survivors and so emotionally empowering that we ultimately received funding from behavioral health organizations as a trauma prevention program.

The survivors' narratives were legendary in nature. Because first-person disaster stories center on events that test the limits of our experience and pit humans against titanic forces, they share some signal traits with *legend*, a genre that depicts human beings in the act of grappling with forces that they cannot control. A legend hits you where you live; as Jacob Grimm famously said,[23] it "knocks at your door" and instantly renders the familiar strange, transforming the known into the unknown and forcing us to ponder the nature of existence itself. When a hurricane arrives, puts your city underwater, instantly obliterates every material manifestation of your security, and threatens your life, your neighborhood is now a legend-scape, and you are living a legend.

Folklorists understand the term "legend" to signify various types of narrative. The survivor narratives evoke two of legend's most common meanings: the *Heldensage*, a story recounting the larger-than-life acts of exceptional heroes in conflict with warriors, supernatural beings, or nature itself; and the "belief legend", in which ordinary people encounter and are often destroyed by forces much greater than themselves. These two very different understandings of legend were recognized the Grimm brothers, whose pioneering collection, *The German Legends*,[24] devoted half of their two-volume work to the *Heldensagen* and the other to tales now often known as "belief legend".[25]

Wilhelm Grimm saw *Heldensagen* as descending from ancient epic tradition stretching back to the *Iliad*.[26] But survivors' stories are also legendary in a second sense – that of the belief legend as understood and interpreted by Linda Dégh, Max Lüthi, and other twentieth-century folklorists. This sort of legend involves nameless "everymen" inhabiting the everyday world, who cross an invisible line to be ambushed by enormous powers that they cannot fathom.[27]

Sidney Harris is one of hundreds of survivors recorded by our project whose acts during the disaster would be lauded as heroic by any listener, but (like every other survivor recorded by our project) he refuses to claim the status of hero. He extends credit to other people for any good he may have done.

Consider how Sidney progressively undercuts the heroic image that his acts manifestly proclaim, how he locates heroism and inspiration only in others, and how he finally dissolves, surrendering his self and his story into the identity and care of his neighbors. Sidney, a guard in the central New Orleans jail, was on duty when Katrina hit, but because no one foresaw that this fortress-like prison would be endangered by the hurricane, he had brought with

23 J. Grimm, 1888, xv.

24 Grimm & Grimm 1981.

25 Ward 1981, 375-78.

26 W. Grimm 1829, 335-37.

27 Dégh 1971 and 2001; Lüthi 1961 and 1976.

him his seventeen-year-old nephew for the boy's safety. After the storm passed, the water rose swiftly and high within the building, prisoners panicked, and the vastly outnumbered guards felt and shared their fear.

> It's … a scary feeling that the water's getting higher and you don't know actually how high it's going to get….
>
> … us being understaffed …, it was only actually one [guard] to a tier [of prisoners]. So, you have no weapon, you … by yourself. It's dark, and you just have inmates surrounding you, trying to break the glass. And you just … praying that none of them break that glass. Cause you can't fight them off.
>
> [T]his went on for three days and the water had got to the second floor, in the jail … and I just had this feeling … I just didn't really care to even try to fight no more. I just laid down and was like whatever going to happen is going to be, you know… It was rioting. People … getting shot. You was just hearing gunfire, … screams, everything… I just gave up…[28]

It is the acts and needs of others that repeatedly lead Sidney to regain his will. His fellow deputies somehow spur him to help herd hundreds of prisoners out of the jail and onto an overpass where they are now dry but the inmates are still starving, desperate, and angry.

> … we were on the bridge, and when the inmates were about to start rioting on the bridge [our commander] gave us shotguns. But it was … twenty of us with shotguns, you know, and all of them inmates. And these guys were at the point where they was like, "You could shoot some of us, but you can't shoot all of us.[29]

According to Sidney, he did nothing brave by standing against the rioters. Again he absolves himself of heroism. Time passes.

> They still had so many people on the bridge with no water, and you had no food. So basically, it was a mind thing. If you could get it up there mentally, you know, you would have been all right.

> So … on the strength of my little nephew, I started getting a little strong, you know, because he kind of broke down and was like, "Man, why can't we just go home?" Because a lot of deputies had *quit* and walked off. But on the strength of him I just found it somewhere in me. I just wasn't scared no more.[30]

Boats come for the prisoners as Sidney guards the bridge. Then helicopters pick up some of the guards. Sidney and his nephew stand by and wave as others are flown to safety.

Sidney and his nephew have been repeatedly offered a helicopter ride to safety. Every time, Sidney turns it down. Every time, his nephew gets more upset. Sidney consents to board a helicopter with his nephew, but there aren't enough seats left for everyone still on the bridge.

> I said, "Well look, take [those other people]." My nephew got mad at me again. I was like, "Man, just bear with me, man."
> He was like, "Man, you lucky that I love you."
> … I was like, "Yeah, I'm *glad you do*".[31]

Sidney and his nephew finally board the helicopter with the three other men still left on the bridge. But Sidney will not finish his story without first undercutting the last hint of his own heroism. Shortly before ending he adds,

28 Harris 2013, 193-94.
29 *Ibid.*, 196.
30 *Ibid.*, 197.
31 *Ibid.*, 201.

> Actually, … why I didn't get on before a lot of people, was like, *dang*, I ain't never rode on no helicopter. I loved riding on airplanes, but I'm like, a helicopter, you know, I ain't really too sure about that. So when it came time, like you either going to stay … in this water, … or you going to civilization? So I finally manned up and it was a relief.[32]

In the end, Sidney gives everything but heroism the credit for his acts. He even credits his fear before himself.

The hero's tendency to surrender all credit reaches its climax in the words of another survivor, 74-year-old Charles Darensbourg, who along with his wife Jackie, survived Katrina, but lost his home of 53 years and everything in it. He spends the first hour of his story describing the beauty of everything he has lost:

> We … didn't safeguard our pictures or our treasures – things we wanted to keep for the rest of our lives, we didn't safeguard these things. And we left them, and they were destroyed.[33]

He then presents a lesson in the value of loss. Just as any real hero must dissolve, anyone who cares for his goods or friends or stature does best to surrender his claim on them:

> But one thing I have found: ever since I can remember, you receive as you give. … It may not be the same that you give that you would receive, but in the long run it comes back to you in one way or another. … the things that we shared with other people, our pictures – some of the poetry I had written and different articles … shared with other people – after Katrina, just started to come back. Our kinfolks and our friends started sending back pictures that we['d] shared with them, poems I had written and some of the mementos that Jackie had given.
>
> The only poems that I did not share … were the poems that I had written for Jackie on our wedding anniversaries, and we did not share them with anybody because I said I want this to be just for Jackie…. I want her to feel something special about these poems.
>
> I did not share them with anybody, so they were completely destroyed … The things that we shared, we got back in return. The things we did not share, we did not get back.[34]

Charles's litany of loss becomes somehow also the sum of all that he can never lose. As his narrative ends, his personal story dissolves into a catalog of the losses of his neighbors. All their houses were destroyed forever. Some who stayed were lucky enough to be rescued from their rooftops. Charles turns his attention, finally, to his neighbors who drowned in their homes. Like Sidney, Charles empties himself into his relatives, friends, and neighbors. They are the heroes; everything *he* has been able to keep is what they have given back to him.

No one could mistake Sidney or Charles for Achilles, yet, in surrendering all claims to heroism, Sidney and Charles are doing something not so distant from what Achilles did thousands of years ago. What Sidney and Charles *unlearn* in the course of their stories is any sense of self-importance. Progressively, as they speak, they do all in their power to diminish themselves. In the process, they heal the whole community. Today in Greece, a huge number of disaster survivors stand in need of a chance to put themselves in their own shoes and allow story to help them retake possession of themselves. One of my great hopes in presenting this paper in Athens at such a tumultuous time is to be able to work out ways in which a survivor project conducted in Greece's enormous refugee culture can allow the newest inhabitants of this country to benefit from

32 *Ibid.*, 203.

33 Darensbourg 2013, 242.

34 *Ibid.*, 242.

one of Greece's oldest lessons for the world: to become greater, more heroic, more generous in and through their losses.

During the last several decades of legend study, folklorists have been vexed in trying to reconcile two types of narrative that share the name "legend": the hero legends of past centuries, that portray giant, nearly superhuman figures performing acts beyond mortal capacity; and the belief legends of today, those depicting nameless little people acted upon by forces much greater than themselves. The narratives of Sidney and Charles bridge the gap between the big old days and our present era of the little people. They have become giant in their smallness, and the best neighbors a soul could hope to have. These men and many of their fellow survivor narrators dissolve themselves into something very big, endless, and happily eternal for those who, like me, cannot abide the idea that such heroism and such *true* hero stories should ever end.

In this age of media narration dominated by one giant, impersonal *me*, it is vital to remember that the essence of story relies on who we give it to. As Megas told us half a century ago, and as great storytellers instinctively know, a story is no greater than the relationship between the teller and the listener, a relationship that allows the narrator to become us, and us to become the story. It is the obligation of folklorists to nurture narrative intimacy. Our best stories need that, and we all need those healing stories.

Carl Lindahl
University of Houston
lindahlcarl1@gmail.com

Bibliography

ANCELET, B. J., M. GAUDET & C. LINDAHL (EDS.) 2013
Second Line Rescue: Improvised Responses to Hurricane Katrina, Jackson, Mississippi.

ANDERSON, A. 1997
'The Girls and the Alligator', in *Swapping Stories: Folktales from Louisiana,* C. Lindahl, M. Owens, & C. R. Harvison (eds.), Jackson, Mississippi, 122-26.

BENNETT, F. 2002
'Jack and the Three Giants', in *Little Jack and Other Newfoundland Folktales,* J. D. A. Widdowson (ed.), St. John's, Newfoundland.

CASHMAN, R. 2008
Storytelling on the Northern Irish Border: Characters and Community, Bloomington, Indiana.

DARENSBOURG, C. A. 2013
'If You Do Not Give, You Do Not Receive', in *Second Line Rescue: Improvised Responses to Hurricane Katrina*, B. J. Ancelet, M. Gaudet, & C. Lindahl (eds.), Jackson, Mississippi, 235-47.

DÉGH, L. 1971
'The Belief Legend in Modern Society', in *American Folk Legend: A Symposium*, W. D. Hand (ed.), Berkeley, California, 55-68.

DÉGH, L. 2001
Legend and Belief: Dialectics of a Folklore Genre, Bloomington, Indiana.

FUGATE, J. M. 2000
Three days of interviews and folktale performances. Melbourne, Florida, 2-4 June. Conducted, recorded, and transcribed by Carl Lindahl. The portions of the interviews cited here are transcribed in Lindahl 2001, 39-43, 81-89.

GLASSIE, H. 2006
The Stars of Ballymenone, Bloomington, Indiana.

GREEN, W. & S. PECKINPAH 1969
Screenplay to *The Wild Bunch*, 145-min. motion picture, Los Angeles.

GRIMM, J. 1888
Teutonic Mythology. Vol. 3, J. Stallybrass (transl.), London.

GRIMM, J. & W. GRIMM 1981
The German Legends of the Brothers Grimm, D. Ward (transl. & ed), 2 vols., Philadelphia.

GRIMM, W. 1829
Die Deutsche Heldensage. Göttingen.

HARRIS, S. 2013
'On the Strength of My Litte Nephew, I Started Getting a Little Strong', in *Second Line Rescue: Improvised Responses to Hurricane Katrina*, B. J. Ancelet, M. Gaudet, & C. Lindahl (eds.), Jackson, Mississippi, 190-204.

HURSTON, Z. N. 1990 [1935]
Mules and Men, New York.

FAGELS, R. 1990 (TRANSL.)
Homer. The Iliad, New York

KAKRIDIS, I. T. 1949
Homeric Researches, Lund.

LINDAHL, C. 1982
'Skallbone, the Old Coon, and the Persistence of Specialized Fantasy', *Western Folklore* 41, 192-204.

LINDAHL, C. (ED.) 2001
Perspective on the Jack Tales and Other North American Märchen, Bloomington, Indiana.

LINDAHL, C. (ED.) 2004
American Folktales from the Collections of the Library of Congress, 2 vols., Armonk, New York.

LINDAHL, C. 2010
'Leonard Roberts, the Farmer-Lewis-Muncy Family, and the Magic Circle of the Mountain Märchen', *Journal of American Folklore* 123, 251-75.

LINDAHL, C. 2012
'Legends of Hurricane Katrina: The Right to Be Wrong, Survivor-to-Survivor Storytelling, and Healing', *Journal of American Folklore* 125, 139-78.

LINDAHL, C. 2016
'Acting on Magic and Winning with Words in Märchen Worlds (and Beyond)', *Fabula* 57, 231-47.

LINDAHL, C., M. OWENS, & C. R. HARVISON (EDS.) 1997
Swapping Stories: Folktales from Louisiana, Jackson, Mississippi.

LÜTHI, M. 1961
Volksmärchen und Volkssage: Zwei Grundformen erzählender Dichtung, Bern.

LÜTHI, M. 1976
'Aspects of the Marchen and the Legend', in *Folklore Genres*, D. Ben-Amos (ed.), Austin, Texas, 17-33.

MEGAS, G. A. 1970
Folktales of Greece. Chicago.

SCHEIN, S. L. 1984
The Mortal Hero: An Introduction to Homer's Iliad, Berkeley, California.

SEITEL, P. 1981
'Proverbs: A Social Use of Metaphor', in *The Wisdom of Many: Essays on the Proverb*, W. Mieder & A. Dundes (eds.), New York, 122-39.

SKRH 2006-9
Surviving Katrina and Rita in Houston audio archive. 433 recorded interviews of hurricane survivors and responders; more than 400 were recorded from survivors by fellow survivors trained by the Surviving Katrina and Rita in Houston project between 23 January 2006 and 30 August 2007; interviewers continued recording fellow survivors until the end of 2009.

SMITH, C. 1995
Urban Disorder and the Shape of Belief: The Great Chicago Fire, the Haymarket Bomb, and the Model Town of Pullman, Chicago.

SOLNIT, R. 2009
A Paradise Built in Hell: The Extraordinary Communities That Arise in Disaster, New York.

TRAHAN, A. 2013
'We Really Did Not Think That We Would Make It', in *Second Line Rescue: Improvised Responses to Katrina and Rita*, B. Ancelet, M. Gaudet, & C. Lindahl (eds.), Jackson, Mississippi, 77-89.

UTHER, H.-J. 2004
The Types of International Tales: A Classification and Bibliography, 3 vols., Folklore Fellows Communications 284-86, Helsinki.

WARD, D. 1981
'Epilogue', in *The German Legends of the Brothers Grimm*, J. Grimm & W. Grimm, vol. 2, 341-84.

ZANKER, G. 1994
The Heart of Achilles: Characterization and Personal Ethics in the Iliad, Ann Arbor, Michigan.

Contributors

MINNA SKAFTE JENSEN

Educated in Greek and Latin at the University of Copenhagen 1956-63; gold medal in 1966; Dr.phil. 1980. Associate professor at the University of Copenhagen 1971-93, leader of a research project in Icelandic, Norwegian, Swedish, Finnish, and Danish Neo-Latin literature 1987-91, and professor of Greek and Latin at the University of Southern Denmark 1993-2003. Since 2017 she has been guest researcher at the University of Copenhagen. Member of The Royal Danish Academy of Sciences and Letters since 1993, of The Royal Norwegian Society of Sciences and Letters since 1994, of The Folklore Fellows since 1995, and of Koninklijke Academie voor Wetenschappen, Letteren en schone Kunsten van België since 1997. She was president of the International Association for Neo-Latin Studies 2009-12. The Gad Rausing Prize in 2014.

Main fields of study: Archaic Greek epic and Scandinavian Neo-Latin poetry, both characterised by important changes of media, from orality to writing, and from handwriting to print. In epic studies she builds on Parry and Lord's oral-formulaic theory and folkloristic methodology. She reads the Neo-Latin poetry in a Renaissance framework.

IOANNA KAFETZIDAKI

An educational professional with a background in psychology, early childhood education, and the integration of new technologies in education. She majored in Psychology at the University of Ioannina and completed her training as a Kindergarten Teacher at the University of the Aegean. She furthered her expertise with two master's degrees, one in Education Sciences with a specialization in Education through New Technologies and one in Special Education. She is currently the head of the 7th Kindergarten in Kos.

MARIANTHI KAPLANOGLOU

Professor of Folkloristics at the University of Athens and director of the graduate program "Folklore and Literature". She studied at the University of Athens and at the EHESS of Paris. She is member of the publication committee of the Catalogue of the Greek Folktales and a scientific partner of the Enzyklopädie des Märchens. With Michalis Meraklis she is co-director of the series of translations on international folklore studies. She is co-editor of *The tale. From the Brothers Grimms to our times. Diffusion and study* (2017).

GEORGE KATSADOROS

Professor of Folklore Studies/Folkloristics at the Department of Primary Education of the University of the Aegean. His main research interests include the diffusion and distribution of folkloric genres through modern media and their appliance in Education. He has taken part in many conferences and acted as a referee for many journals. He has published several works in Greece and abroad.

IOANNIS M. KONSTANTAKOS

Professor of Ancient Greek Literature at the National and Kapodistrian University of Athens. He has also taught as visiting professor at the University of Milan, the Hebrew University of Jerusalem, and the Drama School of the National Theatre of Greece. He has published widely on ancient comedy, narrative, folklore, and the relations between ancient Greece and the Near East. He has received the prize of the Academy of Athens for his scholarly work.

GEORGIOS KOUZAS
Assistant Professor at the University of Athens (School of Philosophy, Department of Philology), where he studied Philology and Folklore. He has worked in research programmes at the University of Athens, at the University of Thessaly, and the Panteion University. He has taught at the University of the Peloponnese, at Hellenic Open University, and at the Democritus University of Thrace. He has published articles in Greek and international journals.

CARL LINDAHL
Professor of English and Folklore, University of Houston. Specialises in oral narrative, folklore in disaster response, and festive folklore, primarily in Britain, Ireland, and the Appalachian and Southern regions of the U.S. His books include Folktales from Louisiana (1997), Medieval Folklore (2000), Perspectives on the Jack Tales (2001), American Folktales from the Collections of the Library of Congress (2004), Second Line Rescue (2013), and We Are All Survivors (2022).

MICHALIS G. MERAKLIS
Professor Emeritus of Folklore at the University of Athens and the University of Ioannina. He is a leading expert in folklore studies and literary studies. He worked as an assistant of Georgios A. Megas at the University of Athens and received his Ph.D. with Kurt Ranke at the University of Göttingen. Meraklis is former President of the Hellenic Folklore Society and editor of the Journal Laographia. He has served as Dean at the University of Ioannina and as President of the Panhellenic Union of Philologists. He was the recipient of the Herder Prize in 1995. He has written many books and numerous articles on various aspects of folklore and literature. His book *Tragedy and folk culture in Ancient Athens* (2017, in Greek) is a monumental study, which analyzes all the tragedies of Aeschylus, Sophocles, and Euripides in the light of folk studies, aiming to show how much the three poets owe to their contemporary folk life and culture.

BIRGIT OLSEN
Studied Modern Greek and Classics at the University of Copenhagen from where she also received her Ph.D. During her Ph.D. studies, she spent a year at the University of Cambridge under the supervision of Professor David Holton. She has taught at the University of Copenhagen, Aarhus University, and Fulbright College, Arkansas.

Her main fields of research have been Early Modern Greek texts and Modern Greek folk tales. She was assistant director at The Danish Institute at Athens 2016-19 and now holds a position at The Royal Danish Academy of Sciences and Letters.

SOPHIA PAPAIOANNOU
Professor of Latin at the National and Kapodistrian University of Athens, Faculty of Philology. Her research interests include Latin epic, especially Vergil and Ovid; the literature and cultural politics of the Augustan Age and the early empire; Roman comedy; Ancient Rhetoric and Performance; and the Greek Epic of the Late Antiquity. She has published several books, articles, and chapters on these topics.

NICOLETTE S. TRAHOULIA
Professor of Art History at the American University of Greece. She was educated at UCLA (B.A.) and Harvard (Ph.D.). Her work on the medieval Greek *Alexander Romance* exemplifies her approach to studying illustrated books as objects that function within larger experiential contexts. She is a former Fulbright Research Scholar and is currently a Fellow of the Institute for Hellenic Culture and the Liberal Arts.

MANOLIS VARVOUNIS

Studied Archaeology and Theology at the National and Kapodistrian University of Athens from where he also received his Ph.D. He did his postdoctoral studies at the University of Louvain-la-Neuve in Belgium. His main fields of research have been Greek Folklore and Religious Folklore.

He is Professor of Folklore in the Department of History and Ethnology and Dean of the School of Classics and Humanities in Democritus University of Thrace, in Greece.

ANDREW WALKER WHITE

A longtime theater artist and performing arts critic, based in the Washington, D.C. area. He received his Ph.D. from the University of Maryland, College Park, and is also a veteran of the Fulbright program, conducting research on post-Classical Greek culture in Greece and Turkey. His chief interest has been the performing arts of the Graeco-Roman world, including the rites of the Greek Orthodox Church, from Late Antiquity to the Middle Ages.

CHRISTOS ZAFIROPOULOS

Associate Professor of Ancient Greek Literature at the University of Patras, Faculty of History and Archaeology. His research interests include Greek Philosophy, especially Plato, the Aesopic corpus, Greek Drama, Greek Mythology and Folklore, History of Ideas, and the Reception of Greek Literature and Culture. He has published books, articles, and chapters on the above topics.

STAMATIS ZOCHIOS

Researcher at the Hellenic Folklore Research Centre at the Academy of Athens. He holds a doctorate from the University of Grenoble. He teaches at the EPHE, is affiliated with the Societies, Religions, Secularities Group and is currently preparing his Habilitation of Research on the subject "Exorcism and possession in the Orthodox Church". He previously worked at the University of Strasbourg. His main area of interest is popular, vernacular, and lived religion, and popular beliefs in Eastern and South-Eastern Europe. He is responsible for research projects at the Hellenic Cultural Center and directs the journal *Études balkaniques - Cahiers Pierre Belon*.